LEADERSHIP & MANAGEMENT STUDIES IN SUB-SAHARA AFRICA

Volume I

Romie F. Littrell and Prem Ramburuth, Editors
Leadership & Management Studies in Sub-Sahara Africa Conferences

University Readers
San Diego, CA

Romie F. Littrell is Associate Professor of International Business at the AUT Business School of Auckland University of Technology in New Zealand and has more than thirty years of experience in the field of international affairs and marketing. His extensive studies of leadership and management in Africa are reflected in this collection of articles and papers.

Prem Ramburuth is Associate Professor and Associate Dean of Undergraduate Programs and Education at the Australian School of Business, The University of New South Wales, Sydney, NSW, Australia. She has conducted expansive research and written on global management issues regarding diversity, expatriation, international affairs, and education.

First published in the United States of America in 2007 by University Readers

11 10 09 08 07   1 2 3 4 5
Printed in the United States of America

ISBN: 978-1-934269-12-1 (paper)

Go to http://www.universityreaders.com/publish/lmssa
for links to the authors' websites.

University Readers
800.200.3908 I www.universityreaders.com

Leadership and Management Studies in Sub-Sahaı

Selected papers presented at the Leadership & Management S
2006 Conference, Stone Town, Zanzi

Romie F. Littrell
AUT Business School
Auckland University of Technolo
Auckland, New Zealand
Email: crossculturalcentre@yahoo.

Prem Ramburuth
Australian School of Business
The University of New South W
Sydney, New South Wales, Aust
Email: p.ramburuth@unsw.edu

Table of Contents

Acknowledgements

Financial support and support in kind for the conference has been provided by:

- Sheraton Kampala-Uganda managed by GoldenLeaves Hotels Management Company
- The Australian Government through AusAID
- Administrative funding and resources were provided by the AUT Business School, Auckland University of Technology, Auckland, New Zealand
- Zanzibar Beach Resort
- Zanzibar Excursions Limited

Scientific Committee of the 2006 Conference

The Scientific Committee was responsible for management of the solicitation, review, and selection of articles, arranging the presentation agenda, and publishing the printed agenda.

CONFERENCE COMMITTEE – 2006

The conference committee was responsible for advising on the venue, dates, organisation, structure, and marketing of the conference.

Conference Chair:
Romie F. LITTRELL
Auckland University of Technology
Auckland, New Zealand
Email: lmsssa2006@yahoo.com

Australia: Prem RAMBURUTH
University of New South Wales
Sydney, New South Wales, Australia
Email: p.ramburuth@unsw.edu.au

Australia: Margaret MATANDA
Monash University, Victoria, Australia
Email:
Margaret.Matanda@BusEco.monash.edu.au

Canada and West Africa:
Armel Brice ADANHOUNME
HEC Montréal, Québec, Canada
Email: armel-brice.2.adanhounme@hec.ca

EU: Temi ABIMBOLA
University of Central England
Birmingham, United Kingdom
Email: Temi.Abimbola@uce.ac.uk

EU: Ashok SOM
ESSEC Business School, Paris
Cergy-Pontoise Cedex, France
Email: Mail: SOM@essec.fr

Nigeria: Augustine AHIAUZU
Rivers State University of Science &
Technology, Port Harcourt, NIGERIA.
E-mail: cimrat@phca.linkserve.com

West Africa: Osarumwense IGUISI
Euro-African Management Research Centre
(Maastricht; Brussels; Paris)
Brussels, Belgium
E-mail: e-amac@cuci.nl

USA: Shawn DALY
Tiffin University
Tiffin, Ohio, USA
Email: SDaly@tiffin.edu

Zimbabwe: Zororo MURANDA
Chinhoyi University of Technology
Bag 7724
Chinhoyi, Zimbabwe
Email: zororomuranda@yahoo.com

PREFACE

The Leadership & Management Studies in Sub-Sahara Africa conferences consist of a voluntary association of individuals interested in development of Africa through improving leadership and management competencies of Africans. Our initial efforts consist of empirical and theoretical research investigations and reviews of studies in the area.

This book consists of articles selected by the editors from the papers presented at the 2006 conference in Stone Town, Zanzibar. All submissions were reviewed by the editors and the authors invited to revised and update their work for publication. The contents of the book consist of the articles from those authors who were invited, agreed to have their work included, and submitted an updated version. The full proceedings publication on CD is available for purchase from lmsssa@gmail.com.

Significant contributions were made to the success of the conference and the book by Anil Kamdar, General Manager of the Zanzibar Beach Resort near Stone Town; Ali Mohammed Ameir, General Manager of the Zanzibar Excursions travel and tourist agency; Vijay Vijeyakumaar, CEO of GoldenLeaves hotel management company and the Sheraton-Kampala, Uganda. We are also greatful to the Government of Australia for supporting attendees through the AusAID programme.

Romie F. Littrell
Auckland, New Zealand
December 2007

Welcome Address from Government of Zanzibar

Honourable Dr. Mwinyihaji Makame Mwadini
Minister of the President's Office of the Government of Zanzibar
Conference Centre, Zanzibar Beach Resort, Stone Town
25 June 2006

Mr. Chairman, organizers and sponsors of the conference, distinguished participants, invited guests, ladies and gentlemen, it is indeed a very great honour for me to officiate the opening of this conference on a very Topical Issue to Africa and the world in general.
May I thank the sponsors and organizers for the invitation.

Allow me at the outset to welcome you all to Tanzania and Zanzibar in particular. I believe you will be taking some time after the conference to tour the Island so as to enjoy its beautiful scenery and the taste, touch and aroma of the Spice Islands. You are welcome to our beautiful Island.

I have been informed that this conference of prominent academicians shall deliberate on the general topic of leadership and management. The list of participants is highly impressive. I note the presence of people with wide experiences from all the continents. There are representatives from Africa, Europe, Asia, Israel, Australia and New Zealand, Canada and the United States of America. I am sure such a mixture will bring a variety of knowledge for not only the participants but it will also benefit organizations, the countries you represent and the world at large. Indeed Zanzibar is fortunate to host such a distinguished gathering.

I am not an academician. I have been a civil servant for many years of my active life, and currently I am in Politics. As such I can not pretend to be academically conversant with the topic of this conference. However, allow me to share a few general ideas from a political perspective.

African countries, similar to other countries on the globe have a rich history in leadership, let alone the pre-history. African countries after independence from the late 1950s have gone through varying forms of leadership and development management. We have seen one party state leadership, military leadership, outright dictators and a few brands of African democratic leaders. Each of these claimed to represent the interests of its people in terms of articulation of the development agenda. Most of these leadership traits however lacked some important virtues of good leadership that is accountability to the people, and people's participation and ownership of the development agenda.

Over the years, with globalization encircling all nations, and especially with the end of global bipolarization at the end of the cold war, international leadership and development management standards exerted pressure for change. Even though it was slow, this change has been positive. Today an African leader is assessed from the way he or she came to power. This is because the democratic electoral institution has taken root in many countries. Pluralism in politics and the existence of opposition political parties have now become an acceptable phenomenon. Elections are carried out at regular constitutional intervals.

With this new development African leaders are now not merely judged on the basis of how they came to power but on how best they are able to articulate the development interests of their people. A good leader is the one who is able to institutionalize an acceptable development agenda. He oversees the building of a participatory mechanism that involves all the segments of society through the public sector, private sector, civil society and community based organizations. Through participation, the people define their own development needs and own the process of their achievements. A good leadership promotes a conducive macro-economic environment, assures society of law and order, provide basic social services to enable individuals to cultivate their talents in the production of goods and services.

Development management is an attribute of good leadership. Good leadership is based on transparent decision making, accountability, integrity, respect for human rights and promotion of the rule of law. Good leaders are seen beyond the ballot box. They actively build a management structure to spearhead development through the implementation of the promises they delivered during elections. We now have come to accept that a good African leader is the one who supervises and manages, through a properly laid down institutional framework that involves the participation of all stakeholders, a poverty reduction strategy that has measurable and achievable targets. A good leader understands the importance of addressing issues concerning vulnerable groups, women, youth, the aged and the disabled. It is also now a creed that a good leader does not tolerate corruptive practices and works to expose and bring to justice corrupt elements.

These are noble and ideal visions of a good African leader and leadership in general. Africa is far from totally achieving this noble vision. Poverty is rampant. In many corners of the continent democratic institutions are being tramped upon. Civil wars, outright genocide, diseases and famines claim thousands of innocent lives annually. The scourge of HIVIAIDS is spreading like bush fire unabated.

Africa needs assistance, assistance toward poverty eradication, assistance to be able to achieve the internationally accepted Millennium Development Goals (MDG). The current pace of change and reforms demand extra thrust to propel African countries towards the attainment of MDG targets by 2015. Good leadership and practical Development Management are crucial ingredients to the needed thrust.

You have a very crucial and interesting agenda before you. I wish this conference the best success. Zanzibar, Tanzania and the African continent are waiting to see what can be achieved from your three days of exchanges.

I once again welcome you all to Zanzibar. Having said that, I now have the honour to declare your Conference on Leadership and Management officially open.

Thank you for your attention.

Plenary Address

Honourable Ms. Samia S. Hassan, Minister of Tourism, Trade and Investment of the Government of the Government of Zanzibar
Conference Centre, Zanzibar Beach Resort, Stone Town
25 July 2006

Mr. chairman, conference participants, ladies and gentlemen, good evening.

At the outset, let me express my gratitude and appreciation for being invited to meet you this evening, for purposes of sharing Ideas and experiences, and, getting to know one another. It is an honour and a pleasure to me.

In my capacity, as a minister responsible for Tourism, Trade and Investment, I feel obliged to take this opportunity to welcome all those who came from far, .outside our country boundaries, to this romantic Island. Allow me at this point, to brief this gathering on the history of Zanzibar.

The name Zanzibar evokes images and dreams of the exotic archipelago, nestled in the Indian Ocean, and a destination that is both legendary and mysterious. Historically, the Islands have been at the hub of the Monsoon trading routes for millennia. It was this very place, where some of the great moments in history were enacted, where journeys of discovery sometime started and some ended, and, where glamorous Sultanates were established. In fact, it is even gossiped, that this is where the first mediaeval global village was founded.

Zanzibar retains the imprint of its historic legacy in the meandering streets of Stone Town, as well as, in the language, Swahili, with its multiple roots, and, in the rare antiques displayed in bazaars and markets.

In general, Zanzibar which enjoys a romantic nature of its name, as well, strategically located for business investment and for tourism. It offers a rich cosmopolitan (African, Arabian, and Indian) culture, which moulds the people of Zanzibar with peculiar characters of softness, honesty, humbleness, intelligence, and charm. Moreover, Zanzibar is endowed with pristine beaches that adorn the coastlines, and the fragrant spice plantations that blossom from the interior and make a thick forest. This is an extraordinary tropical paradise which is a tourism destination that knows the way forward.

I was informed that this convention is for making a thorough analysis on leadership in Africa and the type of leadership that could bring about economic growth. This being the case, allow me now to spend some few minutes to echo my voice on the discussion.

I would like to focus my comments on the concept of ethnicity, which is a quite vital component of leadership in Africa. In pre-colonial Africa subjective aspects of ethnicity started to become more conspicuous with processes of formation and consolidation of centralised state systems. Centralised state systems were characterised by the emergence and growth of ruling aristocracies and dynasties, new forms of ideological and political institutions, and the establishment of standing armies. Class relationships between the ruling aristocracies and the subject people also grew within state systems.

As was the case with the ideology of national unity, the ideology of developmentalism had the tendency of marginalizing ethnic pluralism under the belief that modern development through processes of industrialisation, development of communication and transport infrastructure, modern education and health service, and urbanisation would make ethnicity and ethnic identity disappear[1]. This tendency therefore resulted in contradictions between ethnicity and development, resulting in accentuated ethnic conflicts.

This analysis is also revealing that the disintegrative role of colonial and post-independence states has been facilitated mainly by the system of periphery capitalism in the forms of colonial and neo-colonial relations. Thus during the nationalist struggle for independence and during the post-independence era such capitalist relations have contributed to the growth of contradictions between African nationalism and ethnicity. The contradictions have in turn given rise to the growth of ethnised politics and consequently ethnised leadership.

In discussing the development of a new leadership in Africa all these historical facts need to be taken into consideration. As far as the arguments of development are concerned, the new leadership should be of the type which first and foremost, will facilitate the process of bringing ethnic conflicts to an end in the continent.

Three phases of leadership can be traced in Africa. The first phase was that of the 1960s, soon after the independence of most countries. This was the phase of visionary African leaders who had great ideas for the continent and its people, ideas including complete liberation from colonialism and white minority rule; fight against poverty, disease and ignorance, and the creation of a united continent.

The second phase of leadership also came from the late 1960s to the 70s and 80s. This can be seen as a phase of leadership characterised by neo-colonialism and exploitation, with leaders who in alliance with neo-colonial forces have been looting the wealth of the African continent and its people such wealth to foreign banks in Europe and elsewhere. Such leaders who became millionaires and billionaires were not elected by the people but came to power through military means.

The second phase of leadership came also from the late 1960s to the 70s and 80s. This can be seen as a phase of leadership characterized by neo-colonialism and exploitation, with leaders who in alliance with neo-colonial forces have been looting the wealth of the African continent and its people, and repatriating such wealth to foreign banks in Europe and elsewhere. Such leaders who became millionaires and billionaires were not elected by the people but came to power through military means.

The third phase of leadership is witnessing new leaders who are not corrupt and who do not generally enrich themselves; those who do enrich themselves will invest their wealth in the development of Africa. This is when real Africa is just being born, still weak but gaining strength and confidence.

---

[1] Hettne, Björn. (1993). Ethnicity and development - An elusive relationship. *Contemporary South Asia*, 2:2, 123 – 149.

The leadership of the second phase is in the process of dying. Good and bad leadership is not mainly based on corrupt and non-corrupt, undemocratic and democratic leaders, but a close examination of developments in Africa indicated a close correlation between corrupt and ethnised leadership. Evidence elsewhere in Africa has shown that corrupt leaders are not only dictatorial but also base their political power in ethnic, racial and even religious groups. Today's world is rapidly evolving it is more complex, more interrelated, more interdependent.
The challenges faced by the next generation of global leaders will be more intractable than any that have come before. Confronting these issues will require fresh thinking, as well as innovative and truly global solutions.

Old problems and emerging risks can not be mastered with the current set of strategies, institutions, standards and attitudes. It is time for the new generation - the Young Global Leaders -to step forward with bold and creative strategies to address the deficiencies in the management of global and regional affairs.

And also, to take pre-emptive action before problems ripen into catastrophes, we need to take creative approach to tackle terrorism, economic crises, environmental degradation, cultural annihilation, disease and poverty. We must also define the role and responsibilities of regions and nation states searching for an identity in an increasingly interdependent world.

Technological and scientific advances in such areas as communication and medicine can provide great new benefits, but without proactive management they could also pose tremendous risks and ethnical concerns.

Humankind needs dedicated young leaders to meet such challenges. And so, I urge you diligent Professors to facilitate growth of knowledge on Styles of leadership in Africa that could facilitate growth on socio-economic development, for the betterment of the Continent.

Let me at this juncture applaud the wise decision of making this convention in Zanzibar. I salute the organizers and financiers for catalyzing the process and making this gathering possible. My sincere thanks to you dear participants for accepting to attend this conference in this Island.

I once again welcome you all' to Zanzibar and I would humbly request the organization of the conference to allow sometime for tourism, so that you have an attestation of what I have just told you about Zanzibar.

SECTION 1

INTRODUCTORY DISCUSSIONS OF LEADERSHIP ISSUES IN SUB-SAHARAN AFRICA

BEAUTY, CULTURE AND SPIRIT IN LEADERSHIP: AN AFRICAN PERSPECTIVE

Prof. Lovemore Mbigi

Introduction

The task of leadership throughout the ages has been that of enablers of development or progress in society, communities and organizations. Therefore, the ultimate task of leadership in any given society is that of transformation. Effective leadership must have the capacity to transform individuals by providing role models. Leaders should be able to transform their societies, communities and institutions.

Culture and Leadership

The focus of leadership transformation should be around three key areas of human existence, which are detailed below:

i. **Economics** which calls for the creation of societal value, wealth and brotherhood of humanity or fraternity.

ii. **Politics** which involves the creation of influence and power relations, as well as human rights which may require creating a measure of acceptable comparative equality. Comparative equality should always be characterized by liberty or freedom.

iii. **Culture** whose pillars are education, language and religion.

According to the philosopher Rudolf Steiner, cultural renaissance or renewal is the foundation that determines the quality and quantity of political, social and economic transformation. It is the task of leadership to look after the culture of institutions, communities and society. In ancient African communities and institutions the key of leadership was to look after cultural renewal and preservation to ensure political, social and economic progress. The reality in modern African societies, communities and institutions is that the role of cultural stewardship has been neglected. This has resulted in social and economic decay to a point where African leaders have become funeral undertakers of dying institutions, communities and societies.

The South African political dispensation and reconciliation is home-grown; that may be the reason why it has been sustainable. The resultant shared national rainbow vision is sustainable because it has given South Africans a sense of shared destiny. It is a vision rooted in the indigenous African philosophy of Ubuntu, with emphasis on the values of interdependence. It is important for the modern African leadership to reconnect with their cultural heritage and become guardians of African cultural renewal, as well as becoming positive forces in social, political and economic transformation in their societies, communities and institutions.

Pivotal Role of Culture in Development

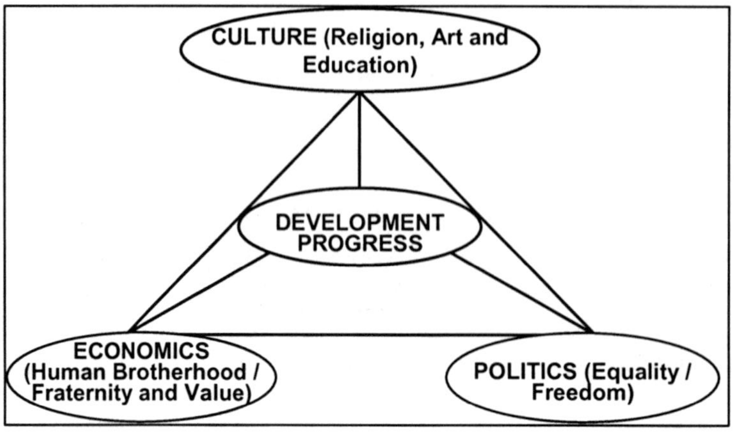

Social, political and economic transformation is determined by the rate of cultural renewal.

Most modern urban Africans have lost their collective identity and memory due to colonialism. They are neither Western nor African. They are in a halfway-house situation; a place where there is no identity. This undermines the possibility of achieving progress, local, national, as well as global identity.

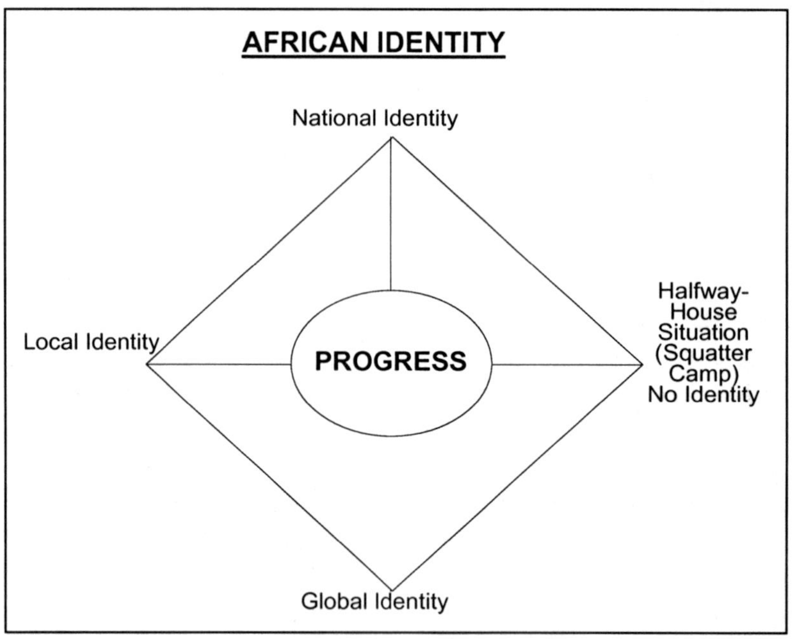

Current State of Cultural Renewal

At the moment African culture is not dynamic. Its development is retarded and marginalized by Western culture, which has undermined **economic and business development**, as well as social and political transformation.

Institutional leadership should focus on cultural renewal to ensure the development of genuine African cultural forces to drive economic and business development as illustrated by the economic history and business revolution of both Europe and Japan. This is well articulated by the Arab philosopher Hisham Sharabi, "Only Europe, being the first to modernise, was the transformation into modernity . . . autonomous and therefore authentic. In all other cultures with the exception of Japan, modernization occurred under dependent conditions, which lead to distorted, inauthentic modernity."

"It is important to note that in the development the various . . . societies were hampered not only by internal structures, but also by the decisiveness with which Europe emerged as the centre of wealth and power in the world."

The inspirational factor for us in Africa is Europe's unique achievement in its ability to transcend its **feudal state** and effect transition to modernity wholly on its own.

The problem of the African elite, both White and Black, is its dependency on the West in economic and cultural terms. There is also a lack of consciousness and appreciation of the importance of cultural capital as a key economic resource. Therefore, there is a need in investment in both cultural intelligence and capital. The result is a halfway-house situation where, as a people, we are neither authentic Africans nor authentic Europeans with no distinct cultural identity which is an important reference point for achieving global, as well as national identity and economic success. It is not by accident that your most enterprising groups such as the Jews, Indians, Japanese and Chinese have deep cultural roots and a distinct cultural identity. Entrepreneurship requires meaningful confidence which can only be inspired by high personal confidence.

Yet again the example of Japan is illuminating, for it was fully aware of the consequences of foreign borrowing and it relied on its domestic, cultural and financial resources to drive its industrialization and modernization process. Again Hisham Sharabi is very explicit about the cultural dimensions of modernity, **"Modernism, consciousness of being modern, is a vision involving the transformation of self and the world, which finds its expression not only in 'reason' and 'revolution' but in art, literature and philosophy as well."**

The ultimate task of leadership in African organizations and communities is to develop intelligent cultural strategies rooted in African cultural belief systems and thought to ensure sustainable development, as well as transformation. The role of leadership is to develop the cultural capital and mindset of the organization to ensure extraordinary performance. Culture is not developed by the front-line employees or by the grassroots masses but by the leaders.

Culture determines the spirit of the organization. It is the role of management to create and nurture the spirit of the organization. Peter F Drucker, the philosopher of modern management, writes in his classic book on management as follows: "For the spirit of the organization is created from the top. If an organization is great in its spirit, it is because the spirit of its top people is great. If it decays, it does so because the top rots; as the proverb has it 'Trees die from the top'. No one should ever be appointed to senior position unless top management is willing to have his/her character serves as a model for subordinates."

In terms of the indigenous African cultural worldview, the primary role of leadership is to nurture the spirit and culture of the societal institutions and communities. Indigenous African chiefs and kings are first and foremost the spiritual and cultural guardians of the communities. They have to be suitable and competent in discharging their cultural and spiritual roles first, above all other roles and duties. Modern African leadership may need to embrace this heritage in order to build effective institutions and progressive communities on a firm foundation of a thriving and attractive African civilization with civilized values characterized by a governance conscience and compassion. For we have to manage transformation with compassion without destroying the hope in our organizations and communities.

Max DePree, the modern management guru, put it very clearly in his book, ***Leadership is an Art*** when he says, "Leaders must take a role in developing, expressing and defending stability and values. In a civilized institution or corporation, we see good manners, respectful persons, and understanding of the way in which we serve each other."

The current emphasis in leadership on scientific aspects of management and analytical tools is ruinous because management is an art and not a science. Leadership should not only have a quest for the truth, but also have a quest for purpose, meaning, good and beauty.

Beauty in Organizations and Communities

Leadership must have a quest for cultural capital. The key pillars of any culture are:

i. Religion (spiritual capital).

ii. Art (beauty).

iii. Education.

In indigenous African cultures, indeed all ancient cultures, the religious institutions looked after culture with the support of the ruling elite.

- Africa needs a new breed of leadership that can look at a beautiful forest with rapture and sanctify its beauty by making it a sacred sanctuary.
- Africa needs a new breed of leadership that can look at the mystery of our existence and be inspired to search for its spiritual meaning.
- Africa needs a new breed of leadership that can look at nature with awe and be inspired by its teachings and its capacity to give unlimited scope to the imagination which can inspire the creation of beautiful products and a beautiful world. The American religious philosopher Thomas Moore defines beauty as follows; **"For the soul, then beauty is not defined as pleasantness but rather as the quality in things that invites absorption and contemplation."**

Modern African leadership in institutions and communities have to understand beauty and give it a more prominent place in life, society and workplaces. Indigenous African spirit nature religions have always understood the value of beauty in a very deep sense as evidenced by their emphasis on beautiful ceremonial regalia, music, dancing and drumming. Thomas Moore says, "Religion has always understood the value of beauty, as we see in churches and temples, which are never built purely on practical considerations, but always for the imagination."

Every manager and every employee in every institution in Africa should understand beauty in a very deep sense if Africa is going to create beautiful products and care for the environment. Everything in the universe is connected. The sacred is always present and standing with an open invitation to us, according to African tribal spiritual traditions. This allows us to see the divinity of all things in the universe, including the products we produce, the services we render and the work we do. Humanity shares a common brotherhood with all things in the universe. We need a sense of shared destiny that extends to all common objects in the universe. It is very difficult to live in the world without an emotional relationship with nature. The divinity of nature African tribal spiritual traditions is not only a possibility but also a reality. As leaders in organizations, we need to foster a relationship with nature in the manner detailed below:

i. Pausing every day for reflection and contemplation through meditation, as well as prayer.

ii. Observing nature.

iii. Listening to the eloquence of silence in nature and absorbing its eloquent teachings.

iv. Being open and prepared to be affected and stirred by its beauty.

v. Meaningful reflection of traumatic events in our personal life in order to find meaning and personal destiny meaning in them.

We discover the person within us and our spiritual path in the darkest zero hour of our life. If, as leaders, we are not making a difference and doing something extraordinary with our life, it does not matter how long we live. If we do not love the common objects on Mother Earth, we cannot love the world. The world only exists in its individual objects. True environmental care is rooted in deep feeling for the universe and a deep personal realization that this world is our shared home and sanctuary. In fact, without this realisation and relatedness we lose our sense of belonging and identity, which will lead to emptiness, as well as a loss of life meaning.

As leaders of our institutions and communities, we have to expose ourselves to the power of beauty and risk the rational emotions it stirs within us. If we can accept the invitation of the great possibilities of life, then we can develop authenticity which will stir the great genius, which can lead to creativity and inspire us to take our organizations and communities beyond the known horizon, as well as boundaries.

Max DePree puts it very clearly when he says, **"To lose sight of the beauty of ideas and of hope and opportunity, to frustrate the right to be needed, is to be at the dying edge."**

As institutional leaders we need to spend a lot of time learning about the beauty and significance of our work, so as to develop a deep feeling for it. Beauty can be understood only through experiential learning, through humanities, performance arts, and art form itself. According to Thomas Moore "Art, broadly speaking, is that which invites us into contemplation, art intensifies the presence of the world. We see it more vividly and deeply. The emptiness that many people complain dominated their lives comes in part from the failure to let the world in, to perceive it and engage in it fully."

Action Pointers on Beauty

- Take time to appreciate all the beauty in the world.
- Take personal responsibility to create beauty in your life.
- Decorate the placed you live at, so as to be the highest expression of beauty.
- Ensure that the clothes you wear are the highest expression of distinctive beauty.
- Ensure that you live an organized life.
- Ensure that your home is orderly, as it is the structural dimension of beauty.
- Ensure that your home is well maintained.
- Ensure that you listen to beautiful music.
- Ensure that you choose a beautiful spouse.

- Ensure that you beautify your children.
- Ensure that you sculpture your body to be the highest expression of beauty through an appropriate diet and exercise.
- Pursue beautiful thoughts and ideas.
- Invest in attractive pieces of art.
- Beautify your workplace.
- Decorate your workplace so that it becomes the highest expression of beauty.
- Ensure that you workstation or office is orderly.
- Put artistic design in whatever work you do.
- Establish a garden so that it can be the highest expression of beauty.
- Design and deliver service in the spirit of harmony and beauty.
- Design and produce beautiful products.
- Beauty can be inspiring and uplifting.

Spiritual Capital in Organizations and Communities

It is a requirement of leadership to create and preserve the good in our institutions and society. Indigenous African spiritual traditions are obsessed with the creation of the good and to draw our attention to what is good in the world and to assist us as leaders to become good people. Our tribal spiritual traditions help us to develop consciousness about what it means to be a good person and what it means to be a good society, for it is the role of leadership to create good progressive institutions and communities. The highest form of consciousness that we can attain as leaders, is spiritual consciousness. This is attained through reflection and silence, by deep personal contemplation over significant events in our life, the organization and community. This will lead to a deep sense of self-understanding and a deep search for meaning, setting in motion a process of personal transformation which gives us the capacity to let go of the tendency to blame others for our misfortune and accept full responsibility for our circumstances.

Thomas Moore says, "Living artfully therefore requires something as simple as pausing. Some people are incapable of being arrested by things because they are always on the move. A common symptom of modern life is that there is no time for thought, or even for letting impressions of the day sink in. Yet it is only when the world enters the heart that it is made into soul. The vessel in which soul making takes place in an inner container scooped out by reflection and wonder."

In African tribal traditions reflection is reached through moments of prolonged silence and reflection which may range from a few hours to a few days which are accompanied by fasting called "Kutsanya" in Shona. Prolonged reflection can also be achieved through a night ceremony or vigil accompanied by trance dancing, music, collective singing and drumming around a key strategic theme, punctuated by insights from psychic visioning experiences. This ceremony in the Shona tribal language is called "Dandaro". At Eastern Highlands Tea Estates I began to apply "Dandaro" procedures to worker and management education to raise and accelerate strategic consciousness or awareness throughout the organization. It was a great success as it dramatically increased both productivity and profitability. "Dandaro" has also been adapted to modern African Christianity through a ceremony called "Vhuserere".

Africa needs leaders who can look at the gift of beautiful mountains and have the capacity to be inspired by them to transcend our unfortunate historical and economic circumstances, then lead us into the promised land of economic prosperity. Africa needs leaders who are capable of listening to the eloquence of silence and the rhythms in their hearts and then transcend the daily pressures and stresses and be able to reach out for the possibilities of life.

In both Eastern and Western thought there is proliferation of literature describing the possibility of profound developmental transformations in our adult life. The most ancient is found in Vedic traditions of India and Asian Buddhist traditions experienced through yoga and meditation. The most eloquent and scientifically validated of these has been in the Vedic psychology of the Vedic spiritual guru Maharishi Mahesh Yogic which is a theory of seven levels of consciousness as an integrated hierarchy of discrete levels of cognitive functioning. Maharishi presents this ancient knowledge in a very simple manner and makes it available through a set of uniform procedures - the Transcendental Meditation (TM) and TM Sidhi programme which requires no change in lifestyle or religious belief system, but are predicted to accelerate the development of consciousness. CIDA City Campus in South Africa has developed a Consciousness Based Educational (CBE) model for training managers which incorporates TM practices with a high degree of success.

Levels of Organizational and Community Consciousness

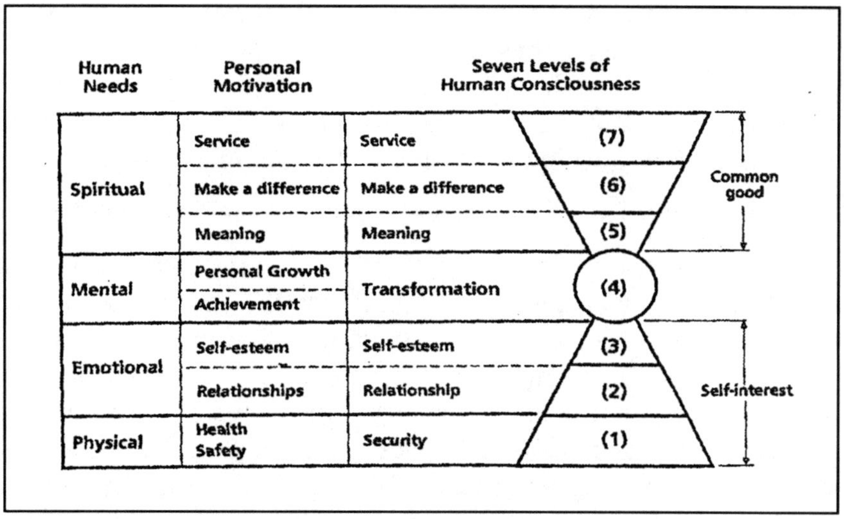

High spiritual consciousness in organizations and communities is achieved when leaders can create and enact an exciting extraordinary story that can shift people's mindsets, which enables them to see possibilities in the world and find new hope in their existence.

Culture and Transformation

Leaders in Africa are called upon to manage change of three levels which are detailed below:

i. **Improvement Change (level one):** This level requires leaders to galvanize their organizations and communities for improvement in order to optimise existing potential by developing best practices.

ii. **Intelligent Copying and Borrowing (level two):** This entails benchmarking against the leaders in a given field. This requires movement from the old to new worldviews, but the new has been done elsewhere. This may involve benchmarking and intelligent borrowing from global systems of cutting-edge practices.

iii. **Mindset Change (level three):** The key element of this type of change is that it involves elements of a paradigms shift. This level requires a lot of self-confidence based on deep cultural rootedness so that people can develop new cultural lenses for them to see the world anew, so as to develop creative and innovative solutions to the problems, as well as the ability to develop revolutionary breakthrough ideas. This is not possible without creating a new level of strategic consciousness throughout the organization and the community. This is not possible without cultural and spiritual renewal, which are the two major keys to organizational, community and personal transformation.

It is the role of leadership to bring presence and profound meaning and hope into any situation and into this confusing world characterized by rapid and chaotic change. In indigenous African spiritual traditions a leader is the ultimate medium or channel of meaning, hope and value. In organizations and communities the concept of servant leadership brings together service and meaning to express the fundamental interdependent values of Ubuntu. This is well expressed by the Archbishop Desmond Tutu:

"Africans have a thing called UBUNTU; it is about the essence of being human, it is part of the gift that Africa is going to give to the world. It embraces hospitality, caring about others, being willing to go that extra mile for the sake of another. We believe that a person is a person through other persons; that my humanity is caught up and bound up in yours. When I dehumanize you, I inexorably dehumanize myself. The solitary human being is a contradiction in terms, and therefore you seek to work for the common good because your humanity comes into its own in community, in belonging."

- Archbishop Desmond Tutu, The Right to Hope: Global Problems, Global Vision (1995) -

There is a need for us to find meaning in our work. We have to accept the personal responsibility for personal meaning and to develop the capacity within us to access meaning. Ancient indigenous African and Eastern traditions may be instructive in this regard. Julian Burger may be correct in saying, "Indigenous peoples are one of the world's most persistent voices of conscience, alerting humankind as to the dangers of environmental destruction. As the world searches for alternative strategies to deal with global problems, it is turning more and more to indigenous peoples. Much of their respect for nature, their methods of resource management, social organization, values and culture are finding echoes in the writings of scientists, philosophers, politicians and thinkers."

Conclusion

Organizations and their leaders attain high levels of consciousness when they operate beyond the bottom-line and personal interest to serve both the host community and society. They enlarge their sense of accountability to include not only their workplace but also the local community and society. They have to be aware of major challenges facing society and are active in finding solutions. They have a sense of shared destiny with the world and are able to see the complex web of our interconnectedness with everything in the universe and attach significant meaning to it. It may be appropriate to conclude with the voice of Danah Zohar,

"To lift the curse of contemporary capitalism, we must envision a broader and deeper view of what it means to be human beings. We are not primarily economic beings; we are fundamentally creatures of meaning. Our brains are designed to ask the existential questions such as, What is the meaning of life? Why was I born?, What am I here for?, Why must I die? We are designed to seek an overarching "story" about ourselves that gives meaning, value and a sense of purpose to our lives."

This can be achieved by bringing back spirituality in our life through the practice of meaningful rituals and ceremonies in organizations as well as in communities. Collective rituals and ceremonies are the sacred technology through which leaders help their organizations and communities remain conscious of spiritual ideas and values.

Application Guidelines

- Redefine the role of leadership to emphasise spiritual and cultural roles in the organization.
- Emphasise cultural, spiritual, artistic, political and philosophical dimensions in the training and development of all levels of leadership in the organisation.
- Ensure the development and implementation of a consciousness-based educational (CBE) model for training and development of managers in the organisation, so as to attain the seven levels of consciousness.
- Pay particular attention to the artistic and beauty elements in the development of the culture of the organisation.
- Ensure that there are a sufficient number of managers with liberal arts educational background with degrees in humanities, the fine and performance arts, as well as the social sciences.
- The curriculum for training leaders and worker education should have a high dose of cultural, philosophical, spiritual and artistic training, as well as liberal education.
- Worker education should also focus on helping employees to develop meaning and purpose in their work, as well as life including personal growth strategies.

Conclusion

Africa needs a new breed of leadership which has the capacity to transcend daily stresses and pressures, as well as the limitations imposed by its history and its current unfavourable circumstances to grasp and create an attractive future. A bold leadership with deep feeling for cultural renewal and a deep appreciation for beauty to create a vibrant African civilization with a sense of legacy and compassion. Our duty is not to condemn African history, but our duty is to transform the collective African story.

References

Alexander, C. et al 1989 Higher Stages of Human Development. New York: Oxford University Press.

Arrien, A. 1993 The Four Fold Way. San Francisco: HarperSanFrancisco.

Barrett, R. 1998 Liberating the Corporate Soul. Johannesburg: Butterworth-Heinemann.

Bloomsbury Publishing 2003 Best Practice. Cambridge: Perseus Publishing.

DePree, M. 1989 Leadership Is An Art. New York: Dell Publishing.

Drucker, P. F. et al 2005 The Daily Drucker. Oxford: Butterworth-Heinemann.

Moore, T. 1992 Care of the Soul. London: Piatkus.

Sharabi, H. 1988 Neopatriarchy: A Theory of Distorted Change in Arab Society. New York: Oxford Press.

Steiner, R. 1999 Towards Social Renewal. London: Steiner Press.

Wallerstein, I. 2003 The Decline of American Power. London: The New Press.

Zohar, D. et al 2000 Spiritual Intelligence: The Ultimate Intelligence. New York: Bloomsbury.

TRIALS AND TRIBULATIONS OF MANAGEMENT AND LEADERSHIP IN (SUB-SAHARA) AFRICA

GIDO MAPUNDA
University of South Australia
School of Management
P.O. Box 2471, Adelaide
South Australia 5000
Australia
Tel: +61 88 302 0482
Fax: + 61 88 302 0512
e-mail: gido.mapunda@unisa.edu.au

ABSTRACT

One of the crucial factors in the economic development of Sub-Sahara Africa is good governance, which falls squarely on management and leadership both in the private and public sectors. This article is primarily a case-based and conceptual work, which can help one understand the dynamics and challenges of management and leadership in Sub-Sahara Africa. I think an examination of the complexities of management and leadership in Sub-Sahara Africa is long overdue. Why? Many African countries have at least been politically independent for more than 30 years, yet their economies are still struggling. Tanzania, for example, has been independent for 45 years. Yet ordinary Tanzanians still struggle to make ends meet. I would argue that this applies to other economies in Sub-Sahara Africa.

It is arguable that the Western media and other international press outlets are obsessed with negative reporting when it comes to Sub-Sahara Africa. However, it is most likely that the mismanagement of African economies plays into the hands of these media outlets. For example, while Africans do not have a monopoly on corruption, it is rampant in Sub-Sahara Africa and it needs to be addressed. This paper is about real people, Africans in this case, with real challenges.

Key words: African management and leadership, Sub-Sahara Africa, brain drain, African renaissance

INTRODUCTION

It has to be said that this paper may not have many positive things to write about management and leadership in Sub-Sahara Africa. However, I have tried to be as objective as possible, and have attempted to state the problems as they are rather than paint a positive picture for the sake of it. This paper explores several critical management and leaderships issues confronting African managers and leaders. Arguably, the economic development and social advancement of African peoples is directly linked to the quality of management and leadership both in the private and public sectors. Put simply, it requires good governance. The latter should be premised on good management and leadership. Apart from its economic woes Tanzania is one of the politically stable economies in the continent and, for the purposes of this paper, is used as a case study and reference point, mindful that the situation in Tanzania is likely to be similar to other countries in Sub-Sahara Africa.

THE PROBLEM

Economic development and social advancement of ordinary African peoples in Sub-Sahara Africa is, in large part, abysmal. Most African countries became independent in the early 1960s, almost the same time as their Asian counterparts. The stark difference is that the latter have made a great leap forward in the development stakes, whereas African countries in the Sub-Sahara region have almost stagnated. Despite having more than their fair share of natural resources, African countries have very little to show for it. In this context, Tanzania is a good example. In contrast, Singapore, with no natural resources (not even water, it buys this precious resource from neighbouring Malaysia), has advanced leaps and bounds to a point where it has now joined the developed world– the first world, as it is called. What has gone wrong with African countries? Can the answer be found in management and leadership?

African countries in the Sub-Sahara region are faced with significant problems of corruption, mismanagement, managerial and leadership incompetence, lack of leadership and limited capacity and a lack of courage and willpower to fight corruption. These problems may give rise to nepotism, brain drain, increased crime rates and other associated problems. Yet one comes across people, including leaders and managers, who talk about 'lack of opportunities', 'lack of money' and 'poverty' as the root causes of African peoples' misery. This is despite the abundance of natural resources such as minerals, rivers, forests, fauna, national parks, fertile lands and a rich African cultural heritage.

The founding father of Tanzania, the late President Mwalimu Julius Nyerere (1967), used to remind Tanzanians that they should not use money as an excuse for being poor, explaining that money was in fact an outcome, which results from a person (or an organisation or indeed a nation) producing goods or services. In other words, to get money one has to produce a product or provide a service and sell it. Clearly, in order to develop, people need to be productive, that is, they have to produce goods and services for the market. I think in Sub-Sahara Africa in particular, this has serious management and leadership implications at the local, regional and national levels. The title *trials and tribulations* is a summation of the significance and seriousness of management and leadership issues and problems (challenges) in Sub-Sahara Africa. Arguably, the economic development and social advancement of African economies in the area of study depends on it.

Capacity building through education, institution building, and the realisation of ordinary peoples' dreams is almost non-existent. In Tanzania, for example, nothing much appears to have changed in regard to economic development and social advancement during the 45 years of political independence. People are still using the same simple tools of production they used before, during and after independence. Ordinary people in Dar es Salaam (the former capital, which still is the de facto capital), for example, are still using mikokoteni (a simple form of wheel barrow made of wood) to transport goods from point to point today, as they did more than 60 years ago. Town and city councils still provide inadequate services to town and city residents. Often the services are non-existent. For example, driving around Dar es Salaam you are quickly treated to potholes, which seem to greet you wherever you go. What is more, there are 'rubbish dumps' almost everywhere, a situation brought about by of lack of adequate provision of rubbish removal services by the Dar es Salaam city council and other relevant local councils. This is not because of lack of money but rather because people are lining their pockets, in one word, corruption.

Hypotheses

In the context of the topic, the paper set out to test the following two relevant hypotheses:

Hypothesis 1: Managers and leaders in Sub-Sahara Africa are preoccupied with serving themselves instead of serving the people – there is lack of servant leadership.

Hypothesis 1: Economies in Sub-Sahara Africa are ill-served due to chronic corruption (which permeates all levels of society) and poor governance.

Theoretical Backdrop

Much has been written on management and leadership in the developed world, the same cannot be said about literature on management and leadership in Sub-Sahara Africa. Consequently, the theoretical basis of this paper is general management literature rather than African management. An examination of the two key concepts – management, and leadership is in order. What is management and what is leadership? Management is the planning, organising, leading, and controlling of human and other resources to achieve organisational goals effectively and efficiently (Jones and George, 2004: 26) In addition, management includes such qualities as persistence, survival, intelligence, analysing, tolerance, reaction, and problem solving.

Leadership is the process by which an individual exerts influence over other people and inspires, motivates, and directs their activities to help achieve group or organisational goals (Jones and George, 2004: 312). Furthermore, leadership includes qualities such as passion, enthusiasm, proactive attitude, vision, trust, obsession and positive aggression. The ability of an individual to communicate a vision successfully, and the ability of an individual to bring people towards a cause and to guide them through that cause, is the essence of effective and efficient leadership. I would add another important attribute of leadership: courage to make tough decisions.

There are significant differences between management and leadership. Zaleznic (1992) identifies these differences:

TABLE 1
Differences between Leaders and Managers

Leaders	**Managers**
Innovate	Administer
Develop	Maintain
Inspire	Control
Long-term view	Short –term view
Ask what and why	Ask how and when
Originate	Initiate
Challenge the status quo	Accept the status quo
Do the right things	**Do things right**

Source: Zaleznic (1992)

Given the state of economic development and social advancement in Sub-Sahara Africa, these differences are critical to the extent that they can help explain the state of affairs in the region. It can be argued that Sub-Sahara Africa is in real need of quality managers and leaders at all levels of society. That is not to say there are no quality managers and leaders in the region. The fact is that there are and there have been examples of excellent leaders in Sub-Sahara Africa. It is arguable that these excellent leaders provide models for not only Africa, but the world. They include Nelson Mandela (Republic of South Africa), Mwalimu Julius K.

Nyerere (Republic of Tanzania), and Nkwame Nkrumah (Ghana). What did these eminent leaders have in common? They led by example, they had integrity and they took their leadership position as a responsibility not a privilege, that is, they were not self-seeking. Instead, they worked tirelessly for their fellow citizens. Above all, they were immune to corruption. In addition, they were pragmatic and honest enough not to make empty promises to the people they served. People are all too familiar with empty promises, especially close to elections.

These were not just leaders for Africa, but they were world class leaders. I try to imagine what would happen if Mwalimu Julius Nyerere or Nelson Mandela was the president of the most powerful nation on earth - America. I think the world would be a much better place. Let me briefly talk about only one of these African leadership stalwarts - Nelson Mandela. In terms of leadership, Nelson Mandela is not only an African icon but an international icon. Writing about Mandela's leadership prowess, Joseph had this to say:

> *... an international icon who was admired and honoured by heads of state, royal families and social elites around the world, but whose commitment to 'the poorest of the poor' never wavered; an African with strong attachments to the continent and its people, and a transforming leader who, like Gandhi and King, had an uncanny instinct for moving and persuading people, changing attitudes and appealing to the best in human nature.*
>
> (Joseph, in Asmal, Chidester and James, 2003: 499)

Arguably, African managers and leaders should provide African solutions to African problems. Former South African President Nelson Mandela argued for African solutions to African problems and was a vigorous cheerleader for President Clinton's statement to the South African Parliament, that the developed world had been asking the wrong question.

> *'We have been asking what can we do for Africa, what can we do about Africa?' President Clinton said. 'We must now ask what can we do* with Africa?'
>
> (Clinton, in Asmal, Chidester and James, 2003: 502)

President Clinton's statement was a clear signal that the United States had heard and understood Nelson Mandela's plea for a partnership between rich and poor nations rather than benevolent big brother domination. Although the other leaders mentioned above did not enjoy the same international prominence and standing, there is no doubt that they had similar qualities as those of Nelson Mandela. Unlike Ghana and Tanzania, the political situation in South Africa was volatile under apartheid. In addition, Mandela had been a political prisoner at Robben Island for 27 years. These two elements were always going to put Nelson Mandela and South Africa in the international spotlight.

African Leaders: Are they Leaders or Managers?

The question is: are they leaders or managers? Based on the differences between leaders and managers shown in the table above, it can be argued that most African leaders are managers not leaders. There are exceptions, which include Mwalimu Julius Nyerere; Nelson Mandela; Kwame Nkrumah of Ghana and Thabo Mbeki, the current president of the Republic of South Africa.

Arguably, the majority of African leaders display management traits rather than leadership traits. An observation of what is happening in Sub-Sahara Africa leaves one with the impression that its 'leaders' are merely managing, not leading. What they seem to be doing is administering, maintaining, controlling, accepting the status quo and doing things right even if they are wrong. Most of them are self-seeking rather than serving the people. Managers do not make things happen, rather they maintain what is in existence. They are not inclined to bring change because they are prone to accepting the status quo and maintaining it. One needs to question and challenge the system in order to change it. I think that is why nothing much seems to have happened in Sub-Sahara Africa, despite the fact that the majority of countries have been independent for over a quarter of a century. In the international community, Africa is largely seen as 'unproductive' and unable to sustain and provide for herself, not because of lack of resources but because of lack of quality managers and leaders. For example, Tanzania has had minerals dug and taken out of the country before, during and after independence. Yet Tanzania and the communities where the minerals are dug from have very little to show for these minerals. Quality leaders would have remedied this situation, which would in turn lead to significant economic development and social advancement.

Leaders make things happen. How? They do this by demonstrating leadership qualities including being inspirational, innovative, and original; having the ability to challenge the status quo; having the ability to develop their economies; and by doing the right things for their people, which results in economic development and social advancement for the citizens. If one looks at economies in Sub-Sahara Africa, how many African leaders fit the bill? Apart from corruption, what is happening in the region? Compared to what is happening in other economies, for example in Asia, perhaps not much. Clearly, there is much to be done on the management and leadership landscape. I think economic development and social advancement can take place in Sub-Sahara Africa, if its managers and leaders take leadership seriously, as a responsibility not a privilege.

Leadership: it is a responsibility not a privilege

In addition to the traits of leadership mentioned above, leadership should be treated as a responsibility not a privilege, in any organisation and at any level. Put simply, leaders should serve their people first and foremost and not themselves. I think there are key questions that should guide their behaviour and conduct, which include: Why am I in this position? What gives me the right to be in this esteemed position in life? What do I want people to remember me for when I am out of office? What will my legacy be when I vacate office? I think these are critical questions especially in the context of Sub-Sahara Africa. There is an argument here that economic development and social advancement in Sub-Sahara Africa is lagging behind primarily because of lack of quality management and leadership.

The founding father of the United Republic of Tanzania, Mwalimu Julius Nyerere (1967) said 'Tanzanians should be running while others (developed societies) are walking" in order to develop a sustainable economy. I think this is only possible if its leaders adopted this philosophy beyond lip service. In terms of economic development, Tanzania, like other countries in Sub-Sahara Africa, is a long way from walking, let alone running. In contrast, Asian countries such as Singapore, Taiwan and South Korea, to name only three, have been running ever since they became independent. This explains the significant economic development those countries have achieved.

Leadership lessons from traditional tribal chiefs can be used to reinforce the view that people in management and leadership positions should treat their position as a responsibility not a privilege. Most traditional tribal chiefs were visionary leaders who had the development of their respective tribes as their primary focus – be it military expansionism or economic development. In Tanzania, these tribal leaders introduced cash crops such as coffee, tobacco, tea, and other crops in districts such as Bukoba, Kilimanjaro, Mbinga, Njombe, Iringa and Songea. These tribal leaders or chiefs were very much a product of the tribal tradition in which they had been brought up, that is, they recognised the need to be responsible and accountable to their people, settling their disputes with careful courtesy, making them feel important and representing them with dignity. Clearly, these chiefs had leadership qualities that would stand any leader in Sub-Sahara today in good stead – they made things happen for their tribes. They served their people and led by example. One of the key elements that is lacking in Sub-Sahara Africa is servant-leadership. To be an effective leader one has to serve the rest. Robert Greenleaf (in Kreitner and Kinicki, 2007: 534) believes that great leaders act as servants, putting the needs of others, including employees, customers, and community, as their first priority. Servant-leadership focuses on increased service to others rather than to oneself. Arguably, African leaders are divorced from this noble mindset and are too preoccupied with accumulating fortunes for themselves, often at the expense of citizens and the economies they are supposed to manage.

Michael Jordan, arguably the best basketball player ever, and a very successful businessman, provides an insightful personal explanation on leading by example:

> *Leaders lead. A lot of people talk about leading, but in the end that's all they're doing, talking. I have always led by example. I don't believe in talking about what I provide to others. The last thing I need or want is to draw attention to myself. That's not who I am.*
>
> (Jordan, in Vancil, 2005: 123)

I think Jordan's stance on leadership mirrors the leadership approach and prowess of African tribal chiefs. They let their actions do the talking and there was no need for them to brag about their achievements or what they did for their people. The adage 'action speaks louder than words' is ever so true. Traditional tribal African chiefs can be useful reference points for managers and leaders in Sub-Sahara Africa, if they are serious about making things happen and hence making positive change for their people. In this context, I wish to argue that addressing corruption, for example, can lead to significant economic development and social advancement in many countries in Sub-Sahara Africa.

Management, Leadership and Corruption

In this article corruption is seen as an economic problem as well as a management and leadership problem. It has to be said at the outset that people in Sub-Sahara Africa do not have a monopoly on corruption. Westerners, and indeed other people around the world, are not immune to corruption. However, there is a key difference, which can be explained as follows: imagine that an African and a Westerner are both given a milk cow. The difference between a corrupt Westerner and a corrupt African is that the Westerner will 'milk the cow' while the African will 'kill it.' In other words, the Westerner does not get rid of the cow that provides him with sustenance - milk, whereas his African counterpart, through greed, gets rid of the cow - bleeding it to death. The following example reinforces the difference. In 1987, a Medical Officer working for Air Tanzania confided to me that "the airline (Air Tanzania) was going broke and was close to being declared bankrupt". My immediate response was "You cannot be serious. The airline is a monopoly in the country. How can it go broke when there are so many passengers waiting to travel?" Basic principles of demand and supply did not warrant that the only airline in the country would go broke. I mean, demand for air travel was very high, which was compounded by poor roads, especially during the rainy season. It was not uncommon, for example, to see passengers sitting on the floor in transit on an airplane. In other words, even if officials were 'helping themselves' the airline should still be profitable.

Luckily, South African Airways saved Air Tanzania from total collapse. Corruption problems are affecting other countries in the study area. For example, Air Zambia has long ceased to exist and as such Zambia is without its own airline service. Travels to and from Zambia rely primarily on South African Airways.

To say corruption in Sub-Sahara Africa is an endemic, serious problem is an understatement. I think African managers and leaders will be judged by their courage, determination and resolve to stamp out corruption. In fact, the problem is so entrenched that stamping it out is rather too ambitious a goal and hence unachievable, certainly in the short-term and medium-term. Arguably, any African leader who can display enough courage, relentlessness, passion and determination to reduce corruption by even 20% will be highly regarded by their ordinary citizens. I assume that in order for them to seriously address this problem, which is easily the major contributing factor to the stagnation of economies in Sub-Sahara Africa, the managers and leaders are themselves not corrupt. On the other hand, if they are, then the task of eradicating corruption has to start by the managers and leaders cleansing themselves ('becoming clean') and beginning to behave and act in a moral and ethical manner – leading by example, as it were.

The situation in Kenya is testimony to the perception that corruption is deeply embedded in the system, which makes it even more difficult to fight. According to Transparency International (New Internationalist, 2005: 22):

> *Transparency International's Kenyan Bribery Index found three-quarters of business people still expected to have to pay bribes. Officials of the Ministry of Public Works demanded the largest sums, closely followed by officials of embassies and foreign organisations. And of the ten most corrupt institutions, six were law enforcement bodies and local government authorities. ...But the real body blow came when President Kibaki's own anti-corruption tsar, John Githoni, resigned in February 2005. Colleagues in the organisation he used to head, Transparency International Kenya, said that Githoni's resignation could only mean that his job was impossible.*

It is ironic that people who should play an active role in fighting corruption are themselves culprits. In a generic sense, these are managers and leaders. To be fair to Kenya, I do not think other countries in Sub-Sahara Africa are much different.

It has to be said that governments in Sub-Sahara Africa are endeavouring to address this endemic problem, at least in theory. In Kenya for example, there are notices aplenty - notices in government buildings that tell people: 'bribes will not be taken; 'stop being corrupt.' (New Internationalist, 2005). These notices are all part of the nationwide anti-corruption campaign to tackle this endemic problem. However, what seems to bother Kenyan citizens most is President Kibaki's reluctance to prosecute wrong-doers both within his own and the previous government. Canadian High Commissioner Jim Wall (New Internationalist, 2005: **22**) sums the Kenyan situation thus: 'what is apparently lacking is...the political will to ferret out and expose the crooks.'

It can be argued that it is much easier for managers and leaders to be corrupt than to fight corruption. Why? The financial rewards are significant and therefore tempting. In addition, given that the problem is widespread (in Tanzania, for example, this is a common talking point for ordinary citizens in urban areas and villages) it is easier to go with the flow than try to go against it. Managers and leaders are supposed to provide solutions to the problem. Unfortunately, when managers and leaders are themselves corrupt they become not only part of the problem but, at least in an African context, the problem.

Put simply, it is difficult and a real challenge for managers and leaders not to be corrupt – it is much easier and personally more beneficial to be corrupt. People in Sub-Sahara Africa are desperate for managers and leaders who can make things happen on the economic development and social advancement front, which means tackling corruption beyond paying lip service. This is a real challenge that requires courage, integrity, honesty, relentlessness, uncompromising commitment and passion to serve (ordinary) citizens. At another level, it is safe to argue that this problem contributes to yet another problem, 'brain drain.' Again, I think managers and leaders in the region need to address it for the economic benefit of the region.

Research results

Hypothesis 1: The Tanzanian case study confirms the hypotheses introduced earlier.

Hypothesis 2: Primarily managers and leaders in the Sub-Sahara Africa are self-seeking and least interested in serving the people – corruption is testimony.

African 'Brain Drain' to the West

For the purposes of this paper, 'brain drain' is treated as a management and leadership problem to the extent that it has significant economic development and social advancement implications in Sub-Sahara Africa. In other words, there is an argument for managers and leaders in the region to look at how to address this problem for economic benefits of the region. Much has been written about brain drain. A detailed account of the problem is beyond the scope of this paper.

Put simply, brain drain is a situation where educated people, mainly from developing nations, migrate to developed countries in search of a better life and better opportunities. There are numerous examples of brain drain. For the purpose of this paper a few examples from World Health Organisation (WHO) Reports (New Internationalist, 2005) will suffice:

- Today there are more doctors from Benin working in France than there are in Benin.
- There are more Ethiopian doctors in Washington DC than in the whole of Ethiopia.
- South Africa loses almost half its qualified doctors to Canada, Britain and Australia. It recruits staff from poorer countries like Kenya, Malawi and Zimbabwe which now account for 80% of South Africa's rural doctors.
- Zambia's public sector retained only 50 out of 600 physicians trained in medical school from 1978 to 1999.
- Britain has saved $117 million in training costs by recruiting Ghanaian doctors since 1998.
- Around 12,500 doctors and 16,000 nurses from Africa are registered to work in Britain.

Clearly, these examples are merely a scratch on the surface, and cover only one profession. There is no question that low wages and salaries in Sub-Sahara Africa, and developing countries in general (Vujicic. Zurn, Adams, and Dal Poz, 2004, 2: 3), play a role in the migration of trained personnel from the region where they are needed most to the West – countries that can afford to train their own personnel compared to their African counterparts. It is no secret that migration of labour from developing countries to developed countries is huge business at the present.

There is no need to labour the brain drain problem, which I have suggested is primarily a management and leadership problem. Put simply, people are forced to leave their motherland because they are desperate and are looking for opportunities for improved economic wellbeing and social advancement. I hold a very strong view that Sub-Sahara Africa is not poor – it is mismanaged. If it is agreed that it is a management and leadership problem, the critical question is: how do nations in Sub-Sahara Africa reverse the trend? I suggest that managers and leaders in the region can address the problem through pragmatic 'brain re-drain' strategies, some of which are discussed in the next section, albeit briefly.

Some 'brain re-drain' strategies

The most wholesome strategy would be one where professionals from the region, who reside in the west and other parts of the world, returned to their countries of origin in Sub-Sahara Africa and played an active role in the economic development and social advancement of their countries. However, this strategy is probably unrealistic for a whole range of reasons and hence not likely to work. It is also probable that this strategy is not in the best interest of both parties – governments in the region, and Africans resident overseas. However, there may be some who may want to return home.

The next best option is for countries in Sub-Sahara Africa to allow for dual citizenship to eligible nationals residing overseas. One of the benefits of this strategy is that it will enable people to play an active role in the economic development and social advancement of their respective countries. Critics may have reservations about dual citizenship, perhaps with some justification in certain cases. However, I think the benefits (positives) would outweigh the costs (negatives). In addition, the dual citizenship legislation could be written in such a way that it addressed some of the concerns. For example, it could stipulate exceptions to dual citizenship for certain categories of people for political, financial and security reasons.

Another pragmatic brain re-drain strategy is what I refer to as the 'going home without going home' strategy. Basically, the essence of this strategy is not to try and get Africans who reside overseas to return to their countries of origin in Sub-Sahara Africa, but to work out ways and means of how these overseas residents (citizens) can contribute to the economic development and social advancement of their respective countries. In fact, I would argue that, if there is good management and leadership, countries in Sub-Sahara Africa can use their overseas nationals (citizens) to great economic and social advancement advantage. The point is managers and leaders in the region need to think laterally and outside the square. The key questions might be: How can we (governments in Sub-Sahara Africa) use these people in our quest for economic development and social advancement? How can we get them involved in our development strategies and efforts?

Clearly, there are numerous ways of using these overseas residents for the benefit of their home countries. Let me cite three examples: they could be used as consultants in a wide range of professions; they could be used as business partners and/or business mentors for local businessmen and women; governments in Sub-Sahara Africa could aggressively encourage these overseas citizens to return home for holidays as often as possible – killing two birds in the process! How? Firstly, they would spend much needed foreign currencies (Euros, dollars, franc marks, pound sterling, yens); and secondly, they could be used as consultants and mentors while they are on holidays. I think this would create a much needed win–win situation for Sub-Sahara countries on the one hand, and overseas nationals (citizens) on the other. I think this strategy can result in productive and positive outcomes, which would give rise to improved economic development and social advancement.

African Renaissance

Arguably, Africa has much to offer, not only its citizens but the rest of the world. South African President Thabo Mbeki (2001) provides a visionary statement when he articulates a sense of the renewal of African greatness in the concept of African renaissance in the new millennium. This vision is premised on good governance – good management and leadership in the private and public sectors in Sub-Sahara Africa. Such vision also assumes unity among African peoples, rooted in their pride of being at the origin of all things which humankind considers important for the human race. Africa is the origin of the human race, that is, the place where man was born and hence it is the place where all peoples of the world can return to visit the site of their origins. The shear magnitude of the greatness that Africa's history represents gives us a glimpse of what Africa can offer again, given good management and leadership. Sub-Sahara Africa can provide world class leaders such as Nelson Mandela, the late Mwalimu Julius Nyerere, Kofi Anan, Thabo Mbeki, to mention only a few. Managers and leaders in Sub-Sahara Africa need to spearhead this renaissance so that Africa can maintain and sustain it greatness. Africa needs to reclaim its greatness, which can be achieved through good governance.

Conclusion

This article has raised issues and problems that are often informally discussed by citizens in their daily lives. The problems are real, sensitive (depending on whether or not one is involved in, for example, corruption) and even emotional. I think there is room for emotions in management and leadership. As mentioned earlier, the paper is about real people. Ultimately it is about addressing their wellbeing. Consequently, emotions are inevitable. Recognition and acknowledgement of emotions in management and leadership is important.

This paper is likely to trigger some negative as well as positive reactions. This is to be expected, given the nature of the issues and problems raised. However, whatever the reactions are, it is hoped that managers and leaders in Sub-Sahara Africa can seriously engage in open and transparent discussions on the issues and challenges or problems facing the region in order to provide practical solutions for the economic development and social advancement of African peoples.

The generic orientation of the paper has directly and indirectly touched on areas such as politics and history without going into detail. There is a strong correlation between management, politics and history. For example, Kanter points out:

> *Politics in business is per se neither good nor bad. The importance of political skills in management is becoming increasingly apparent. All effective managers 'play politics' by developing networks of mutual obligations with other managers in the organisation. They may also have to build or join alliances and coalitions* (Kanter, 1979: 65).

These intertwined disciplines are even more topical in less developed regions such as Sub-Sahara Africa. There has to be a harmonious relationship between them in order for countries in this area to achieve significant economic development and social advancement.

Despite its woes and shortcomings, Africa is still a great continent and has much to offer. However, it can be argued that African leaders are failing their citizens. Many African leaders are resigned to the notion that Africa is poor and seem to have succeeded in convincing themselves and the citizens of this defeatist mindset, which gives them an excuse not to do anything to facilitate economic development and social advancement in the region. They need to change this mindset. Africa is not poor rather it is mismanaged. Its leaders continue to fail African peoples. Its leaders need to have the courage not to be corrupt, to instead stamp out corruption. They need courage because it is much easier to be corrupt – often the benefits to corrupt individuals are huge.

References

Asmal, K., Chidester, D. & James, W. 2003. *Nelson Mandela in his own words: From freedom to the future.* London: Little, Brown.

Jones, G. R. & George, J. M. 2004. *Contemporary management* (3rd ed). New York: McGraw-Hill.

Kanter, R. M... 1979 Power Failure in Management Circuits. *Harvard Business Review,* 57(3): 65–75

Kreitner, R. and Kinicki, A. 2007. Organisational behaviour. (7th ed). Sydney: McGraw-Hill Irwin.

Kreitner, R. & Kinicki, A. 2004. *Organisational behaviour.* Sydney: McGraw-Hill/Irwin.

New Internationalist. 2005. The people, the ideas, the action in the fight for global justice. New Internationalist, 2005(379): http://www.newint.org/issue379/what-is-to-be-done.htm.

Nyerere, J. K. 1967. *Freedom and unity/uhuru na umoja.* London: Oxford University Press.

Vancil, M. 2005. *Driven from within: Michael Jordan.* London: Simon and Schuster.

Vujicic, M., Zurn, P., Adams, O. and Dal Poz, M. R, 2004. *'The role of wages in the migration of health care professionals from developing countries,' Human Resources for Health, Department of Human Resources for Health, WHO, 28 April 2004.*

Zalenic, A. 1992. Managers and leaders: are they different? *Harvard Business Review.* 70 (2): 126-136.

Biographical notes

Gido Mapunda is Program Director at the School of Management, University of South Australia, Australia. His undergraduate degree is from Tanzania and his master's degree is from Monash University, Melbourne and his PhD is from RMIT University, Melbourne. His research interests include management and leadership in developing nations, entrepreneurial leadership, and indigenous and minority entrepreneurship.

RESEARCHING, DELIBERATING, AND APPLYING AFRICAN LEADERSHIP AND MANAGEMENT PRACTICES

BARBARA A. TRAUTLEIN, Ph.D.
President
Systems Research and Consulting
1445 North Maidstone Drive
Vernon Hills, Illinois, USA 60061
Phone: (01) 847.549.6950
Fax: (01) 847.549.6960
E-mail: barbara@trautlein.com

and

CLARENCE D. TROWBRIDGE, M.B.A., P.M.P.
Training Manager
BP West Coast Products LLC
2350 E. 223rd Street
Carson, California, USA 90749-6210
Phone: (01) 310.847.5734
Fax: (01) 310.847.5783
email: clarence.trowbridge@bp.com

ABSTRACT

This chapter distinguishes African leadership and management practices and describes the authors' work to apply this knowledge for the betterment of a global corporation. A key goal is to attempt to overcome an imbalance in international organizational scholarship and consulting: specifically, conducting research on Western organizations and attempting to apply the theories and methods in other regions in the world. Instead, we draw on learnings from a global research program in general and African findings in particular and utilize them to enhance the workings of a Western-based multinational corporation (MNC).

We begin by summarizing findings to date from a global research initiative, "Intentional Dialogue Enabling Action Learning" (IDEAL), aimed at understanding how managers in MNCs in four geographic regions including sub-Saharan Africa perceive: 1) the ideal organization; 2) effective leadership; and 3) what works and does not work in change management. Based on the findings, we propose a previously unidentified *global yearning* among managers that transcends geography, industry, and gender for more *holistic* and *transformational* organizations systematically focused on *people*.

The research suggests that compared with the rest of the world there are distinctive features to sub-Saharan African leadership and management approaches. More specifically, sub-Saharan African managers are more likely to behave in ways that balance and embrace "transformational" leadership behaviors with "transactional" practices. These distinctive features have implications for sub-Saharan African managers, as they are challenged to proactively preserve their people-orientation as they adopt task-focused management tools from the West. Moreover, these findings point to opportunities for Western MNCs to learn and intelligently borrow the transformational practices longed for by their people and lived so seemingly naturally by the managers interviewed in sub-Saharan Africa. We offer a description of how we have applied the IDEAL framework and African-inspired people-practices in BP Refining, a global energy corporation.

Key Words: ***Leadership, Change Management, Africa, Cross-Cultural Research, IDEAL Research Program, IDEAL Framework***

INTRODUCTION

Foundations of the "IDEAL" Research Program and Framework

> *The task of leadership throughout the ages has been that of enablers of development or progress in society, communities and organizations. Therefore, the ultimate task of leadership in any given society is that of transformation... It is important for the modern African leadership to reconnect with their cultural heritage and become guardians of African cultural renewal, as well as becoming positive forces in social, political and economic transformation in their societies, communities and institutions...There is also a lack of consciousness and appreciation of the importance of cultural capital as a key economic resource. Therefore, there is a need in investment in both cultural intelligence and capital...The ultimate task of leadership in African organizations and communities is to develop intelligent cultural strategies rooted in African cultural belief systems and thought to ensure sustainable development, as well as transformation. The role of leadership is to develop the cultural capital and mindset of the organization to ensure extraordinary performance...It is a requirement of leadership to create and preserve the good in our institutions and society.*
>
> (Lovemore Mbigi, African professor, business lecturer, and consultant, keynote speaker at the inaugural Leadership and Management Studies in Sub-Saharan Africa Conference in Zanzibar, 2006)

> *Our challenge...is to understand the cultural identity of the people and places we go to – their unique values, concerns, and desires. I think of inclusion as a leap of humility – a necessary step to help us recognize that there is much we do not know and cannot understand about other individuals, even when we share culture, language and gender. The fewer the common cultural reference points we share with others, the more critical our ability to ask questions, suspend assumptions and seek appropriate help to understand the nuances of others' world views. When we do this well, we are able to recognize, attract and develop talent, however different its manifestation, we are able to operate for mutual advantage in diverse communities...We become a truly great global company.*
>
> (Patti Bellinger, BP Group Vice President, as quoted in BP, 2003: 3)

Mbigi's and Bellinger's comments speak to our purpose here: to offer research- and action-based insights geared toward the positive transformation of organizations operating around the globe, and to do so by asking questions, suspending assumptions and seeking to understand the world views of MNC managers working in vastly different cultural contexts. We offer this research, its findings and our applications with sense of humility and excitement as we attempt to express and explicate the views of a diverse group of managers around the world.

With this aspiration, we report and build-on a research initiative co-launched by the first author during a two-year period from 2004-2006. The research made use of a proprietary interview protocol and analysis methodology designed to catalogue and understand the experiences, views and aspirations of managers employed in multinational companies (MNCs) in North America, Europe, Asia, and Africa. From the research, a framework emerged that helps articulate how managers around the world conceive of "the ideal organization of the future," "effective organizational leadership," and "what works and does not work in change management." The research approach enabled comparisons across geographic region, industry and gender.

The research further elucidated themes in the African interviews that distinguished them from the rest of the world's managers. More specifically, African managers seemed more naturally adept at enacting the types of people-focused, community-oriented, and transformational behaviors longed for by managers globally. Conversely, the North American managers were more likely than those in other regions to focus on issues of profits/process over people, to neglect mention of corporate social responsibility issues, and to report feelings of personal disempowerment to effect meaningful change.

What a rich opportunity, then, to apply these findings in the North American operations of an MNC, to enable its managers to learn from best practices in other cultures, and to transform its organizational and leadership practices closer to the ideals it espouses. Thus, we launched our global- and African-informed action research within BP Refining, a global energy corporation.

Global and Sub-Saharan African Themes

The overarching theme of the research findings is a consistent and intriguing *global yearning* among managers. Their desire is for future organizations and leaders that are more *holistic*, putting at least as much attention on people and relationships as they do on task and profits. This led to positing the *IDEAL (Intentional Dialogue Enabling Action Learning) framework* – to explore and advance this consistency and alignment of managers' experiences, perspectives and aspirations around the world. The research indicates that relatively few of these desired organizations or leaders exist today because specific *organizational barriers* - thought of as inherent and widespread attitudes, mental models, habits and behaviors - get in the way. But we also suggest ways that the barriers can be overcome.

Despite the consistency that the research uncovered, we do not propose that organizations already do or should pursue the future in a uniform way. There are environmental circumstances and aspects of cultural heritage that serve as reasons for individual organizations, countries and regions to pause, dialogue and reflect on the "best" ways to proceed. This appears particularly evident in sub-Saharan Africa, which is at a critical juncture in the evolution of organizational leadership and management. On the one hand, managers in sub-Saharan Africa are drawn to the perceived efficiency and effectiveness of incorporating Western management practices into their organizations. On the other, we detected a consciousness more clearly vocalized in the sub-Saharan Africa interviews than other regions, that leaders and managers have a *responsibility* to proactively engage and develop employees and act as agents of benefit to community and society.

From a South African manager:

> *I think the ideal organization of the future would . . . be aligned with cultural, social, and humanitarian responsibilities. [If] you say human capital is your shareholders and people concerned with the environment and so on, you'll probably have a smooth flight . . .*

Yet, when we asked interviewees in sub-Saharan Africa where managers might explore models of African leadership and management, they responded that such models do not generally exist, are not geographically accessible, or are not relevant in a global world where multinational corporate values are being widely adopted. Accordingly, we suggest that organizations in sub-Saharan Africa risk abandoning outlooks that may be "inherently African" as well as aligned with the holistic, people-centered approaches we identified as a *global yearning*. The opportunity is to initiate leadership dialogues, forums and development experiences that address the questions: "what are distinctive features of African leadership and management?" and "what can the rest of the world in general, and specific MNCs such as our case study firm in particular, learn from these distinctive practices?"

METHODS

Research Design and Data Analysis

The research plan was to first hear manager voices in the three major regions where MNCs are generally headquartered and substantial economic activity is generated (North America, Europe and Asia). Managers in sub-Saharan Africa were included in order to incorporate a region not widely studied or thought of as a source of leadership and management learning. As Adler (2002) noted, in the 1990s, less than 7 percent of organizational and human resource management articles in leading U.S. management journals and less than 18 percent of articles published outside North America were international in outlook, and as Jackson (2004: 7) has commented, "the global academic management community appears to pay little attention to Africa."

With these observations in mind, the research design and analysis methods were developed to be consistent with Wright's (2004: 52) assessment that "international management is still a field characterized by lack of theoretical understanding. This is one of the strongest theoretical reasons for advocating qualitative research in the field, since qualitative research is the most robust way of generating theory." Qualitative methods are also generally well-suited to "explore how individuals or organizational members give meaning to and express their understanding of themselves, their experiences, and/or their worlds" (Yates, 2004: 138). An inductive research process was employed to understand the perceptions of multinational managers with respect to organizational development, leadership, and change management, and the choice of methods was predicated on a grounded theory approach (Glaser & Straus, 1967; Locke, 2001).

The qualitative analysis software package Atlas.ti was used to manage the large volume of data and search for themes. The software's features facilitate sorting respondents by characteristics, coding and retrieval of data, searching for key words and phrases, and clustering codes into higher level core codes. Such software can enable researchers to "do more rigorous, consistent, and thorough analysis than they otherwise might" (Weitzman,

2000: 817). (For a more extensive overview of the IDEAL research program, please see Trautlein, 2007a; for a more in-depth analysis of its Africa-specific findings, please see Trautlein, 2007b.)

Interview Protocol

The interview protocol consisted of ten questions supported with sub-question prompts that focused on managers' experiences with and perceptions of what has changed, is changing, and still needs to change in organizations. The interviews began with questions about demographic information and career experiences. The types of questions relevant to this paper elicited: memories of most and least successful change initiatives/projects; images of the ideal organization of the future; thoughts about a respondent's potential personal role in creating the envisioned ideal organization of the future; and consideration of globalization's impact on managers' work and lives.

Participants

From late 2004 through January 2006, the "core constituency" of 107 managers working in MNCs were interviewed. Selection criteria were as follows: individuals working in an MNC (defined as a company with marketing, sales and/or operations in a minimum of three countries); physically located in North America, Europe, Asia/Oceania and Africa; employed in the Financial Services, Retail Products and Services, and Paper/Printing/Publishing industries; level of manager above supervisor but below CEO; a minimum of eight years work experience; a minimum age of 30 with no explicit maximum. Managers' roles spanned the breadth of the organizational value chain in terms of functional line and staff responsibilities. The 107 interviewees consisted of 46 individuals (43%) from North America; 26 (24%) from Europe; 20 (19%) from Asia; and 15 (14%) from sub-Saharan Africa. Sub-Saharan African interviewees were working in and represented the nationalities of Cameroon, Democratic Republic of Congo, Ivory Coast, South Africa and Uganda.

RESULTS

Global Overview: Cross-Cultural Consistency and Connections

Overall, this research initiative elucidates surprising consistency across the four geographic regions, three industries, and gender - contradicting conventional wisdom and research literature that assumes fundamental national, ethnic, industry and gender differences. Indeed, the research uncovered more similarity than not across these parameters, illuminating a heretofore unrealized alignment of experiences, perspectives and aspirations. At the macro level, this occurs in three areas: 1) images of the ideal organization of the future; 2) observations about effective leadership in the workplace; and 3) experiences with what works and does not work in change management initiatives and projects. The research also unearthed the global consistency of organizational barriers that deter achievement of the ideal organization of the future, adoption of enlightened leadership behaviors and styles, and deployment of effective change management practices. This led to the development of a framework allowing us to conceptualize these similarities and to provide a foundation for reflection and action inquiry with other researchers and consulting clients: the Intentional Dialogue Enabling Action Learning (IDEAL) framework, which we adopted as the name for the overall global research program as well. (See Figure 1 for a description of the IDEAL Framework.)

Analysis and Interpretation: Ideal Organization of the Future

For the most part, managers described workplaces that have evolved into being less "hierarchical," more "democratic," and more "participative," as well as managed with a view toward "meritocracy," "accountability," and "transparency," over the course of their working lives. At the same time, managers described certain structures, processes and behaviors that persist, leaving managers desirous of what is *missing*. Managers collectively characterized the "ideal organization of the future" as one with a more pronounced and proactive emphasis on people – valuing, empowering, investing in and even *nurturing* them. In their interviews, managers explained that the "ideal organization of the future" would be more communicative, collaborative, consensus-building, inclusive, and welcoming of multiple styles and perspectives.

FIGURE 1
The IDEAL Framework

	The Ideal What did people say about their yearnings/longings/ aspirations?	The Barriers What did people say about what gets in the way? What are the paradoxes and tensions people are experiencing?	The Implications What can be done to overcome barriers and achieve the ideal?
Ideal Organization	The ideal is "whole" perspective: that is, balanced perspective; key stakeholder perspective; internal/ external and short/ long-term perspective	Short-term focus, pressure to perform, process & technology valued over people, loss of loyalty to and from organizations	Action Learning – dialogue/reflection on aspired-to aspects of the ideal organization, structure, systems, processes, policies
Effective Leadership	Balance shifts from pronounced task focus to more on people – valuing, listening, collaborating, connecting, aligning	"Lip service" paid to diversity, sense of disempowerment, no time/balance, limited training/people development	Action Learning – dialogue/reflection on shift from transactional "management" to new transformational leadership competencies
Managing Change	Successful change is characterized by communicating, engaging people, integrating cultures, aligning teams	Stuck in a cycle of doing versus being, "change by checklist", constant and ubiquitous change, misaligned cultures	Action Learning – dialogue/reflection on change project insights, integrating cultures and teams, elements of sustainable change

TABLE 1
Ideal Organization of the Future

Ideal Organization Category	ALL %	NA %	Eur. %	Asia %	Africa %
People Valued	92.5	91.3	96.2	85	100
Leadership	52.3	45.7	38.5	65	80
Broad/Integrative Perspective	50.5	52.2	34.6	65	53.3
Consistent/Aligned Focus	43.9	50	38.5	20	66.7
World Citizenship	25.2	8.7	26.9	35	60
Technology	14	8.7	7.7	20	33.3
TOTAL N Per Regional Group	107	46	26	20	15

NOTE: ALL=all respondents combined; NA=North Americans; Eur=Europeans; Asia=Asians; Africa=sub-Saharan Africans.

Managers described signs of people-focused organizations as: adopting more people-friendly HR strategies, empowering individuals and teams, actively including diverse perspectives, offering training and development opportunities, and achieving a spirit of teamwork and more work-life balance. Moreover, the category of "People" and the next most populated category of "Leadership" together paint a picture of a preferred future organization led by people with traits consistent with literature profiles of the "transformational leader" – exhibiting, in other words: intellectual stimulation (fostering learning, risk-taking and joint problem-solving); individual consideration (fostering partnerships between people, making contact with them, and encouraging all to be leaders themselves); and (to a lesser extent) charisma (Bass, 1998).

The third category of responses captures references made by about half of the interviewees and points to an appreciation of organizations that would exhibit more "Perspective," which can also be thought of as "broader perspective," "integrated perspective," or "holistic perspective." This would include organizations where hierarchies, silos and borders fade; cultural and gender diversity is encouraged; and thinking and planning extends beyond the short-term. Just less than half of the interviewees made reference to aligning stakeholders around goals and priorities, categorized as "Focus." About a quarter of interviewees stated that the ideal organization will extend its attention beyond itself to include the wider context and "World" in which it operates, taking into consideration social, community, and environmental concerns. "Technology" was mentioned least frequently (by approximately 14% of respondents) as being a part of the ideal future organization.

Studying the results clearly depicts a unique pattern of responses by African managers. 100% mentioned "people" factors as being critical in the ideal organization of the future, and they were simultaneously more likely to mention the critical role of people-focused leadership. Further, while corporate social responsibility was noticeably absent from the radar screens of three quarters of the world's managers who were interviewed, expanding one's focus to improving the conditions of societies and communities was a key area of concern for the majority of the African managers. As Mbigi (2006: 9), a thought leader on African renaissance/transformational management, observes: "Organizations and their leaders attain high levels of consciousness when they operate beyond the bottom-line and personal interest to serve both the host community and society. They enlarge their sense of accountability to include not only their workplace but also the local community and society. They have to be aware of major challenges facing society and are active in finding solutions. They have a sense of shared destiny with the world and are able to see the complex web of our interconnectedness with everything in the universe and attach significant meaning to it." Finally, as will be described more fully below, while technology was oft-mentioned by our interviewees, it was usually discussed as a constrainer not an enabler. Conversely, African managers spoke positively about the possibility of technology facilitating the ideal organization of the future.

Analysis and Interpretation: Effective Leadership

No questions were asked that used the word "leadership." Instead, content analysis was used to identify what language was used when managers said "leaders" or "leadership" or described situations when someone was exhibiting leader-like behaviors in our interviews. References to leadership behaviors that qualify as "transformational" outpaced those that qualify as "transactional" (see Table 2 below).

TABLE 2

Effective Leadership

Effective Leadership	ALL %	NA %	Eur. %	Asia %	Africa %
Total Leadership Mentions	98.1	97.8	100	100	93.3
Transformational Practices	85	82.6	84.6	85	93.3
-Individual Consideration	63.6	52.2	69.2	70	80
-Intellectual Stimulation	58.9	47.8	61.5	70	73.4
-Charismatic Inspiration	51.4	50	61.5	35	60
Transactional Leadership	33.6	34.8	23.1	25	60
-Goals/Accountabilities	24.3	21.7	23.1	20	40
-Contingent Rewards	16.8	21.7	3.8	10	33.3
TOTAL N Per Region	107	46	26	20	15

NOTE: ALL=all respondents combined; NA=North Americans; Eur=Europeans; Asia=Asians; Africa=sub-Saharan Africans.

And, notably, African managers versus others around the globe were more likely to mention transformational leadership factors, particularly to speak of empowering people by valuing opinions and incorporating offered ideas into organizational solutions. Indeed, the word "listening" was a prominent feature of their interviews. One manager said that it would not be uncommon for him to arrive at the office and spend two hours listening to events occurring in the lives of employees at work and at home.

Additionally, African managers were more likely than those in other regions to also mention the importance of transactional leadership factors. While managers in other regions bemoaned an imbalance of profit/process over people/relationships, African managers described naturally combining listening to and engaging people while managing their performance and holding them accountable to contingent rewards. As Jackson (2004: 115), a noted authority on management and change in Africa, likewise observes, "In order to take account of the expectations and ideals of managers, organizations should be moving towards a people and results orientation and away from a controlling orientation."

Analysis and Interpretation: Managing Change – Success Factors

Again, when asked: "What is the most successful change management initiative or project that you have been involved in or led?" managers' stories underlined that *people not process* determine change management outcomes. The most often-cited success factor – communications and education – was mentioned by over two-thirds of managers (see Table 3). "Leadership" practices, mentioned by approximately two-thirds of interviewees, touched on all the key elements of a transformational leadership style and mindset.

It is not that respondents did not value "transactional" change management. Almost a third mentioned setting goals, holding others accountable, and contingent rewards. But the emphasis was on the critical roles that humans and human dynamics play in successful change. Managers said that change goes well when people are communicated with, energized, and aligned. Change falters when the opposite occurs – a lack of human interaction and engagement.

TABLE 3

Factors Facilitating Successful Organization Change

Success Factors	ALL %	NA %	Eur. %	Asia %	Africa %
Communications/Education	70.1	69.6	69.2	60	86.7
Transformational Leadership	68.2	58.7	69.2	80	80
Engaging People	41.1	37	53.8	25	53.3
Researching Opportunity	38.3	34.8	42.3	40	40
Clear Objectives	30	28.3	30.8	25	40
Transactional Leadership	29	30.4	23.1	25	40
Financial Assessment/Impact	29	30.4	26.9	25	33.3
Reflection/Learning	29	32.6	34.6	15	26.7
Experienced People	28	41.3	11.5	20	26.6
Customer Focus/Satisfaction	25.2	30.4	26.9	10	26.7
Integrating People/Cultures	25.2	15.2	26.9	25	53.3
Team Factors	24.3	23.9	11.5	25	46.7
Performance Management	20.6	17.4	26.9	5	40
TOTAL N Per Regional Group	107	46	26	20	15

NOTE: ALL=all respondents combined; NA=North Americans; Eur=Europeans; Asia=Asians; Africa=sub-Saharan Africans.

Again, a consistent pattern is detected in the responses of African managers – namely, paying primary attention to the people-side of change management. Virtually every change story cited examples of managers deeply, powerfully communicating and connecting with a variety of key stakeholders. Note also the higher percentage of Africans mentioning "integrating people and cultures" and "team factors" than other regions – balanced, again, with a greater focus as well on transactional leadership and performance management to encourage alignment with change goals. During times of change, African managers seem particularly adept at raising the bar to higher performance standards, while simultaneously supporting and engaging their individual employees and teams of people across cultures, levels, and functions.

Aspirations vs. "As-Is": Organizational Barriers

An overarching conclusion of the research is that there exists a longing for evolved organizations that leave people feeling "whole," and where the "ethos of cooperation and integration is very different from the ethos of control" (Zohar, 1997). This leads to the question, "If there is a cross-cultural consistency of views and aspirations, to what extent are they becoming global reality?"

The research unearths a divide between what managers believe works and what more often occurs in their organizations, and a consistency of organizational "barriers" to the achievement of ideals, aspirations and effectiveness in MNCs (see Table 4). These barriers result in paradoxes and tension between a latent hope for evolution toward enlightened leadership and management practices and daily experiences of entrenched power structures, autocratic behaviors, and decisions that run counter to valuing people.

TABLE 4

Barriers – What Gets in the Way

Barriers Category	ALL %	NA %	Eur. %	Asia %	Africa %
Dragging on Diversity	58.9	54.3	57.7	55	80
Treatment/Value of People	50.5	45.7	46.2	40	86.7
Technology	46.7	60.9	46.2	20	40
Expectations of People	37.4	39.1	23.1	40	53.3
HR Practices/Perf. Mgmt.	33.6	30.4	30.8	30	53.3
Loyalty to/from Companies	26.2	21.7	34.6	20	33.3
Organizational Structures	22.4	23.9	19.2	20	26.7
Results Focus	22.4	23.9	23.1	20	20
Work/Life Balance Issues	22.4	28.3	19.2	20	13.3
TOTAL N Per Region	107	46	26	20	15

NOTE: ALL=all respondents combined; NA=North Americans; Eur=Europeans; Asia=Asians; Africa=sub-Saharan Africans.

Furthermore, as we considered the barriers and compared the sub-Saharan African interviews with other regions, three categories emerged as of particular interest, and two others as worthy of mention. These are "Dragging on Diversity," "Treatment/Value of People," "(Elevated) Expectations of People" and "HR Practices/Performance Management" coupled with "Technology."

Dragging on Diversity. The interview protocol did not ask about diversity in the workplace. Yet, 59% of interviewees volunteered that organizations are ineffective at managing diverse workforces, an obvious obstacle to achieving the ideal of people-focused organizations. Managers of many nationalities used the phrase "lip service" to describe attitudes and practices. They also gave unsolicited examples of sexism, racism, ageism, reverse discrimination and subtle cues that those in the minority must adopt behaviors that mimic those in "power" and "authority." African managers, particularly those from South Africa, most frequently spoke of the challenges inherent in managing relationships across ethnic and racial groups.

Treatment/Value of People. Managers in *all* regions suggested that programs, policies and practices that do not translate as respectful treatment and valuing of people would be the most common barrier to achieving the ideal organization of the future. Notably, this sentiment was even more pronounced in the remarks from managers from sub-Saharan

Africa. They consistently expressed greater concern for how decisions and actions affect people than did mangers in other regions.

(Elevated) Expectations of People. While managers reported that people are generally treated better in organizations than in the past, interviews in all regions were nevertheless replete with references to stress, overload, and pressure. Yet, managers in sub-Saharan Africa proved a point of contrast. They spoke of the opportunities afforded by "raising the bar" and "personal branding" and the "end of jobs for life."

HR Practices/Performance Management and Technology. Over a third of interviewees across all regions noted a diminishing of human resource-driven programs including talent management, training and development, rewards and benefits. Yet African managers spoke more positively than other regions about the spread of performance management, personal accountability, and contingent rewards systems. Further, the world's managers gave numerous examples of technology's impact in their organizations, with almost half describing technology in negative or mixed terms. Managers acknowledged technology-enabled enhancements to productivity, information flow and market entry, but they also described how misuse of technology becomes a barrier when it distances people and bombards them with data – basically, when it encumbers versus empowers. In contrast, the majority of African managers were positive about the promise and potential of technology for developing organizations and helping Africa compete on the world stage. These human resource and technological tools were credited by them with instilling discipline in African private and public sector systems.

Analysis and Interpretation: Personal Change Roles

After managers envisioned and described the "ideal organization of the future," they were asked what they could personally do to cause or influence the change (see Table 5).

TABLE 5

Personal Change Leadership Roles

Personal Change Leadership Roles	ALL %	NA %	Eur. %	Asia %	Africa %
Communication/Influence/Education	42.1	26.1	46.2	55	83.3
Role Modeling in Life and Work	27.1	19.6	26.9	20	66.7
Championing Change/Alignment	25.2	19.6	26.9	10	83.3
Setting Strategy/Clear Goals	22.4	17.4	34.6	20	33.3
Fostering People and Teams	16.8	10.9	19.2	5	50
Disempowered	14	19.6	7.7	10	16.7
TOTAL N Per Regional Group	107	46	26	20	15

NOTE: ALL=all respondents combined; NA=North Americans; Eur=Europeans; Asia=Asians; Africa=sub-Saharan Africans.

Almost half of the managers saw themselves in advocacy roles - communicating, influencing and educating others. The second most common response was "role modeling" the change they wish to see, with examples offered by over a quarter of respondents.

Of interest and possible concern is the 14% of managers who could not articulate their role or said that they are not in a position to impact change in a meaningful way, describing themselves in terms categorized as "Disempowered." Against stereotype, North American managers were more likely than those in other regions to express feelings of disempowerment.

In contrast, sub-Saharan African managers were most apt to describe the *active personal role* they would take to achieve their ideal organizations of the future. They talked about sharing their own knowledge as a way to develop others and personally encouraging employees to experiment with new and improved methods. Often, they suggested that their goals include overcoming African employee discomfort with independent decision-making and informed risk-taking. They also detailed new approaches they were already adopting to improve performance management, education programs and rewards systems. This is a pronounced distinction versus regions where managers made references to the "taking away" or scaling back of training and development initiatives.

Analysis and Interpretation: Distinguishing African Leadership and Management

To summarize, sub-Saharan African managers exhibit distinctive features: 1) a more pronounced and inherent inclination toward people-focused leadership; 2) a confidence in and eagerness to adopt "transactional" Western tools and techniques, including in the arenas of information technology, performance management, and rules of governance; and 3) a greater tendency to focus as managers beyond their immediate work roles to make a difference in the home lives of their employees as well as to talk about their organization's responsibility to make a difference in their community and larger society.

Given these distinctions, sub-Saharan African managers were asked if they think there is a model of African leadership, as well as where African managers go for leadership and management development and training. Notions of "African management" were noticeably missing from the mental radar screens of managers in all regions including Africa itself. Most said that skills training is fairly accessible. But they perceived that quality leadership and management development – especially with an "African sensibility" – is not. They also questioned whether a unitary construct of African management exists. Some even seemed perplexed by the questions. For example, a manager from Cameroon asked in reply, "How can there be *an* 'African' management? There are many different countries and cultures in Africa." And another manager working in South Africa for a U.S.-based multinational stated her matter-of-fact view that multinational corporate values have replaced African values.

In keeping with this sentiment, this research points to the global impact of the "North American management model" and U.S.-based MNCs in all four regions. Of interest are the divergent associations managers made with what the North American model represents. Managers credited American management standards and practices with spreading and elevating democracy, meritocracy, transparency, innovation, risk-taking and participative teamwork. They simultaneously attributed Wall Street/investor influences with driving a global focus on cost reduction, efficiency and the bottom line at the expense of people and relationships. The point is not to debate the pros and cons of the North American model. It is to illustrate that the extent to which managers in other regions feel they need to adopt this model impacts other regions' ability to move toward the "transformational" desires that they expressed. And, to point to North American-trained/developed organizations and their leaders as being particularly ripe to learn from African approaches – hence, our case study action learning project described below. But first, we reflect upon the first author's learnings from presenting the research findings at a conference in Africa, and how they inspired us to launch our case study application.

CREATION OF A LEARNING COMMUNITY

Learnings from the Leadership and Management Studies in Sub-Saharan Africa Conference in Zanzibar (LMSSSA 2006)

We have envisioned the positive benefits that could accrue if managers, consulting practitioners and academics proactively collaborate to support leadership and management development in sub-Saharan Africa, prompting the first author to present a paper entitled "Sub-Saharan Africa is Different: Now What?" (Shafer, Trautlein & Sheper, 2006) at the Leadership and Management Studies in Sub-Sahara Africa (LMSSSA) Conference held in Zanzibar, in June 2006 – the initiation of a learning community. In face-to-face discussions at the conference and later virtual dialogues, LMSSSA participants have confirmed the spirit of the findings based on their research and experiences. Several provocative questions have also been raised. For instance:

Is There Such a Thing as African Management? Conference participants noted time and again that Africa is a continent with many cultures spanning thousands of years and dozens of countries. The research described above identified attributes that are "distinctively African." However, a question worthy of discussion is whether or not it is possible to talk about a pan-African leadership and management construct, framework, or set of principles.

Is it Possible to Blend Western and African Approaches? Much debate surrounds this question. There seems to be concurrence that sub-Saharan African managers may be enamored with Western task- and outcome-focused methods at the same time that they appear to naturally focus on people and community – the latter being a quality that managers in other regions aspire to achieve. Yet, talk of "blending approaches" and "intelligent borrowing" naturally creates tension. At the conference and subsequently, discussion and debates have ensued over the purpose of blending or borrowing, their benefits, and how they should be pursued. Moreover, members of this learning community have stressed that thoughtful blending must be preceded by efforts to distinguish and define African versus other approaches.

What Can Managers in Other Regions Learn from Africa? We subscribe to the view that "good management anywhere in the world can draw on cross-cultural experiences from other parts of the globe, as long as this does not take the form of 'intellectual imperialism': African experience is just as valuable as experience from any other part of the world in the pool of knowledge for global managers" (Jackson, 2004: 169). In an era of individuals' search for wholeness and meaning, as well as increasing expectations of corporate responsibility, there is much for managers from sub-Saharan Africa to contribute. Conference participants seemed to agree that managers in industrialized regions seeking a sense of balance and connection when "people seem too busy to be human" might find new role models in sub-Saharan African managers (Mbigi, 2006). Together, we also agreed that the practices of African managers could represent good benchmarks for those who aspire to manage profitably while paying active attention to an organization's impact on employees, the environment, and society.

CASE STUDY: APPLYING AFRICAN LEADERSHIP AND MANAGEMENT PRACTICES IN A GLOBAL CORPORATION

Point of Departure

As researchers and an internal/external consulting team, we sought to capitalize on the IDEAL research findings and apply them for the betterment of an MNC. More specifically, we partnered together to identify what a multinational energy company, BP, could learn from the leadership practices of MNC managers in sub-Saharan Africa. Our case study focuses on a business segment of BP referred to for our purposes here as BP Refining.

BP Refining has eleven wholly owned and operated refineries in the United States, Europe and Australia and has participation in ten other refineries in Europe, Russia and Africa. Being a global company with many assets in Africa, BP Refining may consider an opportunity to study African managers' styles to assist in helping its North American managers achieve the company's expectations. As we will explicate, BP Refining has already identified and imbedded models and practices regarding its vision of the ideal organization and leadership, as well as has several critical change initiatives underway, and we will suggest specific areas where the company may look for opportunities to leverage those ideals and processes informed by the IDEAL framework and by research findings concerning the behaviors and mindsets of African managers.

African managers have demonstrated much in terms of balancing transformational and transactional practices for the positive benefit of their employees, organizations, and communities. Conversely, the North American managers interviewed report the lowest frequency of transformational and people-oriented leadership behaviors. Western managers and their corporate universities espouse a leadership style that coaches, mentors and cares for employees. But they often sense that they may be more task-focused than people-focused. Studying the behaviors of African managers allows Western managers opportunities to see examples of "business caring" for people.

Applying the IDEAL Framework

Consistent with our philosophy, our first step in applying our learnings was to create dialogue around the IDEAL framework. Such dialogue centers around deliberating three sets of inter-related questions:

- What is our vision of the "ideal organization"? What barriers are we encountering in attaining the ideal? What are action learning opportunities to move closer to the ideal?
- What is our vision of "effective leadership"? What barriers are we encountering in enacting effective leadership behaviors? What are action learning opportunities to move closer to the ideal?
- What is our vision of powerfully "managing change" to enable us to survive and thrive as a global organization? What barriers are we encountering to sustaining meaningful change? What are action learning opportunities to move closer to the ideal?

BP Refining's vision of the ideal organization is captured in its definition of the "High Reliability Organization" (HRO). The vision of effective leadership is modeled in the description of the "Level 5 Leader" (L5L). Each of these plays an important role in BP Refining's daily operations. Our questions concern: to what degree of fidelity are these ideals being practiced in the field? What can we learn from identifying the gap between the vision and reality? And, finally, what can we learn from the global research findings in general and African managers in particular? (See Figure 2.)

BP Refining's Vision of the "Ideal Organization"

BP Refining has explicated a vision for itself as the "ideal" organization, a model called the "High Reliability Organization" (HRO). BP defines an HRO organization as one which "conducts relatively error free operations over a long period of time" and "makes consistently good decisions resulting in high quality and reliable operations" (BP 2006: 3; see also Weick & Sutcliffe, 2001). Such characteristics are critical in refining, an inherently hazardous industry. Although the ideal of an HRO might imply a predominant focus on operations and process, a study of the nine areas of emphasis that BP Refining depicts as comprising an HRO indicates a simultaneous focus on people and management practices to enact the ideal. For example, the HRO model states such things as "*encourage individual contribution*", "*create capacity for training*", "*focus is on giving people the right information at the right time to allow them to make the right decision*", and "*do not punish employees who are trying to do the right thing*". BP Refining's HRO model's nine elements are reward and recognition, process auditing, migrate decision making to appropriate person, senior managers who see the big picture, work systems, formal rules and procedures, depth/organizational capacity, training and risk perception.

Research demonstrates the impact of "people practices" such as positive employee relations and extensive training on fostering HROs (Vogus & Welbourne, 2003). Solomon Associates, the leading refining industry benchmarking consultants, identified a common theme across refineries which excel as HRO models: "Becoming a pacesetter is a lot about cultural change, how people think about themselves, their job and the people they work with." (BP, 2006: 14) Underscoring this theme is a supporting thread that people at all levels and functions are trained, empowered, and rewarded to contribute and do the right thing. Similar to the case study firm, African managers in our research cited ideal organizations characterized as investing in their people. To quote a South African manager:

> *I believe it is crucial for each and every organization, to succeed. You can come with technology, you can come with good brands and good products, but if you don't have the management skills to lead people and to make sure that the culture and the environment are such that they can succeed, and they feel part of it – so it's not a top-down approach – you will never succeed. You can have ten quick successes, but long-term you won't succeed...It shows that if you invest in people and if you listen to them, and you make sure they understand what you expect from them, and then you understand what their capabilities are, you can turn them around successfully...For me, the organizations that are going to succeed in the future are the ones which have got cooperative leadership and the ones which invest in human capital and making sure that each and every individual contributes and gets heard. Because you employ the people for them to come and think, and whatever they do they must think and contribute – it's all part of it.*

FIGURE 2
The IDEAL Framework Applied to BP Refining

	The Ideal *Application to BP Refining*	**The Barriers** *Application to BP Refining*	**The Implications** *Application to BP Refining*
o **Ideal Organization**	High Reliability Organization consists of nine elements: o Reward and recognition o Process auditing o Migrate decision making to appropriate person o Senior managers who see the big picture o Work systems o Formal rules and procedures o Depth/organizational capacity o Training o Risk perception	o Dragging on diversity and valuing employees: ▪ Prioritization/preferences of functional expertise undermines the valuing of all employees and diversity and inclusion o Elevated expectations: ▪ Initiative overload ▪ Focus more on technical best practice sharing than on people- or community/social responsibility-practices ▪ Limited time for reflection	Dialogue and action around: o Valuing employees (in all functional areas) o Identifying opportunities for the organization to encourage employees to "give back" to and mutually learn from their indigenous countries o Leveraging Communities of Practice to actively pursue diversity and inclusion goals and stakeholder engagement
o **Effective Leadership**	Level 5 Leader model is defined by six competencies: o Operates from intrinsic motivation and inner will o Thinks strategically o Catalyzes change o Thinks and acts systematically o Creates space and empowers others o Embodies self-management and humility	o Imbalance of transactional over transformational practices o Frenzied pace - initiative overload – focus on projects over people	Dialogue and action around: o The concept and application of "space" with North American and African managers o Driving Level 5 Leadership down and around o Leveraging the Level 5 Leader model to the selection and training processes for future first line supervisors
o **Managing Change**	While there is no BP-sanctioned overarching change management model, the "ideal" approach within BP Refining may be characterized as: o Driven from experience at local levels o Driven by standard good project management practices (and supported by an internal Project Management Academy) o Supported by an embedded "Capital Value Process"	o Feelings of disempowerment o Limited manager/supervisor involvement in change effort o Lack of sharing best practices	Dialogue and action around: o Stakeholder participation - increasing manager and supervisor direct personal involvement and influence in change initiatives o Identifying existing successful change management models and best practices within BP, balancing the need to achieve results with reflective learning and "soak time" to enable change to become institutionalized

Dialoguing around potential barriers to achieving the HRO ideal, BP Refining shares some of the challenges as noted in the global research, including progress on diversity and inclusion. For example, the company may be challenged by a culture that places intense value on operational expertise relating to its manufacturing processes, which may dilute a parallel value for expertise in supporting disciplines, such as the maintenance function. Yet, HRO mandates that the workplace be characterized by a "disproportionately" high level of spending on training and development and the creation of learning capacity at all levels of the organization. This vision should extend beyond expertise in manufacturing operations and find robust expressions in maintenance and other functional groups. The implication here is that MNCs may find it valuable to reflect on how well they are actually valuing each employee regardless of their function/discipline, and look to managers in Africa to understand how they keep the functional discipline of employees from interfering with their behaviors that tend to value each employee. Similarly, the content of African managers' discussions with their employees as captured in the research often centered around challenging them to contribute to more demanding performance expectations, step outside their comfort zone to participate in higher-level business decisions, and take appropriate risks. Therefore, North American managers have an opportunity to learn from African managers about the frequency and content of communicating with their workforce related to challenging, business-focused initiatives.

A complementary vision of the ideal organization BP Refining aspires toward is explicated in its Code of Conduct. Similar to the Codes of Conduct of other firms, BP Refining's affirms its commitment to integrity, health, safety, security, the environment, employee treatment, treatment of business partners, interaction with governments and communities and financial integrity. The underlying theme is not just to abide by laws, good business practices and mandates, but to refrain from even the appearance of inappropriate conduct. It may be interesting to spur dialogue considering not only how the firm is progressing toward its vision of HRO, but also toward its Code of Conduct – and moreover, how the two visions intersect and mutually support each other.

While BP Refining's ideals speak to corporate social responsibility, in our research North American managers were least likely than others around the world to speak of such issues. Conversely, African managers were most likely to do so, particularly with respect to providing tangible assistance to employees' families and the communities in which businesses operate in Africa. As expressed by a manager in the Ivory Coast:

> *At [our firm], our commitment [is] to be connected with the neighborhood and community and community schools. For instance, we made part-time work on the weekends for high school students so that on Saturday they didn't stay home and do nothing. There was something for them [that created] a willingness to work and do something productive . . . We have to convince kids that if they didn't have the chance, they can still have it if they go to school.*

Given the primacy placed on diversity and inclusion by HRO and the Code of Conduct, what can the company learn about how African managers in general and its own African managers in particular take on such corporate social responsibility opportunities? BP Refining may develop opportunities to encourage employees working outside of their country of origin to "give back" to their indigenous country. For African employees working in North American facilities, there exists a particularly valuable opportunity to coordinate and lead a mentoring process with African counterparts. To encourage and even provide resources to an employee to mentor peers in their indigenous country is to "value the employee," and to acknowledge all that the employee has to offer as a unique individual with a unique heritage. Further, as shown through the IDEAL research program, it is also an opportunity for mutual learning, particularly with respect to the people-oriented practices of African managers.

Considering the company's global presence offers other opportunities. For example, BP Refining has a number of "Communities of Practice" (CoPs). These global networks of professionals are grouped according to functional discipline. The role of each network is to identify and replicate best practices. Since most CoPs are groups of technical experts, their replications consist almost solely of technical advancements such as applying a new and improved burner design at a replicating facility. CoPs may be challenged to use their multi-national reach to further BP Refining's model of the ideal organization within their technical discipline by identifying and applying approaches to diversity and inclusion – thereby, promulgating "non-technical" best practice replications, for example, in the arena of mentoring others. According to BP's group vice president, Patti Bellinger, "creating a successful business able to sustain itself over many years depends as much on the ability to build deep and lasting relationships as on technical innovation and commercial strength" (BP, 2003: 8). CoPs may encourage business groups and functions to take on any number of initiatives, such as developmental activities for individual members through short-term exchanges of personnel across countries and even including mentoring relationships with members of local communities. Appropriate metrics of diversity and inclusion may even become part of a network's scorecard. Utilizing CoPs to facilitate such dialogue and opportunities could be very instructive, as BP has many current examples of successful mentoring initiatives, including for apprentices at certain business units, engineers, high potential managers, and members of diverse groups – again, an opportunity for dialogue, reflection, identification, cross-pollination, and action on BP Refining global "best practices."

BP Refining launched its vision of HRO in 2000 with this statement: "Our Refining system is very diverse. We have seven different company heritages represented and we operate in six countries…Such diversity creates many opportunities for learning and creativity. It is also important for any business to have a common way to define itself" (BP, 2006: 1). Further, during the period from 2003-2006 several different geographic regions engaged in reflective dialogue sessions, such as whole systems meetings in North America and learning cafes in Europe, to begin to take action toward the vision in locally relevant ways. The IDEAL framework-based dialogue we are now initiating is a way to reflect upon, several years into installation, lessons learned – in a way that engages multiple regions and fosters joint conversations and mutual learning. What, we ask, are the organizational processes and management practices that facilitate or inhibit HRO principles and outcomes?

BP Refining's Vision of "Effective Leadership"

BP Refining's vision of its ideal leader is captured in its "Level 5 Leadership" (L5L) model. The L5L model for BP Refining arose out of the executive's quest for the best management approach for its unique business. Their approach borrowed heavily from the research and writings of Collins (2001) and Goleman (Goleman, Boyatzis & McKee 2001). This model offers six core competencies of leaders, with each competency containing applications to "managing self" and "leading others," and supporting a balanced focus on task and people as well as short- and long-term thinking and acting. Blended in this model are both transformational and transactional examples of behaviors. The six competencies are operates from intrinsic motivation and inner will, thinks strategically, catalyzes change, thinks and acts systematically, creates space and empowers others, and embodies self-management and humility.

As consultants and trainers, we have had the opportunity to deliver L5L training to first line supervisors and senior hourly employees at two North American refineries. During these sessions, we unearthed barriers to enacting the ideal behaviors specified in the L5L model. One first level supervisor noted:

> *Talking about taking the time to mentor employees and get their input is fine and well. But how am I supposed to do that when I have back-to-back meetings to attend, am on three major projects, and have 100 emails to respond to everyday? I'd like to get out in the refinery and talk to the people, but that's not what my boss is holding me accountable for. I get my priorities handed to me, have my own little box to perform in, and that's as far as my ability to influence goes.*

Thus, this supervisor touched candidly on key themes noted in the global research: initiative overload, not enough time, and a perceived limited span of control.

Yet African managers expressed very positive perceptions of their workload, their ability to make the time to connect with others, and their sense of personal empowerment. So why is there such a significant difference between the two groups of managers? And, as identified in the research, how did the African managers arrive at their unique people-focused behaviors? Especially since there appears to be no "universally-embraced" African model of leadership and no corresponding centers for training and development, we may consider that African managers come to it naturally. That is, their behaviors reflect their culture. The purpose here then is to highlight the striking differences identified in the global research between African managers and others. To say that African managers have a natural propensity to demonstrate care and value at work must be underlined with the real-life understanding that moving a North American manager closer to those same behaviors may be a significant challenge. That is why we propose that African managers offer examples or glimpses of understanding regarding what it can mean to care about others at work, and that this caring may constitute a giant behavioral leap beyond what many other MNC managers can do. For a company like BP Refining to expect a manager to behave in people-focused ways, then, requires more than a leadership model. It requires supporting human resource systems, examples/modeling from superiors and unique opportunities for training and development.

Most importantly, people-focused behaviors are supported by dedication of "time". This is a significant hurdle for most North American organizations. The African managers note clearly that their way of behaving takes time. Some may argue that "good management theory" has always suggested that a manager gets his or her work done through others, and that time spent with others will provide a reward or even achieve a better reward in getting work done than not. But once again, the African managers were not driven to behave in people-focused ways in order to get more work done. Their behaviors were not disguised transformational acts to accomplish transactional goals. Their behaviors were much more about a non-business goal: caring about others. Indeed, African renaissance management has been described as characterized by a more humanistic value orientation to people (Mbigi & Maree, 1995).

A critical area for action inquiry is discussion and analysis of managers' allocation of time, energy and what BP refers to as "space". Within BP, the term "space" is often used with a unique meaning, referring to the relative freedom or opportunity for a manager/employee within the work context to pursue an area of interest and activity. The term does not refer to the nature or volume of an employee's workload. The term appears to be an expression and understanding that exhibiting transformational behaviors takes both time and energy. It would be enlightening to hear BP managers from North America and BP managers in Africa talk about their company's application of the concept of "space".

In addition to looking for opportunities to understand/address time and "space" relating to transformational leadership behaviors, it may be valuable to step back and survey the overall implementation of the leadership model within the company. It would be advisable to take the pulse of how deeply imbedded the L5L model is and then to identify opportunities to drive that ideal down and around. A clear opportunity for BP Refining is to leverage/increase the use of the L5L model while looking to African managers, especially BP's African managers to increase dialogue around potential transformational behaviors. We suspect that the value of the L5L model could be furthered by increased training of leaders, inclusion in supervisor performance expectations and evaluation processes, and as a focus area for the company's reward and recognition program. Again, African managers may be role models for how this might be done, as their behaviors elucidated a simultaneous focus on listening to and valuing people while at the same time holding them accountable to higher standards and providing rewards contingent upon performance (that is, balancing transformation and transactional leadership practices). And, moreover, they seem able to not simply just espouse leadership ideals and human resource practices, but are willing to enact them in a very hands-on manner every day with their staff. To quote a South African manager:

> *I am passionate about people development. I am happy when I see someone who I have helped with a mentoring approach succeeding and being successful in life…I believe that every person has got the potential. If you coach them or mentor them appropriately, they can succeed in life. We went out team-building and what came out of that helped me, because I could see from each and every individual what their potentials were and those people, obviously, who didn't fit into the culture of performance-driven, results-driven, they would have to leave, if they can't cope. So I sat down with each and every individual and went through what their career history was, what their potential was and what their strengths and weaknesses were. And came up with a program to make sure they could succeed in life. And most of them succeeded and most of them are still here.*

Further building on the strength of BP Refining's L5L model, the company may find significant value in utilizing that framework in the selection and training of its future first line supervisors. During 2000-2001, the company engaged in a global dialogue to develop a standardized curriculum for its "first level leaders" (Priestland & Hanig, 2005), and now it may benefit from taking a similar action learning approach to extending and integrating this well-received program to "linked" aspects of its leadership pipeline – and in particular, succession planning from the hourly to the salaried ranks. Like other process industries that require deep technical expertise to operate its facilities, BP Refining looks to its hourly ranks to raise its future first line supervisors. Opportunities for BP Refining may include the installation of a robust process for identifying, selecting and training its supervisors. BP Refining could follow a process that refrains from merely selecting the most technically proficient employee, but that instead identifies a balance of both technical and "people" skills in its candidates. Also, parallel to the selection process should be an effective training and development process. Even before an opening exists in the supervisory ranks, progressive companies invest in development opportunities for "high potential" hourly employees. All of these processes offer excellent opportunities for the company to further is visions of both the ideal organization and the ideal leader.

BP Refining's Vision of "Change Management"

The authors had the opportunity to participate in a key initiative within BP Refining's North America organization, namely succession planning for the hourly maintenance workforce. Through facilitating the design and implementation of several "apprenticeship programs," we assisted BP Refining towards it vision of "people-focused" systems and practices. Here we will discuss the company's change management practices with reflection on these apprenticeship programs.

From 2001 onward, a BP Refinery in North America embarked on a journey to develop apprenticeships, after having no such programs for over twenty years. We facilitated a joint union-management oversight committee to design the structure, governance and implementation of the programs. The programs consisted of several unique characteristics, particularly the deep and pervasive involvement by a wide variety of key stakeholders, most notably the hourly employees themselves. Such participation is perhaps best exemplified by the program's most unique and critical "success factor," its mentoring program (Trowbridge & Trautlein, 2006). The mentoring program was designed to include hourly journeymen mentoring new apprentices, senior apprentices mentoring their junior peers, and supervisors mentoring all involved. Hourly and salaried personnel partnered together for on-the-job training, task sign-offs to ensure qualifications, coaching to ensure safety, and giving/receiving feedback to ensure learning. Indeed, the program was designed to be heavily "bottom-up" driven.

At BP Refining the implementation of apprenticeship programs went relatively smoothly. The process was developed and driven by both experienced consultants and "good project management practices" as opposed to an overarching change management process provided by the company. Two of the few barriers included a lack of time for the managers and employees to reflect on learning from one craft line to another as well as limited involvement by management personnel due to multiple priorities.

In the global research MNC managers cited several characteristics of good change management practices. At the top of the list is an emphasis on communications/education of the workforce relative to the change effort. Second, managers cited behaviors characteristic of transformational leadership as a critical success factor. Overlapping these characteristics is engaging people. Taken together, African managers were more likely to cite those success factors than others around the world.

The implementation of the apprenticeship programs benefited from the same good practices noted in our research. Specifically, the programs included the early involvement of affected employees, and a joint union-management committee provided a forum for discussion and the evolution of ideas and processes. Further, a clearly articulated "business solution" was identified, proposed and sanctioned. Communication within the craft lines regarding the program was very good, and many journeypersons volunteered to participate in the programs as mentors. Virtually all mentors attended extensive training to support their unique roles, and the mentors themselves developed the discrete tools and activities that they then used to train the apprentices on the job.

At the individual level, African managers described their participation in change management initiatives as direct and personal, and as a group exhibited more influence and impact than their counterparts in other regions. For example, in the words of a Congolese manager:

When you do something like this you have to sell it internally and get everyone's commitment and all be moving in the same direction. That's very important because you can't be everywhere. When you have invested yourself 100%, it's necessary for others to take ownership. For change, that is what's important. They shouldn't feel it's something they "have" to do. One thing I do generally is, I don't give injunctions, I explain, "look at what we want to achieve, look at the motive, here's the why, here's what might happen, etc." So that the person does not receive this as if he were a robot – he knows where we are, where we want to arrive, he knows what might happen – we give him the "global picture." These are not low level workers. Once they are committed, I can leave, I can go to sleep. They won't sleep any longer, because they have appropriated the project, it's for them, and they push.

As noted earlier, North American managers were more likely in our research to express feelings of disempowerment. During our participation in the implementation of apprenticeship programs, we observed that some managers and supervisors exhibited effective personal participation while others appeared and acted less empowered, demonstrating various behaviors that indicated confusion or disempowerment regarding the process, expectations and roles. The managers in the global research cited six clear and overlapping challenges to change management. These include a sense of being stuck in a cycle of "doing" versus "being" where they noted that the change outcome was more process and transactional in nature as opposed to a change in people's beliefs or a change in the organization's culture. Also, there was a sense that change management methodology consisted primarily of a "change by checklist" process that achieved short-term outcomes ("checks") but fell short of achieving buy-in by the employees/users and did not get fully imbedded into the organization as the "way we do things here." Further, managers were consistent in their discussions that change seemed both constant and ubiquitous, and that the changes did not allow complete implementation and a time for "soaking" into the culture.

These observations lead us to wonder if MNCs recognize the perceived lack of span of control and influence by their managers and the impact this has on change initiatives. In an evaluation of the apprentice program, we obtained insights from major stakeholders about what was working and what could be improved. The journeymen mentors rated the program very highly, and virtually all cited the positive benefits to themselves around being able to mentor others, sharing their expertise, giving back to the company, and making a contribution to the younger generation. Interestingly, they also valued the opportunity to coach apprentices on non-work aspects of their lives – such as how to balance priorities outside of work with their new responsibilities as employees. In these ways, they sound very similar to the day-to-day behaviors of African managers. In the words of a manager from the Ivory Coast:

Spending time on employees was important…On a daily basis, my job was to listen to the employees and find out if they have any problems and find a solution together. This is important to make sure they bring a good mind and morale to work – and that also means knowing what problems they might have at home. Most of them, when they get to work in the morning, they may not have their minds quiet so that they can accomplish their goal. This involves a lot of individual talking with them to make sure they can clear their minds and focus on the goal.

Similarly, apprentices described the most positive aspects of the program as the mentoring received from the journeymen, and how valued they feel by being tutored, listened to, and moreover, included in non-work "social/family" events. Interestingly, the lowest rated aspect of the apprentice program – by journeymen, apprentices, and even management – was the involvement by managerial personnel, particularly first level supervisors. Hourly workers at all levels, and the supervisors themselves, long for more active engagement in the day-to-day work lives, training, and development of the workforce. As our case study demonstrates, it is not only managers around the world who long for more people-focused organizations, leadership practices, and change management processes – but also the people themselves.

What is unique about African managers that they view their potential influence and participation so positively? Would an overarching change management model assist managers? To what extent do managers need a personal ability to influence change? It follows that a potential goal is to identify opportunities aimed at increasing manager and supervisor direct personal involvement in change initiatives.

At the organizational level, we find that although BP Refining expresses clear direction in its HRO and L5L models, there does not appear to be a similar overarching model for change management, thus exposing the company's initiatives to the barriers noted above. BP has a well-defined "Capital Value Process" that is embedded deeply into the organization and used to identify and manage projects. In addition, the company has a strong Project Management Academy to further project management competencies in its workforce. Both clearly touch on change management, but a clear model that provides guidance and advice to managers and supervisors on how to implement and imbed changes to work processes at the business unit level appears to be lacking.

And, harkening back to the barrier of "dragging on diversity," sub-Saharan African managers were more likely than those in other regions to describe "integrating people and cultures" as a change management success factor. The apprentice programs brought together members of several racial and ethnic groups as well as members of both genders, multiple generations, and diversity on many more levels. The training modules we incorporated to the apprentice program on "understanding differences" was one of the most positively received, as it got to the essence of understanding, appreciating, and effectively working with members of diverse groups. Again, learning more about how sub-Saharan African managers approach the issue of "integrating people and cultures" may provide valuable insights for North American change leaders grappling with similar challenges and opportunities.

Given the IDEAL research program/framework and BP Refining's aspirations, it may prove valuable to engage in action inquiry research to understand the organization's effectiveness at managing change and imbedding new structures, systems, processes and policies. What efforts can be made to increase the perceived span of control and influence of the managers associated with a change initiative? What lessons can be learned from relatively recent change efforts such as the apprentice programs? Further, what change management processes exist within individual business units that may be replicated for best practices and developed into an overarching model for the company? And, how can dialoguing with our African counterparts inform all these areas of inquiry?

Next Steps at BP Refining: Dialogue, Reflection, and Action

Our suggestion for BP Refining is to continue to expand dialogue, reflection, and action learning as described in this chapter and as offered in the IDEAL proposition. That is, the organization may have much to gain by conducting a focused series of discussions leading to new insights in each of several areas outlined above. Many organizations utilize a "plan-do-check-act" model for continuous improvement. It may now be time to take an organizational look or "check" how well things are going. Taking the pulse of various organizational structures and processes, both "inside" to BP Refining's own sites, and then looking "outside" to others, particularly African organizations and managers, for insight may yield significant opportunities to move closer to espoused ideals. It has been said that, like many global corporations, "BP's culture did not traditionally support a reflective pace" but at other points in its lifecycle, the organization has reaped rewards from "going slow to go fast" (Priestland & Hanig, 2005), and this may be one of those critical junctures – at a time when high reliability, strong leadership at all levels, and effectively managing mission-critical change initiatives – are simultaneously in demand (Schwartz, 2006).

We summarize that BP Refining has significant structures and processes in place to make even further progress towards its espoused vision of the ideal organization in its HRO framework and of the ideal leader in its L5L model. Further, we see that the organization has significant opportunities to learn from within as it already possesses an organizational language and models beneficial to conducting dialogues with key stakeholders in various geographic regions around the world.

The managers in the IDEAL research expressed a "global yearning" for the ideal company, leader and change management process. What about BP Refining? Do the managers of this multinational organization yearn for similar characteristics, such as a focus more on "being" than "doing", more on "transformational" than "transactional" behaviors? And how would their collective thoughts and yearnings compare and contrast with the organization's current ideal models? The organization's stated vision appears to encourage and even demand that the company and its leaders engage in this dialogue and effort. The IDEAL research and its unique methodology may present a starting point for their journey.

IMPLICATIONS AND DISCUSSION

Opportunities in Sub-Saharan Africa

What does this mean for sub-Saharan Africa's organizations and managers? If there is an emerging global concept of the ideal organization in the future, but sub-Saharan African managers have distinctive features, then what is to be done to build and inform leadership and management practices in the region?

We assert that Africa is at a crucial juncture in its organizational development lifecycle. Managers we spoke with acknowledge an increase in MNC activity in their countries. They themselves represent a crop of dynamic private sector managers who are among the intellectual and economic elite in the region. And they are optimistically attempting to incorporate Western-style business practices and tools, some of which they were exposed to in studies abroad. The issues they face include retaining their cultural and organizational heritage of communal relations and social responsibility while experimenting with new technologies, methods and standards. They are advocating living wages to educate employees' children while engaging in performance management discussions that eliminate the idea of permanent placement. They are practicing listening and engaging while training employees to make more independent decisions without "checking in." From a research vantage point, their environment and experiences represent a living learning lab for creating blended cultures and programs, or at least how to strategically adopt beliefs, systems and practices from elsewhere.

We advise that while MNC managers in sub-Saharan Africa may be excited about the utility of Western practices and tools, they should be cautious about ceding their leadership and management identities. As our case study demonstrates, there are many aspects of day-to-day African managerial practices that North American managers and their staff long to be able to include in their "tool bag." Reflection and intentionality are called for in that sub-Saharan Africa may be experiencing the "early adoption phase" of new management techniques, including some sense of relief at the possibility of bringing order to chaos. The risk is misapplication with unintended consequences. As one reference point, Japanese managers in their interviews described how it has been necessary for competitive reasons to incorporate Western concepts of performance management. Yet, they also described distress at losing the traditional emphasis on consensus-building, long-term commitments, trust, loyalty and harmony.

Indeed, through the interviews we saw glimpses that this may already be occurring to some degree. Take for example the words of a Congolese manager, bemoaning the impact of changes imposed on his firm recently acquired by a Western-based MNC, and pondering what could be done to move his organization closer to the ideal:

> *It would be necessary to return to the situation that once existed, to place more focus on the human being, on the personnel. I know we need profit, that companies need to grow, need to be the most successful, but we need to stop for a bit and return to the well-being of the individual. It's the personnel that are the cause of the company functioning; it is the personnel who consume and who are the reason for a flourishing economy. The more we put pressure on people...the more they will fear the future. So we need to return to the primary importance of the human being. If this were done, coming to work would no longer be a problem. Of course, we know there is work that has to be done, but we would know that at the end of the month we had something, some satisfaction.*

A Time for Action Inquiry in Sub-Saharan Africa

Those committed to the development of organizations in sub-Sahara Africa have a unique opportunity to dialogue around these issues and help create *intentional* strategies, structures and systems. As Jackson (2004: 48) states, "research must be ongoing, and reflect an action dynamic that is able to make interventions into management processes, and which in their turn may inform our unfolding theory." What would an indigenous African leadership and management development institute look like? What fields of thought and study would be offered in a blended institute? From an organizational standpoint, it could be quite thrilling to try and integrate the heritage of a rich tapestry of sub-Saharan African culture with new business tools, technologies and practices. The quest would be the same as the emerging global quest to find balance in a leadership and management model that embraces the whole. It is just that the journey in sub-Sahara Africa begins from a different place, literally and figuratively. There is a window of opportunity for sub-Saharan African managers to engage in self-reflective questions of organizational identity including: What are enduring or continuing features linking present organizations with the past and presumably the future? (Gioia, 1998). What interventions are necessary and what would be our continuous journey of innovation? (van de Ven, Polley, Garud & Venkataraman, 1999). As Mbigi (2006: 8) writes:

> *The key element of this type of change is that it involves elements of a paradigms shift. This level requires a lot of self-confidence based on deep cultural rootedness so that people can develop new cultural lenses for them to see the world anew, so as to develop creative and innovative solutions to the*

problems, as well as the ability to develop revolutionary breakthrough ideas. This is not possible without creating a new level of strategic consciousness throughout the organization and the community. This is not possible without cultural and spiritual renewal, which are the two major keys to organizational, community and personal transformation. It is the role of leadership to bring presence and profound meaning and hope into any situation and into this confusing world characterized by rapid and chaotic change.

It would be exciting and advisable to conduct such dialogue on a regional basis, as well as within individual MNCs operating in Africa as we have done in our case study firm. Such activities bring together three essential elements of disciplined leadership development: *intentional inquiry*, *research*, and *action*. Together, they hold the promise of transformational learning (Torbert, 2004), because they involve real managers (and as our change management case study demonstrated, even potentially line and staff personnel) working on real tasks as learning experiences (Vince & Martin, 1993). And they are consistent with key aspects of the internationalization process, which can be conceived of as a hybrid of experiential learning, systematic planning and contingency – embedded with a spirit of innovation and adaptive choice to solve strategic and structural dilemmas (Li, Li, & Dalgic, 2004).

A Time for Action Inquiry Globally

As demonstrated in our case study above, one may challenge the conventional wisdom that people across the globe have differing ideals regarding organizational, leadership and change management practices and pursue dialogue that capitalizes on research and opportunities to learn from each other within and between firms and regions. As such, we offer the following ideas for contemplation for key players in the global leadership and management arena:

MNC Leaders. Reconciling paradox and making sense of organizational experience is a role of leadership (Quinn, 1988; Weick, 1995). This begs the question consistent with the research findings of whether those in defined MNC leadership roles should be proactively charting a "new way" of organizational development and change management. If they choose, they can lead discussions of how best to blend global corporate practices with local realities and intelligently borrow business processes developed in one region to other regional operations. This is particularly true for CEOs and leaders in MNCs with responsibility for global strategy or global human resources.

Consultants. Discussions of organizational transformation, as we have facilitated for BP Refining with respect to its vision of HRO, L5L, and succession planning, call for reflection, agreement and alignment. Guiding this sort of inquiry is a continuing opportunity for consultants in the 21st century. And unlike the United States and parts of Western Europe, sub-Saharan Africa is not a market that would be considered "over-consulted" in the arena of leadership and management development. Consultants who are comfortable leading strategic conversations in cross-cultural environments can help shape reflective dialogues, deep experiences and action learning in sub-Saharan Africa, and in MNCs globally. However, consultants opting to simply teach or transfer frameworks from other regions would have a decidedly counter-productive effect.

Academia. University undergraduate and graduate business education programs teach belief systems and approaches to leadership and change. They are places of learning and appropriate hosts for the types of inquiry here advocated. Ultimately, leadership models are merely social constructs that can be reinterpreted and changed. There is an opportunity and need in programs around the world to incorporate alternative methods, views and voices and consider what *truly global* leadership models look like. Goldsmith, Greenberg, Robertson & Hu-Chan (2003) suggest that qualities and capabilities of a successful leader with "global business understanding" include flexibility and the ability to refrain from labeling different perspectives as right or wrong. In this same vein, we have offered a set of people-oriented practices that managers around the world deemed as comprising a globally-relevant model of *effective leadership.* In the ideal scenario, managers in sub-Saharan Africa and beyond would become aware of some of the best aspects of management approaches from Africa, just as there is awareness of qualities of North American, European and Asian leadership and management.

Concluding Comments

Taking "employee empowerment and buy-in" to "employee caring and cultural relevance" is not a stepped change, but a dramatic difference in perspective. This is the essence of the difference between the Western and African managers we studied. For example, African managers offer "*empowering people by valuing opinions*" and "*incorporating offered ideas into organizational solutions*" as hallmarks of their styles. What does that look like? It may be clear to African managers, but it is just as likely to be unclear to Western managers. Western managers talk about empowerment and team decision making, but the realities are often tied to specific team or project events, and do not necessarily spread to the daily decision making processes used by a manager. Dialogue with African managers and reflection may provide insight to Western managers who are intent to give more than just lip service to such ideologies.

The global pattern of the IDEAL research program and framework suggests opportunities to dramatically re-think and re-prioritize approaches to leadership and management development in the 21st century. Some might think of it as a quantum leap forward, intriguing to contemplate and complex to propagate – that is, a global sense that transactional management approaches are necessary but not sufficient to leading organizations that are *successful, sustainable* and *satisfying.*

This represents the spirit of our proposition: that there is an unrealized but awakening cross-cultural alignment of experiences, views and aspirations in three areas: 1) images of the ideal organization of the future; 2) observations about effective leadership in the workplace; and 3) experiences with what works and does not work in change management. More specifically, there is a latent global *yearning* for organizations that are more actively engaged with the "people side" of organizational development, leadership, and change. Managers revealed through their responses that organizations in the past and present have focused on "doing" (tasks of "transactional management"). But when invited to freely envision a future, the interviewed managers shifted focus to a new way of "being" (humanistic orientation and skills related to "transformational leadership"). As our case study demonstrates, there is much the rest of the world can learn from African leadership and management practices, and their penchant for forging a sense of wholeness and connection between people, organizations, and communities.

REFERENCES

Adler, N. 2002. *International dimensions of organizational behavior* (4th ed.). Cincinnati, Ohio: South-Western, a division of Thomson Learning.

Bass, B.M. 1998. *Transformational leadership*. Mahwah, NJ: Lawrence Erlbaum Associates.

BP Refining and Pipelines Leadership Fieldbook. 2006. bpdistributionservices@bp.com

BP Diversity and Inclusion in Action. 2003. bpdistributionservices@bp.com.

Collins, J. 2001. Level 5 leadership: The triumph of humility and fierce resolve. *Harvard business review*. January.

Gioia, D.A. 1998. From individual to organizational identity. In *Identity in organizations: Building theory through conversations*. Thousand Oaks, California: Sage Publications.

Glaser, B. & Strauss, A. 1967. *The discovery of grounded theory: Strategies for qualitative research*. London: Weidenfeld & Nicolson.

Goldsmith, M., Greenberg, C.L., Robertson, A., & Hu-Can, M. 2003. *Global leadership: The next generation*. Upper Saddle River, New Jersey: Pearson Education, Inc., publishing as Financial Times Prentice Hall.

Goleman, D., Boyatzis, R., & McKee, A. 2001. Primal leadership: Hidden driver of great performance. *Harvard business review*. December.

Jackson, T. 2004. *Management and change in Africa: A cross-cultural perspective*. London: Routledge.

Li, L., Li, D. & Dalgic, T. 2004. Internationalization process of small and medium-sized enterprises: Toward a hybrid model of experiential learning and planning. *Management international review*. 44(1): 93+.

Locke, K. D. 2001. Grounded theory in management research. *London: Sage Publications.*

Mbigi, L. 2006. Beauty, culture, and spirit in leadership: An African perspective. *Leadership and management studies in sub-Saharan Africa*, Zanzibar, Tanzania.

Mbigi, L. & Maree, J. 1995. *Ubuntu: The spirit of African transformational management*. Randburg, South Africa: Knowledge Resources.

Priestland, A. & Hanig, R. 2005. Developing first-level leaders. *Harvard business review*. June: 113-120.

Quinn, R. E. 1988. *Beyond rational management: Mastering the paradoxes and competing demands of high performance*. San Francisco, CA: Jossey-Bass.

Shafer, P., Trautlein, B.A., & Sheper, J. 2006. Sub-Saharan Africa is different: Now what? *Proceedings leadership and management studies in sub-Saharan Africa 2006 conference*, Zanzibar, Tanzania. LMSSSA@gmail.com.

Schwartz, N.D. 2006. Can BP bounce back? *Fortune*. 154(8): 91-99.

Torbert, B. 2004. *Action inquiry: The secret of timely and transformational leadership*. San Francisco, CA: Berrett-Koehler Publishers.

Trowbridge, C. & Trautlein, B.A. 2006. Succession planning for the maintenance workforce, *National Petrochemical and Refiners Association Annual Meeting*, Salt Lake City, Utah.

Trautlein, B.A. 2007a. Ideal *organizations, leaders, and transformations: Lessons from the IDEAL research program and framework*: Working Paper. Vernon Hills, IL: Systems Research and Consulting.

Trautlein, B.A. 2007b. What *the world can learn from African leadership and management practices*: Working Paper. Vernon Hills, IL: Systems Research and Consulting.

van de Ven, A., Polley, D.E., Garud, R. & Venkataraman, S. 1999. *The innovation journey.* Oxford, United Kingdom: Oxford University Press.

Vince, R. & Martin, L. 1993. Inside action learning: An exploration of the psychology and politics of the action learning model. *Management education and development.* 24(3): 205+.

Vogus, T. J. & Welbourne, T. M. 2003. Structuring for high reliability: HR practices and mindful processes in reliability-seeking organizations. *Journal of organizational behavior.* 24(7): 877+.

Weick, K. E. & Sutcliffe, K. 2001. *Managing the unexpected.* San Francisco, CA: Jossey-Bass.

Weick, K. E. 1995. *Sense-making in organizations.* Thousand Oaks, CA: Sage Publications.

Weitzman, E. A. 2000. Software and qualitative research. In N. K. Denzin & Y.S. Lincoln (Eds.), *Handbook of qualitative research.* Thousand Oaks, CA: Sage Publications.

Wright, L. L. 2004. The need for international research. In B.J. Punnett and O. Shenkar (Eds.), Handbook for international management research. *Ann Arbor, MI: University of Michigan Press.*

Yates, S. 2004. *Doing social science research.* London: Sage Publication.

Zohar, D. 1997. *Rewiring the corporate brain: Using the new science to rethink how we structure and lead organizations.* San Francisco, CA: Berret-Koehler Publishers.

Acknowledgements

The authors gratefully acknowledge the contributions of Patricia Shafer for her role in the original global research, and of Jason Sheper for his role in conducting several interviews with sub-Saharan Africans and co-facilitating dialogue surrounding the research findings and their implications during the LMSSSA 2006 Conference in Zanzibar.

AFRICAN SUSTAINABLE LEADERSHIP DEVELOPMENT: A CULTURALLY INTELLIGENT LEADERSHIP MODEL FOR SERVICE ORIENTED LEADERS AND ORGANIZATIONS

MARCO TAVANTI, Ph.D.
Management of International Public Service
DePaul University Chicago
mtavanti@depaul.edu

Abstract: *As a new generation of African leaders is emerging, so is the need to create appropriate and effective leadership paradigms for personal and organizational development. Servant leadership and cultural intelligence are essential pillars for identifying, developing and sustaining value-based leadership practices. Drawing from the Service Leadership model that emerged from the DePaul Leadership Project (DLP); this article outlines the competencies, orientations, methods and strategies for establishing effective and culturally intelligent sustainable leadership development programs. The DePaul leadership development model proposes that a collaborative, value-centered, and service-oriented perspective be at the center of an effective and sustainable African leadership development program. This innovative and cross-cultural leadership development model bridges theories and best practices from the sustainable development, service leadership and cultural intelligence paradigms in leadership and organizational development. National or international institutions committed to effective organizational and leadership development can adopt and adapt this African sustainable leadership development model to fit their needs.*

Keywords: cultural intelligence, leadership, development, service, sustainability

Leadership is a universally recognized concept, but at the same time the practice and interpretation of it is culturally framed. During the past 50 years, there have been countless development initiatives empowering marginalized and impoverished populations in Sub-Saharan Africa. With the growing presence of nongovernmental organizations (NGOs), and more recently of local civil society organizations (CSOs), the leadership development work of churches has expanded into a collaborative global agenda fostering sustainable development initiatives. Yet, many still struggle to identify what does and does not work. Systems thinking applied to personal and organizational leadership is a fairly new field (Fullan 2004). This paper attempts to introduce and integrate the characteristics of three innovative paradigms in leadership and management: servant leadership, cultural intelligence and sustainable development.

Recent international and cross-cultural analysis of managers and leaders has shown how limiting the "one-size-fits-all" approach to management can be. Several questions need to be addressed: "How can the servant-service leadership paradigm be applicable in culturally diverse contexts?" "What African values reflect or contradict the servant-service leadership paradigm?" "How can this innovative, but still Western based and Christian inspired, model become more culturally intelligent?" The integrated leadership development model presented here bridges these insights of servant leadership with the cultural intelligence and sustainable development paradigm.

Through a comparative study of 42 in-depth interviews of leaders working in the United States, Latin America, Europe and East Africa, the DePaul Leadership Project (DLP) has formulated culturally appropriate assessments measuring personal, collective, organizational and international leadership practices (Tavanti 2005). The cultural relevance and validity of this emerged leadership model is placed here in relation to the needs and best practices of African leadership development. The three leadership paradigms that emerged during the interviews, namely servant leadership, cultural intelligence and sustainable organizations are combined to formulate an African sustainable leadership development model adaptable by individuals and organizations. In the examination of the service-servant paradigm with the cultural-intelligence and sustainable development paradigm we suggest an integrated model for sustainable and organizational leadership development. This framework analysis on the emerged DLP paradigms, orientations and competencies could serve as a system thinking template for evaluating African best practices in leadership development.[2]

The Servant-Service Leadership Paradigm

Robert K. Greenleaf, the creator of the servant leadership principles, affirms that "leaders must be servants first." This strong statement suggests that authentic leadership development programs need to orient their efforts to form service-oriented leaders and organizations. Such leaders are less concerned about personal achievements or past failures and are more excited about serving their countries and organizations in the challenges of the future. What does service-orientation mean in the cultural, political and socio-economic contexts of Africa? Before answering this question, let's examine the meaning of this paradigm as applied to personal and organizational leadership development.

As explained by Robert K. Greenleaf in his essay 'The Servant as Leader' in 1970, servant leadership emphasizes the need for leaders and organizations to focus on meeting the needs of others. Current personal and organizational leadership studies put an emphasis on a sense of community, empowerment, shared authority, and relational power. These elements have been recognized by numerous authors as indicators of the great promise represented by servant leadership (Bass 2000). Despite the fact that to date there are very few solid research studies on the application and characteristics of servant leadership (listening, empathy, healing, awareness, persuasion, conceptualization, foresight, stewardship, commitment to the growth of people, and building community) the notion of servant leadership has been gaining momentum across value-oriented people and institutions (Northhouse 2003: 308).

Servant leadership is an understanding and practice of leadership that places the good of those led over the self-interest of the leader. Greenleaf believed that the servant-leader is one who is servant first. In his book *The Servant as Leader* he wrote: "It begins with the natural feeling that one wants to serve, to serve first. Then conscious choice brings one to aspire to lead. The best test is: do those served grow as persons; do they, while being served, become healthier, wiser, freer, more autonomous, more likely themselves to become servants? And, what is the effect on the least privileged in society; will they benefit, or at least, not be further

[2] The African sustainable leadership models and paradigms illustrated in this paper serve as frameworks for the consultative and leadership development initiatives of the Depaul Leadership Project (DLP) in East Africa. They also serve to evaluate and plan initiatives of the East African Institute of Collaboration (EAIC) and for the Vincentian Family's Think Tank initiative for the analysis of organizational best practices in poverty eradication.

deprived?" (Greenleaf & Spears 2002: 24). The servant-leadership paradigm has inspired leadership and management authors like Stephen Covey, Scott Peck, Ken Blanchard, Peter Block, James Hunter, and Max DePree among others.

The servant-service leadership paradigm has been applied in the business, government and nonprofit sectors. School administrators and higher education institutions have also applied this paradigm to their missions and curriculums. The current popular “service-learning” program across universities emerged in the 1980s as a synthesis between the learning-by-doing or experiential learning, with the insights of civic engagement and servant leadership. Several large, medium and small sized corporations have successfully applied and integrated the servant-service leadership paradigm into their practices of managing-by-values (Blanchard & O’Connor 1997; Spears 1996).

The servant-leadership paradigm has been applied to the study of corporations and other service-oriented organizations. Several Fortune 100 companies have applied and advocated for servant leadership as a new paradigm for success. According to the study of Sen Sendjaya and James C. Sarros (2002) six criteria identify these servant leadership companies: openness and fairness, camaraderie/friendliness, opportunities, pride in work and company, pay/benefits, and security (Sendjaya & Sarros 2002: 57). In the attempt to study and assess the health and service orientation of organizations, Dr. Jim Laub developed the Organizational Leadership Assessment (OLA) in 1998. The purpose of this assessment, originally called SOLA (for servant), is promoting the valuing and development of people, the building of community, the practice of authenticity, the providing of leadership for the good of those led and the sharing of power and status for the common good of each individual, the total organization and those served by the organization (Laub 1999). In the OLA model, healthy servant leadership organizations reflect the following six characteristics: (1) display authenticity, (2) value people, (3) develop people, (4) build community, (5) provide leadership and (6) share leadership. The uniqueness of the OLA instrument is to align personal self-perceptions of practices with the culture of the organization.

TABLE 1

Service Leadership Characteristics

o Display Authenticity	• Open & Accountable • Willing to Learn • Honesty & Integrity	o Build Community	• Build relationships • Work collaboratively • Value differences
o Value People	• Serve others first • Believe & Trust in people • Listen receptively	o Provide Leadership	• Envision the future • Take initiative • Clarify goals
o Develop People	• Provide for learning • Model appropriate behavior • Build up through affirmation	o Share Leadership	• Share the vision • Share the power • Share the status

The SERV*OR model is another application of the Servant-leadership paradigm to personal and organizational leadership assessments. The SERV*OR model of organizational service orientation is developed and validated. The model measures employee perceptions of an organization's service practices, policies and procedures. It incorporates 10 dimensions of service orientation including servant leadership, service visions, customer treatment and employee empowerment. The model also emphasizes service encounters, servant leadership by management, human resource management and service systems created for quality customer service (Lytle, Hom & Mokwa 1998). The analysis of this model suggests that servant-leadership and service vision are foundational leadership elements within the practice and development of service-oriented individuals and organizations. Although SERV*OR focus on customer service interpretation of servant leadership, it attempts to bridge the individual's "servant leadership" characteristics with the service-orientation and mission of the orientation.

These types of assessments are important contributions to the empirical and systematic studies of servant and service leadership paradigms applied to personal and organizational practice. Yet, they often fail to assess the intercultural validity as well as the sustainable application of such models into leadership development programs. The "one-size-fits-all" approach of management has proved to be wrong by more recent international and cross-cultural analysis of managers and leaders. Therefore the questions should be "How can the servant-service leadership paradigm be applicable in culturally diverse contexts?" "What African values reflect or contradict the servant-service leadership paradigm?" "How can this innovative, but still Western based and Christian inspired, model become more culturally intelligent?" The integrated leadership development model suggested here bridges the insights of servant leadership with the cultural intelligence and sustainable development paradigm.

The Cultural Intelligence Paradigm

David C Thomas and Kerr Inkson, the authors of Cultural Intelligence, argue that leaders and managers must develop skills for recognizing cross-cultural difference and choosing appropriate behaviors according to each cross-cultural context (Thomas & Inkson 2004). The term 'Cultural Intelligence' or CQ, relates to Daniel Goleman's Emotional Intelligence (EQ). The two concepts are actually comparable in the sense that they both involve high levels of self-awareness, as well as an ability to connect with and understand others (relational awareness). Both types of intelligences are rooted in the concept of social intelligence (Goody 1995).

Leadership is a concept more or less universally recognized, but the practice and interpretation springs from a unique cultural context. Local cultures and contexts interpret leadership across multiple meaning-making and value-belief systems (Ciulla 2003). The GLOBE model proposed by House, Javidan, Hanges, and Dorfman (2002) is based on the premise that leaders and followers in specific cultures behave, assume and expect differently across different cultural contexts. Because of the increased speed and intensity of connections in our global era, leaders and organizations must strive to recognize and adapt to local differences and the ever changing demands of local-global (glocal) contexts.[3]

A number of scholars have recognized the importance of cultural variables in leadership and organizational processes and behaviors (Hofstede & Hofstede 2005; Lucas & Chambers 2003; Thomas & Inkson 2004; Earley & Ang 2003). Cultural diversity is interpreted in its large sense not limited to national and ethnic notions, but as "shared motives, values, beliefs, identities and interpretations or meanings of significant events that result from common experiences of members of collectives and are transmitted across age generations" (House, Javidan, Hanges & Dorfman 2002: 5). This definition obviously includes the cultures and subcultures of organizations.

Earley and Mosakowski (2004) suggest a definition of CQ that has to do more with skills and techniques than attitudes and values. Our interpretation of cultural intelligence is more comprehensive than this. Cultural intelligence includes what is also known as intercultural competencies and, even more, intercultural awareness. Ata Karim (2003) suggests intercultural consciousness in leadership as a "synergistic combination of essential cognitive, emotional, and behavioral knowledge and skills for intercultural competence and a commitment to consistent, caring, and ethical application of those skills and knowledge" (Karim 2003: 37). The concept of intercultural consciousness indicates the moral and ethical responsibility that leaders and organizations have to engage in cultural intelligence programs and collaborative relations.

TABLE 2
CQ Development Characteristics

o **Cultural Awareness**	• Self Awareness • Identity with own culture • Personal interpretation and practices of culture • Ethnocentric thinking
o **Cultural Knowledge**	• Salient knowledge of particular culture of other • Health belief, practices and behavior • Stereotyping of other culture • History and traditions • Power distribution
o **Cultural Sensitivity**	• Empathy • Interpersonal communication skills • Acceptance and trust • Respect • Appropriateness
o **Cultural Competency**	• Assessment skills • Diagnostic skills • Clinical skills

[3] *Glocalization* as a term, though originating in the 1980s from within Japanese business practices, was first popularized in the English-speaking world by the British sociologist Roland Robertson in the 1990s.

Throughout the 1980s and 1990s most NGOs and church missionary projects operating in the African continent focused their work on the importance of acculturation and local adaptation. Yet, most schools, hospitals and other large institutions remained tied to a dependent and somehow unsustainable model. The cultural intelligence paradigm offers new criteria for interpreting the cultural feasibility and intercultural effectiveness of leadership and organizational related projects and initiatives. The cultural intelligence paradigm requires extensive critical analysis of individual and collective identities and actions.

The Sustainable Development Paradigm

The sustainable development paradigm emerged in the 1980s in an attempt to explore the relationship between development and the environment (Dresner 2002). The application of the sustainable development paradigm to leadership and organizational development is essential for establishing the connection between economic progress and societal development and environmental concerns. Sustainability is, therefore, closely connected to the triple bottom line (TBL) concept (Henriques & Richardson 2004). The TBL notion emerged in the 1990s as a deepening of the organizational applications of the sustainability paradigms (Edwards 2005). The TBL notion suggests that leaders must pay attention to development that is equally driven by economic interests, and the respect of human dignity and of local contexts. Today numerous organizations are active in their annular TBL reporting which entails reporting on economic, social, and environmental issues (Laszlo 2003).

According to the World Commission of Environment and Development (Brundtland Commission) report, sustainable development is "a process of change in which the exploitation of resources, direction of investments, orientation of technological development, and institutional change are made consistent with future as well as present needs" (WCED 1987: 9). Apart from attempting to reconcile economic growth with environmental protection, the sustainable development agenda of Brundtland also focuses on social justice and human development within the framework of social equity and the equitable distribution and utilization of resources (Banerjee 2003).

Sustainability and sustainable development, which are used interchangeably in both academic and popular discourses, mean different things to different people. While some stress social relations in particular ecological contexts, others stress the primacy of social justice (Edwards 2005). In an attempt to clarify the sustainability concept and explore its relevance to management, Thomas N. Gladwin. James J. Kennelly and Tara-Shelomith Krause (1995) identified several themes, including human development, inclusiveness (of ecological, economic, political, technological, and social systems), connectivity (of sociopolitical, economic, and environmental goals), equity (fair distribution of resources and property rights), prudence (avoiding irreversibilities and recognizing carrying capacities), and security (achieving a safe, healthy, and high quality of life).

There is a need to identify and promote an integrated approach to sustainable development. Theses terms can be seen as contradictory. To sustain suggests to support from below, to supply with nourishment; while development resembles more an act of control, an induced process, often promoted and managed by external agents operating under the tenets of modern Western science (Banerjee 2003). This idiosyncrasy, more than a dualism, is what is needed for attaining an integrated model of effective leadership and organizational development in the African contexts.

TABLE 3
Human Development Sustainability Themes

o **Inclusiveness**	• Ecological Systems • Economic Systems • Political Systems • Technological Systems • Social Systems
o **Connectivity**	• Sociopolitical goals • Economic goals • Environmental goals
o **Equity**	• Fair distribution of resources • Property rights
o **Prudence**	• Avoiding irreversibilities • Recognizing carrying capacities
o **Security**	• Achieving a safe life • Healthy life • High quality of life

Towards an Integrated African Model of Leadership Development

How do these leadership development paradigms relate to African contexts? In his recent visit to Ghana, Henry Mintzberg challenged the assumption that "we" westerners can develop leaders as we think to develop countries (Mintzberg, 2006). The fact that some best practices in leadership development work in Chicago does not necessarily mean that they fit the local needs and specificity of other contexts in Africa. As sustainable development theories and practices suggest, we cannot have a true socio-economic development unless there is true understanding of local needs and possibilities. Imposed top down leadership development models or "best practices" may obviously raise reactions from the part of African leaders. How would managers in Chicago react to a team of consultants arriving from Tanzania with their list of "best practices"? In his analysis of "cross-cultural" leaders such as Kofi Annan, the Ghanaian seventh Secretary General of the United Nations, Mintzberg suggests that an "engaging" model of leadership, rather than heroic, would work best to promote leadership development in African contexts. The concept of engaging leadership resembles the characteristics previously described in the servant-service leadership paradigm. In Mitzberg's words, "true leaders engage others with their thoughtfulness and humility because they engage themselves in what they are doing – and not for personal gain. Such leaders bring out the energy that exists naturally within people. If there is a heroic dimension to their behavior, it is not by acting heroically as much as by enabling other people to act heroically." (Mitzberg 2006: 4).

The diverse cultures of the African continent present common dimensions comparable to the values expressed in the service, cultural and sustainability paradigms. Mbigi (1995) invites organizations in Africa to build their programs in a more open dialogue with indigenous cultural practices. Several concepts, ideas and metaphors drawn from African culture fit well with the transformational and servant leadership model. The author describes the African value and practice of "Ubuntu," the solidarity or brotherhood which arises among people within "marginalized" or "disadvantaged" groups (Mbigi 1995: 7). Although expressed in various languages and cultural worldviews, this "sense of service to the poor" is a value embedded in the collective shared experience of African people. "A thumb working on its own is useless" is one among many proverbs that reflects the collective African identity. Mbigi advocates that effective leadership development programs and approaches to training in organizations must take into account the interconnectedness of African people (Mbigi 1995: 18-24).

People in management and leadership positions in African nonprofit and social service organizations often find themselves pulled in two different directions. They are expected to be transparent and accountable like private businesses but their "customers" or "clients" do not expect them to operate like businesses. An appropriate way of handling this situation is for organizations to focus on leadership development. Only an integrated model of leadership development that would reconcile Western and African management values would be capable of fostering sustainable leadership development programs in African contexts. The service paradigm applied to leaders and organizations in Africa serves as an example. While hierarchical systems in organizations are a functional reality, leaders must undergo a change in how they perceive themselves and their role in an organization as well as how the organization operates. Quoting Drucker and Pollard, "leaders will have to see themselves as students… (and) must always be prepared to serve and never ask someone to do something that they are not ready to do themselves," (Garone & The Conference Board 1999: 18). Due to the partnerships that many indigenous, African civil society organizations (CSOs) have with larger, multinational organizations, it is important that CSOs recognize that the leadership structures of their partners are changing away from a command-and-control model and that CSO leaders may have to do the same in order to maintain the partnership.

In the Handbook for Leadership Development, the Center for Creative Leadership (CCL) defines leadership development as "the expansion of a person's capacity to be effective in leadership roles and processes" (McCauley, Moxley & Velsor 2003: 4). The right process for cross-cultural and effective development programs is not designing a "shopping list" or "fast-forwarding" types of programs. Rather, they need to integrate the development leaders with organization and team development. The emphasis is not on developing a list of skills but to increase the capacity to learn from experience and be open to change if necessary. This attitude of humility encourages a willingness to learn and is an essential component for both the individual's and the organization's capacity building. Neither leaders nor organizations can become great, unless they go beyond striving to be the best and enter into an ongoing process of integrated development. Hoppe (2003) argues that effective and integrated leadership development program must be cross-culturally intelligent. The essential components of the development experience (assessment, challenge and support) as well as the development process at the organizational level must be adapted and sustained through intercultural dialogue.

The leadership model that emerged from the ongoing research of the DePaul Leadership Project (DLP) is an example of an integrated model. Through the multilevel comparative research and leadership development programs the DLP aims to gather and learn from value-oriented personal and organizational best practices. Since its foundation in 2003, the project has assessed and trained more than 650 participants worldwide. Based on the inspiring values and modern applications of St. Vincent de Paul (1581-1660), the DLP identifies the characteristics of Vincentian leadership in four orientations (mission, task, people and service) and 12 competencies (Vision, Value, Innovation, Commitment, Pragmatism, Risk-taking, Inclusiveness, Collaboration, Communication, Service, Empowerment and Social Justice). Throughout the international collaboration with nonprofit organizations and service institutions worldwide, the DLP has identified a fifth orientation measuring five cross-cultural leadership competencies: Openness, Flexibility, Identity, Empathy and Respect. These orientations and the corresponding competencies reflect Geert Hofstede's cultural dimensions of masculinity, individualism, risk-taking, power inequality, and short-term orientation (Hofstede & Hofstede 2005; Tavanti 2005).

The DLP model is a comprehensive and inclusive service-oriented leadership model assessing and promoting value-service oriented leadership practices of people in organizations. Their service, mission and value oriented leadership practices are evaluated in balance with their commitment and accomplishments of tasks, and their ability to engage in collaborative, communicative and inclusive interpersonal relations. The servant-servant leadership paradigm and the cultural intelligence – intercultural consciousness paradigms are embedded in the orientations and competencies of the DLP model. The sustainability paradigm, when combined with the service and culture paradigms, forms an integrated model of three intersecting circles that can be used to understand both personal and organizational leadership development practices.

TABLE 4
DLP Orientations and Competencies

o Mission Orientation	• Vision Competency
o	• Value Competency
	• Innovation Competency
o Task Orientation	• Commitment Competency
	• Pragmatism Competency
	• Risk-taking Competency
o People Orientation	• Inclusiveness Competency
	• Collaboration Competency
	• Communication Competency
o Service Orientation	• Service Competency
	• Empowerment Competency
	• Social Justice Competency
o Cross-cultural Orientation	• Openness Competency
	• Flexibility Competency
	• Identity Competency
	• Empathy Competency
	• Respect Competency

This integrated model for leadership development goes along with Jim Collins' (2001) findings of what makes good organizations become great. His "hedgehog" concept is exemplified in three interconnecting circles of (1) What you are deeply passionate about? (2) What can you be the best in the world at doing? (3) What drives your economic engine?

These three questions reflect the service, culture and sustainability paradigm of our leadership development integrated model. It is suggested that African leadership and organizational development programs can reach their best efforts if they follow and re-evaluate their practices through these three frameworks.

FIGURE 1
The Integrated Leadership Development Model

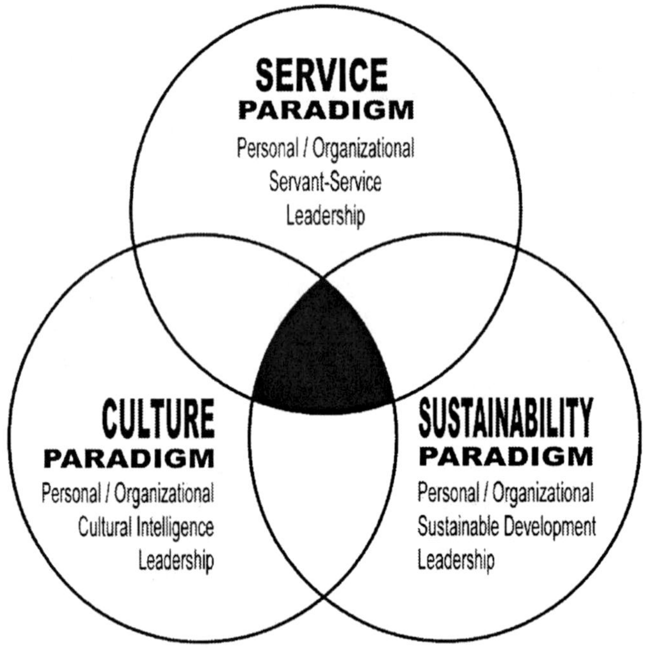

Vincent de Paul, the founder of organized charity used to say "It is not enough to do good, it must be done well." Many times, it is the small things that count; like an act of charity. But in organizational leadership development it is a well-thought-out plan and deliberate actions that make a difference. Vincent understood this and dedicated his leadership vision, managerial skills and organizational inventiveness to making a sustainable impact to serve disadvantaged populations worldwide. He understood the idea that the good intensions of a few heroic leaders are not enough to alleviate world poverty (Sacks 2005). This integrated model suggests that good mission statements, plans and visions of individuals have the possibility to become great organizations and best practices when developed and thoughtfully discerned through economic, cultural and service paradigms. Using Collins' vocabulary and cultural context, the intersection of these circles provides teams and organizations across the three sectors with "Big, Hairy, and Audacious Goals" (BHAG) to do great things (Collins 2001 and 2005). In the African context, each organization has to come up with their own version of "big, risk-taking and bold" goals to achieve great things. The three paradigms are not about settings specific goals but help ask the hard questions and gain an understanding of an individual and organization's leadership development assumptions and practices.

In Conclusion:

In this article, we have analyzed three recent trends in leadership development theory. The Greenleaf Center suggests that the servant leadership paradigm can be applied as an institutional philosophy, a model in for-profit as well as not-for-profit organizations, trustee education, community leadership organizations, experiential and leadership education, and, finally, in training programs related to personal and spiritual growth (Spears & Lawrence 2001; Spears & Greenleaf 1998). We have argued that the service-servant leadership paradigm is relevant across sectors, beliefs and cultural contexts. We suggested that certain characteristics of African philosophies and cultures fit (if not extend) the concept and values of servant leadership. We would suggest that a service-oriented organizational leadership development approach could be even more appropriate for African contexts. Our integrated leadership development model suggests how the service, culture and sustainability paradigms resemble Jim Collins' good-to-great and hedgehog concept.

A follow up of this framework analysis paper would be to create a matrix that showed the overlap between the three paradigms as well as their unique characteristics. A critical analysis of this model would suggest its limitations and simplifications. Nevertheless the refinement of this model will occur as our research goes into the application and analysis of best practices in the East African context of nonprofit and service sector organizations. To analyze the model in a broader perspective, the DLP will apply a comparative analysis across contexts and sectors. We anticipate that the service paradigm will receive more acceptance than the sustainability model across nonprofit, volunteer and religious organizations that often operate in a more defined environment and attract motivated employees. We also anticipate that these organizations will resist undergoing appropriate evaluation processes of their intercultural competencies and sustainability impact.

The need for understanding the nature of leadership development and implementing effective leadership development practices will likely be greater than ever before. At the same time, we find ourselves hopeful by looking at the possibilities of integrating personal leadership development with organizational development. We are also optimistic that the integration of systems thinking, contextual learning and personal development will become better and more articulated in the years to come. The learning and comparative analysis of many "engaging" African best practices in organizational leadership development will have a profound effect on poverty reduction strategies, democratization, decision making and human rights.

REFERENCES

Ata U. Karim. 2003. A developmental progression model for intercultural consciousness: A leadership imperative. *Journal of Education for Business,* 79 (Sept-Oct): 34–40.

Avolio, B. J. 1999. *Full leadership development: Building the vital forces in organizations.* New York: Sage Publications.

Banerjee, Subhabrata Bobby. 2003. Who sustains whose development? Sustainable development and the reinvention of nature. *Organization Studies,* 24(1): 143–180.

Bass, B. M. 2000. The future of leadership in learning organizations. *Journal of Leadership Studies,* 7(3): 18–40.

Blanchard, K., & O'Connor, M. 1997. *Managing by values.* San Francisco: Barr-Koehler Publishers.

Ciulla, J. 2003. *The ethics of leadership.* Belmont: CA: Wadsworth/Thomson.

Collins, J. 2001. *Good to great: Why some companies make the leap ... and others don't.* New York: Harper Business.

Collins, J. 2005. *Good to great and the social sectors: Why business thinking is not the answer.* A Monograph to Accompany Good to Great.

Dresner, S. 2002. *The principles of sustainability.* London and Sterling, VA: Earthscan.

Earley, C. & Soon, A. 2003. *Cultural Intelligence: Individual Interactions Across Cultures.* Stanford, CA: Stanford University Press.

Earley, C. P. & Mosakowski, E. 2004. Cultural intelligence. *Harvard Business Review,* (Oct): 139–146.

Edwards, A. R. 2005. *The sustainability revolution: Portrait of a paradigm shift.* Gabriola Island, BC, Canada: New Society Publishers.

Fullan, M. 2004. *Leadership and sustainability: System thinkers in action.* Thousand Oaks, CA: Sage Publications.

Garone, S. J. & The Conference Board. 1999. Conference. *The Future Organization: New Leadership and Employee Roles: Conference Report of the 1999 Organization of the Future Conference in New York, USA, 18-19 February, 1999.* New York: The Conference Board, 1999.

Gladwin, T.N., Kennelly, J.J., & Krause, T.S. 1995. Shifting paradigms for sustainable development: Implications for management theory and research. *Academy of Management Review,* 20(4): 874–907.

Goody E, (Ed.). 1995. *Social intelligence and interaction.* Cambridge: Cambridge University Press.

Greenleaf, R. K., & Spears, L. C. 2002. *Servant leadership: A journey into the nature of legitimate power and greatness.* (25th anniversary ed.). New York: Paulist Press.

Gudykunst, W. B., & Hammer, M. 1996. Designing intercultural training. In D. Landis & R. Bhagat (Eds.), *Handbook of intercultural training* (2nd ed.) Thousand Oaks, CA: Sage.

Henriques, A., & Richardson, J. (Eds.). 2004. *The triple bottom line, does it all add up?: Assessing the sustainability of business and CSR*. London: Earthscan Publications.

Hofstede, G., & Hofstede, G. J. 2005. *Culture and organizations: Software of the mind: Intercultural cooperation and its importance for survival.* Columbus, OH: McGraw Hill.

Hoppe, M. H. 2003. Cross cultural issues in the development of leaders. In C. D. McCauley & Velsor, E. V. (Eds.), *The Center for Creative Leadership Handbook of Leadership Development* (2nd ed.). San Francisco, CA: Jossey-Bass.

House, R., Javidan, M., Hanges, R., & Dorfman, R. 2002. Understanding cultures and implicit leadership theories across the globe: An introduction to project GLOBE. *Journal of World Business,* 37(1): 3–10.

Jackson, T. 2004. *Management and change in Africa: A cross-cultural perspective.* London: Routledge.

Laszlo, C. 2003. *The sustainable company: How to create lasting values through social and environmental performance.* Washington: Island Press.

Laub, J. A. 1999. *Assessing the servant organization: Development of the servant organizational leadership (SOLA) instrument.* Unpublished doctoral dissertation, Florida Atlantic University.

Lucas, N., & Chambers, T. 2003. Editorial comments: Special issue, "Leadership in diverse societies." *Journal of Leadership and Organizational Studies,* 9(3): 1

Lytle R. S., Peter W. H., & Mokwa, M. P. 1998. SERV*OR: A managerial measure of organizational service-orientation. *Journal of Retailing,* 74(Winter): 455–458.

Mammo, T. 1999. *The Paradox of Africa's Poverty: The role of indigenous knowledge, traditional practices and local institutions.* Trenton, NJ: Red Sea Press.

Mbigi, L. 1995. *Ubuntu, the spirit of African transformation management.* Randburg, South Africa: Knowledge Resources.

McCauley, C. D., Russ S. Moxley & Ellen Van Velsor (Eds.). 2003. *The Center for Creative Leadership Handbook of Leadership Development* (2nd ed.). San Francisco, CA: Jossey-Bass.

Mintzberg, H. 2006. Developing countries? Developing leaders? Learning from another place. To be published in *Development in practice.* Available at http://www.mitzberg.org.

Northhouse, P. G. (Ed.). 2003. *Leadership: Theory and practice.* Thousand Oaks, CA: Sage Publications.

Ntseane, P. G., & Youngman, F. 2002. *Leadership in civil society Organizations in Botswana*. DPMF Policy Brief Series, No. 7. Addis Ababa, Ethiopia: Development Policy Management Forum.

Nwoye, K. O. 2000. *Corruption, leadership, and the dialectics of development in Africa: An exploratory perspective*. Enugu [Nigeria]: Associated Printing & Litho. in conjunction with Center for African Development and Political Strategy.

Ronan, N. J. 1993. Developing the African manager: The good, the bad and the competent. *Management Education and Development,* 24(4): 388–394.

Sacks, J. 2005. *The end of poverty: Economic possibilities for our time.* New York, NY: Penguin Press.

Sendjaya, S., & Sarros J. C. 2002. Servant leadership: Its origin, development, and application in organizations. *Journal of Leadership & Organizational Studies,* 9 (Fall): 57–65.

Spears, L., & Greenleaf, R. K. 1998. *The power of servant leadership: Essays.* San Francisco, CA: Berrett-Koehler Publishers.

Spears, Larry C. & Lawrence, Michele. 2001. *Focus on leadership: Servant leadership for the 21st Century* (3rd ed.). New York, NY: Wiley.

Spears, L. 1996. Reflections on Robert K. Greenleaf and servant-leadership. *Leadership & Organization Development Journal,* 17(7): 33–36.

Tavanti, M. 2005. Cross-cultural Vincentian leadership: The challenge of developing culturally intelligent leaders. *Vincentian Heritage,* 23-25 (2) 26 (1): 01-225.

Thomas, D., & Kerr Inkson. 2004. *Cultural intelligence: People's skills for global business.* San Francisco, CA: Berrett-Koehler.

World Commission of Environment and Development (WCED). 1987. *Our common future.* New York: Oxford University Press.

SECTION 2

MANAGEMENT AND LEADERSHIP EDUCATION

CULTURAL MANAGERIAL HYBRIDIZATION: THE CASE OF AFRICAN MANAGEMENT EDUCATION ENTREPRENEURSHIP [4]

DR. JEAN-PAUL LEMAIRE
ESCP-EAP
European School of Management
79avenue de la République
75011 Paris
France.
E-mail: jplemaire@escp-eap.net

DR. NATHALIE PRIME
ESCP-EAP
European School of Management
79avenue de la République
75011 Paris
France.
E-mail: prime@escp-eap.net

Abstract

In most countries of Sub-Saharan Africa (SSA), the authoritative statements of the international financial institutions have led to a removal of trade and investment barriers and, above all, to a withdrawal of the State from many sectors of the economy, therefore creating new opportunities for local and foreign private initiatives. Within the context of this fast evolving environment, developing management capabilities has become a crucial agenda to address the transition of the continent, and to accompany both the necessary reforms to be implemented in the mismanaged public sector and the rapid growth of private initiatives more often lacking well-trained modern senior and middle managers. Compared to this challenge, the issue of modern advanced management education has received very little attention, therefore the two purposes of the research. First it aims to explore the stratification of various managerial references in SSA, relying on the historical and acculturation perspectives that show how different management systems may interact in today's management practices of the modern African enterprise. Second, it aims to rely on an in-depth case study related to the creation and growth of an indigenous initiative of management education in Senegal in order to illustrate the development of hybrid systems of people management and organizational development and to see what has been successful and what has not been successful in terms of the adaptation and synthesising of the different management systems observable in SSA.

Key words

Cultural hybridization, management education, entrepreneurship, Senegal

---

[4] The authors express their gratitude to Amadou Diaw, Founder and President of the Institut Supérieur du Management (ISM) in Dakar, and Mouhamed M. Dieye, Professor of Sociology at the University Cheikh Anta Diop in Dakar and academic advisor of the doctoral program of ISM, for the trust, time and data provided to develop the case study.

Introduction

In most countries of Sub-Saharan Africa (SSA), the authoritative statements of the international financial institutions have led to a removal of trade and investment barriers, and, above all, to a withdrawal of the State from many sectors of the economy, therefore creating new opportunities for local and foreign private initiatives. Within the fast evolving context of the political regulatory, economic and social, as well technological environment (Lemaire, 2003), developing management capabilities has become a crucial agenda. This is to address the transition of the continent, and to accompany both the necessary reforms to be implemented in the mismanaged public sector, and the rapid growth of private initiatives that are often lacking in well-trained modern senior and middle managers.

The issue of management education development in Africa has received little attention however, although it has the potential to make substantial contribution to improving prospects (Financial Times, 2004). Therefore, the first aim of the research is to identify the possible various managerial references to which SSA has been exposed, drawing on the joint historical and acculturation perspectives, in order to better understand how different management systems may integrate into "hybrid" or "cross-vergent" dynamic management practices (Ward et al., 1999) within the specific context of the modern African enterprise.

Secondly, in order to focus, as suggested by Jackson (2002), on the development of hybrid systems of people management in Africa, the research aims to illustrate how local exigencies of environmental pressures, combined with several managerial influences, led to a form of cultural managerial hybridization, both in the institutional model adopted and in some key aspects of the Institute's management approach. It aims to do so by means of a case study on the creation and growth of an indigenous entrepreneurial initiative in the sector of management education in Senegal.

Methodology

In a region dominated by oral traditions, by the relative lack of written historical and archaeological records, and by the successive traumas brought by slave trade, colonialism and often disappointing Independences, the historical perspective becomes a precious tool to develop a future orientation capable of anchoring future projects in the multiple legacies of the past, as well as dealing with the present challenges to be met in Africa. Understanding the historical background is, therefore, important for those who want to develop management education in Africa with the Africans (Kiggundu, 1991).

After reviewing the literature on the successive management systems that co-exist in today's SSA, the paper uses a case study to illustrate the hybridization of management systems in the creation and growth of the leading Senegalese management institute, ISM (Institut Supérieur du Management, Dakar). The single case design has been chosen in order to facilitate the deep understanding of the relatively little known research phenomenon (Ghauri 2004) of cultural "hybridisation" and "cross-vergence" of African management. It relies on a longitudinal approach of an institution, which is in charge of diffusing managerial values and practices, and, as an organisation, submitted to managerial constraints.

Following the multi-methods approach to ensure validation (Campbell & Fiske 1959), several methodological tools have been combined in order to throw light on the creation and growth of the Institute:

- participant observation and action research, initiated by the authors during 3 successive years of teaching seminars targeted to 3 out of 4 promotions of the young Assistant Professors committed in the pre-doctoral and doctoral programs of the Institute, and representing the newly created permanent faculty ;
- triangulation through in-depth interviews with the founder and President of ISM, as well as with the Professor in charge of the Academic coordination of the research activities of the nascent permanent faculty; those interviews have been checked with interviews of various Assistant Professors;
- a longitudinal observation of the evolution of this pool of Assistant Professors during 3 years parallel to the growth of the Institute, and with its strategic and organisational adjustments, bearing in mind the changes occurring through times in the management education sector in Africa and especially in Senegal since the early nineties.

The stratification of managerial references in Sub-Saharan Africa

Even if Africa is undoubtedly "at the edge of the world" (Smith, 2005), it is also the most "globalized" continent. In 2003, the share of African trade in the African GDP was 52.7% (compared to 41.5% for the world average, 16% for the Europe zone – intra European exchanges excluded, 19% for the USA and 19.9% for Japan)[5]. As a result, a long tradition of interactions with foreign powers and corporations can be found, that has reflected, up to now, the colonial legacy rather than an indigenous approach to management activities (Jackson, 2002). Still, several "ideal-type" management systems have been evoked in previous research, especially in the domain of management development (Kiggundu, 1991) and HRM in Africa (Jackson 2004). Understanding the prevailing values, beliefs, attitudes and behaviours in the society at large, can help us understand the kind of cultural patterns that employees, as well as managers, bring into the organization (Granovetter, 1985). In other words, understanding how Africa exhibits different layers of management systems is an important key, if one wants to acknowledge the complexities of the combined effects of different cultures on African societies in general, and on management and organizational practices in particular (Horwitz, Kamoche & Chew, 2002). "If anything, 'African management' is cross-cultural management" (Jackson, 2002: 999).

We emphasize, from the most recent to the most traditional management systems, the following layers to which 'African management' has been successively exposed (cf. figure 1):

- the current upper crust composed of the global environment forces (i.e. emerging from the unstable worldwide "declustering" economy);
- the hegemonic Western management principles composed of colonial and post-colonial historical legacy;
- and the deep African management patterns rooted in pre-colonial time.

The Current Upper Crust of the Global Environment Forces

Despite considerable environmental variations across countries (historical, economic, social, political), all African economies are going through a stage of transition that started with the fall of the Berlin wall in 1989. This period is not specific to Africa, but the rapid pace and radical degrees of change observed in SSA have probably not reached similar levels elsewhere.

[5] Source: World Bank, Country Data Profiles, http:///www.worldbank.org/data/countrydata/countrydata.html

It is characterized by a shift from overstaffed public organizations to more publicly accountable organizations, and to private companies that have to be competitive and profitable in a global open competition (Jackson, 2002). Economic structural adjustment programs, imposed by international financial institutions as pre-requisites for the allocation of new international loans, have led to a reduction of government spending. Subsidies have been removed, and goods, labour and money markets deregulated. Prices have been decontrolled to respond to international market forces and liberalization of trade. Finally, the political-legal deregulation and economic liberalization have been supported by rapid technological changes, including new communication means capable of progressively abolishing time and space barriers.

These political regulatory, social and economic, as well as technological pressures can be observed in most sectors of activity and, overall, African economies are being progressively "de-clustered" (Lemaire, 2000; 2003). The operating environment of African firms is, therefore, largely dependent on international turbulences and uncertainties of the global marketplace. But it is also influenced by the traditional presence of former colonial European powers, challenged by the increased influence of the USA, as well as by the sustained efforts of Asian economies in developing Africa. These include countries such as Japan, and, more recently, emerging economies such as Korea, Malaysia, Taiwan, India and China.

From the management development point of view, the liberalization of African economies has led to a number of challenges: How to develop predominantly under-skilled people, with little awareness of consumer economy, in countries where universities are bankrupt or financed by international institutions under the condition of radically rationalizing their administration? How to retain the African elite who can now afford, physically and financially, to study and work, not only in the old Europe, but also in the US or in Asian countries (like Australia or Singapore)? How to develop human capabilities to ensure the flexibility and responsiveness required to face global competition?

From the cultural point of view, economic globalization translates into a growing exposure to a variety of cultural patterns from the dominant economic zones (the Triad economy composed of North America, the European Union and Japan) that have shaped the nature and expressions of capitalism in each of these regions. In the Western areas (North America and Europe), in spite of important nuances between the USA and Europe (see e.g. Brewster, 1993), as well as between the European countries (Hickson, 1993), the dominant value orientations profile underlying management systems is based on values that were originally created by the European Renaissance. These found their first propitious milieu in Anglo-Saxon Protestant countries, where experiences of large scale industrialization and urbanization processes first took place. Typically, these give precedence to individualism over communalism, internal over external locus of control, egalitarianism over hierarchy, universalism over particularism, doing over being, "economic" linear clock time over "eventual" cyclical natural time (Prime, 2003).

Given the economic domination of the USA since the Second World War, these values are often assimilated into the modern "global culture" values, at least in the American rhetoric, too often exhibiting a crude ethnocentric idea that "West is best". This is in spite of a number of persuasive critiques drawing on cultural arguments about the culture-bound nature of management thinking and practices promoted by the North American view of the world of work, essentially based on a dominant functionalist paradigm (see e.g. Blunt & Jones, 1997) or "post-instrumental" management system (Jackson, 2002). Japanese management thinking, in spite of the enormous success of the Japanese economy since the Second World War, has never reached the same degree of idealization and self-satisfied rhetoric worldwide, except maybe in the domain of quality management and lean manufacturing.

FIGURE 1
New African Hybrid Managerial Patterns

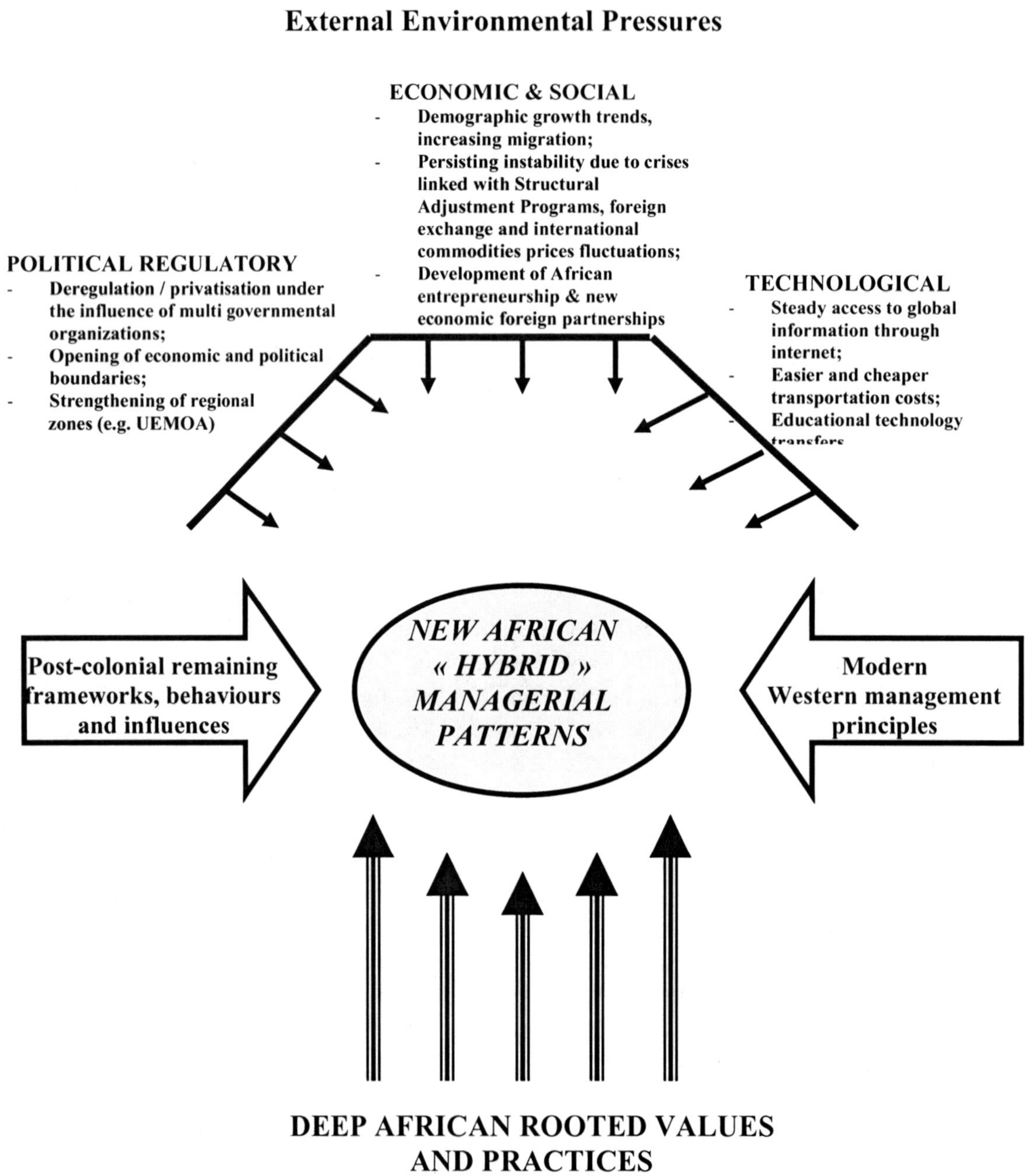

These "global values", to which Africa is exposed (as well as most other countries) through the global economy environmental forces, are not consistent with traditional SSA values. Still, they are familiar to the latest generation of African managers or entrepreneurs who have been trained outside Africa and are well aware of international (American) management standards. This management style is more likely to be observable in MNCs operating in Africa, as well as in new private companies that are progressively emerging from the transition time with a results and market orientation.

The Hegemonic Western Management Principles in Colonial and Post-colonial Times

As suggested by Jackson (2002), "African management" in the description of the post-colonial management system in Africa, is informed by the developed/developing world dichotomy ("African management" is a "developing country management") underlying the convergence assumption by which the developing world, through industrialization, should become more like the developed world. In reality, it is more likely that this "African management style" reflects a theory X style of management (from McGregor) or a "Jacobinism" (Zadi Kessy, 1998) typical of the management systems imported by colonial powers. These have been "tacked-on" to African society (Dia, 1996), and then perpetuated after the Independences, probably because it was simply the way managers were trained in the colonial era or because of vested political and economic interests.

This management thinking mistrusts human nature and therefore imposes controls on workers, encourages little initiative, and rewards a narrow set of skills by financial means only (Jackson, 2002). Therefore the "African management style" is described as centralized, bureaucratic, authoritarian, etc. (see e.g. Blunt and Jones, 1997). But formal management development in Africa owes its origins to Western management theory and practices (Kiggundu, 1991). Indeed, the first task of the colonial powers was to systematically destroy local pre-existing institutions and management practices in order to develop their own colonial administrative systems. This destruction resulted not only in the practical domination of the colonial powers over Africa, but also in the psychological destruction of the African self-esteem (Zadi Kessi, 1998).

From the management development point of view, a large body of civil servants was developed in order to carry out the administrative responsibilities of the colonial state, emphasizing literacy and lower clerical and administrative functions, along with kinship and loyalty to the colonial authority (Kiggundu, 1991). No local senior management was ever developed since the Africans were not expected to assume any managerial responsibilities. As a consequence, Africa had no capacity to manage at the time of independence. This colonial management style hangover is more likely to be observable in the remaining large public administrations and private companies, led by educated management elite with low managerial expertise. These organizations are characterized by a lack of motivation, low productivity and labour strife (Jackson, 2004).

The case of South Africa must be outlined, since it illustrates particularly well the hegemonic influence of a Western colonial and post-colonial "Eurocentric" management approach as opposed to the "Afro-centric" approach developed in the South African Ubuntu philosophy (Mbigi, 1997). Khoza (1994) speaks about the Whites being "individualistic exclusivists", building "exclusive institutions". The dominant corporate style is dominated by the idea of a form of opposition: decision-making is informed by power relations, and adversarial relationships are fostered between managers and the managed, buyers and suppliers, whites and blacks, etc. To Jackson (2004), Western management style is characterized by its instrumentalism where people serve the ends of organizations. Finally

Mbigi (1997) insists on the rationalism of Western management systems as expressed in job descriptions, job evaluations, disciplinary codes, grievance procedures and in the lack of place for dreams by constantly making the workers aware of the practical limitations and realities of companies.

The Deep rooted African Values and Schemes

One of the consequences of the systematic destruction of indigenous administrative systems by colonial powers in Africa is the relative lack of knowledge about organizational forms and management styles used in pre-colonial Africa (Kiggundu, 1991). Moreover ancient Africa's many cultural complexities are often forgotten or slighted in the annals of history (Frobenius, 1933). While Egypt may be discussed, and most ancient Nubia sometimes mentioned, little is known of the many other states that have contributed to African history, such as the medieval states of West Africa, the ancient state of Zimbabwe and the antiquity and power of Abysinnia. Still, as outlined by the African scholar Cheikh Anta Diop (1960), it is evident that, if starting from Nubia and Egypt, continental geographical direction had been followed, such as Nubia-Gulf of Benin, Nubia-Congo, Nubia-Mozambique, the course of African history would have appeared uninterrupted. This is the perspective in which the African past should be viewed. On the basis of the cross-fertilization of data coming from a variety of domains (ethnographic accounts, palaeontology, linguistics, artefacts analysis, journey telling, morphological analyses), and the use of a comparative approach between different SSA sub-regions, the research approach of Cheikh Anta Diop is crucial for the understanding that there was no interruption of African history. The African and 'nigger' origin of humanity and of the Egyptian/Nubian civilization is established, as well as the identification of the major migration roads and the formation of African ethnos.

Cheikh Anta Diop also provides us with a detailed analysis of the economic organization of pre-colonial Africa, in contrast with the prevailing views of a pure subsistence economy, where the individual is dominated by nature, where no currency, credit, or accumulation of wealth could exist at the supposed state of primitive development of pre-colonial Africa. If primitive tribes existed, he shows the existence of a modern kind of commercial organization, a highly developed social and economic structure based on a rigid cast organization, import-export practices between the different Kingdoms, definite trade routes and economic wealth. Like India, or other countries before the colonial presence, Africa was rich (this being actually the best argument explaining why the foreign powers came).

Kiggundu (1991) describes chiefs, emperors or hereditary kings imbued with both secular and divine authority, showing a highly personalized and authoritarian leadership still observable in post colonial regimes. They were absolute rulers whose power came from conquests, special relationships with the supernatural or descent from the original occupants of the territory. Still some forms of democracy were exercised with "constitutional" procedures for removing unsuitable rulers.

From the management development perspective, this period was characterized by extensive informal apprenticeships and on-the-job training. Learning was generally viewed as a passive process relying heavily on extensive observation (Sawadogo, 1995). The elders progressively identified the most promising leaders among the youth. Therefore, the elders played a crucial role and would act as life-time mentors or role models.

In South Africa, the need for an "Afro-centric" approach to management in African organizations has been acknowledged by several authors, immediately after the abolishment of the apartheid political system. Afro-centricity remains a broad concept, but it has largely to do with usage of African home-base solutions in addressing challenges, including economic challenges (Khoza, 1994). African home base conceptual knowledge about people and their predispositions to work and productivity are all connected with Africa's inclusive Ubuntu-based value system. Ubuntu covers the cultural propensity for African people to be community and inclusively oriented. It is a concept that brings to the fore images of humanism, supportiveness, cooperation and solidarity within the community. Mbigi (1994) points out that Ubuntu means fundamentally relying on traditional African management values and practices, like leading as an oral culture using parables and African proverbs as well as traditional healers, folk singers, market women and traditional peasant farmers as role models for inspiring and empowering leadership. Other African based Ubuntu principles are about creating an inclusive enterprising community and establishing intimate relationships. Lessem (1994) notes that the view in Africa is that a group needs stroking, nurturing and attention.

Much has been written about individualism-collectivism philosophies and their impact on management, but the large body of literature does not provide an adequate explanation of African communalism although generally traditional African society may be regarded as being low in individualism (Blunt & Jones, 1992). To Khoza (1994), Ubuntu is an orientation to life that is opposed to individualism and insensitive competitiveness, and not comfortable with collectivism, where collectivism stresses the importance of the social unit to the point of depersonalising the individual.

Though the Ubuntu South African concept may probably be valid for other African countries, Zadi Kessi (2003) adds two important dimensions associated with deep African traditional values that have a major impact on managing African organizations. First, time is not money, since it is not measured by the clock, but rather by the natural time of seasons that give rhythm to agricultural work and social-religious rituals. Second, Africans tend to have an external locus of control grounded in a sacred and magical vision of nature and human life.

CULTURAL HYBRIDIZATION IN MODERN SSA MANAGEMENT

The African continent, due to its high degree of openness, its high level of migration, and its current transition state, is a propitious place where culture change phenomena and culture contact results can be observed. Having presented the different layers of cultural influences to which Africa has been successively exposed, it is important to explore how these various patterns of management thinking and practices may have integrated into modern SSA management.

Culture Change and Modern Africa: The Impact of Changes in the Environment and of Contact between Societies

All cultures are inherently predisposed to change and, at the same time, to resist change. From this perspective, there are dynamic processes operating that encourage the acceptance of new things and ideas, while there are others that encourage changeless stability. A holistic approach to culture change is necessary, to fully acknowledge the three general sources of influence or pressures that are responsible for both change and resistance to it: forces at work within a society, contact between societies and changes in the natural environment (cf. table 1).

TABLE 1
Culture Change Processes

	Within a society	*Between societies*
Processes leading to change	- invention - culture loss	- diffusion - acculturation
	Stimulus diffusion	
Processes resulting in resistance to change	- habit - string integration of culture traits	- in-group/out-group dynamics

(Adapted from http://anthro.palomar.edu/change/)

Today's 'natural' environment of African organizations is characterized by the impact of the strong pressures related to the globalization drivers (political regulatory, social and economic, technological "de-clustering" forces), leading to increased possibilities of diffusion or movement of things, ideas and people from one culture to another (from the rest of the world to Africa, between African countries especially at the sub-regional scales, and from Africa to the rest of the world). Within this context, a reasonable assumption is that *acculturation* in African management should be high. This acculturation is based on the diffusion on a large scale of alien cultural traits (in our case, of managerial ways of thinking and doing resulting from the successive periods of culture contact exposed earlier), thus substantially replacing deep traditional African rooted cultural management patterns. Changes within African societies (but maybe also within most other open modern societies) should therefore be understood best in the light of dominant changes *between* societies rather than *within* societies. Thus things coming from outside eventually stimulate invention or culture loss (change processes), or culture resistance when old habits or traditional cultural traits integration are reinforced (resistance processes).

The 'between societies' process of in-group/out-group dynamics is also very important to consider, since they target issues of ethnocentrism that are relevant to the African context in general. Ethnocentrism can result either from universalism or particularism (Todorov, 1989). We probably have both forms in the African context. Universalism is associated with the mimesis frequently observed in post colonial societies (Zadi Kessi, 1998), but also in modern times, when people from less economically developed countries want to fit with the dominant ideal – American – model (Blunt & Jones, 1997). Particularism, as an expression of the need to resist rapid and overwhelming change by revitalizing old habits or cultural traits, is also a frequent reaction to modern culture contact in a de-clustering environment (e.g. the "Afro-centric" approach proponents within the African context).

The Acculturation Process: Towards Hybridization and Cross-vergence

Focusing on the acculturation concept, it has classically been defined as "those phenomena which result when groups of individuals having different cultures come into continuous first hand contact, with subsequent changes in the original culture patterns of either or both groups" (Redfield, Linton & Herskovits, 1936: 149). The outcome may include not only changes to existing phenomena, but also some novel phenomena that are generated by the process of cultural interaction (Sam & Oppedal, 2002). Acculturation changes can happen at the individual and group levels and refer to changes in languages, identity, values, behaviours, attitudes, habits, social institutions and the like. Acculturation changes are normally geared towards adaptation, i.e., to ascertain that the individual or the group is able to meet the challenges arising from living in the midst of two (or more) different cultures.

Focusing on the research issue of acculturation in the social sciences disciplines (sociology, anthropology, linguistics, psychology and others), Rudmin (2003) notes the profusion of acculturation constructs on the basis of the use of the fourfold framework promoted by John Berry to organize the acculturation constructs into four generic types, depending on the relative importance of the first-culture (F) and the contact culture (C). These four ideal types have been symbolized as: (1) -F+C, (2) +F-C, (3) +F+C, and (4) -F-C, with attached meanings: 1) that the contact culture is favoured, or 2) that the first-culture is favoured, or 3) that both are favoured, or 4) that both are disfavoured.

Concepts elaborated to describe the "+F+C" option are actually numerous. Rudmin (2003) finds in this category constructs like "hybridity", "cultural pluralism", "syncretism", "multiculturalism" or "fusion". But in any case, this "+F+C" third option goes beyond the traditional debate in management studies between convergence/divergence advocates, and recalls the "cross-vergence" alternative proposed by Ralston, Terpstra & Kai-Cheng (1997).

Decades of research have been devoted to the study of culture contact on the basis of a dual conceptualization of values formation (England & Lee, 1974; Kelly, Whatley & Worthley, 1987; Hofstede, 1999). Those who follow the "convergence" theory perspective (Negandhi, 1975; Kelley & Worthley, 1981) believe that economic ideology drives values, and therefore managers embrace values with regard to economic activity and work-related behaviour. Convergence implies that developing countries will progressively assimilate values equating to Western industrialized capitalistic countries, managers from global companies being change agents in favour of the adoption of Western management techniques, behaviour and business systems. Conversely, advocates of the "divergence" approach (Ricks, Toyne & Martinez, 1990) argue that national culture, not economic ideology, drives values. Consequently, the value systems of countries adopting capitalistic values would remain largely unchanged (e.g. in Eastern countries Shaw, Fisher & Randolph, 1991).

Cross-vergence is an integrative alternative arguing that neither the convergence - divergence polar extreme views is adequate to explain the dynamic interaction of economy and national culture. In an open de-clustering environment, the cross-vergence viewpoint sees managerial culture change as a continuum between the polar extremes of convergence and divergence by which an integration of cultural and economic ideological influences happens. This integration results in a unique system that borrows from both national culture and economic ideology. The "synergistic approach" of cultural diversity management (Adler, 1991) conveys a similar rationale (maximizing "my" culture *and* "their" culture), as well as the grid of analysis of the integration end state in Mergers and Acquisitions proposed by Marks and Mirvis (2001), in the case of maximum and joint degree of change, both in the acquired and acquiring company, leading to "transformation" (i.e. new ways to operate).

Hybridization in Modern African Management

There is latitude within Berry's generic type "+F+C", depending on the aspects of managerial culture focused upon and whose perspective is considered (Rudmin, 2003). In the study of modern African management, we will consider the acculturating "minority's" perspective (African manager and entrepreneurs), and we will focus on the acculturation results favouring the combination of both traditional African and foreign cultures. It is assumed that this type of acculturation can best provide Africa with the capacity to meet the challenges arising from living at the crossroads of cultural influences in a turbulent global economic landscape. The success of fast growing East Asian economies shows that Confucian values are indeed intrinsically contributing to Asian economic growth, and that economic success must take traditional values into account (Hofstede & Bond, 1988). Japan and other tigers and dragons from the Pacific Rim have achieved a high level of industrial development because they have largely kept their languages, traditions, and historical references.

There is no reason why Africa should be an exception to that rule (Dia, 1991), and Zadi Kessy (1998), CEO of the first class performing companies CIE (Compagnie Ivoirienne d'Electricité) and the SODECI (Société de Distribution d'Eau de Côte d'Ivoire) provides a very relevant analysis and implementation guidelines of how traditional African values can be positively enacted to serve the needs of the modern African enterprise. From the cross-vergence point of view, this managerial approach calls more for a "cultural reform", rather than an "African renaissance" as Jackson (2002) does, since the issue is the *transformation* on the basis of the energy emerging from sound cultural ground. This is precisely what Zadi Kessy advocates - for the capacity of African management to transform communalism into group spirit, hierarchy into the sense of discipline, oral commitment into contractual trust, hospitality into integration, and enthusiasm into commitment.

In the SSA context, several authors have advocated this conceptualisation of cross-vergence as a hybridization process from which emerges new and mixed forms of management, capable of combining the best of traditional African values and foreign high performance management systems. The South African post-apartheid period provides an especially fruitful setting for the expression and implementation of such an integrative view of culture contact and change even if problems and obstacles are numerous (Prime, 1999). Thus Koopman (1994) describes the new South African organization to be developed under a pragmatic humanism approach, in which the way to incorporate inclusiveness is to seek unity in diversity. It means building trust and respect for different values, building common values, and learning.

Mbigi (1997) describes the challenge of synthesising different tribal, racial, economic, social, political and cultural values in South African management, for there is a need for management as a discipline to have a strong value base and philosophical base as a foundation of practice. He draws a parallel between the spirit of the feudal African hunter's attributes and the modern entrepreneur's attributes (emotional resilience, persistence, hunch, instinct, an eye for chance, enthusiasm, and the capacity to work hard, take risks and improvise). Then Mbigi describes the implementation of what he calls inspirational management. The process of management change goes through four major stages: releasing the Hunter's spirit, releasing the communal spirit, developing a village spirit, and releasing a productive spirit. The company has to be driven by a powerful vision and rational management systems.

THE ISM DAKAR: A CASE OF CULTURAL HYBRIDIZATION IN MANAGEMENT EDUCATION ENTREPRENEURSHIP

Based on the often neglected historical and acculturation perspectives, the identification of the possible various managerial references to which SSA has been successively exposed, suggests how different management systems may integrate in a hybrid or cross-vergent dynamic characteristic of management practices in the modern African enterprise. We will now illustrate the development of hybrid managerial systems in SSA by means of a case study focusing on the creation and growth of an indigenous entrepreneurial initiative in the sector of management education in Senegal. The purpose is to show how environmental pressures combined with several managerial references led to a form of cultural managerial hybridization, both in the institutional model adopted and in some key aspects of the Institute's management approach.

The Creation of ISM and the Sector of Management Education in Africa

ISM was created in Dakar in 1992. It has developed rapidly in terms of student numbers, programs offered and geographical locations. Numbers have risen from 25 students in 1992 to 2500 in 2005 and are still progressing at a very steady pace. The programs have flourished. The initial "bachelor" degree, a three-year program which is still the core program of the ISM, has been complemented by a wide range of Masters' programs, as well as by an International MBA and a doctoral program. Dakar remains the major ISM educational platform, but the Institute has already expanded at the national level (with new regional centres delivering the bachelor program in Saint Louis, Ziguinchor, Thiès, and Koalak, thus providing the Institute with a national coverage). It has expanded outside Senegal as well, with two Masters programs initiated in Niamey – Niger - and Wagadugu -Burkina Faso.

At the origin of the project lie the shortcomings of the overcrowded and almost permanently on strike Senegalese public universities in Dakar and Saint Louis. During the 1980's and the 1990's, permanent strikes took place, for a large number of social as well as pedagogical reasons. Recurrent disorders still persist (Tamba, 2004). These institutions were graduating many students, in Law, Economics, Sociology, Ethnology, Literature, Linguistics, etc., who were ready to apply for corporate positions, but with a mostly theoretical knowledge and methodological background that did not fit the needs of existing industrial and business structures. Furthermore the number of graduates exceeded, by far, the available positions offered in the well-established Senegalese organizations. Therefore, these academic curricula appeared inappropriate to stimulate and serve entrepreneurship, business development as well as basic managerial qualifications expected by employers.

But, beyond these immediate incentives to develop a new business education system, some more structural issues were pressing for change in Senegal during the early 1990s. These can be organised into three types of "external pressures": political regulatory, economic and social as well as technological.

The Evolving Political Regulatory Environment

Environmental changes for a renewed managerial education, at first, stems from political-regulatory measures. In 1994, a law on private higher education was passed in Senegal, to implement the Educational Structural Adjustment Plan designed in conjunction with the World Bank and the International Monetary Fund in October 1994. Previously, another law of February 1991 encouraged private individual or collective initiatives to create a Technical and Professional Training School. The major principle of the reform was the restriction, through selection, of the previously open access to university for any Senegalese "bacheliers" (end of 12th Grade diploma), in order to proportionate the number of students in the public universities to their physical capacities and pedagogical resources. Some regulations applied to the new private higher education establishments ("Etablissements Privés d'Enseignement Supérieur", EPES), under the control of a special department of the Ministry of Education which defined some conditions of agreement that were generally not fully respected. This explains why almost none of the new EPES had received, and still have not received, the official recognition from the Ministry of Education today (Tamba, 2004)[6].

[6] In December 2005, ISM Dakar was the first EPES to obtain academic recognition from the CAMES (Conseil Africain et Malgache pour l'Enseignement Supérieur), under the form of the accreditation of its Bachelor in Management three year program.

The WB and the IMF, by means of their structural adjustment programs, tended to encourage privatisation in many sectors and to stimulate the development of more efficient structures, which would be eager to recruit a staff possessing appropriate competencies. Some other incentives to change management education came from the development of regional economic organizations, such as UEMOA, among West African countries, and, on a larger African scale, from the NEPAD initiative providing a perspective for increasing flows of trade and investment in more integrated economic areas, requiring new and increasing business and management capabilities based on shared language, principles and processes.

The Changing Social and Economic Environment

Economic and social incentives also explain the steady growth of the private management education sector. In a long-term perspective, the increase of the post independence demographic growth rate is an important factor. In a shorter-term perspective, the devaluation of the CFA franc currency in January doubled the cost of studies abroad.

As a matter of fact, quantitative pressures – demography as well as standards of living – contribute to understanding the steep increase of the local demand for higher business education standards. Likewise, from a more qualitative point of view, middle class families wished to have access to more operational curricula leading to better employment perspectives for their children. Tamba (2004) stresses the point that, for girls, two or three year management programs were considered by families as the most appropriate. Beyond Senegal, in countries like Burkina, Mali, Mauritania, Gambia and Niger, suffering from political instability and/or less developed education institutions, comparable quantitative and qualitative drivers attracted significant flows of students to Senegal.

The Evolving Technological Environment

A third set of external pressures on the management education sector came from the technological environment. The development of the sector was certainly stimulated by the spread of internet ADSL access, which offered new perspectives together with all other new information systems and communication developments. This led to the development of new businesses based on new technologies of information and communication, associated with traditional activities or with activities exhibiting new business models, such as call centres created in Senegal or other African countries (Mauritius, Morocco etc.). Management knowledge and education diffusion could also benefit from these new technological means.

Overall, these external pressures combined and gave rise to new challenges for management education, in Senegal as well as in the west-African sub-region. This paved the way for a quick expansion of private higher education establishments, universities and professional training schools. In 2004, almost 50 such institutions existed in Senegal, mostly in Dakar, training about 13,000 students (Tamba, 2004). In such a context, ISM appeared, among them, as a pioneer, as early as 1992. Most other major competitors came later, among them being the pioneer group of private professional training schools, Sup de Co Dakar or ISFG, created in 1993, and the private Université Dakar-Bourguiba, created in 1995. ISM was initiated with the support of the Senegalese Employers' Club, and was aimed at locally training African managers in close connection with companies. The initial professional supporters provided the students with internships during their schooling period and with a job after graduation.

The Institutional Model: A Pragmatic Accommodation of Many Cultural Influences

Turning to the institutional model of ISM, observations suggest that several cultural influences have been pragmatically accommodated. We will address (a) the post-colonial persistent heritage; (b) modern Western management education inputs; and (c) the appeal to African rooted educational values.

(a) Post-colonial persistence Post-colonial legacy in West African management education models is manifest, as it is in management practices. African management education appears relatively new, dating back to the late nineties, prior to which management education was only accessible abroad (in Europe as well as in North America) for a very limited group of privileged future local managers. Apart from the historical reasons discussed earlier, this can be explained from the institutional point of view, at least in French speaking Africa, by the highly selective benchmark of the French or Belgian "Grandes Ecoles de Commerce", whose level tended to appear out of reach of the locals. The reference model for the EPES, ISM's direct competitors, has been, and still is the French "Grandes Ecoles de Commerce" model, with one to two years "preparatory classes" leading, after an advanced selection process, to a three year program, hopefully in the top range of French leading Business Schools located in Paris, but more generally to medium range schools, such as the French "ESC" ("Ecoles Supérieures de Commerce") located in province. Since its creation, ISM has offered a preparatory class whose access (up to 80 participants) was restricted by financial conditions resulting from the competitive exam and living expenses in France.

In addition, post "Baccalauréat" French private management education institutions provided ISM with a more operational benchmark in reference to university curricula in the first two years' applied studies cycle –such as the "Brevet Technique Supérieur" (B.T.S.) and the "Diplôme Universitaire de Technologie" (D.U.T.) developing managerial profiles well appreciated by the private sector. In particular, this was appreciated by the banking sector where employees in West Africa were ageing by the end of the nineties, and by the new information technology sector which was starting to grow in Senegal.

Overall, ISM has adopted several benchmarks through the early program design with the help of French "Ecole de Commerce" consultants, but very quickly a one to two years applied managerial curriculum was accessible after the university two years general studies curricula. These developments gave birth to the Diplôme Supérieur de Gestion, soon unified (in 1998) under the name of the ISM Bachelor diploma, referring clearly to the American managerial education system. The executive MBA program, previously created in order to always be ahead of competitors, referred to an Anglo-Saxon standard.

Post colonial influences, therefore, remained strong as cultural and business connexions remained close between France and West Africa. Today, they tend to decrease as the public sector's grip on Western African economies is loosening and the modern private sector, as well as multinational companies, is expanding within the region. This development in the West and Central French speaking Africa followed, in a way, the changes of the former colonial country's business education adjustments. But it has also left room for other influences from North America, the UK and the English speaking African zone.

(b) Modern Western management education inputs *American and Anglo Saxon influences have been important since the early stages of ISM. The contribution of diverse Afro-Americans academics belonging to the most prestigious institutions, such as Columbia, Georgetown or Harvard University has been strong through very early invitations to teach and visit the ISM facilities. They have been able to help acquire the management education* *patterns and tools that could be implemented in the newly created organization. Since the mid nineties, a set of key African universities from the English speaking Africa, for example from South Africa, Nigeria, Ghana, have also provided teachers and training programs to ISM.*

The recent membership of ISM to the private sector investment arm of the World Bank, the Global Business School Network (GBSN), also allows for a regular meeting between the Deans and faculty of sixty business schools of the continent, as well as with a large set of institutions from the Western hemisphere. At a more operational level, some training has been offered, such as case studies method seminars gathering a wide range of scholars from diverse African business schools (e.g. the GBSN seminar co-organised in May 2005 in Johannesburg by the Gordon Institute of Business Science and Lagos Business School, to which academics from South Africa, Kenya, Tanzania, Senegal, Nigeria and Ghana attended, including four Assistant professors from ISM).

Other academics from the USA, the EU and Asia have also been associated with the development of programs, especially for the Executive MBA (recently transformed into the International MBA, and teaching 30 executives on a part time basis). Executive training was also, in the early stage of ISM, and until the late 1990s, a useful complement to provide additional resources to finance the young structure. It also inspired, from the early stages of the institution's development, new patterns and product launches which have been exploited through time. Among the executive programs organised by ISM, there are those that have been sponsored by USAID, the World Bank and other multi-governmental institutions.

As a matter of fact, US imported modern managerial education principles tend to be introduced smoothly, directly as well as indirectly, without harsh conflicts with the post colonial influence since the evolution is comparable in France among the leading business schools. It creates a balanced and combined approach of program design, pedagogical style as well as of Faculty management. It is that kind of "soft" melting process that tends now to combine in the doctoral program adding influences grounded in rooted African values.

(c) African rooted educational values The initial idea of the ISM Doctoral program is directly related to the need to be able to rely on a permanent faculty, stemming from the dramatic increase in student numbers: the institution could not afford to work solely with part time practitioners and professionals, given the teaching burden of the different programs (Bachelor students represent 1500 students and the Masters more than 400). The point was to cope properly with these quantitative challenges as well as with qualitative criticisms commonly linked to many African management programs: "There are few MBA programs here, but most are mediocre. The teaching is still too theoretical and relies heavily on textbooks and lectures. Pedagogy needs to move more towards hands-on consulting experiences and cases. We need more faculty with real world experience" (America, 2003; 31). The African rooted managerial influence has come indirectly in the implementation conditions of this doctoral program, by means of the academic sponsorship, of the recruitment process and of the research orientation adopted.

The development of the doctoral program relies heavily on the University of Senegal in Dakar, with the special contribution of Cheikh Anta Diop University, which provided the doctoral coordinator and the initial group of experienced faculty, ready to transmit their research practices to the four successive yearly intakes which have been successively involved in the process since 2001. The recruitment initially targeted students in Sociology and Ethnology who were interested in business teaching. They usually possessed a corporate or administrative background, and expressed strong interests in African organizational realities and specificities, as well as in good practices, bearing in mind remaining pre-slavery and pre-colonial practices as important explanation factors of today's realities. The recruitment has also been highly multicultural since the beginning, with participants coming from a variety of countries of the sub-region (Ivory Coast, Mali, Guinea...).

The research orientations favour the study of indigenous research issues relating to the local sectors, local formal and informal business practices, the adjustment to imported managerial principles both by foreign companies and by local actors educated abroad, etc. These research orientations were developed in connexion with the concerns of local companies and public organizations. Research projects were also undertaken with the help of data collected by ISM Bachelor and Master students during their internships in companies. Research is also initiated and supported by some alumni experiences.

Overall, the hybrid African educational management model stems from these diverse influences converging in the doctoral program, which epitomizes them and shapes ISM as a new and genuine African private university model, training African managers, both for local organizations and for foreign business partners, by an African grown faculty.

Hybridization: Managing the Institute and the Indigenous Faculty

Turning to the management system progressively implemented at the ISM, especially for managing the pool of new Assistant professors constituting the permanent nascent faculty, the hybridization process is particularly obvious in the domains of decision-making, teamwork, mentoring and time management.

Corporate decision-making very clearly combines individual as well as collective principles. It is customary for the CEO to rely on frequent lengthy committee meetings, in order to openly discuss the different aspects of an issue or decision with a large body of employees of ISM. Typically, some faculty, as well as some administrative support people, will be involved. In parallel, the daily observation of decision-making in the Institute shows that the CEO's hierarchical role is very much pronounced: for most decisions, people in charge, even for routine tasks, tend to look for the CEO's validation (and the CEO tends to accept this practice). His responsibility is therefore dual. He must at the same time implement the traditional "chief" behaviour combining heavy and long (and genuine) consultation with a strong hierarchical-individual based decision-making (ultimately, decision-making is his).

Teamwork is another domain where cultural hybridization operates among the ISM permanent faculty of Assistant professors who are also doctoral students. If conducting doctoral research is clearly an individual commitment, the way the process has been implemented at the ISM relies also on traditional communal values and practices. First of all, each doctoral student works as a team member in a group composed of other doctoral assistants gathered on the basis of the commonalities of their thesis agenda (from the theoretical or the empirical point of view). The purpose is to stimulate economies of scales, lateral information exchanges, identification to a group sharing similar "academic" preoccupations. It is grounded in African orientation enhancing supportiveness, cooperation and solidarity. Also, each doctoral student is in charge of teaching and coordinating work projects with the different Bachelor and Master students of the Institute. In this format, one can note that their teamwork is managed in such a way that the doctoral student in charge plays the role of a mentor for the undergraduate teams. He/she orients pedagogical exercises in the direction of his/her own data collection for the thesis. This associates pedagogy to research in order to serve the respective interests of the various members of the community.

The role of seniority remains a key reference in the ISM management system. In daily management, some 'wise men' (former army officers) are involved in the staff on a permanent basis: they provide advice on strategic and structural orientations to the higher executive team. They act as facilitators among the staff members as well as vis a vis the students in order to solve many key issues stemming from the regular education process. Besides, another field of association of African values with managerial needs in ISM is the empowerment process handled by the eldest – among the students as well as among the fast expanding permanent faculty members. The eldest provide the youngest or the new comers with clear advice, help and support. This fits well with the seniority based African social system that is also observable in the way the permanent faculty is in charge of the regulation of students' initiatives, as well as in the way teamwork and pedagogical projects (e.g. students' company projects or faculty research groups) are managed.

Finally, first hand observation of daily management in ISM shows a striking hybridization of time management patterns combining a sense of emergency with the capacity to 'give' uncounted time to interlocutors provided that a relationship exists. Therefore, the contrasts between an economic monochromic vision of time grounded in task orientation, and a general feeling of sincere 'propitious' time, sometimes predominate over abstract clock time.

Conclusion

The purpose of this research was to explore the cultural hybridization process observable in modern SSA management with an illustration chosen in the domain of management education entrepreneurship. After reviewing the many layers of successive managerial influences to which modern African managers and entrepreneurs have been successively exposed, the research suggests that culture change processes (leading to culture change and/or to resistance) should be considered, especially as a result of contacts between societies with a focus on the "synergistic" acculturation, by which traits from the first culture (i.e. African) and contact culture (foreigners), are creatively combined to result in a new way of thinking or doing things.

The case study developed through the multi-methods approach at the ISM in Dakar is particularly useful to understand how the Institute has been evolving over time at the crossroads of many influences, be they in the institutional model or in the management of the Institute and of the young nascent permanent faculty. Thus the historical background of the Institute demonstrates that its institutional vision has constantly evolved in a number of directions. From a corporate employer led organization, it has become an autonomous organization directly connected to individual expectancies of students and corporate needs. The French "Ecole de Commerce" model has shifted to a genuine educational structure combining a diversity of other local and foreign influences. The centralized organizational structure has moved to a regional and international network. Finally, ISM has evolved from a professional education institution to a fully-fledged private university, including a doctoral and research program, catering for local needs and problems of African management today.

Managerial implications of the research target the need for the foreign partners of the Institute, especially in France, to better understand the complexity of management education models emerging in modern Africa today. The old imperialist approach is not possible anymore. The level of education of African managers, entrepreneurs, faculty members as well as students has considerably increased over the last 15 years, and all have relatively good access to 'what's going on' outside Africa, be it on the basis of a personal or family first-hand experience, or via the use of new communication and information technologies, especially the Internet.

Limits of the research are first related to the literature review on acculturation that has remained very general in scope. Future research should focus on this issue within the context of the fast growing emerging economies, rather than on the more classical context of immigration from less developed to more developed countries that are very much represented in the acculturation literature. Regarding the field study, we have focused on synergistic acculturation, which is one out of four options (in Berry's classification scheme) of the acculturation change process, itself being only one 'between societies' culture change processes among several others. Cultural change has to be seen through a holistic approach, and the observation provided in the paper of the ISM creation and growth patterns does not account for such a complexity, especially for the in-group/out-group dynamics.

Another important limitation is associated with the difficulty to codify, over a long period of time, in an evolving environment and organizational setting, the major dimensions for which hybridization has been particularly active. We have outlined the development of the institutional model, as well as some key managerial variables characteristic of the ISM management style, but others should be explored (e.g. motivation of the faculty, the leadership style of the CEO, and the corporate culture of the Institute).

Future research areas on managerial cultural hybridization in SSA involve evaluation of key variables in implementation of cross-cultural diffusion, adoption and transformation of managerial references and practices of modern enterprises in the sub-region. There is a need to focus on contingency approaches and mediating variables affecting organizational level application, as well as theoretical approaches on the importance of contexts (Horwitz, 2002). A second important research area concerns identification of the potentially best acculturation types to fit with the fast changing African business environment. What would be, among the original African values and management practices, those practices which should be kept as they are? Would they have to be slightly changed or radically modified in order to best cope with the types of modern global economic and managerial challenges that African companies are increasingly confronted with? This issue echoes another that has paramount implications for management academic and educative production in a "de-clustering" business and academic community: what, in our managerial systems (concepts, tools, methodologies etc), can be said to be universal, partly local *and* finally implacably local? Just as managerial ideologies have tended to spread from the North to the South over the past centuries, with more or less success, what could the North learn as a result from the new opportunities offered by lateral exchanges ('South-South') as well as by 'reverse diffusion' processes from the South to the North?

References

Adler, N. 1991. *Cultural dimensions of organizational behavior*. Canada: South-Western.

America, R. 2003. Advancing Africa. *BizEd*, May-June: 28–33.

Anta Diop, C. 1960. *L'Afrique noire précoloniale*. Paris: Editions Présence Africaine.

Berry, J.W. 1990. Psychology of acculturation: Understanding individuals moving between cultures. In R. Brislin (Ed.), *Applied cross-cultural psychology:* 232–253. Newbury Park, CA: Sage.

Blunt, P., & Jones, M. L. 1992. *Managing organizations in Africa*. Berlin: De Gruyter.

Blunt, P., & Jones, M. L. 1997. Exploring the limits of Western leadership theory in East Asia and Africa, *Personnel Review*, 26 (1-2): 6–23.

Brewster, C. 1993. Developing a European model of human resource management. *International Journal of Human Resource Management*, 4 (4): 765–784.

Campbell, D. T, & Fiske, W. 1959. Convergent and discriminant validation by the multitrait-multimethod matrix. *Psychological Bulletin,* 56: 81–105.

Dia, M. 1991. Développement et valeurs culturelles en Afrique subsaharienne. *Problèmes économiques*, n°2.281: 28–32.

Dia, M. 1996. *Africa's management in the 1990s and beyond*. Washington D.C: World Bank.

England, G. W., & Lee, R. 1974. The relationship between managerial values and managerial success in the United States, Japan, India and Australia. *Journal of Applied Psychology*, 59: 411–19.

Financial Times. 2004. Schools on a mission to teach, Monday December 13.

Frobenius, L. 1933. *Histoire de la civilisation africaine* (6th ed.) Paris: Gallimard.

Ghauri, P. 2004. Designing and conducting case studies in international research. In R. Marschan-Piekkari & Welch C. (Eds.), *Handbook of qualitative research methods for international business:* 109–124. Cheltenham UK / Northampton MA USA: Edward Elgar.

Granovetter, M. 1985. Economic action and social structure: The problem of embeddedness. *American Journal of Sociology*, 82: 929–964.

Hickson, D. J. (Ed.). 1993. *Management in Western Europe: Society, culture and organization in twelve nations*. New York: Walter de Gruyter.

Hofstede G. & Bond, M. S. 1988. The Confucius connection: From cultural roots to economic growth. *Organizational Dynamics*, 16 (Spring): 5–21.

Hofstede, G. 1999. Problems remain, but theories will change: The universal and the specific in 21st-century global management. *Organizational Dynamics*, 28(1): 34–44.

Horwitz, F. M., Kamoche, K., & Chew I. K. H. 2002. Looking East: Diffusing high performance work practices in the southern Afro-Asian context. *International Journal of Human Resource Management*, 13 (7): 1019–1041.

Jackson, T. 2002. Reframing HRM in Africa. *International Journal of Human Resource Management*, 13 (7): 998–1018.

Jackson, T. 2004. *Management and change in Africa: A cross-cultural perspective*. London: Routledge.

Kanungo, R. N., & Jaeger A. M. 1990. Introduction: The need for indigenous management in developing countries. In A. M. Jeager & R. N. Kanungo (Eds.), *Management in Developing Countries:* 1–23. London: Routledge.

Kelley, L., Wathley, A., & Worthley, R. 1987 Assessing the effects of culture on managerial attitudes: A three-culture test. *Journal of International Business Studies*, 18(2): 17–31.

Kelley, L., & Worthley, R. 1981. The role of culture in comparative management: A cross cultural perspective. *Academy of Management Journal*, 24: 164–73.

Khoza, R. 1994. The need for an Afro-centric management approach – A South African-based management approach. In P. Christie, R. Lessem & L. Mbigi (Eds.), *African management, philosophies, concepts, applications:* 117–124. Randburg, SA: Knowledge Resources.

Kiggundu, M. N. 1991. The challenges of management development in Sub-Saharan Africa. *The Journal of Management Development*, 10(6): 32–47.

Koopman, A. 1994. Transcultural management, a search for pragmatic humanism. In P. Christie, R. Lessem & L. Mbigi (Eds.), *African management, philosophies, concepts, applications:* 41–76. Randburg, SA: Knowledge Resources.

Lemaire, J-P. 2000. *Measuring the international environment impact on corporate marketing and strategy: The PREST model.* Proceedings of the 16th IMP Conference, Bath.

Lemaire, J-P. 2004. *Stratégies d'internationalisation* (2nd ed.). Paris: Dunod.

Lessem, R. 1994. Four worlds – The Southern African business sphere. In P. Christie, R. Lessem & L. Mbigi (Eds.), *African management, philosophies, concepts, applications:* 17–40. Randburg, SA: Knowledge Resources.

Marks, M. L., & Mirvis P. H. 2001. Making mergers and acquisitions work: Strategic and psychological preparation. *Academy of Management Executive*, 15 (2): 80–94.

Mbigi, L. 1997. *Ubuntu: The African dream in management.* Randburg, SA: Knowledge Resources.

Neghandi, A. R. 1975. Comparative management and organizational theory: A marriage needed. *Academy of Management Journal*, 18: 334–44.

Prime, N. 1999. *Cross-cultural management in South-African companies: Problems, obstacles, agenda.* Proceedings of the 7th Cross-Cultural Consumer and Business Studies, Cancun, Mexico, December 12-15.

Prime, N. 2003. Cultural value. In R. Rugimbana & S. Nwankwo (Eds.), *Cross-cultural Marketing:* 3–24. London: Thomson.

Raltson, D. A., Holt D. H., Terpstra R. H., & Kai-Cheng, Y. 1997. The impact of national culture and economic ideology on managerial work values: A study of the United States, Russia, Japan and China. 28 (1): 177–207.

Redfield, R., Linton R. & Herskovits, M. 1936. Memorandum on the study of acculturation. *American Anthropologist*, 38: 149–152.

Ricks, D.A., Toyne, B. & Martinez, Z. 1990. Recent developments in international management research. *Journal of Management*, 16(2): 219–253.

Rudmin, F. W. 2003. Catalogue of acculturation constructs: Description of 126 taxonomies, 1918-2003 (www.document). In W.J. Lonner, D.L. Dinnel, S.A. Hayes & D.N. Sattler (Eds.), *Online Readings in Psychology and Culture* (Unit 8, Chapter 8), (http://www.wwu.edu/~~culture), Centre for Cross-Cultural Research, Western Washington University, Bellingham, Washington, USA.

Sam, D. L., & Oppedal B. 2002. Acculturation as a developmental pathway. (www.document). In W.J. Lonner, D.L. Dinnel, S.A. Hayes & D.N. Sattler (Eds.), *Online Readings in Psychology and Culture* (Unit 8, Chapter 6), (http://www.wwu.edu/~culture), Centre for Cross-Cultural Research, Western Washington University, Bellingham, Washington USA.

Sawadogo, G. 1995. Training for the mind. *International Journal of Intercultural Relations*, 19 (2): 281–293.

Shaw, J. B., Fisher, C. D., & Randolph, A. 1991. From materialism to accountability: The changing cultures of Ma Bell and Mother Russia. *Academy of Management Executive*, 5(1): 7–20.

Smith, S. 2005. *L'Afrique paradoxale*, RAMSES 2005: Paris, pp. 111-124.

Tamba, M. 2004. *L'enseignement supérieur privé au Sénégal.* Note de synthèse, Faculté des Lettres et Sciences Humaines, Université Cheikh Anta Diop de Dakar, Sénégal.

Todorov, T. 1989. *Nous et les autres*. Paris: Editions du Seuil.

Ward, S., Pearson, C., Entrekin, L., & Winzar, H. 1999. The fit between cultural values and countries: Is there evidence of globalization, nationalism or cross-vergence? *International Journal of Management*, 16 (4): 466–473.

Zadi Kessy, M. 1998. *Culture africaine et gestion de l'entreprise moderne*. Abidjan: Editions CEDA.

EXPLORING SCHOOL LEADERSHIP IN A PLURALISTIC SOUTH AFRICA

RIKA JOUBERT
JEAN W VAN ROOYEN
University of Pretoria
Department of Education Management and Policy Studies
Groenkloof Campus
Pretoria, 0002
South Africa
Tel: 27 12 420 5514
Fax: 27 12 420 3723
Email: rika.joubert@up.ac.za
jean.vanrooyen@up.ac.za

Abstract

This paper examines aspects of effective leadership in the Sub-Saharan context with reference to South Africa and the South African Education System as representative examples of the diversity of Africa. It provides a brief overview of school leadership in a pluralistic South African society in a post-apartheid dispensation; it explains the relevant background with reference to the heritage of apartheid regarding the separation of the peoples of South Africa. School leadership in South Africa currently faces two major challenges; ensuring equitable access to education and improving the quality of education in general. Theories on leadership are contextualized with the Euro-centric and Afro-centric leadership debate; leadership practices in effective schools; and addressing diversity in South African schools. This paper concludes by introducing the concept *contextual leadership* in an effort to bridge the polarisation between the Euro-centric, Afro-centric and trans-cultural approaches to effective leadership.

Key words: ***contextual leadership, cultural diversity, education, integrated schools***

BACKGROUND

South African society is essentially heterogeneous and multicultural. Historically, South African society was divided into four major racial groups[7]: black, white, coloured and Indian. A number of cultural, linguistic and religious groups could be discerned within these four groupings.

According to the results of the second democratic census (Census 2001), which were released in July 2003 there were 44 819 778 people in South Africa on 10 October 2001. Of these, 79% classified themselves as African (black); 9.6% as white; 8.9% as coloured; and 2.5% as Indian/Asian. The census indicated that at the time a total of 21 685 415 people in South Africa were male, and 23 662 839 female.

The South African population currently consists of the following black groups: the Nguni people (Zulu, Xhosa, Ndebele and Swazi), the Sotho-Tswana people, who include the

---

7 In the South African Apartheid system people were classified in terms of white, Indian (people who originally came from India and surrounding countries) , coloured (people from mixed black and white descent) and black (African descent).

Southern, Northern and Western Sotho as well as the Tsonga and the Venda groups. A large percentage of black people in South Africa are immigrants from Nigeria, Mozambique and Zimbabwe. The heterogeneous white population includes the Afrikaners; the English, the Portuguese, the German, the Greek and various other language groups. The coloured group includes both Christians and those who follow Islam. Indians, and those who immigrated to South Africa from Asia, still maintain a strong cultural identity.

Due to this differentiation, separatism and later structural pluralism became part of South African society. A host of legislative mechanisms enforced segregation in all walks of life. Separate educational opportunities, in which cultural differentiation was prominent, were provided for each race group (Christie 1991). Segregated education never was equal education, because education for white learners was, in contrast to black education, free and compulsory and benefited disproportionately from state expenditure. As a result educational provisioning for black learners was inferior to provisioning for white learners (Meier, 2004). After 1994 there was a significant increase in the education budget allocation under the post-apartheid democratic government, from R31.8 billion in 1994 to R69 063 billion in 2003. At almost 6% of Gross Domestic Product, South Africa has one of the highest rates of government investment in education in the world (Burger, 2003).

By mid 2003, the South African public education system accommodated more than 11,7 million school learners, 448 868 university students, 216 499 technikon students, and over 356 000 FET (Further Education and Training) college students. There were 27 458 primary, secondary, combined and intermediate schools with 354 201 educators (Burger, 2003).

A summative look at the respective provinces reveals the following demographic and education information.

TABLE 1
Summative Breakdown of Some South African Demographics (Department of Education, 2005)

PROVINCE	WCape	ECape	KZN	NCape	FS	NW	GP	MP	Lim
Capitol	Cape Town	Bisho	Ulundi / Pietermaritzburg	Kimberley	Bloemfontein	Mafi keng	Johannesburg	Nelspruit	Polokwane
Languages%	A 55.3 X 23.7 E 19.3	X 83.4 A 9.39 E 3.69	Z 80.9 E 13.8 A 1.9	A 68.0 Tw 20.8 X 6.2	SS 64.4 A 11.9 X 9.1	Tw 65.4 A 7.5 X 5.8	Z 21.5 A 14.4 SS 13.1 E 12.5	Sw 30.8 Z 26.4 Nd 12.1	Se 52.1 Ts 22.4 V 15.9
Population	4.53m	6.44m	9.43m	8.23m	2.77m	3.67m	8.84m	3.12m	5.28m
% Popul.	10.1	14.4	21.0	1.8	6.2	8.2	19.7	7.0	11.8
Learners	956 836	2 116 426	2 783 051	202 010	696 155	891 036	1 661 817	914 739	1 816 852
Schools	1 597	6 165	5 788	454	2 186	2 253	2 225	1 926	4 251
Educators	27 248	64 865	77 829	6 179	22 596	30 319	53 749	25 515	54 298

Abbreviations used for Languages: A = Afrikaans; **E** = English; **Nd** = isiNdebele; **Se** = Sepedi;
SS = Sesotho; **Sw** = siSwati; **Ts** = Xitsonga; **Tw** = Setswana; **V** = Tsivenda; **X** = isiXhosa; **Z** = isiZulu.

The termination of separatism or apartheid did not automatically ensure mutual understanding and acceptance among races and cultures in South Africa. Education leadership is burdened with the task of ensuring that educators are equipped to facilitate cultural understanding and cooperation both in schools and society at large. The legacies of racial domination and other forms of discriminatory practices still linger in the ten year democracy. There is a critical need for all education managers to engage in the new society imbued with the values and principles of an enlightened, modern and democratic constitution (Nkomo, Chisholm & Mc Kinney, 2004).

The South African Constitution, 1996, states that everyone has the right to use the language and to participate in the cultural life of their choice, but no-one may do so in a manner inconsistent with any provision of the Bill of Rights (sections 6, 30 and 31). To cater for South Africa's diverse peoples, the Constitution provides for 11 official languages. According to Census 2001, isiZulu is the mother tongue of 23.8% of the population, followed by isiXhosa (17.6%), Afrikaans (13.3%), Sepedi (9.4%), and English and Setswana (8.2% each).

Freedom of religion and belief is guaranteed by the Constitution. Based on the 2001 statistics, the majority of South Africa's population follows the Christian faith. Other religions include Islam, Hinduism and Judaism. A major component of the Western Cape coloured community is of the Islam faith as well as 20% of people from Indian decent (Burger, 2003).

Although cultural diversity exists between races, ethnic, language, gender and religious groups, as well as between groups of varying social status, the transformation of education in South Africa is concerned mainly with the integration of the various races into a single, united education system. This means that cultural diversity that exists among the people of Africa and those of Western and Eastern extraction now has to be accommodated in a single, integrated education system. It is important to realise that cultural diversity regarding norms and values gives rise to diversity in gender, religion and language. Furthermore, education managers differ regarding the implementation of new legal principles in schools. The heterogeneity of the South African community makes it difficult to interpret and apply specific leadership styles in integrated schools (Joubert, 2004).

South Africa has experienced a rapid rate of Westernization since the dawn of the new millennium and the concomitant, rapid erosion of its cultural heritage. Forje (2003) states that today the South African is neither an African nor a white. South Africa is caught at the crossroads of cultural transformation or acculturation and cultural decay. Kgomo (2004) points out that cultural diversity was, in the past, used as a tool to separate people and diminish the caring emotions of people in South Africa.

SCHOOL LEADERSHIP AND CHANGE IN SOUTH AFRICA

A hallmark of the South African government's approach to education and training has been a commitment to address two key priorities:

- achieving equitable access to education; and
- improving the quality of education (Department of Education, 1996).

Improving the quality of teaching and learning requires strategies, which focus broadly on change in schools and at classroom level. The successful implementation of this strategy depends on the transformation of school management. Managers can no longer wait for instructions or decisions from government. The pace of change and the need to be adaptable and responsive to local circumstances requires that managers develop new leadership skills and management styles. They must be capable of providing leadership to diverse teams and be able to interact with heterogeneous communities and stakeholders. The findings of leadership studies in the United Kingdom have demonstrated that effective leadership is determined and driven by individual value systems, rather than by instrumental managerial concerns (Day, Harris & Hadfield, 2002).

What is the challenge? Changing South Africa's education and training system is possible only if there is harmony between the vision for transformation and the day-to-day realities of those working in the new, integrated education system. In many schools the decades of resistance to apartheid have discredited many conventional education practices such as punctuality, lesson preparation, innovation, individual attention and accountability (Department of Education, 1996). The changes to the education system have resulted in school principals being unprepared for their new role as leaders.

It is common knowledge that some schools perform better than others, or seem to be more successful. This success is not always linked to the quality of the school buildings, the resources available or even the area in which the school is situated. To isolate those leadership behaviours, habits and practices that contribute to a school being effective necessitates an understanding of the leadership styles prevalent in schools.

Lessem (1996) believes that the social, political and economic transformation of South Africa has not been accompanied by a purposefully differentiated and subsequently integrated approach to leadership. He says South African leaders have to recognize and harness the full potential of the cultural diversity of the workforce. Lessem, in Christie *et al.* (1994), makes reference to the integration of four worlds in the South African business sphere:

- *world 1* is what he calls the Western world of Personal Enterprise under strong Anglo-Saxon influence;
- *world 2* is what he calls the Northern world of Managerial Hierarchy under strong European influence;
- *World 3* is what he calls the Eastern world of Cooperative Industry under strong Germanic-Nippon influence; and
- *World 4* is what he calls the Southern world of Communal Network under strong African influence.

According to him, business enterprise in South Africa has drawn strongly on the influence of the competitive and personalised dimension (World 1) and weakly on the coordinated and managerial dimension (World 2), while more or less ignoring the cooperative (World 3) and communal dimensions (World 4). He continues to say that South Africans will need to acknowledge their diverse cultural roots, and for the first time purposefully connect them to their respective managerial attitudes and behaviour, should they wish to differentiate and integrate African management. He further refers to a wholesome set of generic constituents of Africanness, in other words, extensions of empiricism, rationalism, idealism and humanism.

African management as a whole represents an interplay between four psychological or cultural types, albeit with different shades of emphasis. All four factors are requisite for integrated managerial learning and organisational development. When space is transformed into time, experientially based enterprise develops into professionally based organisation; thereafter, and in turn, the developmentally oriented industrial association ultimately develops into a convivially networked economy and society.

Day, Harris & Hadfield (2001) demonstrate the important influences of socio, political, economic, personal and professional contexts on effective leadership. Successful school leaders are able to combine the management of internal and external change with a strong development and achievement orientation. Their practices are based upon clear, communicated values to which all in their community subscribe.

If one accepts culture as an immense, dynamic structure of behaviours, ideas, attitudes, values, habits, beliefs, customs, language, rituals, ceremonies and practices peculiar to a people, and which provides them with general designs for living and interpreting reality,

Khoza's (1994) view, namely that one cannot hope to devise an effective management approach for such people without a profound understanding of their culture, seems valid.

Against this background the main purpose of this paper is to explore different dimensions of diversity and leadership perspectives in an effort to reconcile the tensions between the so-called Euro-centric and Afro-centric schools of thought on leadership and management.

LEADERSHIP PRACTICES ASSOCIATED WITH EFFECTIVE SCHOOLS

South African school leaders have to deal with many mindsets in a diverse country. Every school has to confront the entire litany of societal problems – race relations, developed and developing world disparities, change dynamics, haves versus have-nots and inequalities in education and career potential. The search for practical managerial philosophies and programmes has been long, faddish, cosmetic and fragmented (Beck & Linscott, 1994). The lists of fads, quick fixes and flavours of the month seem endless. Examples are: the managerial grid, management by objectives, situational management, brain dominance, transactional analysis, one-minute managing, systems thinking and managing change. Leaders have to brace themselves not to be confused by the plethora of paradigms.

Various authors currently distinguish between Euro and Afro-centric approaches to management (Lessem 1996, Broodryk 1995, Mbigi & Maree 1995). When attempting to identify Afro-centric leadership features or characteristics it might be wise to keep in mind the words of the South African Minister of Public Service and Administration, Geraldine Fraser-Moleketi (2003):

We need to be careful to label something as 'African' simply because it is voiced, demonstrated or embraced by a person from African origin. If the Zulu warrior Shaka believed in a particular management philosophy, does it make it African by definition or is it Shaka's personal philosophy?

No single leadership style that can be applied equally effectively in diverse schools exists. Broodryk (1995) provides practical guidelines for schools where the role-players represent a variety of cultures, e.g.

- cooperation is preferable to competition;
- reward teams and not individuals;
- democracy means consensus and not a majority vote;
- flexibility is preferable to stability;
- mirror management has to be avoided, i.e. managers should not take for granted that employees are like them and that they will behave as the managers do; and
- set management patterns should be avoided, since flexibility is important.

Beck and Linscott (1994) warn against the "three blind mice of management" i.e. three management fallacies South African leaders could adopt to address the challenge of diversity. First "mirror management", where leaders assume that employees are "like them" and project their own values onto them. Second the "car- wash" mentality, where the leaders assume that what works for one, must work for all. Third, leaders fall into a state of "paralysis" when they believe in an ideal, fixed pattern of mangement, viz. their philosophy is that the way they managed in the past is best because it worked then,

The increase in interaction and collaboration among people with different ethnic and cultural backgrounds is creating a need for the redefinition of both human resource management practices and personnel training issues. On the whole, three factors in particular, are paramount:

(1) diversity management skills; (2) transfer of professional skills; and (3) intercultural interaction and communication skills. The increase in cultural multiplicity is characterised by new organisational designs and work environments in which the human resource management practices of the past no longer function. It is important for managers to be able to work successfully with people from different cultural backgrounds.

According to Lindsay (1999) every educator must acquire five essential elements of cultural proficiency: valuing diversity;

- assessing one's own culture;
- managing the dynamics of difference;
- institutionalizing cultural knowledge; and
- adapting to diversity.

ADDRESSING DIVERSITY IN SOUTH AFRICAN SCHOOLS

Research completed by Roberts and Roach (2006) identifies the following key features associated with effective schools:

- purposeful leadership by the school principal;
- shared vision and purpose;
- high, but realistic expectations of staff and learners;
- effective cooperation and an atmosphere of trust between stakeholders; and
- creating a caring and stable school environment.

School managers are expected to fulfil an extremely wide variety of duties: managing staff, financial management, setting policies and developing relationships with parents, learners and staff. According to Roberts and Roach (2006) effective leaders function in the following domains:

- self management;
- the school;
- human capital;
- relationships with stakeholders; and
- systems and procedures.

The emphasis in each of the above mentioned leadership domains is on the leader's personal traits. Personal traits are determined by a person's culture and value system. Kushner and Brislin (1996) explain that difficulties arise during extensive cross-cultural interaction. People are socialized to label actions 'right' or 'wrong' When they interact with people from other cultures, their perception of proper behaviour is not always manifest. Behaviour considered improper by one group may be practised routinely by another. Common responses to such manifestations include a dislike of culturally different others, negative labels and refusal to interact with others.

Although people adapt, multiple demands within short periods cause frustration during cross-cultural interaction. It is therefore important for effective leaders to assess their own culture and to gain knowledge about other cultures. The misinterpretation of events or the misunderstanding of the subjective meaning of particular behaviour is at the root of the problem. Understanding a person's intentions accurately when s/he behaves in certain ways, requires the leader to understand the context in which the behaviour occurs - culture provides an appropriate context.

Managing the dynamics of difference is very difficult because most people have little knowledge about themselves and the culture of others. One way of regarding culture is to consider it a set of hidden, recurring patterns of behaviour and thought. It is hidden because people learn to behave appropriately in a given culture. It is therefore difficult to explain why people act in certain ways and how they acquired specific behavioural patterns (Kushner & Trifonovitch, (1989).

Leaders also have to distinguish between objective and subjective components of culture. Objective components refer to tangible aspects which are visible, such as clothing, artefacts and food preferences. Subjective cultural components are more subjective, e.g. values, attitudes, norms of behaviour and the roles people assume. Since it is at this level that most misunderstandings and communication problems occur, this should be the focus of intercultural interactions.

A reasonable goal for managing cross-cultural interaction in a school is to acquire the ability to understand and accept that different world views and behaviour exist. Learning to lead a diverse school is akin to learning a new language. Few people receive formal instruction, they learn about cultures by observing others, by trial and error, and by continuous reinforcement. In other words, culture is learned affectively, not cognitively.

Qualitative research completed by Roberts and Roach (2006) to determine the leadership styles of effective school principals describes effective leaders as humble and dedicated, with a passion for education and learning. In addition, they were described as loyal to their schools, tolerant of others' views, and willing to allow their decisions to be challenged.

The findings also show that most successful school leaders have high behavioural and performance expectations of themselves and others that it is important to lead by example, to have a vision for the schools in their communities, and to show compassion and care for learners.

These findings reflect a combination of instrumentalism and humanism as explained by Jackson (2004): instrumental management system leaders focus on results and have a competencies approach, while in a humanistic management system people are valued, participation is encouraged and there is tolerance for other views.

THEORIES OF LEADERSHIP

Leadership as a Concept

This paper focuses on leadership as the ability to influence the actions of others and to guide an organization to a desired state of being or functioning (Roberts & Roach, 2006). Leadership is not a monolithic behaviour or one that is demonstrated only at particular times, it permeates all aspects of the school's operation.

Fuglestadt and Lillejord in Calitz *et al.* (2004) regard leadership not as a fixed static 'ability', but as an unpredictable and ever-changing process. The successful execution of leadership takes into account the particularities of situations and the culture of the specific organisation.

The concept of leadership is complex and evolving. Most of what is written about leadership draws on Western culture, particularly that of Northern America (Coleman, 2003). Leadership, however, is likely to be viewed differently in different cultures. Harber and Davies (1997) contend that leadership in education in developing, specifically African countries tends to be authoritarian. Defining leadership is not an easy task, especially as there is no generally accepted definition (Bush & Glover, 2003). Leadership is essentially the process of building and maintaining a sense of vision, culture and interpersonal relationships, whereas management is the co-ordination, support and monitoring of organisational activities. To enact both roles successfully requires a careful balancing act (Day, Harris & Hadfield,

2001). Leadership is about having vision and articulating, ordering priorities, motivating others to go along with one's decisions, constantly reviewing what one does and holding onto that which one values.

According to Schein (1996) one of the most consistent findings regarding leadership by historians, sociologists and empirically oriented social psychologists, is that leadership should depend on the particular situation, the task to be performed, and the characteristics of the leader's subordinates. One reason for the existence of multiple theories of leadership is that different researchers focus on different elements. Schein (1996) believes institutions of the past may become obsolete and that new forms of governance and leadership will have to be learned. Future leaders will therefore be required to have:

- extraordinary levels of perception and insight into the realities of the world and themselves;
- extraordinary levels of motivation to enable them to experience the inevitable pain of learning and change, especially in a world with looser boundaries, in which loyalties are difficult to define;
- emotional strength to manage their own and others' anxiety, as learning and change become common;
- new skills to analyze cultural assumptions and processes that expand culture by building on its strengths and functional elements;
- willingness and ability to involve others and elicit their participation, because tasks will be too complex and information too widely distributed for leaders to solve problems on their own; and
- willingness and ability to share power and control according to people's knowledge and skills, that is, to permit and encourage leadership to flourish throughout the organisation.

Leadership Theory

Sergiovanni *et al.* (1980) mention an increasing interest in the notion of contingency or situational theory, saying that the essence of this theory entails that *no one best way which can be used in every instance to plan and lead exists.* Blanchard, Zigarmi and Zigarmi (1986) posit that a situational leader needs to learn three skills: flexibility, diagnosis and contracting And that *for a long time people thought that there were only two leadership styles – autocratic and democratic. Democratic managers were accused of being too soft and easy while their autocratic counterparts were often called too tough and domineering. But I have always felt that managers who restricted themselves to either extreme were only "half a manager"* Several writers focus on "situational" leadership style or "contingency" leadership (Hersey & Blanchard, 1983; Gibson & Marcoulides, 1995) where leaders adapt their style to the situations at hand .This means that leadership styles vary according to the nature of participants in an interaction as well as the relative balance of power between them and the outcome sought by the leader.

Although the Hersey and Blanchard situational leadership theory (1983) takes the following situational variables into account: the task, the (job) maturity of the people involved, task behaviour and relationship behaviour in determining the leadership style to adopt, and it disregards culture.

Recently, leadership studies have focussed upon values—the 'moral purposes' and moral craft of leadership (Sergiovanni 1992) the roles of leaders in creating a 'community of learners' (Barth 1990; Senge 1990); and the capacities of leaders to 'make a difference' through their ability to 'transform' (Sergiovanni 1995; Leithwood et al., 1999) or 'liberate'

(Tampoe 1998) rather than simply 'transact'. The most popular theories are located in the 'transactional' and 'transformational' models identified more than twenty years ago (Burns 1978) and lately reinvented through such terms as 'liberation' (Tampoe 1998), 'educative' (Duignan & McPherson 1992), 'invitational' (Stoll & Fink 1996) and 'moral' leadership (Sergiovanni 1992). What is clear from the preceding and effective schools literature is that successful leaders not only set direction, organise and monitor, build relationships with the school community and are people-centred; they also model values and practices consistent with those of the school (Sergiovanni 1995).

Leadership styles described by different authors often overlap, and comparisons between leadership styles tend to exaggerate differences. From the above it clearly shows that a school principal should display behaviour associated with the full range of leadership styles.

Afro-centric Leadership

The social, political and economic transformation of South Africa has not been accompanied by a purposeful, differentiated and subsequently integrated approach to management (Lessem, 1994). Eleven years after the first democratic elections with a huge movement toward black management advancement and cross-cultural teamwork, South Africa is still struggling to develop an integrated South African management and leadership approach.

Initially Afro-centric approach to management was emphasised. The typical Afro-centric management approach which took account of the traditions and culture of African participants in organisations is referred to as the community concept (Khoza, 1994) which perceives the organisation as a community to which the individual belongs. It requires management to be approachable, an informal atmosphere to be established and a free flow of information. Everyone has the right to know what is happening.

The community concept has a philosophical base in the concept of Ubuntu, literally translated: 'a person is a person through other human beings". One of the meanings of Ubuntu, a Zulu word, is "humaneness" and it includes images of supportiveness, cooperation and solidarity. Roberts and Roach (2006:5), postulate that two key themes emerge from the literature on African leadership, namely the importance of the Ubuntu concept and the consultative nature of African leadership. They explain Ubuntu in the words of Boon (1996) as "morality, humaneness, compassion, care, understanding and empathy, sharing and hospitality, honesty and humility". This is also alluded to by Jackson (2004) when he refers to this as the humanistic management approach. Khoza (1994) regards the advantages of the community approach as a way to resolving a preoccupation with individual excellence, which often leads to a reckless individualism in organisations.

In response to the possibility of identifying practices or behaviours that could be described as characteristic of a uniquely African style of leadership Roberts and Roach (2006:7) believe that:

It is very difficult to label the consultative actions of principals in the study as particularly 'African' behaviours - especially as management books written in the rest of the world have also recognised the importance of collegial management styles. One can, however, conclude that many of the practices promoted by the new legislation (in South Africa) *have greater resonance with African practices.*

The development of Afro-centric leadership styles in the last decade has infused a racial essentialist ethos into discourses about the essence and utility of existing education management development programmes. An Afro-centric leadership genre was supposed to have provided black school managers with a countervailing and culturally empowering leadership style to counteract European autocratic management systems (Kgomo, 2003).

Afro-centric leadership insists on congruence between understanding and experiencing to solidify black cultural autonomy. Knowledge and understanding of the apartheid experiences (history and culture) is deemed incomplete and inauthentic without appreciation or more appropriately, empathy. Furthermore, the language of communicating has to be grounded in the African, as opposed to, what is deemed to be a Eurocentric and hegemonic worldview. Afro-centric rejection of the 'management' language of the previous dominant power has widened the gulf between cultures, and problematized intercultural communication (Kgomo, 2003). Although it is important that organisations retain their corporate identities within their respective continents, it is equally important to recognise that leadership and management theory has, over time, developed an international vocabulary. It is important to provide for the uniqueness of Africa and the leadership challenges of Africa, but it is not in the best interests of Africa to be isolated from the rest of the world in the current era of globalisation.

Whiteness has historically embodied distinct attributes: dominance and privilege. Whiteness has been actualised and normalised to the point of invisibility through language, media culture and schooling. "Despite its invisibility, whiteness possesses content inasmuch as it generates norms, ways of understanding history, ways of thinking about self and other, and even ways of thinking about the norm of culture itself"(Lindsay *et. al.*1998).

Afro-centric management may be compared with what Jackson (2004) calls the "African Renaissance". The focus of this management system is firstly people and then results. Belonging and personal development are motivators, while commitment to the group and trust of human nature are basic principles. In practice, participation, transparency and communication are more valued than objectives and control mechanisms. While respecting Jackson's viewpoint it is necessary to point out that leadership and management are not an exercises in semantics. Any situation demanding leadership and management arises because of either an individual or a collective need and such a need will continue to exist, until it is satisfied. This is true of leadership and management on all the continents of the world. How it is done varies according to the context. Afro-centric and Eurocentric approaches to leadership and management should therefore not be mutually exclusive. We are of the opinion, and have cited numerous authors in this paper, to substantiate our view that future leaders will be obliged to lead in a participative manner, taking into account ALL the variables particular to a given situation and context.

Eurocentric Leadership

Lessem (1996) distinguishes between pragmatism, rationalism and holism as typical Western management styles. The focus in Euro-centric management falls on free-spirited individualism, analytically based management, impersonal structures of hierarchical organisation and quality. A positive aspect of its meritocracy lies in the emphasis on quality and process focus. A negative aspect is the manifestation of bureaucracy in all spheres of management.

According to the Western paradigm all knowledge is acquired through experience (Lessem, 1996). In the pursuit of excellence the focus is on self-help and sharing of knowledge, while experience is less favoured. Each person is deemed to be the best judge of his/her own interest. A Eurocentric leader attaches overriding importance to freedom of expression and individual initiative is encouraged as opposed to depersonalised management and conformity. Involvement with the company and others is of a "calculative", rather than "moral" nature (Lessem, 1996). Conflict and competition are used constructively in the organisation. Self-discipline is oriented toward the realisation of self-interest through performance and productivity.

The rational-centred executive sets clear objectives. Effective conduct depends on the concentration of power in the hands of a small number of exceptionally able people (Lessem, 1996). Quality and achievement are sharply focused and therefore planning and exercising control receive constant attention.

Transcultural Leadership

There are two different levels of personal engagement in multiculturalism: one involves the level of knowledge and information that a leader has about other cultures, the other the attitudes, feelings and emotions that the culturally and ethnically different arouse in the leader. Once the multiculturalism of societies is accepted as a fact, diverse approaches to and ways of understanding and interacting with cultural differences can be developed.

Transcultural leadership competence can be defined as: "The ability to recognize oneself operating in cultural context, the identification and appreciation of cultural differences, and the development of general strategies for adapting to cultural difference (Bennett, Bennett & Allen, 1999: 15)."

To Dimmock and Walker (2000) the significance of culture, especially at the societal level, stretches beyond its importance as a mediating influence on theory, policy and practice. They believe both conceptually and empirically that societal culture a potentially powerful analytical tool with which to lay the foundation for developing a new branch of educational leadership, management and policy.

Competent education leaders therefore need to

- become aware of the role of culture as manifested in *inter alia*; language, values, attitudes, and learning styles in teaching and learning in an integrated school;
- develop an understanding of the problems likely to occur when persons from different cultural backgrounds attend an integrated school; and
- become familiar with techniques and materials that will enhance the actions of others.

Contextual Leadership

It is not possible to create a single, uniquely South African leadership style for education leaders based on certain behaviours and practices. This does not mean that that which is African must be discounted. Colonialism and intellectual imperialism relegated indigenous knowledge and practices that originated outside the European context. As a result, through the notion of an African Renaissance, African traditions have been afforded greater status and are seen as worthy of intellectual inquiry. Competent education leaders need to become aware of and sensitive to cultural differences, to develop an understanding of the problems and to adopt techniques that will enhance effective teaching and learning in integrated classrooms.

John Work (1996) stipulates five fundamental challenges for true future leaders.

They must:

- be willing to become more sensitive and understanding with respect to the ethnic, cultural and gender differences in the workplace and should demonstrate that sensitivity and understanding;
- have a vision for the workplace that ultimately results in a significant broadening of that corporate culture and the workplace environment;
- be willing to craft and implement new, different employment and communication processes to enhance and promote perceptions of fairness and equity;
- be willing to bring full and unquestionable commitment to the effective utilization of a diverse workforce; and
- be the linchpin between their organization and the larger community.

In the turbulent and unpredictable climate of uncertain and changing challenges which characterized schools of today and tomorrow the room for manoeuvre is constrained and inevitable tensions arise. Consequently, effective leadership in the 2000s and beyond is essentially concerned with adapting strategies and tactics (but not values) to address unanticipated events and new demands. The capacity of leaders to make a difference will, then, depend upon their interpretation of and responses to the constraints, demands and choices that they face.

Education leaders have to adapt to an education system that moved from being autocratic and bureaucratic to social and humanistic. The new, integrated education system strives for the creation and support of conditions under which educators and learners are able to achieve learning. (Department of Education, 1996).

The challenge education leaders face is the societal reconstructing of their schools. Societal reconstruction is informed by knowledge and understanding of other cultures. Achieving cultural synergy in a pluralistic society requires effective leadership.

One of the most daunting challenges education leaders face is the ability to talk about and learn about other cultures. What needs to be unlearned is the assumption that "white is right" and "West is best", or that European theories are better than those African theories.

Bryson (1991) postulates that the situational leadership theorists, especially Paul Hersey and Kenneth Blanchard, in Management of Organizational Behaviour (1988 edition), developed the complex Situational Leadership Grid III that in reality became a unified field theory accommodating all human potential, motivational and needs theorists. The practice of Situational Leadership Grid III encapsulates the finest empirical and polemic efforts of Abraham Maslow's hierarchy of needs, Frederick Herzberg's hygiene factors and motivators, Douglas McGregor's Theory X and Theory Y, Chris Argyris' immaturity/maturity continuum, Eric Berne and Thomas Harris' transactional analysis concepts, Erich Fromm's humanising organisations, Viktor Frankel's search for meaning and Martin Buber's theory on the relationship between individuals.

Binedell in Christie *et al.* (1993) refers to Drucker's assertion that the concepts driving the systems and structure of an organisation are in an independent sense universal. The primary questions and answers to basic effectiveness apply, irrespective of the context. He, however, also asserts that beyond this the other, more powerful reality is the context in which an organisation operates. The above-mentioned contexts are not universal, but particular. Drucker's challenge to South African leadership, according to Binedell, is to question the universal notion of management effectiveness and to propose that the realities that lead to success vary considerably from one context to another.

The entire preceding debate points to what we would like to call ***Contextual leadership.*** Contextual leadership in our opinion constitutes a combination of all of the above. There are no simple recipes or single leadership style for any country or situation in the world. To be effective, leadership in any given context, anywhere in the world, and therefore in Africa as well, requires the leader to:

- apply all the complex principles underpinning the Situational Leadership Grid III as developed by Hersey and Blanchard; evolving from the work of their peers referred to previously in this paper;
- take cognisance of the culture(s) of the people involved in any endeavour;
- be sensitive to cultural differences in the group of people to be led;
- acquire a working knowledge of the different cultures of the people involved;
- actively allow for the possibility that there are more ways than one of solving problems and making decisions, by following an invitational/collegial approach; and

- allow for and actively take into account all the variables encompassed in the situational/contingency leadership theories (the task at hand or the need to be addressed, the situation, time limits, resources available, maturity levels and experience of the individuals or group members responsible for task execution, etc.) before deciding on a leadership approach in any given context.

CONCLUSION

According to Binedell (1993) three broad approaches are required to develop South Africa's education management orientation, viz.:

- the need to understand the specific nature of the South African environment (the so-called 'engine room');
- to develop exogenous conceptual models related to the indigenous realities of South Africa, transferring endogenous management concepts to the African context; and
- in the process of turning vision into reality, it is necessary to engage in action research in the frontline of education.

Because of the constantly changing demographics of the entire world, and of Africa as well, it is imperative that everybody in a leadership position, on a permanent basis, be tuned in to, be sensitive to, and become progressively knowledgeable about the cultural profile of the group they are leading, as well as the profile of every individual member of the group. Tapping into knowledge of leadership theory, calling on the combined resources of one's experience as a leader and displaying an attitude of respect for the individual member and his/her maturity and cultures, the leader can make an informed choice on how to lead in any given context. This infers that every situation in any given context demands a unique leadership response from the leader. It further implies that no two leaders will necessarily lead in exactly the same way in the same context, because they too, are different and may have completely different profiles, which would influence the situation. There is therefore no single simple generic leadership style that can be adopted or serve as a model for the complex demands made on the leaders of the world. However, if the concept of contextual leadership is applied every leader should be able to find the most suitable leadership approach suited to the context within which leadership is required.

The characteristics of successful leaders and their ability to be simultaneously people-centred whilst managing a number of tensions and dilemmas highlight the complexity of the kinds of values-led contingency leadership exercised by these successful heads. This study illustrates that there are no neat solutions to situations which hold within them so many variables; that successful leadership is defined and driven by individual and collective value systems rather than instrumental, bureaucratic, managerial concerns.

The absolute necessity to allow for openness and a creative approach to every situation is well illustrated by Binedell (1993) with reference to the work of Nonaka (1986), which explains the reason for Japan's defeat in the Second World War as the inability of the Japanese command structures to change and adapt their strategic and tactical thinking, and to respond creatively to technological and military changes that preceded the Second World War. Contextual leadership also links up closely with Peter Senge's (1990) concept of learning organisations.

Having explored leadership in a pluralistic world, we believe that a **contextual approach to leadership** opens opportunities to capitalise on the rich possibilities of cultural diversity, thus creating synergistic opportunities for effective leadership and management. The problem is that many of the training models focus upon managerial rather than leadership functions. In doing so they fail to build capacities of heads to reflect upon their own values and those of the whole school community and do not provide sufficient emphasis upon building the range of interpersonal qualities and skills necessary and appropriate to effective leadership.

REFERENCES

Barth, R.S. 1990. *Improving Schools from Within: Teachers, Parents and Head Teachers Can Make the Difference*, San Francisco, CA: Jossey-Bass.

Beck, D. & Linscott, G. 1994. The African Crucible. In Christie, P., Lessem, R. and Mbigi, L. *African Management.* Randburg, South Africa: Knowledge Resources.

Bennett, J.M., Bennett, M.J. & Allen, W. 1999. Developing intercultural competence in the language classroom. In R. M. Paige, D. L. Lange & Y. Yershova (Eds.) *Culture as the core*: Minneapolis, MN: CARLA.

Binedell, N. 1994. Vision and reality – Business in the new South African environment. In Christie, P., Lessem, R. and Mbigi, L. *African Management.* Randburg, South Africa: Knowledge Resources.

Blanchard, K. Zigarmi, P. & Zigarmi, D. 1986. *Leadership and the One Minute Manager.* London: Willow Books.

Broodryk, J. 1995. *The Afro-centric leadership process*. Pretoria: Ubuntu School of Philosophy.

Bryson, J.E. 1991. Creative Leadership: Theory and Practice. In Basson, C.J.J. and Smith J.A.J. 1991. *Educational Management.* Pretoria: Unibook Publishers.

Burger, D. (Ed.), 2003. *South African Yearbook 2003/04*. Government Communications (GCIS). Pretoria.

Bush, T. & Glover, D. 2003. *School Leadership: Concepts and evidence*. London: NSCL.

Christie, P. 1991. *The right to learn. The struggle for education in South Africa.* Cape Town: Raven Press.

Coleman, M. 2003. Theories of leadership. In Thurlow, M., Bush, T. & Coleman, M. (Eds.) *Leadership and Strategic management in South African Schools.* London: The Common Wealth Secretariat.

Cushner, K. & Brislin, R.W. 1996. *Intercultural Interactions: A practical guide*. London: Sage.

Cushner, K. & Trifonovitch, G. 1989. Understanding Misunderstanding: barriers to dealing with diversity. In Cushner, K. *Human Diversity in Action.* U.S.: McGraw-Hill College.

Day, C., Harris A. & Hadfield, M. 2001. Grounding knowledge of schools in stakeholder realities: A multi perspective study of effective school leaders. *School leadership and management*, 21 (1): 19 –42. University of Nottingham.

Department of Education, 1996. *Changing management to manage change*. Pretoria: Department of Education South Africa.

Department of Education. 2005. Education Statistics in South Africa at a glance in 2003. Pretoria: Department of Education.

Duignan, P.A. & Macpherson R.J.S. 1992. *Educative leadership: A Practical Theory for new Administrators and Managers.* London: Falmer Press.

Forje, J.W. 2003. Non-violence as a way to social justice in fragmented societies in Africa. In Lasonen, J. & Lestinen , L. (Eds.) *Teaching and learning for intercultural Understanding, Human Rights and a Culture of Peace.* Jyvaskyla: Institute for Education Research.

Fraser-Moleketi, G. 2003. Speech at anniversary colloquium of the School of Public Administration at the University of Pretoria. http://www.info.gov.za/speeches/2003/03/102109461002.htm, posted 20 October 2003.
Fuglestadt, O.L. & Lillejord, S. 2004. Culture as process: Leadership challenges in the construction of productive learning cultures. In Calitz, L., Fuglestadt, O.L. & Lillejord, S. (Eds.). *Leadership in Education – Productive Learning Cultures*. Sandown: Heinemann.
Gibson, C.B. & Marcoulides, G.A. 1995. The invariance of Leadership Styles across Four Countries. *Journal of Managerial Issues,* 7 (2).
Harber, C. & Davies, L. 1997. *School Management and Effectiveness in Developing Countries: The Post Bureaucratic School*. London: Cassell.
Harris, A. 2002. *Effective Leadership for School Improvement*. London: Routledge.
Hersey, P. & Blanchard, K. 1983. *Management of Organizational behaviour*. New Jersey: Prentice-Hall.
Jackson, T. 2004. *Management and Change in Africa: an Introduction*. London: Routledge.
Joubert, R. 2004. *Enhancing leadership capacity in a Pluralistic South Africa through effective training programmes*. Paper read at the Common Wealth Council for Education Administration and management, Regional Conference in Hong Kong, 20-22 October 2004.
Kgomo, F.T.J. 2003. Vision for the future-the rainbow nation of South Africa: using the economic, social- cultural, ethnicity and national diversity dimensions to build an extraordinary inclusive national identity. In Lasonen, J. & Lestinen, L. (Eds.) *Teaching and learning for intercultural Understanding, Human Rights and a Culture of Peace.* Jyvaskyla: Institute for Education Research.
Khoza, R. 1994. The need for an Afro-centric management approach – A South African based a management approach. In Christie, P. (Ed.) *African Management.* Randburg: Knowledge Resources.
Leithwood, K. & Jantzi, D. 1990. *Transformational leadership: how head teachers can help reform cultures.* School Effectiveness and School Improvement, 1(4):249–280.
London: The Industrial Society.
Le Roux, J. 2004. Educational Leadership in multicultural schools. In Calitz, L., Fuglestadt, O.L. & Lillejord, S. (Eds.) *Leadership in Education – Productive Learning Cultures*. Sandown: Heinemann.
Lessem, R. 1994. Four Worlds the Southern African Businessphere. In Christie, P., Lessem, R. and Mbigi, L. *African management.* Randburg, South Africa: Knowledge Resources.
Lessem, R. 1996.The Southern African Businessphere. In Steyn, M. & Motshabi, K. *Cultural Synergy in South Africa.* Randburg South Africa: Knowledge Resources.
Lindsay, R.D., Robins, K.N. & Terrell, R.D. 1999. *Cultural Proficiency: A Manual for School Leaders.* California: Corwin Press.
Mbigi, L. & Maree, J. 1995. *Ubuntu: The spirit of African Transformation Management.* Randburg: Knowledge Resources.
Meier, C. 2004. Teacher Training For Intercultural Cooperation in a Changed Socio Political Context: The South African Experience. In Lasonen, J. & Lestinen, L. (Eds.) *Teaching and learning for intercultural Understanding, Human Rights and a Culture of Peace.* Jyvaskyla: Institute for Education Research.
Nkomo, N.M., Chisholm, L. & Mc Kinney, C. 2004. *Reflections on School Integration*. Cape Town: HRSC Publishers.
Republic of South Africa. 1996. *The Constitution of the Republic of South Africa.* 1996. Pretoria: Government Printers.
Roberts, D.V. 1999. Cultural Proficiency In A Multi-Cultural Society –A South African

In Lasonen, J. & Lestinen, L. (Eds.) *Teaching and learning for intercultural Understanding, Human Rights and a Culture of Peace.* Jyvaskyla: Institute for Education Research

Roberts, J. & Roach, J. 2006. *Leadership Styles and Practices in Effective Schools.* Johannesburg: Matthew Goniwe School of leadership and Governance.

Schein, E.H. 1996. In Hesselbein, F., Goldsmith, M. & Beckhard, R. (Eds.).*The Leader of the Future. New visions, strategies, and practices for the Next Era.* San Francisco: Jossey-Bass Publishers.

Senge, P. 1990. *The Fifth Discipline.* New York: Doubleday.

Sergiovanni, T.J., Burlingame, M., Coombs, F.D. & Thurston, P.W. 1980. *Educational Governance and Administration.* Englewood Cliffs, New Jersey: Prentice-Hall.

Sergiovanni, T.J. 1998. Leadership as pedagogy, capital development and school effectiveness. *International Journal of Leadership in Education,* 1(1): 37–47.

Stoll L & Fink D 1996. *Changing our Schools.* Buckingham: Open University Press.

Tampoe, M. 1998. *Liberating leadership: Releasing Leadership Potential throughout the Organisation.* London: Falmer.

Walker, A. & Dimmock, C. 1999. A cross-cultural approach to the study of educational leadership: an emerging framework, *Journal of School Leadership,* 9(4): 321–348.

Work, J.W. 1996. Leading a Diverse Work Force. In Hesselbein, F., Goldsmith, M. & Beckhard, R. (Eds.) *The Leader of the Future. New visions, strategies, and practices for the Next Era.* San Francisco: Jossey-Bass Publishers.

TRAINING AFRICAN LEADERS AS A POWERFUL LEEWAY TO REBUILD STATE-CAPACITY IN POST-WAR CONTEXT: THE CASE OF THE BURUNDI LEADERSHIP TRAINING PROGRAM (BLTP)

ANTOINE FOUCHER
Manager of the "Negotiators of the World" Program, ESSEC IRENE
foucher@essec.fr

ALAIN LEMPEREUR
ESSEC Business School & ESSEC IRENE Director

Abstract

Over the last 40 years, Burundi has experienced acute political problems in relation to both wealth and power sharing between the most pre-eminent ethnic groups of the country, the Hutus and Tutsis. Often quite violent, these conflicts led to an estimated 300,000 deaths and 1.5 million people endured displacement either inside or outside Burundi.

The 2000 Arusha Agreement aimed to end relentless and large scale violence throughout the country. It also constituted a consensual political framework that paved the way in Burundi from political turmoil to peace, stability and democracy. The free and democratic election of President Nkurunziza in August 2005 and the successful integration of formerly armed movements, including the CNDD-FDD combatants, in the national defense forces (FDN) are strong evidences that Burundi underwent a remarkable political transformation.

How did this transformation happen? Decades of deadly conflicts had resulted in widespread and profound feelings of mistrust within the various social layers, and most of all amongst leaders of influence. If Burundi was to cope with the political challenge it was still confronted with, its leaders had to go beyond this feeling and accede to a common vision.

The present paper shows how valuable the training in **collaborative decision-making, motivation-based negotiation, communication, mediation, visioning, strategic planning, and the management of organizational change** can be to support a transitioning country like Burundi. Though this paper primarily focuses on the example of the Burundi Leadership Training Program (BTLP) initiative, other programs notably carried out in Democratic Republic of Congo for example currently help designing an intervention pattern adaptable to a wide range of former protracted conflicts.

Burundi's Post-Conflict Situation: Initial Assessment Findings

Today known as the Burundi Leadership Training Program (BLTP), this post-war capacity-building initiative has come to enjoy a very broad support of Burundian leaders of all ethnicities and social sectors and is believed, by many, to be playing an important role in advancing the Burundian peace process and transition to democracy. How did this buy-in take place?

The BLTP initiative was built on a broad consultation process that the assessment team, headed by Ambassador Howard Wolpe from the Woodrow Wilson International Center for Scholars (WICS-Washington DC) led, both in Burundi and with other concerned actors (i.e.

donors, regional leaders, and international NGOs), in the aftermath of the 2000 Arusha Peace Accord, the 2000 Arusha Agreement mentioned in the Abstract.

The Arusha Accord was intended to provide the framework for an end to a seven-year civil war waged mostly between the Tutsi-led government and regular army, and Hutu political and armed rebel groups. **The consultation process was intended to evaluate the needs of Burundian leaders to rebuild their state capacity and promote economic recovery. It also aimed at insuring a very broad buy-in for a training initiative that would strive to reinforce leadership skills among the most influential leaders in Burundi.** The assessment team got early support for this initiative from Burundian top leaders of all parties and political persuasions, even beyond the early signatories of the Arusha agreement. Additional support was enthusiastically offered by the African regional facilitation team and the international community of diplomats and donors.

Initial consultations and later interviews have allowed for the patternization of post-conflict's spheres of leadership, as they apply to the Burundi case[8]:

> (1) A "winner takes all" war mentality, with a minimal sense of inter-dependence or common ground among key actors of the society;
> (2) Major social inequalities that tend to reinforce the lines of ethnic division;
> (3) A regional dimension that complicates the situation, including cross border incursions and arms flows, borders dividing ethnic communities, staging areas in neighboring states, and illegal resource flows through neighboring states;
> (4) Political mobilization along ethnic and regional lines;
> (5) The absence of trust among key leaders;
> (6) A huge gulf between a privileged and wholly discredited political class and the impoverished mass of the population;
> (7) A failure of communications at all levels, as well as a rhetoric of demonizing the "other";
> (8) An absence of agreement on the "rules of the game" to ensure inclusive democratic governance after an election;
> (9) A history of mismanagement and bad governance; and,
> (10) A security sector that is not seen as serving the interests of the whole nation.

From Mistrust to Cooperative Visioning: The BTLP Objectives

On the basis of the early consultation, the BLTP was to inaugurate training in collaborative decision-making – in motivation-based negotiations, communications, mediation, visioning, strategic planning, and the management of organizational change. **Because of the project's intention to address simultaneously both the ethnic divide within the political elite and the wide gulf between the country's political class and the mass of the population, the initial 95 key Burundian leaders were drawn in equal measure from the political class and civil society.** They were selected on the basis of cross-listing the lists that Burundian key leaders provided. They were asked to provide lists that contain leaders from all backgrounds who could influence, for better or worse, the future of Burundi.

Based on the abovementioned findings, four main post-war reconstruction objectives were assigned to the BTLP initiative:

---

[8] "Rebuilding Peace and State Capacity in War-Torn Burundi", (with Howard Wolpe and alii), *The Round Table,* Vol. 93, n°375, July 2004, 457-467

(1) Enabling former belligerents to shift from a zero-sum paradigm of winners and losers to one that recognizes **interdependence** and common ground, and urges for new ways of diagnosing and addressing the current challenges of a divided society, while brainstorming solutions to create value together;
(2) Developing **trust and confidence** among key leaders, while starting an honest dialogue on the negative impacts of many past actions by one (or both) side(s) against the other (each other), whatever the intentions may have been;
(3) Strengthening the skills of communication required for effective collaboration, to circumvent a competitive rhetoric of divisiveness and confrontation, and acknowledge the power of a **cooperative rhetoric** and language for reconciliation and unity; and,
(4) Re-building a **consensus on the "rules of the game",** i.e., on how power will be shared, and organized, as well as how decisions will be made in a country where all groups are respected and able to rebuild together a renewed vision for the future of their social compact.

Aiming at a Critical Mass of Trained Leaders

Burundi has a population of 6 million inhabitants. It was essential that during the post-conflict stage, many leaders be trained in the mentioned skills, while they were defining the target groups who had to be trained next. The Burundi program started with seed money from the World Bank to train a hundred key leaders from all sectors of the society, and ended up training several thousands of them, thanks to the support of the Burundians themselves who indicated the need, for example, to train the security sectors in priority.

From 2003 until 2006, seven IRENE trainers, led by Alain Lempereur, in cooperation with Liz McClintock (CMPartners) and Howard Wolpe (Woodrow Wilson International Center for Scholars), have facilitated workshops for about 4535 people:

- **Ngozi Process**
  - March & September 2003, May 2004 => **Burundian Leaders** **95 participants**

- **Other workshops: Security Forces and Political Parties**
  - November 2003 (Nairobi) => **Commanders of Armed Movements and Regular Army (Forces Armées Burundaise - FAB) 37 participants**
  - February 2004 (Bujumbura) => **Cease-Fire Commission (CMC)** **33 participants**
  - May 2004 (Gitega) => **Integrated Command of the Army (FDN) 30 participants**
  - September 2004 (Bujumbura) => **Joint Liaison Teams for DDR**
  - **(United Nations and Burundian Forces)** **95 participants**
  - February 2005 (Gitega) => **Integrated Command of the National Police (1) 35 participants**

- May 2005 (Gitega) => **Integrated Command of the National Police (2) 35 participants**

- **Training of Trainers**
  - March-April 2004 (Gitega-Ruyegi) => **Leaders Facilitators at the Communal Level 30 participants**
  - July 2004 (Paris) => **Training of Trainers 45 participants**
  - July 2005 (Washington) => **Training of Trainers 40 participants**

- **Community Based Leadership Project**
  - 2004-2005 (Gitega-Ruyegi) => **Burundian Leaders at the Communal Level 4000 participants**

- **Political Parties**
  - November 2004 (Gitega) => **Leaders of political parties 31 participants**

- **Government Workshop :**
  - September 2005 (Bujumbura) => **President, VPS, Ministers, Key Advisors 28 participants**

- **TOTAL : +/- 4535**

Because the initial leaders of the "Ngozi process" helped identify who should be trained next, and because of the capacity of Ambassador Wolpe to convince the donor community that this was worth investing in, it became possible to accompany the transition, including in some of its most delicate aspects, like the contribution to an integrated command of the army and of the police.

A further spin-off of the initial Burundi training program is a two-year OTI pilot project launched in the provinces of Gitega and Ruyigi in February 2004, directed at the community reintegration of refugees, displaced persons and ex-combatants. Under this initiative, 20 Burundian "master trainers", selected on the basis of 30 facilitators who were trained, have themselves been training 4000 local leaders (formal and informal) in the same skills and techniques that are being provided to national leaders. All of this training is conducted in Kirundi (rather than in French), and Liz McClintock, as well as ESSEC IRENE facilitators Ricardo Perez-Nückel and Liliane de Andrade, developed materials that are accessible to illiterate and semi-literate populations.

In November 2004, the BLTP, in partnership with the Burundi Independent Electoral Commission and the UN Mission to Burundi, organized two workshops for the top leaders of thirty-one Burundian political parties. Designed to reduce tensions in the lead-up to elections, these workshops in collaborative decision-making were enthusiastically received by the party leaders and led to important new collective initiatives: the writing by the leaders themselves of an Electoral Code of Conduct; a joint press communiqué signed by all of the leaders assuring the public of their joint determination to work for elections without violence or intimidation; and a request that the BLTP facilitate periodic gatherings of the party leaders, so that they might be able to sustain their new relationships through the election cycle and beyond.

In September 2005, following the conclusion of a remarkably successful – and for the most part, violence-free – election process, the newly elected President, Pierre Nkurunziza, convened a BLTP Cabinet Retreat in collaborative decision-making. The President, the Vice-Presidents, the Ministers and some of their key advisers reflected together during several days to deepen methods and key issues to ensure government success. The President also asked that another workshop be held for party leaders, because he does not want the losing parties to feel marginalized by their defeat.

Using a Methodology for Experiential Learning and Off-the-Classroom Melting

The BTLP employs a non-traditional, interactive pedagogy, with trainers who are skilled in the techniques of institutional and conflict transformation, and who have extensive experience working with both private sector and public institutions to create more cohesive and effective organizations.

However, all of these workshops require more than "book learning" and a cognitive understanding of concepts. A paradigm or mind-set cannot be taught; it must be experienced - The same is true of trusting relationships that develop only over time and involve personal emotional investment. Likewise, an appreciation of the importance of process will emerge only through direct experience with others. What the BLTP training provides is an opportunity for experiential learning – through interactive exercises, simulations, and role-playing – all designed to enable the participants to learn and build upon their skills, not only through lectures and reading but more importantly through their own experiences.

It also involves the creation of an environment where leaders (re)learn to live together – a weeklong "retreat" in which meals, coffee-breaks, storytelling around a beer, and nightlong conversations offer participants the opportunity to (re)build trust in one another. It means a total experience, where progressive or sudden shifts happen in the perception of "the other". Participants, who sometimes had never talked to each other during years as official representatives of their respective delegations in peace talks, find new spaces and times to recognize each other as human beings. The rebirth of the other side's humanity is one of the cornerstones of the "training process".

Trainers participate in all of these activities merely as facilitators of process (not of content), and, because they are seen as fair catalysts of these meetings, at times, participants confide in them, off the record, sharing their fears but also their hopes. This phenomenon also contributes to the healing process, and to the recognition that there IS a possibility for a better future, which needs to be tried.

Workshop exercises reinforce this out-of-the-classroom experience. For example, they are designed both to demonstrate the power of conditioning on perceptions and to strengthen participants' communication skills, including the need for active listening and active speaking. They also seek to transform the way in which the participants define and understand their "self-interest," such that they come to see their long-term security and welfare as being not in opposition to, but directly dependent upon, the larger society of which they are a part. The objective is to enable the participants to comprehend that collaboration with others is not a matter of altruism or of adherence to some abstract notion of "good governance," but is a matter of enlightened self-interest that can be embodied in the pursuit of the collective interest for the entire society. This requires an understanding of the concept of "motivation-based negotiations," in which decision makers distinguish between their "positions," or idealized aspirations, on the one hand, and their underlying "motivations," or fundamental needs, fears and interests, on the other. Sustainable decisions are far more likely to result from a decision-making process that turns not on attempts to impose one's position on others but, instead, on the search for means of satisfying the interests of all.

Recognizing that adults learn more effectively through hands-on experience, the training also tries to combine different tools for adult-education:

(1) **Role-plays and simulations** are frequently used in training. Some very well-known simulations, like the Harvard PON "Oil Pricing" exercise, may be used to illustrate internal and external tensions within or between groups. Other simulations are sometimes adapted or rewritten, as the Conflict Management Group did for "Sally Soprano", which is played in an African context with a football player. Some new cases are also produced in order to fit the African context such as a negotiation about a grant between country officials and donors. Debriefings always follow the use of simulations or exercises, and are focused on the lessons that the participants themselves have drawn from the simulation.

(2) **Micro-exercises** follow the same path: adoption, adaptation or pure creation. The pure creation of exercises often comes from the experience of the participants, as was done for an exercise on rumors, or using the example of a negotiation between a medical official and a guard to let through a convoy with medicine to illustrate the importance of balancing active listening with active speaking.

(3) **Films** have also been used. For example, in order to illustrate mediation techniques and success, the "Médiateurs du Pacifique" movie was used; it describes how in New Caledonia a mediation process helped the population from French descent (Caldoches) and the indigenous population (Kanaks) to rebuild dialogue in a quasi civil war context. The "Our Friends at the Bank" movie was used to illustrate the need to improve the need for both donors and country officials to build stronger partnerships with each other.

(4) **PowerPoint presentations** are used throughout the workshop for a dual purpose: on the one hand, to structure the key learning points and, on the other hand, to capture "on-line" the works of the participants during the discussions and plenary sessions. At the end of each workshop, the PowerPoint slides, including the contributions made by participants during the seminar, are distributed to all participants, along with suggested readings and the final report.

(5) **Application sessions** are an important part of the learning process. During the last days of a workshop, *current issues or challenges* that are chosen by participants themselves are addressed using the tools, so that participants can return to their responsibilities with illustrations of how the tools are relevant to their reality, and how they could apply them effectively and successfully. Tools that have emerged from HNP, PON, ESSEC IRENE and elsewhere, such at the Four Quadrant Tool or the 10 Asset Preparation Framework form the basis of the application sessions.

From "Track 2" to "Track 1": Generating Issues and Ideas Together and Follow-Up

Given the nature of the retreat and the constraints of the original invitation, (participants are invited in their personal capacity, not as decision-makers), we are always careful not to get too deep and too early on commitments. However, we've found that participants welcome the opportunity to use this approach, especially the application sessions, to get as close as is reasonably possible to the decision-making process. This way the "track two" approach and brainstorming process gets very close to the so-called "track one" diplomacy and decision-making process.

It is also worth mentioning that participants always choose the issues and challenges they want to work on, and that our role as facilitators is limited to that of a coach on process to help them select the issues and on methods to help work on them, when they have selected them. Occasionally participants have asked for external experts on content to be present to help inform the application session. The more specific the challenges, the more such experts are needed. For example, when the training for the key military leaders or integrated command was organized, participants requested that they work on such specific issues as the definition of the combatant, the harmonization of rank or the allocation of posts in the newly unified army. The presence of a technical expert on issues of DDR (disarmament, demobilization, and reintegration) then became useful during the workshop. But in no way is our training the place where decisions are made, or a substitute for the existing institutions. At best, it becomes a think tank or a platform where many ideas are raised, discussed, deepened, criticized, and it all paves the way for the actions that participants then undertake in their respective institutions. This "non-commitment" mode will unleash creativity in an atmosphere of trust.

Deepening understanding of each other and of issues also happens "beyond" the training retreat during the follow-up sessions that are organized every two months, following the initial workshop. This follow-up principle nurtures the continued efforts of the network when participants share the ways in which they have applied the skills acquired in the interval. Stories include impacts in their professional and often their private lives. These follow-up sessions aim at reinforcing the skills and tools learned as well as insuring sustainability of the process of a paradigm shift in decision-making. The constitution of a Yahoo-Group also strengthens the network and the capacity for all the members to interact constructively.

Another on-going step "beyond" the training which has contributed to reinforcing the sustainability of the program has been the work that Howard Wolpe undertakes to share what was learned from the training process, updating top leaders on the progress that has been made during the workshops. He was also the participants' spokesperson with top leaders, and with donors, when further activities were advised.

We must reemphasize the fact that in the three year training process of more that 400 top leaders and 4000 communal leaders, a major shift was dictated by participants – from a focus on a mixed group to a strong emphasis on the security sector – because participants saw these groups as key for a stable transition of the country, and as those who most needed the skills of effective collaborative decision-making.

On the basis of this approach, one that combines adaptable teaching methods with an ongoing consultation and buy-in process, some of the recent work of the team has been devoted to determining what it would take to possibly replicate the Burundi project in other post-conflict or conflict situations. There are three places where the applicability of such methods is being investigated: the DR Congo where a pilot program was started at the beginning of 2006, as well as in Liberia and in the Ivory Coast.

Next Activities in Burundi

Originally, as was explained, only 95 leaders were trained. But the impact of what has come to be known in Burundi as "the Ngozi process" (named after the original training venue) in rapidly building unprecedented cohesion among leaders who had been bitterly polarized by four decades of inter-communal violence led to requests from the Burundian government that the experience be quickly extended to army and rebel commanders, to prepare for the implementation of the cease-fire, for DDR, and for unification of the Army. This led recently, in turn, to:

> (1) A request from the former Army Chief of Staff (now the newly appointed Minister of Defense) that a two-year training program be established to build cohesion in the newly integrated army high command;
>
> (2) A related request for the "training of trainers," so that the Ngozi process might be institutionalized within the national military academy of Burundi;
>
> (3) A request that a two-year training program be similarly established for the top one hundred officers of the new national police force; and
>
> (4) A request by the UN Force Commander that 84 former combatants be trained to serve as mixed teams of observers to monitor the demobilization process.

All of these security sector initiatives have been underwritten by the British Department for International Aid (DfID).

Assessing the Impact of Leadership Training in the BLTP

Peter Uvin, when he assessed the first year of BLTP achievement in his World Bank report, distinguished between different possible levels of impact of such a project. These different categories remain more useful than ever, and can be extended.

- *Level 1:* personal impact, eye-opening for individuals

Leaders who participated in the workshop undertook some dramatic experiences, where suddenly leaders "on the other side" could be seen, at least in the moment, as potential partners and no more as arch-enemies. Some eye-openers and methods contribute to this new awareness, but it is still to be proved that beyond that very experience during the workshop, participants will actually change some of their "old" views and patterns of behaviors and behave with the "others" as partners.

- *Level 2:* relational impact, towards reconciliation

Leaders who spent so much time together started creating a relationship together, and built a capacity, at least during the workshop, to work together. The existence of follow-up sessions, as well as the Yahoo-Group, continued to play a similar role of deepening the relationship. This was confirmed by the willingness of many participants to turn up at the next meeting, be it for work, for further training or for socializing. BLTP also becomes a resource center, with books and computers, which will reinforce the "institutional aspect" of the BLTP, so that it is more and more Burundian, and less and less a Western import.

- *Level 3:* sustainable impact for the participants

Whether the early changes in people will be confirmed in these very people is harder to assess. At the very least, some participants have become strong partisans of the BLTP process, and have used the methods themselves in their work and asked for these methods to be shared with as many people as possible beyond the circle of those who were initiated. If the training had only been a one-off activity without any interest and sustainable helpful change for the participants, it is very unlikely there would be have been such a drive from trained participants for further involvement of the BLTP in the transition process.

- *Level 4:* sustainable impact for the institutions to which participants belong

If training had been limited to the early 95 participants of the 'Ngozi process', it is doubtful that it could ever have a sustainable impact on institutions themselves. But when participants drove the process towards institutions – cease-fire commission, integrated command of the army or the police –, it is clear that there was a strong potential for influence on these institutions themselves. For example, the commission that had been working for several months on the integrated command of the army had been in deadlock on three key issues: the definition of the fighter, the harmonization of grades and the allocation of the posts in the new FDN (National Defense Force). Following the workshop, there was a quick solution that participants found together on the first issue, and then the next two issues were also addressed, until appointments in the new army actually took place. Similarly, gathering political leaders from 31 parties helped them draft the electoral code of conduct.

- *Level 5:* sustainable impact for populations

At an early stage of the BLTP, it aimed, beyond people and network, to lead to concrete bankable projects. As the different leaders often belonged to several institutions and regions, it is not clear that this intuition to draft projects that would immediately benefit the populations was well founded. Though some efforts have been made by participants in that respect, only the CBLP (Community Based Leadership Project) seems to have direct impact on the populations in two provinces. It still needs to be proved that the BLTP will have a long-term positive impact for the populations. At the very least, a peaceful transition has been observed: it includes non-violent elections and aftermaths, and the constitution of a national army, based on the two key components of the country security sector (former regular army and CNDD-FDD armed movement). This has enough of an impact on the populations that the BLTP can be seen as positive, even for them.

For a Remake: BLTP 2, BLTP 3, BLTP 4, etc.

In a nutshell, if the BLTP could be differentiated from other programs in which ESSEC IRENE has been involved in Africa, it is by:

(1) The actual cohorts of participants in the workshops – a critical mass of trainees;

(2) The high status, awareness and drive of participants;
(3) The choice of a long-term approach – not a single workshop but a retreat with follow-ups;
(4) The capacity to be responsive to key transition issues at turning points – for an integrated security sector, free elections;
(5) The permanent buy-in. Nothing would have been possible without the incredible pugnacity of Ambassador Wolpe, who knew all the key diplomats (and potential supporters and donors) in the region, but also all the key Burundians;
(6) The involvement of two wonderful Burundian leaders, who have become friends: Eugène Nindorera, former Minister of Human Rights, and Fabien Nsengimana, former presidential adviser and current director of the BLTP. Their advice was precious at all times; and,
(7) The substantial leap of faith of donors, who have built success on the basis of success.

Sometimes, it can be said that the capacity to combine all these forces can hardly be replicated. This does not seem true. If, instead of doing little programs here and there, which are disconnected, and without follow-up, more forces were united, the BLTP could be replicated more often and Africa could be a better place for all.

SECTION 3

ENHANCING BUSINESS COMPETITIVENESS IN SUB-SAHARA AFRICA

AFRICAN REGIONAL CO-OPERATION AND GROWTH TRIANGLE STRATEGIES

Evariste Habiyakare
Åbo Akademi University
Department of Business Studies
Henriksgatan 7
Turku 20500
Finland
***E-mail*: ehabiyak@abo.fi**

Richard Owusu[9]
Swedish School of Economics and Business Administration
PB 479, Arkadiankatu 22
Helsinki 00101
Finland
***E-mail:* richard.owusu@hanken.fi**

Abstract

Whereas Africa has witnessed failure to achieve economic growth through formal regional co-operation efforts, Asia combined these efforts with other strategies and has been able to achieve positive results. Through formal regional co-operation and conscious support to key potential growth zones, Asian countries used growth triangle (GT) strategies that were aimed at increasing their competitiveness. This paper discusses the GT concept and proposes that African countries could benefit by adopting GT strategies. We illustrate our key arguments by comparing two regional co-operation processes in Africa: the East African Community (EAC) and the Economic Community of West African States (ECOWAS).

Key words: East African Community (EAC), Economic Community of West African States (ECOWAS), Growth Triangles.

Introduction

Regional economic co-operation is widely seen to be an important catalyst for regional development. Apart from the political effects of peace between co-operating neighbours, various economic effects have been suggested. The abolition of intra-regional barriers and the creation of an economic zone, as in the case of the European Union (EU), create a bigger market area for both local and foreign companies. Local companies can easily expand to the neighbouring countries thereby specialising, achieving economies of scale and passing on the benefits of cheaper prices to consumers. Greater competition could lead to greater innovation and effectiveness. Greater intra-regional trade will lead to faster economic growth and create jobs based on regional catalysts. Foreign companies may be more inclined to enter a country if they can do business in the whole region from there.

---

[9] Corresponding author

So far, African countries have not been adequately attractive to foreign investors for production for the local market or for export. Among the reasons adduced for this situation is their small economies and perceived instability (Commission for Africa, 2005; ECA, 2002; World Bank, 2000; UNCTAD, 1999). Thus, one could forecast that an economic union of the whole of Africa or regions like East and West Africa would be more attractive to foreign investors. Regional economic integration strategies consist of both formal and informal processes and policy measures. The catalysts are the legal frameworks and policy measures as well as the consequent formal processes. They provide legal, economic and political backing to the informal processes, thereby enabling the captains of informal processes to work openly on developing them. On their own, the formal policies of regional economic co-operation are important but inadequate. The European Union (EU) is an example of a highly ambitious project that has brought increased economic development, political co-operation as well as integration to Europe. The Association of South East Asian Nations (ASEAN), on the other hand, has not attempted the far-reaching political and economic policies attempted in the EU, but has succeeded in increasing the area's economic growth (Kakazu, 1994). In both of these cases, apart from the formal process there are also "informal" business processes of regional integration, which cement the formation of trans-border industrial districts, economic growth areas or "growth triangles".

According to the EAAU (East African Analytical Unit) (1995) a growth triangle (GT) is defined as:

> "*... an economic concept underpinned by political motivation. It involves linking adjacent areas of separate countries with different endowments of factors of production such as, land, labor and capital and different source of comparative advantage, to form a sub region of economic growth. GT seeks to reduce regulatory barriers to the exploitation of economic complementarities in order to gain a competitive edge in attracting domestic and foreign investments, and to promote exports for mutual benefits of areas and countries involved. While GTs are facilitated by governments, they must have strong private sector involvement to succeed*"

We compare the Asian experience to the African because we find many similarities between the Asian economic, cultural and social situation and the African context. During the wave of independence from European colonialism, some Asian countries were at a comparable level of development with some African countries at the moment. Therefore the role of GT strategies in the economic success of some Asian countries is informative.

Aim and Method

In this paper, we examine the evolution of African regional economic integration schemes and we analyse the potential of growth triangle (GT) strategies to be implemented and to succeed in Africa. The ultimate aim is to increase the understanding and the debate on the conditions under which African countries could benefit mutually from adopting GT strategies. We use the Asian example to argue that by using formal integration processes combined with GT strategies to support informal economic processes, African countries may achieve positive results. Using the East African Economic Community (EAC) and the Economic Community of West African States (ECOWAS) as examples of formal regional co-operation, we examine how far these strategies have been applied in these regions.

African Regional Co-operation

The African continent has witnessed various regional co-operation efforts. Their declared aims have been, mainly, to promote trade, security, prosperity and growth for their members. They have different origins – one type is linked to colonial influences (ex. CEMAC, CEPGL, CEEAC, CFA, EAC) another is linked to post-colonial geographical regions (ECOWAS), and a third to South Africa's post apartheid position and influences (ex. SACU, SADC,COMESA).

The East African Community (EAC)

Economic co-operation between Kenya, Uganda and Tanzania dates back to the colonial period. A Uganda/Kenya Custom Union was established in 1917 and was joined by Tanzania in 1927. Inter-territorial co-operation between these countries was first formalised in1948 by the East African High Commission. This provided a customs union, a common external tariff, currency and postage; and also dealt with common services in transport and communications, research and education. Following independence, these integrated activities were reconstituted and the High Commission was replaced by the East African Common Services Organisation (EACSO) established in 1961, which many observers thought would lead to a political federation between the three territories (www.crwflags.com). The new organisation ran into difficulties because of the lack of joint planning and fiscal policy, separate political policies and Kenya's dominant economic position. In 1967 the EACSO was superseded by the East African Community. This body aimed to strengthen the ties between the members through a common market, a common customs tariff and a range of public services so as to achieve balanced economic growth within the region. The East African Community collapsed in 1972 following political differences between the member states (www.crwflags.com/). It was revived through the signing of the East African Cooperation Agreement in 1993. Since then, various co-operation treaties have been signed leading to the formal re-establishment of the East African Community (EAC) on July 7, 2000 by a treaty among Kenya, Tanzania and Uganda. This set into motion further collaborative protocols between the nations and included agreements on standards, crime prevention, establishment of a free trade area, economic development strategies, scientific and technological collaboration, and establishment of a legislative assembly and courts. Furthermore, the East African Customs Union was formally established in November 2004 and will have the objective of creating a customs-free internal market and harmonised external tariff rates. The community has a population of about 100 million (www.crwflags.com/). Furthermore, Rwanda and Burundi, being landlocked and heavily dependent on these EAC countries for land transit of foreign trade, have initiated talks to join the community. The potential for deepened economic integration within the current EAC membership, and even together with potential members Rwanda and Burundi, is relatively good. The three countries are united by the use of Swahili and English and their business law is mainly based on the British model. There are many traditional ties between the people. So far, Kenya is the leading economy in the region.

The Economic Community of West African States (ECOWAS)

ECOWAS was formed in 1975 and currently consists of 15 nations and 230 million people. It has an estimated total Gross Domestic Product (GDP) of $80bn (2002) (Siddioi, 2003). The regional powerhouse is Nigeria whose population is bigger than all the other 14 countries put together and makes up 51% of the region's GDP. However, there are several other medium-sized economies that are important partners for Nigeria's development – particularly Cote d'Ivoire (13%), Ghana (7.4%), and Senegal (6.7%) of the region's GDP (Siddioi, 2003). The aim of ECOWAS is to integrate the economies of the region and create mutual development (www.ecowas.info). The formation of the organization was initially seen as a success in uniting the Francophone and Anglophone countries. The former French colonies were initially linked through various customs and economic policies and had a single currency. Externally, their economies were linked to France. In the same vein the English-speaking countries were linked to Britain externally but did not have as close formal economic links as their Francophone neighbours. However, the first 20 years of ECOWAS were characterised by empty promises and very little was achieved in the form of economic integration. The French-speaking countries continued their co-operation in the form of the monetary union (CFA) while the English-speaking countries lacked any unified policy. In the early 1990s attempts were made to overcome hurdles and accelerate integration. A new treaty signed in 1993 aimed to achieve a common market and a single currency. It envisaged the establishment, among other things, of a West African Parliament, as well as a court to enforce the decisions of the community. However, the biggest achievement of regional integration has been in peace-keeping and conflict-resolution where it has set an example for regional co-operation and peace maintenance in the world.

Entrepreneurship, Investment and the Economic Integration Imperative in Africa

It is widely believed that economic growth could be achieved through promoting local entrepreneurial capacity and local and foreign direct investments. In the African case, apart from growing but inadequate foreign aid, foreign investments have been insignificant and have been confined to extractive industries. Regional economic integration could attract more foreign direct investment to these regions. Regional integration is also helping countries at war to make peace and the politicians are at least waking up to the need to promote business in their regions. It is clear that African countries need to improve the business environment fast and radically, since the investment absorption capacity depends on building the institutions to deal with increased financial and legislative demand (Commission for Africa, 2005). Furthermore, free interregional trade is inevitably crucial to the success of major investments as most African countries are economically too small to attract significant foreign direct investments to only their own local markets. It also seems a logical assumption that these sub-regional integrations (would/could?) move to bigger and wider pan-African regional integration. We would believe that the recent proclamations of leaders, for example within the framework of the African Union, will lead to long-term policy change within these regions.

The South East Asian Example

Dahles (2003) argues that Asian growth triangles (AGT) are distinctly Asian forms of regional co-operation, which have evolved from the area's experience in export processing zones (EPZ), industrial and technological parks. These growth triangles are localised economic co-operation zones that exploit complementarities between geographically contiguous areas of different countries to gain competitive edge in export promotion. Consequently, trans-border areas are comprised of elaborate network relations, public-private partnerships in the form of subcontracting, outsourcing and franchising. Thus, these relations of economic co-operation bind together large-scale enterprises as well as multinational corporations. Hiroshi (1997) outlined some of the factors which determined success of growth triangles in the Asian context: 1) strong cultural and social ties; 2) an ideology of shared growth and benefits; 3) a high degree of political commitment; 4) existence of complementary relationships in the resource endowments; 5) easy access to inter-regional boundaries or complete permeability within regions; 6) a reasonably well-developed infrastructure; 7) the existence of metropolitan centres that are able to create and diffuse dynamism within the GT. One important factor in the creation of Asian growth triangles has been informal cross-border business networking, particularly that of the Chinese business Diasporas (Ramström, 2004), although official support aided these ongoing processes.

Comparisons of Asian and African Development and Economic Integration Initiatives

In Africa, despite a number of efforts towards inter-regional links between different countries and regions, a conscious development of growth triangles have not yet taken off. One of the most apparent reasons for failure could be identified as a lack of political and entrepreneurial commitment on the side of the implementers within the member states. Most efforts have remained as political forums, with very little resources, capabilities and mechanisms to foster economic growth within them. Non-democratic leadership has worsened political rivalries between leaders, for example Tanzania invaded Uganda (with the tacit support of the African and international community) to overthrow Idi Amin's dictatorship. In West Africa the recent civil war in Cote d'Ivoire has strained relations with its Northern and Western French-speaking neighbours. In Asia, as Japan combined western technologies with its own home-grown technology and management techniques (Ramström, 2004), it acted as a knowledge source and a role model for most of the Asian countries. Asian supply side and demand sides developed at the same time and, above all, there was willingness from the United States of America to disseminate Asian growth stimuli and to provide demand for Asia's trade surplus in the 1970s and 1980s, as predicted by Vernon' s Product Life- Cycle theory (1966, 1979*).* In the case of Africa, the Republic of South Africa (RSA) in the south and Nigeria in the west are expected to act as role models for Sub-Saharan Africa. The RSA in particular, with its advanced industries and economic development, is expected to act as an engine for fostering business activities through providing relatively cheap technologies and as a conduit for investment in African countries. On the other hand, despite industrial progress in Nigeria, the country is still troubled by perceived corruption and ethnic as well as religious divisiveness.

Whereas US and EU firms moved their production to Asia and have also been favouring cheap imports from Asia in some cases, African manufacturing has not taken off and their exports have been mostly in raw materials. After their independence, in the 1960s and 1970s, most of the African governments acted to protect their infant industries, but these policies did not bring positive results. This failure could be attributed to many factors, such as: a lack of managerial and technical know-how which was a direct result of a lack of education during colonialism, and a lack of African entrepreneurship under colonialism.

For the sake of comparison between Asia and Africa, we can see that the liberalised trade regime, export-oriented FDI and actors' commitments to export characterises the Asian development, which means making use of the free market elsewhere. In Sub-Saharan Africa, (except the RSA), there is a lack of well-developed production industries. When they exist, it may be hard to find markets outside their borders. In the Asian growth triangles, the quest for macro-stability led to state control of personal consumption and standard of living. For the sake of the "general good" democracy was constrained as far as commercial expansion was not hurt. Further, the Asian growth triangles were characterised by a relatively high level of national saving, while resources were geared towards industrial growth (Dahles, 2003).

In the EAC and the ECOWAS on the other hand, political developments indicate that most of the country members have been hurt by internal and regional instability and conflicts that have deterred FDI. The existence of powerful state authorities in Africa is similar to the

Asian countries; however, the African regimes have failed to foster industrial growth within their national boundaries. Asian governments played the role of benevolent decision maker, protecting their industries where necessary and implementing policies to allow their firms to upgrade their products and technologies through learning (Dahles, 2003). This included the capacity to change the policy framework within which the economy operates without undue social upheaval. In contrast African countries are now being pushed towards extreme laissez-faire policies by the World Bank and other financiers and donors. There are fears that this would not give their industries the time to develop properly.

Discussion

According to Foroutan (1992), there are more than 200 regional co-operation organisations in Africa of which more than 80% are inter-governmental. As a result, there has been a proliferation of schemes operating within the same geographic area with overlapping membership and duplication of mandates, which has made regional investment, trade and political and economic integration rather slow. However, looking at the EAC and ECOWAS, we believe that the foundations for informal processes exist in these two African sub-regions. It is well known that African borders are unnatural in the sense that they frequently divide ethnic and cultural groups. There are ongoing traditional connections and networks; in both the EAC and ECOWAS, there is a large amount of unreported border trade. However, genuine official support policy is lacking. In the ECOWAS region, the previously more advanced co-operation between the French-speaking countries has been hurt by the crisis in Cote d'Ivoire. Workers and immigrants, particularly from French West Africa, working in the country are reported to have been targeted and considered allies of the opposition (www.kaiptc.org). This destroys the essence of economic integration since free movement of people is not made possible. Previously, there have been mass deportations by Ghana and Nigeria of each other's citizens.

On the other hand, the experience of Asia also includes political conflict and instability. Examples are problems between Malays and Chinese in Malaysia, the deportation of Indonesian workers from Malaysia, political instability in the Philippines and the continued war of words between South Korea and China on one side and Japan on the other, which is due to the Japanese colonisation of both countries and alleged atrocities (Ramström, 2005).

The Asian experience has shown that economic development and the development of infrastructure and education are symbiotic processes. In that sense one can express optimism for Africa too – as soon as economies start to take off, the promise of economic betterment may suppress ethnic, religious and political tension as in the case of Asia. The promise by the international community to support infrastructural projects as well as good governance, including debt reduction measures, may give African countries the breathing space for development. Potentially, Africa has natural resource endowments, and complementary development relationships can be developed. Africa is a contiguous geographical area without significant natural boundaries, and cultural and ethnic groups span across national borders. The difference in Asia seems to have been a successful local entrepreneurship and foreign investment interest in the area, which have overcome the problems caused by national and ethnic conflicts and political instability. Besides Japan, the successes of newly developed Asian countries like South Korea, Singapore, Taiwan and China are, at the moment, a distant dream for African countries.

Conclusions and Propositions

We strongly believe that the experiences of Asian growth triangles could be applied in Africa as well. If applied properly, we believe that it could enhance competitiveness and improve levels of employment. Strategies may be directed towards attracting new investments from local, national and foreign investors which in turn, create new job opportunities as well as increased incomes. We believe that, with regional cooperation, African countries would be able to cope better with shifting and volatile patterns of international demand. In other words, we believe that by clustering, by sharing work, expertise, collective services and risk, inter-regional and inter-firm networks should be able to demonstrate their ability to jointly resist market shocks and adapt to rapid worldwide economic and political changes. The ultimate goal of these co-operation efforts and clustering would be to improve economic performance and the standard of living of the population in these areas. We propose that regional co-operation schemes like EAC and ECOWAS could move further to manage economic interdependencies through the adoption of conscious GT strategies. We believe that the mode of interest formation, aggregation and articulation of policy response to regional and international dynamics by participating countries affect and are affected by the nature of regional co-operation as well as the production profiles of the involved countries. However, to apply a growth triangle strategy requires further strong interaction between business, social and political actors. As growth triangles emerge, they affect and are affected by continued regional co-operation policies, new production profiles and new political, social and business formations. We believe that the societal groups and state institutions continuously affect domestic interest formation, aggregation and articulation of policy responses as domestic production profiles change in participating member states. Therefore, the participating countries' policies and the consequent regional co-operation models that develop will have deep influences on the emergence or non emergence of a sub-regional growth triangle.

However, we would caution that constructing greater comparative advantage, through using GT strategies, would require an understanding of the social and political institutions of the country members because a simple assessment of relative resource endowments will not indicate which states or regions have comparative advantages in different industries. All in all, doing business across borders implies not only relocation of production process but also relocation of labour and management models and strategies, i.e. dynamic relationships between organisations and people with different cultural backgrounds, both within and outside their states. Lastly, we suggest the west could explore the possibility of assisting Africa in applying an African version of GT strategy.

References

Awuah, G. B. 1997. Promoting infant industries in less developed countries. *International Business Review*, 6: 71– 87.

Chong, A. 1996. *Theory, methodology and history for growth triangles analysis*. Presented at Acadia University for the October Order & Disorder Conference of the Atlantic Political Science Association

Commission for Africa. 2005. *Report of the Commission for Africa*. www.commissionforafrica.org (accessed 5 January 2006).

Dunning, J. H. 1995. Trade, location, and economic activity and the multinational enterprise: A search for an eclectic approach. In J. Drew (Ed.), *Readings in International Enterprise:* 250–274. London: (publisher?).

East Asia Analytical Unit, 1995. *Growth triangles of South East Asia*, Australian Department of Foreign Affairs and Trade, East Asia Analytical Unit, Canberra.

Economic Commission for Africa, 2002. *Economic report on Africa, 2002.* Addis Ababa: ECA. www.uneca.org

Foroutan, F. 1992. Regional Integration in Sub-Saharan Africa, Experience and Prospects. The World Bank, Policy Research, Working Papers, Trade Policy, Country Economics Department,WPS 992.

Kakazu, H. 1994. Growth triangles *in ASEAN, a* new approach *to regional* co-*operation. Hong Kong: Oxford University Press.*

Kojima, K., 2000. 'The Flying Geese' model of Asian economic development: Origin, theoretical extensions and regional policy implications. *Journal of Asian Economics*, 11 (4): 375–401 Winter.

Prahalad C.K. & Hamel G. 1990. The core competence of corporations. *Harvard Business Review,* 66 May/June: 79–91.

Ramström, J. 2005. *West meets East. A study of cross-institutional business relationships between Finnish /Swedish and overseas Chinese firms.* Unpublished Ph.D. Dissertation, Åbo Akademi University, Turku, Finland.

Siddioi, M. 2003. Is a common currency for West Africa feasible? *African Business,* July 2003; 289.

Vernon, R. 1966. International investments and international trade in the product life cycle. *Quarterly Journal of Economics,* 80(2): 190– 207.

Vernon, R. 1979. The product life cycle hypothesis in a new international environment, *Oxford Bulletin of Economics & Statistics*, 4 (4): 255–267.

Woo, C. Y., Deallenbach, U. & Nicholls-Nixon, C. 1994. Theory building in the presence of "randomness": The case of venture creation and performance. *Journal of Management Studies,* 31(4):507–524.

World Bank 2002. *African development indicators 2002: Making monetary work for Africa.* Washington, D.C World Bank

World Bank 2003. *World development report.* Washington, D.C World Bank.

World Bank 2000. *Regional brief: Sub-Saharan Africa.* Washington, D.C: World Bank. www.worldbank.org

Zhang, K. H. 2001. Does a foreign direct investment promote economic growth? Evidence from East Asia and Latin America. *Contemporary Economic Policy*, 19(2): 175–185.

http://www.crwflags.com, accessed on 18.12.2005

http://www.commissionforafrica.org , accessed on 30.12.2005

http://www.kaiptc.org, accessed on 01.01.2006

GHANA BECOMING 'BANGALORE OF AFRICA': THE ROLE OF SERVICING CAPACITY AND MARKET ACCESS

VIPIN GUPTA
Simmons College School of Management
300 The Fenway
Boston, MA 02115
USA
Tel: 1-617-277-3692
Fax: 1-617-521-3138
Gupta05@gmail.com

SUSAN D. SAMPSON
Simmons College School of Management
409 Commonwealth Ave.
Boston, MA 02215
USA.
Tel: 1-617-521-3895
Fax: 1-617-521-3138
Sampson@Simmons.edu

Abstract

Over the past few years, Ghana has been able to gain accolades from many as the rising Business Process Outsourcing (BPO) center of Sub-Saharan Africa, and even a potential Bangalore of Africa. In this paper, the case of Ghana and its pioneering technological firms is examined, to draw valuable lessons on how to develop initial technological capability for servicing global customers from a condition of competitive deficiency. This study has important implications for other nations in Sub-Saharan Africa looking to play an important role in the global economy.

Key words: Technological Capability, Ghana, Servicing Capacity, Telecommunications, BPO, Sub-Saharan Africa

INTRODUCTION

In a survey released in January 2006, rating the most promising Business Process Outsourcing (BPO) centers in the world, Ghana was ranked 22nd among 40 nations, and 1st in Africa. Ghana was ranked ahead of South Africa, which is ranked 32nd (World Bank, 2006). Ghana's rising as the Bangalore of Africa will be a sign of hope for the whole of Sub-Sahara Africa. The Western nations, particularly the US, appear to be ready to support Ghana by way of market access and immigrant diaspora.

The rise of Ghana as a BPO center was unexpected as recently as just a few years ago. In 2003, South Africa had more than 500 call centers, which was triple the number in 1997, employing about 70,000 employees (De Vynck, 2004). In contrast, Ghana employed less than 5,000 employees in its BPO sector including call centers and claim processing in 2003, although the sector was growing very rapidly. At the time, it had only about 300,000 fixed phone lines, 550,000 mobile subscribers, 400,000 computers, 20,000 Internet subscribers and 325,000 Internet users, with a population of about 20 million (Osiakwan & Foster, 2004).
Using data from around 2000, Ifinedo (2005) assessed technological readiness of nine African nations. Ghana scored below average on seven of the eight factors: (1) culture, understanding and effectiveness, (2) knowledgeable citizens, (3) industry competitiveness, (4) access to skilled workforce, (5) willingness and ability to invest, (6) advanced infrastructure, and (7) macro economic stability. It was rated above average and the best in only one factor – cost of living and pricing. Overall, it was ranked second to the last, above only Cote d'Ivoire. South Africa was rated the best on the eight factors.

Along with economic factors, work culture played a part in the lack of development in Ghana. Traditionally, Ghanaian work-culture has been summed up in terms of a local saying, "If I can't get ahead, I won't let you get ahead either." (Oster, Goodman, Osiakwan, & Bernstein, 2004). The saying is generally represented by the image of an alligator with two heads, each trying to go in a different direction. Therefore, Ghanaians have historically avoided going into business and instead sought support from the government. Ghana's founding president, Kwame Nkrumah, once declared, "Seek ye first the political kingdom and all else shall follow." (Thompson, 2002).

Given the economic and cultural factors working against Ghana, how did they rise to become a promising BPO and quite possibly the next Bangalore? This paper traces the process by which the development of technological capability in Ghana was managed by various actors and the inter-play of market forces. First, a brief review of the literature on the concept of technological capability and the technological background of Ghana is presented. Second, the research methodology is identified and successive stages in the information and communications technology enabled services are classified. Third, the technological base available to the actors in each succeeding stage of servicing is investigated. Finally, there is a discussion of the factors that enabled success, despite the technical deficiencies in technological capability.

LITERATURE REVIEW

Technological Capability

Technological capability is a multi-faceted ensemble of human, physical, social, emotional, organizational, institutional, and financial capital. According to Bell and Pavitt (1993: 163), "Technological capabilities incorporate the resources needed to generate and manage technical change including skills, knowledge and experience, and institutional structures and linkages." National technological capability confers the absorptive capacity on a nation's people, and provides a base to exploit for added value. Absorptive capacity refers to the capacity to appraise, acquire, apply, and adapt the acquirable technology (Cohen and Levinthal, 1990).

In the case of Ghana, the technological base has been extremely deficient, not only from international standards, but also from the minimalist African norms. As such, the absorptive capacity conferred on Ghanaian firms is of a very poor quality, and cannot be credited to be the factor in the rise of Ghana as the potential BPO center of Africa.

While the concept of absorptive capacity is an acquisitive one, it is suggested here that the need for incorporating an additional concept, that of servicing capacity, is necessary to capture the experiential and application aspect of technological capability. "Servicing capacity" refers to mobilizing, assembling, and offering a range of appropriate and relevant technological servicing to the involved players. This servicing capacity helps the players become demanding customers, sophisticated vendors, developers and purveyors of factor endowments, rival competitors, and enables government and institutional agencies. Even when a nation's technological base is very deficient, the devotion and dedication of its firms to service their targeted constituencies, in a way that enhances the value-adding knowledge and skills (including awareness of new possibilities), can contribute substantially to a nation's technological capability.

Background of Ghana

A review of the background of Ghana confirms the fundamental technical deficiencies in the national and organizational technological base. Ghana has an agricultural orientation with 70% of its 20 million plus population living in rural areas. Cocoa and gold are its primary sources of foreign revenue (World Fact Book, 2006). After independence in 1957, Ghana set up a number of state-owned enterprises producing a range of previously imported consumer goods for the domestic market. The Pioneer Industries and Companies Act of 1959 committed to develop an attractive environment for foreign direct investment and identified this environment as a critical factor for development. By 1970, Ghana had a diverse, dynamic manufacturing sector, although only on the surface (UNCTAD, 2003).

In reality, little servicing capacity had been created and Ghanaian aspirations remained low. Aspiration is essential to building community cultural wealth and can be defined as the ability to maintain hopes and dreams for the future despite real or perceived barriers (Yosso, 2005). The major national firms were concentrated in the refining and aluminum smelting sector where the nation had a natural resource advantage. Foreign firms operated primarily in food processing and industrial intermediaries manufacturing. African-owned firms in the formal sector were small scale, running on simple machinery and on low-level technical and managerial skills. The output tended to be of lower quality and focused on the domestic market. These firms lacked capital for refurbishing, upgrading, and modernizing facilities. Most African-owned firms were in the informal sector, operating essentially as home-based enterprises using very simple technologies and personal and part-time family labor (UNCTAD, 2003).

The weak foundations led to disastrous macro dynamics. In 1978, the nation's first president was overthrown through a military coup. The fragile manufacturing sector disintegrated, output fell to about 40 percent of the 1977 level by 1984, and inflation surged to 120 percent in 1983. Faced with huge national debt, a freer market system was adopted under World Bank guidelines. More than 250 of the 300 state owned enterprises were divested. Yet, even after this freer market system was adopted, the share of private sector in the national income rose from 4.5 percent to only 10 percent in 2003. This occurred, despite the fact that as many as 80 percent of the economically active population was engaged in the private informal sector, 8 percent in the private formal sector, and 6 percent in the public sector (UNCTAD, 2003).

Since the early 1980s, Ghana emphasized education, increasing allocations from 1.5 percent to 5 percent of GDP. In 2004, five hundred odd public senior secondary schools graduated a total of 90,000 students, up from 27,000 students graduating from three hundred schools in 1987. Yet, 70% of the 3.7 million school students in Ghana studied at the primary level, and only 30% of junior secondary school graduates had access to senior secondary school education. Further, the number of students graduating from universities was only 10,000, with total enrollments in tertiary education at 100,000. With these limited education options, the minimum wage in Ghana was $1 per hour (World Fact Book, 2006).

Most workers in Ghana's manufacturing firms had middle or secondary education. However, because of the deficiencies in the education system, firms had to incur the costs of remedial training for two thirds of these workers (Verner, 1999). Consequently, Ghana's firms were smaller in terms of structure and staffing, employing a less educated and less trained workforce that had only a quarter of labor productivity relative to Sub-Saharan African nations such as Zimbabwe and Kenya (Bigsten, et. al. 1998). Ghana suffered from a high brain drain with 43 percent of its skilled workforce estimated to have migrated overseas (Docquier & Rapoport, 2004).

RESEARCH METHODOLOGY

Gupta and Wang (2004) suggest a Process Tracing Congruence technique to uncover the process of transformation. In the congruence method, an existing formal or informal theory is used to make predictions regarding the outcome of the dependent variable in a particular case, given the value of the independent variable relevant to that case. The inference is then triangulated using 'process tracing', i.e. by identifying a causal sequence that clarifies how the independent variables contribute to the outcome of the dependent variable (Bennett and George, 2001). In deciding on a case study, one should look not for a 'typical' case, but rather for a 'critical' case that has a low probability of holding out in relation to theory, so as to uncover one or more missing steps in a causative relationship through intense observation and theoretical arbitrage.

In this article, the general theory of technological capability that attributes further development to prior absorptive capacity, giving rise to an evolutionary multi-staged process, is used. In South Korea for example, studies suggest that in Stage 1, foundations were established by the assembly of finished products locally. In Stage 2, absorptive capacity was built through R&D to understand technology either to produce on license or to copy, and through development of public sector university and research centers. In Stage 3, the government vastly increased its R&D funding, and the private sector pursued small scale advanced R&D effort to create new products. Finally, in Stage 4, the firms were able to make large research investments, in both basic as well as applied domains (Mahoney, Lee & Yun, 2005).

The case of Ghana and its firms is used for conducting within-case analysis. Ghana represents a 'critical case' because it has a low probability for strengthening of foundations using R&D and academic centers, thereby limiting absorptive capacity between development stages. Ghana is among the most impoverished nations of the world and is substantially dependent on the aid from bilateral and multilateral sources for even basic development. The case of Ghana is of high relevance because it shares these characteristics with several nations in Sub-Saharan Africa that are seeking to develop their technological capability with few resources for building even basic absorptive capacity. Given limited resources, jobs in technology would substantially raise the standard of living for citizens of Ghana and other Sub-Saharan African nations.

To trace the process of technological capability in Ghana, three levels of servicing capacity are identified in congruence with the staged evolutionary theory:

FIGURE 1
Staged Evolutionary Theory for Ghana's Technological Capacity

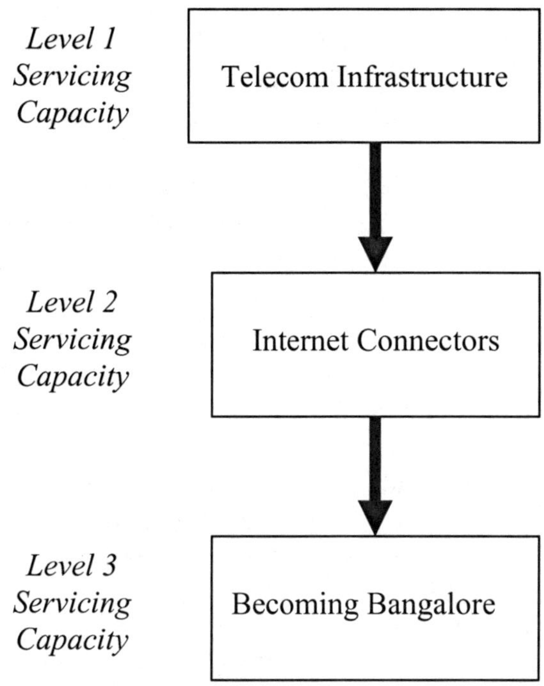

This paper will also examine if sufficient absorptive capacity was accessible to the nation for the development of each level and, if not, then what factors enabled the observed servicing capacity of the firms at each level.

BUILDING ICT-ENABLED SERVICING CAPACITY

First Level Servicing Capacity: Telecom Infrastructure

Telecom infrastructure is among the most basic requirements for servicing capacity in ICT-led value-added services. Until 1994, market penetration of telephones in Ghana stayed around 0.3 percent. In the 1970s and 1980s, the government launched two telecom rehabilitation projects sponsored by the World Bank. These projects helped replace obsolete equipment and supported improved institutional governance and management at the state-owned monopoly, Ghana Posts and Telecommunication, which was founded in 1974 (Godfred & Henten, 2004).

As part of 1983 Structural Adjustment Program of the World Bank, the government adopted the Accelerated Development Plan in 1994. Post and Telecoms were separated and converted into Ghana Post and Ghana Telecom in 1995. In 1996, a strategic equity stake of 30 percent of the Ghana Telecom was sold off to G-COM, a consortium led by Telecom Malaysia with full management control. A competitive duopoly was created, by licensing a second national network operator with similar rights and obligations as Ghana Telecom. Both operators were given five-year exclusive rights over the years 1997 to 2002. A third operator was licensed for the rural areas. The National Communications Authority was set up as the regulatory body in 1996. Value-added services such as mobile telephone services, data transmission, paging, and pay phones were offered. The corporate users were allowed to develop their own private networks by investing in satellites (Frempong & Henten, 2004). Mobile operators were allowed to operate starting with Mobitel (now Buzz) in 1991, Celltel (now Kasapa) in 1993, ScanCom (now Areeba) and later the incumbent Ghana Telecom affiliate, One Touch.

Between 1995 and 2000, there was rapid growth in phone usage in Ghana. The nation had about 750,000 phone lines in 2000, up from 50,000 in 1994. By 2000, when the five-year Accelerated Development Plan ended, tele-density had risen from 0.34 lines per 1000 inhabitants in 1994 to 1.16 lines, and public phones had risen from 0.001 lines per 1000 inhabitants in 1994 to 0.16 lines (Ministry of Communications, 2004).

Land-line operator. Ghana Telecom, with a subscriber base of 280,000, was the largest fixed line telecom operator in 2003. Since its partial privatization, its management was under the control of Telekom Malaysia (the minority shareholder). The new 2001 government refused to renew the management contract of Telekom Malaysia in 2002, because of deteriorating service quality and failure to fulfill investment promises. Telekom Malaysia asked for a buy back of its 30 percent shares bought at US$38 million in 1996 for US$100 million, though the Ghana government disputed this valuation (Frempong & Henten, 2004). Meanwhile, the Norwegian operator Telenor received the new management contract. A loan of US$150 million was obtained from China to fund new investments. Telenor committed to 400,000 new phone and Internet lines to all towns and villages that contain a secondary school (Frempong & Henten, 2004). Ghana Telecom reduced the loss of revenue leakage in the billing system from 25 percent in 2001 to 10 percent by 2005 (myjoyonline, 2005c). In 2001, receivables over 180 days constituted almost one-third of the total revenues resulting in a huge amount of bad debt. Under Telenor, Ghana Telecom achieved a turnaround from substantial losses to growing profits.

Along with introducing better systems for preventing fraud and bad debts, a Ghana Telecom Training Centre was also founded. This centre trained 822 people in 2003; 2,995 in 2004; and 3,936 in 2005 to improve individual and institutional efficiency, and planned to eventually obtain university status (myjoyonline, 2005c). Thus, there was substantial improvement in the efficiency of customer service, and the majority of Ghanaians could get access to telecom services by 2005 (Botwe, 2005).

The second largest telecom operator was Westel, which was set up in 1997 with majority equity from the US-based Western Wireless Company. Westel was expected to invest about US$50 million for the first five years of operation. However, its actual investments were only US$26 million and they generated a subscriber base of less than 3,000 in 2002, as compared to its target of 50,000 subscribers (Frempong & Henten, 2004). Most of Westel's revenues derived from its international gateway license that it used to connect some of the mobile operators who were not allowed to directly connect overseas. Westel planned to operate a pre-paid system whereby the users would have access to Ghana Telecom's network. However, Ghana Telecom contested this, forcing Westel to set up its own network, which delayed its operations and its viability.

The third telecom operator, Capital Telecom, was wholly Ghanaian owned and had license to operate in the underserved rural areas. However, its subscriber base was only about 500 in 2002. It secured a $275,000 grant from the United States Trade Development Agency for a pilot project, to test the viability of new technologies in providing low cost wireless service in a rural environment (Frempong & Henten, 2004). Overall, the landline telecom capacity in Ghana was very limited, and the quality poor. As seen in Table 1, the call completion rate deteriorated in the late 1990s and early 2000s, as the number of subscribers increased without expanding the network infrastructure.

TABLE 1

Quality of Service for Ghana Telecom, 1998-2002, in Percentages

	1998	1999	2000	2001	2002
Fault incidence rate/month for 100 lines	5.2	6.1	5.0	3.9	4.0
Fault clearance rate in 48 hours	62.0	56.9	58.5	59.9	65.7
Local call completion rate	81.1	78.8	77.6	78.5	77.6
Long distance call completion rate	63.4	54.7	47.0	59.8	55.2
International call completion rate	50.3	69.0	73.0	70.4	63.5

Source: Frempong & Henten (2004)

In summary, there is little evidence that the new telecom operators benefited much from the absorptive capacity created by the preceding player. Moreover, the absorptive capacity of the first telecom operator itself was very limited. It was not until servicing capacity in the form of pay phones, mobile phones, paging, and data transmission were added by competing contractors, financed through foreign investment, that there was any capacity built beyond the basic landline infrastructure.

In Africa, a significant amount of telecom services are distributed to users who did not have telephone or International Direct Dialing. To serve these users, small entrepreneurs resold Ghana Telecom services through some 2,000 tele-centers. Often, Ghanaians living abroad or returning from abroad invested in tele-centers as safe investments. A survey by Falch and Anyimadu (2003) indicated that 67.6 percent of the tele-center owners established the business through their own funds, 15.5 percent from friends/relatives, 4.2 percent from the banks, and 12.5 percent from the other sources.

Mobile operators. Given the limited capacity of the landline operators, mobile telephony grew more rapidly in Ghana, as shown in the Table 2.

TABLE 2

Number of Cellular Mobile Subscribers, 1993-2003, in thousands

	1993	**1994**	**1995**	**1996**	**1997**	**1998**	**1999**	**2000**	**2001**	**2002**	**2003**
Mobitel/ Buzz	1.7	3.3	3.6	10.0	16.9	22.3	33.0	40.0	50.9	53.0	45.8
CellTel/ Kasapa	-		0.8	1.9	2.6	2.8	2.2	0.9	0.9	8.7	10.5
ScanCom/ Areeba	-		-	0.4	7.0	13.0	38.0	90.0	140.0	160.0	300.0
OneTouch	-		-		-	-	-	-	30.0	78.2	175.0
Total	1.7	3.3	4.4	12.3	26.5	38.1	73.2	130.9	221.8	299.9	531.3

Source: Frempong & Henten (2004)

Mobitel (now Buzz), Ghana's first mobile operator and 90 percent owned by Milicom International, launched the first prepaid service in Sub-Saharan Africa in 1998, which accounted for two thirds of its customers by 2002. The second mobile operator was CellTel, founded by a Ghanaian Company Kludjeson International, which later sold an 80 percent equity stake to Hong Kong-based Hutchison Wampoa, and was renamed as Kasapa. Inspired by these, ScanCom, a subsidiary of Luxemburg-based Investcom, entered the market. ScanCom estimated its potential customer base at 3,000 in 1996, but grew rapidly to become highly successful with 300,000 subscribers by 2003; the company was later sold off to Areeba (Frempong & Henten, 2004).

The mobile telephony resulted in a changing cost structure for Ghana Telecom. In 2005, 37 percent of its revenues and 90 percent of the cost of goods sold were comprised of the connectivity fees paid to the mobile operators, for the calls made from its networks to other mobile networks (myjoyonline, 2005c). Therefore, Ghana Telecom launched its own mobile phone service – OneTouch. It also sought to push the pre-paid system to mitigate its bad debts. Though OneTouch grew very rapidly with a capacity of 600,000 subscribers in 2005, Areeba maintained its lead, and under new ownership, Buzz became number 2.

For all mobile operators, landline operators controlled international connections via its congested submarine fiber cable; therefore, the international call quality of the mobile operators was very poor. Overall, the pace of growth of mobile telephony in Ghana until 2003 was below that of many other African nations like Kenya, Tanzania, and Uganda (Frempong & Henten, 2004). Thus, the basic telecom infrastructure capacity in Ghana was quite impoverished.

Second-level Servicing Capacity – Internet Connectors

Internet service providers. While the absorptive capacity of the telecom sector remained minimalist, the improvements in the telecom servicing capacity began to inspire new entrepreneurial leaders. National Computer Systems (NCS) was started by Dr. Nii Quaynor in 1988, using his own personal savings. Quaynor was a senior software engineering manager of Digital Equipment Corporation (DEC). In 1994, NCS allowed its subscribers to dial-in to its computers, and access the global Internet over a dial-up link to Pipex, the largest ISP in England. It thus became the first company in Sub-Saharan Africa to offer TCP/IP connectivity, including to the government and its agencies. Later in 1996, NCS used a PanAm satellite for establishing a connection to the global Internet backbone in the USA for more reliable service. NCS also hosted web pages for over 125 organizations in Ghana, mostly non-government organizations (Foster et al, 2004).

Ghana's second ISP, Internet Ghana was founded in 1996 by Electromod, a local computer company run by Leslie Tamakloe. It leased a line from Ghana Telecom for a dedicated connection with the MCI's Internet backbone in the USA. It focused primarily on the corporations, growing its corporate customer account from 20 in 1996, to 40 in 1998, 60 in 2000, and 84 in 2003. It pioneered the use of DSL in Ghana, and supported 150 subscribers on DSL by 2003, over existing phone lines by using a splitter. It used fiber optic backbone operated by Volta Communications, which supplied electricity to Ghana, to offer high speed Internet in many regional capitals of Ghana (Foster et. al, 2004).

Soon, one more ISP entered the market. Africa Online had been set up in Kenya by three MIT/Harvard-educated Kenyans. An operation in Ghana was started in 1996 by MIT-educated Ghanaian Mawuli Tse, using a leased line from Ghana Telecom to connect to the company's hub in Boston. Africa Online used VSAT to connect many of the regional capitals of Ghana. The emphasis of Africa Online was to rapidly build its absorptive capacity through funding support from Prodigy. However, after the dot com crash, it was forced to focus on premium-priced high quality service to fund its strategy, as the funding from Prodigy dried up. Its position was therefore relegated to 5th position in the Internet market (Foster et. al, 2004).

Ghana Telecom also made substantial investments in creating Internet infrastructure; however, it was unable to introduce an Internet service by 2003. Overall, by 2004, over 52 ISPs had been licensed with only about 23,000 dial up accounts because of a shortage of functioning dialup phone lines. Five companies accounted for about 22,000 dial up accounts, and 70 percent of about 1000 corporate leased line DSL accounts. These were: NCS, ITS, Internet Ghana, IDN, and Africa Online. Most corporate accounts were comprised of Internet cafes. Most users relied on these Internet cafes, and the total number of internet users in Ghana was estimated to be 500,000 in 2003. The cost for unlimited dialup Internet service declined from over US$100 a month to US$25 by 2003, after the government made access to ISP licenses automatic in 1999 (Foster et. al., 2004). These initiatives also attracted two companies offering satellite connections – Veristar and Intelset. These planned to integrate into the ISP market, as the competition between them was reducing the prices of global IP connectivity over satellite (Foster et. al, 2004).

In addition to weaknesses in organizational design and human capital training, a major challenge facing ISP entrepreneurs was the cost of capital, with interest rates at over 30 percent. Therefore, many ISPs accepted Voice over IP international calls over their international satellite connections, and some even terminated these international calls illegally on the local exchange network of Ghana Telecom. The government allowed such termination on the private networks of the ISPs, but a number of illegal ISPs had neither their own private networks nor leased lines from Ghana Telecom. Consequently, Ghana Telecom suffered a huge reduction in its revenues from incoming international calls by 2000 with the losses from the actions of 32 unlicensed and illegal VoIP operators in 2002 estimated at US$15 million (Coomson, 2003). These illegal ISPs, however, found it difficult to grow because Ghana Telecom took an aggressive stand and got many of them shut down and their owners imprisoned.

Those adopting a legal route took advantage of the fact that their international connections offered better and more reliable solutions for voice, data, as well as video, compared to the international network of Ghana Telecom. Therefore, most multinationals and diplomatic missions preferred to use the dedicated leased lines offered by these ISPs for their voice needs over the direct service offered by Ghana Telecom (Osiakwan & Foster, 2004).

Within Ghana, many of the regional capitals were linked through a combination of VSAT, wireless, and fiber optic connections. However, in most towns, the only way to access the Internet was through a long distance call to an ISP in one of the regional capitals served by the Internet. Moreover, the ISPs in Ghana were not connected through any Internet exchange. Only about 4 percent of total Internet traffic in Ghana was between ISPs in Ghana. Most Ghanaians accessed hosts outside Ghana, and sent emails to other users in Ghana using international servers primarily like Yahoo and Hotmail. The Ghana Indian Kofi Annan Center of Excellence planned to establish the Ghana Internet Exchange by 2005 (Foster et al, 2004).

Internet cafes. While the capacity of the ISPs was low, it was further hindered by an even lower capacity of the general users to benefit from the services of these ISPs. Therefore, many ISPs focused on offering Internet service to the Internet Cafes, the first of which was founded in 2001. By 2004, there were about 2,000 Internet Cafes, charging between 0.60

cents to US$1.20 per hour, although most of these were small (Foster et. al, 2004). The greatest entrepreneurial leadership in this domain was enacted by now the largest privately owned ICT company in Africa - BusyInternet, founded in Ghana by Mark Davies and his French partner Alex Rousselet in 2001. BusyInternet started with $1.7 million of funds, partly personal savings from an earlier venture of Davies in the UK, and partly from a local non-banking financial institution called Fidelity Group and Databank. BusyInternet was based on the model of the EasyEverything chain of Europe (Hale, 2003b).

BusyInternet's mega cybercafé centers, the first of which was in a 14,000 square foot building, included entertainment such as fashion shows, live music and movies, thus becoming a popular hang out place in the locale (Hale, 2003b). In addition to a one hundred computer public Internet access area, they included an incubator to provide start up Internet businesses with phone and high speed internet service. There was also a 60-seat learning center for workshops and seminars, equipped with video conferencing and web design classes. A $30,000 generator, a back up battery, and an $18,000 transformer protected BusyInternet against the frequent power outages and power surges in Ghana (Hale, 2003b). The BusyInternet, led by Eselle Akofio-Sowah, generated positive cash flows within four months of its opening. However, because of the high costs of the satellite link, the original plan to open two technology centers every year, including centers in other Sub-Saharan African nations, had to be put aside. Instead, the company partnered with local software house SOFT Tribe to develop a software product Limpopo to run accounting functions for African cybercafés. By 2003, the BusyInternet employed 90 people from across West Africa, with 1,800 customers paying US$1.20 an hour. Six out of the ten person management team were women (Phillips, 2002).

In a 2002 survey, about a fourth of the company's users reported e-mail as the preferred reason for Internet use and about 12 percent each identified search, research, education, and business as their preferred use. About 8 percent of users used it for music and for news. About half the users spent half of their Internet time on email. About half the users spent their time emailing primarily to family members (BusyInternet, 2002). BusyInternet included a vision for socio-economic servicing.

BusyInternet's incubator program, BusyIncubator, was headed by Lesley Dodoo, formerly of the Ghanaian Ministry of Finance. BusyIncubator was the first of its kind of small business incubation program in Sub-Saharan Africa. The program was started with a $300,000 grant from the World Bank and the Government of Japan's InfoDev (Information for Development) program (Phillips, 2002). BusyIncubator paired incubates with local businesses that provide a range of financial, technical, management and marketing support services. In its first thee years, BusyIncubator graduated five companies:

1. eShopAfrica.com: founded by Cordelia Slater-Nour in Ghana in 1999, to help promote African arts and crafts into global markets and to secure artisans adequate compensation that was reflective of their talents and the quality of their products. Products included hand-carved Ga coffins shaped like airplanes, shoes and howitzers, which were all designed to reflect the earthly interests of the recently deceased. Cordelia gave hope to numerous African artisans, by recognizing that, "... if you're an artisan in Africa your 'hand-made' thing won't command a high price... you'll be made to feel inferior... Perceptions and economics will force you to accept a low price for your work and you may not be able to feed your family. When they get sick you won't be able to afford medicine, and schools cost too much.... This is the scenario for traditional African artisans all over the continent and in this way centuries old skills are being lost." (Global Knowledge Partnership, 2003: 49).

2. Data Management International Inc. (www.dmi-inc.com), of Delaware, USA. In 2002, it employed 40 Ghanaians at $72 monthly, which was twice the per capita income and thrice the minimum wage, to process environmental fines for the City of New York for about US$500,000 revenues annually. The workers typed in data from computer images of scanned citations handed out, for example, to food vendors who smoked while serving. The transcribed information was returned within 48 hours with an error rate less than 1 percent (Worth, 2002).
3. Interface Technologies (www.interfaceghana.com): A US-based web and software development company that worked with the local offices and dealers of multinationals like Volkswagen to develop their local websites.
4. SOFT Internet Solutions (www.sis.gh): A subsidiary of SOFT, focused on web design and development for companies and organizations in Ghana. Its clients included Ghana Breweries Ltd., Integrated Tamale Fruit Company, Goldlink Tours, Nescafe, Nestle, and First Pharma Ghana.
5. Graphicolor (www.graphicolorghana.com). A Michigan-based company set up a print fulfillment operation in Ghana, which printed the electronic materials on demand from the US-based clients and shipped it to their customers.

In 2004, BusyIncubator launched an 18-month intensive program for incubation, and selected four companies from a pool of seventeen applicants (InfoDev, 2005). The participating companies received a minimum of US$45,000 in technical assistance, including assistance with ICT-based product design, marketing, branding, managerial skills, and technology requirements, low cost infrastructure and a conducive entrepreneurial environment, support for financing and networking opportunities, and access to legal and corporate advice. It encouraged the government to set up the Incubator Governing Council, and offered advice to the Ministry of Communications on setting up of the government's technology incubator at the Ghana Multimedia Centre. Its portfolio of incubates in 2005 included (InfoDev, 2005):

1. Childnet Electronic publishing Co.: interactive educational software development on CD-Roms in Ghana;
2. Event PmG: sells unique invitation cards for all occasions;
3. Top Up Business Services: sells integrated business services through a chain of outlets;
4. Runway 14: An international media firm comprised of animators, copywriters, designers, musicians, new media artists, programmers, television producers, video jockeys, and conceptual urban philosophers;
5. BusyLab: web-based software solutions developer for the Ghanaian market;
6. Cyterra Solutions: offering advanced web development, elearning, and database applications;
7. Ecoband Networks: the local agent/distributor of connectivity services for the ISPs;
8. African Learners Online: offers electronic books for individuals and organizations in collaboration with European and African content providers; and
9. Teledata: a distributor of mobile phones and phone cards.

Overall, BusyInternet became the model of Sub-Saharan African servicing, making a range of technology-focused services accessible to the general users as well as foreign and local firms seeking to establish ICT-enabled services in Ghana. It allowed the nation to dream big dreams, and generated aspirational capital for mobilizing the third level servicing capacity.

Third Level Servicing Capacity – Becoming the Bangalore of Africa

The success of Bangalore, first in software and later in BPO, is often credited to the absorptive capacity fostered by a diverse range of academic, research, and basic industry capabilities in the region, and the supporting institutional environment. Below we trace the process of the development of capacity in software and BPO in Ghana. It will become clear that absorptive capacity was not as important as servicing capacity in the development of software and BPO in Ghana.

Software sector. A few universities in Ghana started offering degrees in computer science, but these lacked computer labs and expert faculty. The private sector entrepreneurs took up the challenge. i2000 Ltd., founded in 1999, collaborated with NIIT of India to offer NIIT benchmarked software development and IT training in Ghana. Within a few years, NIIT became the largest training institute in Ghana, with three centers and a capacity to train 2,000 students annually, though its training was reported to be of mixed quality (Soderberg, Jensen, & Sintim-Misa, 2003). With the help of the government of India, the Ghana India Kofi Annan Centre of Excellence was also set up to develop academic and industry skills in ICT, which started producing graduates that could be absorbed into industry immediately as employees or employers (Osiakwan, 2004).

In the interim, entrepreneurial leadership created a few large local software business houses in Ghana. The largest was SOFT Tribe, founded by the UK-based Ghanaian, Hermann Hesse. Starting with only one computer that various software developers shared, SOFT adopted an industry by industry approach, designing software tailor-made for African situations. SOFT Tribe evolved a "shotgun business strategy," offering between 15 and 30 programs at any given time, including the best seller which was a payroll program called Akatua. This shotgun business strategy allowed the company to grow very rapidly (Zachary, 2005). SOFT Tribe also offered special software for micro-finance management (e-SuSu software), payroll, cybercafé billing and the Ndua system for the timber industry.

In Ghana, SOFT Tribe became the software system of choice, as compared to Microsoft. Its programs were small enough to work with the Intel 486- and even 386-based PCs available for as little as $100. The programs wrote frequently to disk, reducing the chances of losing data if power is lost, as it often was. To combat the rampant piracy, finished products had to be installed by a SOFT technician. The code was not open source like Linux, to prevent people from learning it and then using it for fraud (Zachary, 2005). The company formed partnerships in Nigeria, Gambia, Senegal, and Kenya, for expansion into the region. After growing to a staff of 70, the founder sold a 40 percent stake to private international investors. SOFT Tribe also formed an agreement with Infosys – India's largest software firm – for helping with the marketing and support for Infosys products in Ghana (Hale, 2003). Hesse himself became a revered role model and a savior not only in Ghana, but whole of Sub-Saharan Africa. Guido Sohne, for instance, left SOFT Tribe to launch his own business as an independent programmer in Ghana, and observed, "Many young code writers get their start at SOFT Tribe, learn the ropes, and then hone their skills" (Zachary, 2005).

Growth of servicing options in the software domain also had a positive impact on the domains where the need for absorbing know-how from overseas was more critical. In 2003, there were only about 400,000 computers in use in Ghana, a significant number of which were refurbished. Ghana had no personal computer manufacturing plants, yet a few companies assembled computers using imported parts, though they needed to tap software options to be viable. For example, Racom of the Czech Republic formed Arrow Network Systems to manufacture and market a low cost/low speed networking equipment, but also offered remote branch, point of sale, and telemetry applications (Arrow Networks, 2006).

BPO sector. Given the high costs and interconnectivity problems facing the ISPs in Ghana, the use of Internet by businesses was very limited. However, some entrepreneurial leaders leased private voice over IP networks and offered BPO services, thereby starting a revolution.

A model start-up operation was that of AQ Solutions, a US and Ghana-based firm that started its operations in 2000. The founder, Awo Qaison-Sackey, is the daughter of Ghana's former ambassador to the United Nations (1960's) and a US citizen. She wanted to help bring jobs to her native Ghana. She combined on-site project management in the US with a Ghana-based offshore software development model to deliver cost-effective, high quality solutions to client companies. The firm employed 6 people in the US and assigned them as on-site strategic account managers to each of its Connecticut-based clients including General Electric and Northeast Utilities. This account manager then liaised with the developers in Ghana. The firm consciously incorporated international project management and software development standards into a framework to ensure quality in every step of a client engagement. The Ghanaian managers were flown to the US to meet clients, and clients were allowed to phone the programmers in Ghana directly (Garigga, 2003). Its 30 employees in Ghana were paid an average of $2,400 annually, compared to the local market average of $1,200 annually. The firm planned to hire 500 employees in 2005, and to seek subcontracting jobs from larger Indian companies handling software development for American companies. Joseph Aivano, director of application development at Northeast Utilities, noted, "We picked it up to increase our investment in minority (owned) firms and to get a better understanding of offshore software development... AQ Solutions was more of a pilot test. The test was successful" (Garriga, 2003: www.ghanaweb.com).

The first and the most successful call centre was Affiliated Computer Services (ACS). ACS, a Texas-based Fortune 500 firm with Ghana operations, set up the centre in 2000 with 20 workers. It quickly grew to 1,000 workers within 18 months. The call centre had about 2,000 workers in 2005, earning an average of $2,400 annually plus health insurance, meals, and subsidized transport; and had built a new facility. The employees entered the data on hand-written doctor notes and health insurance claims for Aetna and United Healthcare, working in three 8-hour shifts. This information was then transmitted them back via a satellite link to the US (Thompson, 2002). The founder of the Ghana operation, Tom Blodgett, noted "People didn't believe we could carry this off... We made a bold move, and it worked." (Zachary, 2003: www.ghanaweb.com) Site manager Damon Larson noted. "We have a turnover rate below 3% and an absentee rate also below 3%." (Zachary, 2003: www.ghanaweb.com) The accuracy rate was 99.7 percent (Zachary, 2003). The success of ACS encouraged other companies to follow, of which two were notable:

1. Rising Data Solutions: a Maryland, USA-based firm which opened the first English-speaking call center in Sub-Saharan Africa in 2001. Initially, it focused on telemarketing of mobile phone plans for T-Mobile to US households, using voice over Internet protocol using 15 employees. Later, it landed another contract from Haier America, the appliance manufacturer. Rising Data Solutions implemented Skills-Based Routing to make certain contacts are directed to agents specifically trained to provide that service ensuring quality and efficiency. In addition, it expanded into business process outsourcing and business process reengineering, including medical billing. Sambou Makalou, CEO, noted that "Ghanaian temperament is more suited for customer care (because of patience) than for telemarketing, which requires a bit more aggressive approach." (Mainsah & Ikezi, 2004: 13) Karim Morsli, co-founder, added "We're about leveraging technology to help people on both sides of the ocean" (Slayter, 2004: E05).

2. Global Response Corp: a Florida, USA-based customer contact center and fulfillment services business which had a joint venture partnership with a Ghanaian entrepreneur. Global Response recruited several Ghanaian French and Spanish speaking workers, to service Canada, the US, and France. It planned to hire 2,500 employees by 2005 (Yarney, 2003).

Beyond BPO. As a result of these servicing initiatives, new players with stronger absorptive capacity are being attracted to Ghana. In 2005, Artspage International, an online portal for the sale of music that is linked to approximately 200 distributors, identified Ghana as the hub for its West African subsidiary Afrofile (Myjoyonline, 2005d). It negotiated a deal, whereby Nokia Africa offered US$500,000 dollars to promote Ghanaian music through concerts and training programs. The individual musicians and their publishers would enter their copyrighted works on the portal, which could then be downloaded by consumers for ring tones in their mobile phones. Thus, musicians would be connected with worldwide Internet Service Providers, phone service providers, media houses and entertainment centers, and would receive deserved royalties for the use of their works (Myjoyonline, 2005d).

Institutional support. The principled leadership and aspiration-building servicing by the companies like Busy Internet, AQ Solutions, and Affiliated Computer Services is also beginning to generate a notable change in the mindset of the institutions. In 1998, government of Ghana had laid a Vision 2020 with a science and technology policy aimed at, "lifting Ghana to a middle-income status by the year 2020 through the perpetuation of a science and technology culture at all levels of society, which is driven by the promotion of innovation and mastery of known and proven technologies, and their application in industry and other sectors of the economy." (Yawson, 2003: 3) However, little progress could be made on that front.

The new government, led by President John Kufuor in 2001, recognized that ICT-led value-added services could be the key to future development strategy. The government also planned to modernize and improve eGovernment applications for internal revenue service, immigration, payroll, and procurement. A pilot project called GCNet helped the Customs Department increase custom revenues by 40 percent annually, and cut processing time from 3 days to four hours at the Kotoka International Airport, and from up to two weeks to 2 days at the Tema port (Government of Ghana, 2005). The government of Ghana portal (Ghana.gov.gh) was launched to "provide across the board information to the public and elicit their feedback and suggestions toward the attainment of good governance". (Soderberg et al, 2003: 18)

In 2000, the US signed the African Growth and Opportunity Act to allow more than one thousand products, including such things as textiles, to be sold in the US without paying any tariffs. Given the perceptions of Africa as a 'dark continent' little results would have accrued. However, the entrepreneurial leaders in Ghana provided credibility for dreaming big dreams.

The first company to act was Network Knitwear Fabrics (NKF), which combined the power of free trade with the Internet to set up a sock-seaming factory in Ghana in March 2003. NKF was founded by the US-educated Prosper Adabla, in collaboration with a Ghanaian cotton businessman who formed a joint venture by approaching the third largest sock manufacturer in the US, the Southern Textile Exchange. The relocation of the factory to Ghana was estimated to save $12 million a year (Myjoyonline, 2003). The quality of the products was on par with the US manufacturing operation. The socks originated semi-processed and duty-free from the US factories and were closely coordinated over the Internet.

Within 2 years, NKF grew rapidly to employ 700 people, who knit, sew, seam, bleach, iron, shape, sort, package according to vendor, and then ship duty-free approximately 60,000 dozen socks per week to the United States. The workers were paid $700 annually and supervisors $2400. They produced 23 different brands, including Lee and Wrangler, producing $75m worth of socks per year. The firm made an initial investment of $700,000 from a Bank loan and was profitable (Saki-Addo, 2003).

Several other smaller Ghanaian companies also benefited. Linda Yaa Ampah, a clothes designer and entrepreneur, used email at the Internet café to connect with American customers. She employed 50 tailors to meet the orders worth $40,000 from Africans living in the US. 70 percent of her business was generated through email from the US. She held that "the internet is beautiful, easy and clear… I wouldn't have got nearly so far without it" (Hale, 2003b: newswww.bbc.net.uk).

As a member of the Economic Organization of West African States, Ghana has a dream to be the Gateway of Sub-Saharan Africa. In 2005, the United Nations made Ghana its biggest investment destination in Africa with direct support for the small and medium enterprises. More private and public sector initiatives, with multinational, bilateral, and multilateral support, are sustaining the entrepreneurial leadership in Ghana. Ghana Cyber Group, Inc., founded by Yaw Owusu, secured $10 million of funds from the United Nations and companies such as Oracle Corporation for an upscale technology park at the University of Science and Technology in Ghana. In collaboration with Columbia University and MIT, the park would be identifying, developing, and helping commercialize the early stage client companies through incubation, and for brokering contracts with buyers of outsourcing services in the US. It will include a digital lab for research and development and a two-hundred PC cybercafé.

> *Many other US companies have also committed developmental funds for IT infrastructure in Ghana. Google committed to $1 billion for developmental projects at Technoserve in Ghana in October 2005. In the same month, General Electric donated $4 million of medical equipment, as part of its $20 million GE Africa Product Donation Program, to Ghana's Komfo Anokye Teaching Hospital (KATH). The donation allowed KATH to become the first hospital in Africa to start tele and e-medicine serving many nations in Sub-Saharan Africa (Myjoyonline, 2005b).*

The government of Ghana also sought technical assistance from India, offering Ghana as a cost-effective and quality subcontractor for the Indian companies doing business with the US. It asked for the funds to pilot technology to create an efficient telecom infrastructure for rural areas in Ghana, in addition to the support for building a comprehensive Information Technology Park and related infrastructure for software development, training of software professionals, assistance with technology analysis and marketing, and design of necessary legislative guidelines.

As Ghana sought to develop into the BPO center of Africa, it has also attracted several non-Ghanaian Africans seeking to use its growing reputation and technological capabilities for fraudulent activities. In fact, some have described Ghana as "the rising star of Internet fraud", and in early 2005, the nation was banned from using credit cards to shop via the Internet after over $5 million of online fraud was detected to have been generated from the country. In response, Internet cafes in Ghana, including even the small ones, have instituted several measures to check the level of fraud and to restore the image of the nation (Myjoyonline, 2005a).

DISCUSSION & CONCLUSIONS

The case of Ghana, and its pioneering technological firms, provides invaluable lessons on how to develop technological capability for servicing global customers from a condition of competitive deficiency. This paper traces the process by which the development of technological capability in Ghana got managed by various actors and the inter-play of market forces. This case shows that in the stages of development, absorptive capacity was not as important as the development of servicing capacity. This is especially important to many nations in Sub-Saharan Africa, who have little to offer in the way of infrastructure and hope to build themselves into BPOs. The evidence of technological development in Ghana points to the critical role played by a number of pioneers, many of them native Ghanaians who had emigrated overseas, particularly to the US, and who brought their technological, organizational, entrepreneurial, networking, and global cultural experience to Ghana. These entrepreneurs built aspirational capital in Ghana.

In addition, institutional support was offered by several national governments. Many companies in the US, Europe, and Asia brought to Ghana big dreams and converted these dreams into reality by offering various infrastructure, technological, and subcontracting options. The multilateral institutions, such as the United Nations, worked closely with the government of Ghana to promote a mindset change, oriented towards private sector development and enabling institutional policies.

Despite the challenges associated with the fraudulent activities of some, the result has been a unique hybrid of profit-oriented business orientation and social-oriented community orientation, or what has been termed as "principled leadership". In addition to the unique influence of international and national principled leadership in many parts of Ghana, we also see the emergence of a nascent form of regional clustering. This regional clustering goes beyond the network of competing firms, innovative supporting and related firms, sophisticated customers, and advanced factor endowments, as in the Porter's (1990) diamond model of national competitive advantage.

For most firms, a number of these factors, and several elements in these factors, are lacking in Ghana. The evolving regional clustering is also different from the neo-diamond models, where the firms in a nation could outsource some of the diamond factors, such as by taking advantage of the rivalry among firms in other nations, of the collaboration with international channel partners, and of the demanding customers and large demand scale overseas. In most cases, the foreign customers of Ghanaian firms begin with very low expectations of servicing capability – generally out of a benevolent act of generosity or a heroic symbol of passion for Africa. Similarly, the international channel partners have little strategic interest in Ghana, which remains a very small market because of its limited purchasing power – which, on per capita basis at US$300, was the same in 2003 as in 1960. In addition, it would be a mistake to attribute the increasing foreign direct investments in Ghana to primarily an outgrowth of intense rivalry among firms in other nations. The global rivalry pressurizes the firms to search for sites where very large-scale operations could be established for servicing customers on a worldwide basis. Ghana, with its limited servicing scale, did not qualify by any measure.

Our analysis suggests a need to re-evaluate the traditional interpretations of technological capability. Servicing capacity model, as articulated here, shifts the research lens away from a deficit view of emerging communities as places full of absorptive capacity disadvantages, and instead focuses and learns from the array of cultural knowledge, skills, abilities, and contacts possessed by internationally marginalized groups that often go unrecognized and unacknowledged (Yosso, 2005). Using a Critical Race Theory lens, Yosso (2005) emphasizes how in marginalized groups, such as communities of color, various forms of capital are nurtured through community cultural wealth via inter-related processes.

The model of aspirational servicing articulated here provides a systematic approach for mobilizing the community cultural capital and for converting the aspirations into reality. In addition, one must acknowledge that aspirations can degenerate into fraud and unlawful activities, when they are deprived, rather than enabled and realized. Therefore, aspirational servicing itself is a necessary, but not sufficient condition for development. One also needs principled leadership, which is committed to offering the connections in the form of access to market – both for services, as well as for training and resources, and then mobilizing the aspirational servicing to tap, and even enhance, this market.

In summary, we conclude that the nascent technological clustering in Ghana has germinated from a distinctive model of aspirational servicing, which combines a confidence in the basic human potential even in most deficient contexts with a prudently crafted servicing capacity, which would help germinate the foundations known to be the key to the national competitive advantage.

A major limitation of our work is the use of a single nation case study. It would be desirable to conduct comparative cross-national work and to conduct statistical analysis. Despite these limitations, the case of Ghana as analyzed here does offer a ray of hope to the people of Sub-Saharan Africa, and to other nations that have limited capacities to absorb the increasingly sophisticated, specialized, and costly global know-how.

REFERENCES:

Arrow Networks 2006. www.arrownetworks.net/company_profile.html, accessed April 2, 2006.

Bell, R.M. & Pavitt, K.L.R. 1993. Technological accumulation and industrial growth: contrasts between developed and developing countries. *Industrial and Corporate Change*, 2(2): 163-210.

Bennett, A. & George, A. 2001. Case Study methods and political science: similar strokes for different foci. In C. Elman and M.F. Alman (Eds.), *Bridges and Boundaries: Historians, Political Scientists, and the Study of International Relations*, MIT Press, Boston, MA.

Bigsten, A., Collier, P., Dercon, S., Fafchamps, M., Gauthier, B., Gunning, J.W., Isaksson, A., Oduro, A., Oostendorp, R., Pattillo, C., Soderbom, M., Teal, F. & Zeufack, A. 1998. *Rates of return on physical and human capital in Africa's manufacturing sector.* Working Paper, Centre for the Study of African Economies, University of Oxford.

Botwe, D. 2005. Telenor option justified – Botwe. http://www.myjoyonline.com, accessed 2 April 2006.

BusyInternet 2002. Survey on Why People Use the Internet. *Busy Internet Publications.* www.busyinternet.com, accessed 2 April 2006.

Cohen, W. M. & Levinthal, D. A. 1990. Absorptive Capacity: A New Perspective on Learning and Innovation. *Administrative Science Quarterly*, 35:128-152.

Coomson, J. 2003. 32 ISPs caught in NCA dragnet. *The Ghanaian Chronicle.* http://www.ghanaian-chronicle.com, accessed 2 April 2006.

De Vynck 2004. Telecoms liberalization will boost call centers. Business Report. http://www.busrep.co.za, accessed 2 April 2006.

Docquier, F., & Rapoport, H. 2004. *Skilled Migration: The Perspective of Developing Countries*. Policy Research Working Paper 08/001, Washington, D.C., The World Bank.

Falch, M. & Anyimadu, A. 2003. Tele-centres as a way of achieving universal service – the case of Ghana. *Telecommunications Policy*, 27: 21-39.
Frempong, G. & Henten, A. 2004. *Telecom developments and investments in Ghana*. Discussion Paper, World Dialogue on Regulation for Networked Economies. http://www.regulateonline.org, accessed 2 April 2006.
Garriga, M. 2003. New Haven software company's workers live in Ghana. *New Haven Register*. www.nhregister.com, accessed 2 April 2006.
Global Knowledge Partnership 2004. *ICT Success Stories in Development*. Kuala Lumpur, Malaysia: Global Knowledge Partnership.
Government of Ghana 2005. *E-Ghana Project*. Project Information Document, Ministry of Communications.
Gupta, V. & Wang J. 2004. From Corporate Crisis to turnaround in East Asia: A Study of China Huajing Electronics Group Corporation. *Asia Pacific Journal of Management*, 21: 213-233.
Hale, B. 2003a. Ghana Trumps Mighty Microsoft. *BBC News*. http://news.bbc.co.uk, accessed 2 April 2006.
Hale, B. 2003b. Dot.com tycoon turns to Africa. *BBC News*. http://news.bbc.co.uk, accessed 2 April 2006.
Ifinedo, P. 2005. Measuring Africa's e-readiness in the global networked economy: A nine country data analysis. *International Journal of Education and Development using ICT*, 11. ijedict.dec.uwi.edu, accessed 2 April 2006.
InfoDev 2005. Busy Internet – Ghana. *The info Dev Global Network of Business Incubators*. http://www.infodev.org, accessed 2 April 2006.
Mahoney, R., Lee, K., & Yun, M. 2005. Intellectual Property, Drug Regulation, and Building Product Innovation Capability in Biotechnology: The Case of Hepatitis B Vaccine in Korea. *Innovation Strategy Today*, 1(2): 33-44.
Mainseh, M & Ikezi, E. 2004. Is Ghana an Attractive Proposition for IT Services and Business Process Outsourcing? *Chazen Web Journal of International Business*. http://www.gsb.columbia.edu/chazenjournal, accessed 2 April 2006.
Ministry of Communications 2004. Draft, Committee on World Summit on Information Society. Ghana, Ministry of Communications.
Myjoyonline 2003. Multi-million Cedi Socks Factory Inaugurated. http://www.myjoyonline.com, accessed 2 April 2006.
Myjoyonline 2005a. Internet Service Providers Call on Govt to Reverse Ban. www.myjoyonline.com, Accessed April 2, 2006.
Myjoyonline 2005b. KATH goes hi-tech with tele and e-medicine. http://www.myjoyonline.com, accessed 2 April 2006.
Myjoyonline 2005c. GT threatens legal action to recover 400 billion cedis debt. http://www.myjoyonline.com, accessed 2 April 2006.
Myjoyonline 2005d Nokia to use Ghanaian music as ring tones. http://www.myjoyonline.com, accessed 2 April 2006.
Osiakwan, E.M.K. 2004. *Access to Computers and Communication networks in Ghana*. Paper presented at 2nd International Wide Open Access Workshop in Sweden, May 11. Accra, Internet Research.
Osiakwan, E.M.K. & Foster, W. 2004. *Negotiating the 'Net: The Case of Ghana*. Working Paper, Centre for International Development & Conflict Management.
Phillips, M.M. 2002. On Ghana's Tech Frontier, Internet Start up Flourishes. The Wall Street Journal. http://www.wsj.com, accessed 2 April 2006.

Saki-Addo, K. 2003. US Socks Made in Africa. BBC News. http://news.bbc.co.uk, Accessed April 2, 2006.
Slayter, M.E. 2004. Company takes outsourcing to new level in Ghana. *Washington Post*, E05.
Soderberg, B., Jensen, M. & Sintim-Misa, M.A. 2003. *Investment Opportunities in Western Africa ICT and Internet Sectors – Ghana*. Stockholm, Spintrack IT Advice AB.
Thompson, N. 2002. Rising with Keyboards. Newsweek International. http://www.newamerica.net, accessed 2 April 2006.
UNCTAD 2003. *Africa's Technology Gap: Case Studies on Kenya, Ghana, Uganda, and Tanzania.* New York, UNCTAD.
Verner, D. 1999. *Wage and Productivity Gaps: Evidence from Ghana*. Policy Research Working Paper Series 2168, Washington DC, The World Bank.
William F., Goodman S., Osiakwan E., & Bernstein, A. 2004. Global Diffusion of the Internet IV: The Internet in Ghana. *Communications of the AIS*, 13, article 38.
World Bank 2006. BPO Center of Africa - Ghana among preferred countries for offshore services. Quoted by Martin Walker, UPI Editor. http://www.upi.com, accessed 2 April 2006.
World Fact Book 2006. Ghana. http://www.cia.gov/cia/publications/factbook/geos/gh.html, accessed 2 April 2006.
Worth R.F. 2002. In New York Tickets, Ghana Sees Orderly City. *The New York Times*. http://www.nytimes.com, accessed April 2, 2006.
Yarney, J. 2003. Ghana Jumps into BPO. IDG News Service. http://www.idgnews.net, accessed 2 April 2006.
Yawson, R. 2003. *Management of Technology in Ghana: Problems and Prospects*. Working Paper, CSIR-Food Research Institute, Accra.
Yosso, T.J. 2005. Whose Culture Has Capital? A Critical Race Theory Discussion of Community Cultural Wealth. *Race Ethnicity and Education*, 8(1): 69-91.
Zachary, G. P. 2003. Dialing for Dollars: How Ghana is learning to cash in on data services. Fortune. http://www.cnn.com/fortune, accessed 2 April 2006.
Zachary, G. P. 2005. The African Hacker. http://www.ghanaweb.com/GhanaHomePage/NewsArchive/artikel.php?ID=87421, accessed 2 April 2006.

A CHAOS/COMPLEXITY THEORY APPROACH TO MARKETING IN THE TURBULENT SOUTH AFRICAN BUSINESS ENVIRONMENT

ROGER MASON
Durban University of Technology
Department of Marketing
South Africa
and
University of Wolverhampton
Honorary Research Fellow
U.K.
P.O. Box 1334
Durban, 4000
South Africa
Tel: +27 31 373 5385
Fax: +27 31 373 5480
e-mail: rogerm@dut.ac.za

Abstract

This paper is based on the thesis that the choice of marketing tactics is determined by the nature of the company's external environment. Examining this from the perspective of chaos and complexity theories, the literature indicates that in complex, turbulent environments, destabilising marketing activities are more effective, whereas stabilising type activities are more effective in simple, stable environments, and therefore companies that use predominantly destabilising type tactics are more likely to be successful. The study was exploratory, using qualitative depth interviews with two companies in the complex and turbulent information technology (IT) industry. The results tentatively confirmed that the more successful company tended to use more destabilising marketing tactics, and suggest that using chaos and complexity theory as a guide to the development of marketing tactics could be very helpful in turbulent business environments as are experienced in Africa.

Keywords: Marketing, turbulence, business environment, South Africa, chaos theory, complexity theory.

INTRODUCTION

Marketing involves being able to anticipate, cope with and adapt to changes in the external environment. In a stable and predictable business environment this coping and adapting is relatively easy, but as the environment becomes more complex, and changes happen more rapidly, coping becomes more problematic and difficult. The global environment of business is becoming extremely complex and has been experiencing continuous, rapid change (Chattell, 1995; Ahmed, Hardaker & Carpenter, 1996; Narus & Anderson, 1996; Gilmore & Pine, 1997; Doherty & Delener, 2001). This escalating rate of change is probably being experienced in South Africa to a greater degree than in most other countries (Nasser & Vivier, 1995; Puth, 1996).

Traditional methods such as strategic planning, scenario planning, strategic visioning, market research and forecasting are becoming inadequate to cope with the speed and volume of continuous change and with the unpredictability of discontinuous change (Wall & Wall, 1995; Lane & Maxfield, 1996; Edgar & Nisbet, 1996). Understanding and finding new ways of coping with such continuous and unpredictable changes has become necessary. One way of finding new methods of coping with this volatility is by applying theories from outside the field of marketing in order to obtain fresh insight into the problem (Coffey & Atkinson, 1996). An ever-increasing number of authors believe that the new sciences, specifically chaos and complexity theories, can provide a better understanding of the current environment. This is because such environments can be viewed as complex adaptive systems (Black & Farias, 1997; Peters, 1999; Tedesco, 1998; Prendergast & Berthon, 2000; Doherty & Delener, 2001). It is therefore possible that these theories can cast new light on management and marketing problems (Dolan, Garcia & Auerbach, 2003). Some work has been done internationally in applying these theories to strategic planning, but little research has been done in applying them to marketing tactics (Holbrook, 2003), and even less research on their use in Africa.

The emphasis of this research is to identify which of the marketing mix elements are most effective in coping with complexity and turbulence, such that the probability of marketing success is increased. This paper reports on an exploratory study of a highly complex and turbulent industry, namely Information Technology, in order to identify the marketing mix variables used, and to assess whether the extent of use of these variables can be associated with success in the industry.

South Africa as a turbulent/complex environment

The lifestyles, values and expectations of South African society have changed perceptibly in the past twenty years (Van der Walt, Strydom, Marx & Jooste, 1996). Burgess (1998) maintained that the Indian Ocean Rim area was changing rapidly, with the competitive environment of this region increasing in turbulence. Many authors have shown South Africa as having a complex, turbulent and changing external environment, even before the demise of apartheid (Nasser & Vivier, 1993; Morris & Schurink, 1993; Morris, Marks, Allen, Peery & Newman, 1996; Joubert, 1998). Such complexity and turbulence exists in all seven components of the external environment in South Africa:

Legal The withdrawal of sanctions against South Africa resulted in export markets being opened up and the rewriting of legislation to suit the new South Africa (Terblanche, 1998). Laws have been passed on unfair competition, consumer protection, gender equality, sexual offences, human rights, discrimination, employment equity, access to information and labour relations (**SA 2000: South Africa at a Glance, 1999**; Lamb, Hair, McDaniel, Boschoff & Terblanche, 2000; **South African Yearbook 2001/02, 2002**).

Environment (physical) Despite the growth of the green movement and efforts towards improving the physical environment, rapid industrialisation, population growth and urbanisation pose a serious threat to South Africa's physical environment, with air, water and marine pollution and land erosion being particular problems (**South African Yearbook 2001/02, 2002**). As a result, more pressure is being placed on businesses in terms of pollution control, waste management, recycling, and environmental impact assessments (Lamb et al., 2000).

Political In the political arena the South African environment has experienced a new Constitution, a change in governing party after 46 years, new parliamentary structures and an increased democratisation of government (**SA 2000: South Africa at a Glance, 1999**). The political transformation is not complete, which implies further changes resulting in associated impacts on the economy and organisations. Continuing aggressive privatisation could have a further significant impact (Van der Walt et al., 1996; **South African Yearbook 2001/02, 2002**).

Economic The South African economy has changed from a long-term, predictable, slow decline (du Plessis, Rousseau & Blem, 1994), to uncertainty as to what the future trend will be, indicated by the 30% devaluation of the Rand (**SA 2000: South Africa at a Glance, 1999**), to current relatively high growth levels. Important features of this turbulence are the uneven, but changing, distribution and expenditure of personal income, the influx of foreign immigrants from neighbouring states and the unpredictability of the inflation rate (Van der Walt et al., 1996).

Socio-cultural The South African population is complex in its composition and changing in its socio-cultural make up (Cronje, du Toit & Motlatla, 2000). The total population is declining. Traditional African cultures are breaking down (Morris, 1992), with emphasis on South African and urban first and ethnic group second, resulting in increasing Westernisation and rapid urbanisation. Further affecting these changes is the unpredictable impact of HIV/Aids (du Plessis et al., 1994), the millions of foreigners living legally and illegally in South Africa (Ministry of Welfare and Population Development, 1997), the changing role of women (Cronje et al. 2000: 85), the growth in white-collar jobs (Ministry of Welfare and Population Development, 1997), increasing crime (Peron, 1999; **SA 2000: South Africa at a Glance, 1999**), smaller and more non-traditional families (Ministry of Welfare and Population Development, 1997), and increasing levels of education (Cronje et al., 2000), but with an associated 'brain drain' (Peron, 1995).

Technology The emphasis in technological development in post-apartheid South Africa has been diverted from energy generation and military development to social and economic problems, namely, competitiveness, quality of life, environmental sustainability and information technology for improving society and the economy (**South African Yearbook 2001/02, 2002**). An example of such improvements includes Eskom electrifying 1.44 million houses between 1994 and 2000 (Lamb et al., 2000).

Competition Developing countries provide global corporations with large opportunities, so the deregulation and globalisation of the past few years has meant that South African companies face increasing competition from global corporations - more aggressive competitors chasing fewer customers (Manning, 1998: 24). Increased competition has been encouraged by new laws that outlaw restrictive business practices (**South African Yearbook 2001/02, 2002**) and have increased foreign participation in the South African market. Competition from new sources has also increased, for example convenience stores at petrol stations grew by 25% per year (Terblanche, 1998), 'spaza' or home shops account for 25% of retail sales (Lamb et al., 2000) and the franchise industry grew by 36% between 1995 and 1996 (even before the entry of major international franchisors).

Clearly the nature of the external environment is changing significantly, and it is questionable whether South African firms have the level of competitive strength to cope with this increased environmental complexity and turbulence. Many authors feel that in such "chaotic" environments, traditional management and marketing approaches are inappropriate, and that new methods informed by the new sciences of chaos theory and complexity theory are required (Stacey, 1996;.Brown & Eisenhardt, 1998; Briggs & Peat, 1999; Kelly & Allison, 1999; Koch, 2000).

Chaos/complexity theory

A collection of theories makes up the body of knowledge known as complexity and chaos theory (Boisot, 1999). The underlying idea "is that all things tend to self organise into systems" (Kelly & Allison, 1999: 5). These systems develop patterns that are created when a number of simple rules are applied over many iterations. Small differences at the start of the process can eventually result in large differences in the system's performance. Many interactions in a system can produce unexpected patterns or behaviours (Goldberg & Markoczy, 1998) because stimulating one part of the system can have unexpected effects in other, unanticipated, parts of the system. Such unexpectedness is because of the nature of non-linear feedback networks (Stacey, 1996), the interconnected and interdependent nature of complex systems (Bar-Yam, 2000) and the fact that the system's parts interact and adapt to each other (Meade & Rabelo, 2004). Complex behaviour is orderly, yet full of surprise. In other words, despite apparent uncontrollability, the system is not totally chaotic. The rules that generate this behaviour are part of the system, are not enforced by a single agent, or manager, and cannot be predicted from examining any single part of the system. The system spontaneously self-organises as the various decentralised parts of the system interact. This emergence of adaptive behaviour happens at the edge-of-chaos where there is enough stability to sustain existence, but enough turbulence for creativity to overcome inertia (Waldrop, 1992). Although the behaviour of complex adaptive systems cannot be predicted, it can be influenced by encouraging mutually beneficial relationships between members of the system (Baskin, 1998).

Several chaos and complexity concepts have relevance to business. The central concept is **self-organization**, the process of a pattern of order emerging from a set of simple rules in an interconnected network. The process is not controlled through conscious awareness by an outside 'manager', but spontaneously self-organises from the bottom up through the inter-relationships of the system's parts (Holbrook, 2003). As a result, individual managers cannot predict and plan longer-term outcomes (Wilkinson & Young, 1998; Frederick, 1998; Kelly & Allison, 1999), but by fine-tuning the simple rules that determine the system, it can be moved between stability and chaos (Lewin, 1993). This continuous self-organisation allows and encourages a variety of creative and innovative responses to emerge from changing environments (Dolan et al. 2003).

This **emergence** is the second important concept of complexity theory. It happens when the system's parameters change, leading to a movement towards disorder – important because too much order causes the system to become ossified. The implication is that to cope with change the system should be kept at the edge-of-chaos, where innovation enables it to reorganise itself into new patterns of relationships and from these new patterns, new actions emerge (Merry, 1998), resulting in new order 'for free' (Holbrook, 2003). Examples include new strategies (Conner, 1998), marketing tactics for specific prospects (Forrest & Mizerski, 1996), self-directed teams (Gault & Jaccaci, 1996) and strategic alliances (Wilkinson & Young, 1998).

The third important concept is **feedback**. Negative feedback damps changes, pushing the system back to its original state and producing regular, predictable behaviour - stability (Stacey, 1995; Thietart & Forgues, 1995; Glass, 1996). On the other hand, positive feedback amplifies many small changes (McGlone & Ramsey, 1998), pushing the system away from equilibrium at an escalating rate (Oliver & Roos, 2000), leading to explosive instability, or chaos, in the form of a turbulent market (Doherty & Delener, 2001). Together, positive and negative feedback act as countervailing forces, pushing the system towards instability and at the same time damping changes to increase stability, thereby balancing at the 'edge-of-chaos'

(Thietart & Forgues, 1995), the best position for a company in a turbulent market (Doherty & Delener, 2001). Positive feedback enables a firm with an early small advantage to enjoy exponential growth until the advantage is so great that the advantage becomes 'locked in', and becomes an industry standard, as happened with VHS video recorders and Microsoft Windows (Holbrook, 2003). Positive feedback has been shown in customer defections (Rasmussen & Mosekilde, 1988), product development (Millier, 1999), mass customisation (Saisse & Wilding, 1997) and advertising (Stacey, 1992; Glass, 1996).

The fourth important concept is **sensitive dependence on initial conditions** (Phillips & Kim, 1996; Briggs & Peat, 1999). In a stable system, small changes have small effects, but in a complex adaptive system small changes or errors can grow exponentially with each iteration, until no prediction accuracy is possible (Diamond, 1993; Doherty & Delener, 2001; Holbrook, 2003). An infinite amount of precise data would be required to produce accurate long-term predictions (Mix, 1993). However, many authors suggest ways of using the concept to cope in turbulent environments. Using small nudges to guide an event, rather than dramatic actions to control it are suggested (Gibson, 1996; Wheatley, 1996). Traditionally a small change would be ignored in business. However, the right kind of 'nudge' at the correct time (the initial condition) can lead, through positive feedback, to major changes (Nilson, 1995). Being a 'first mover' is essential because sensitive dependence on initial conditions and positive feedback create a 'flywheel **affect**' that reinforces early success, providing a significant advantage over the long-term (Hamel, 2000; Koch, 2000). To be a successful first mover, a company must recognise the patterns and spot the environmental clues that indicate which small changes to 'nudge' (Morrison & Quella, 1999) and when to nudge them, the 'tipping point' (Gladwell, 2000). Such companies are able to influence environmental changes in ways that are favourable to themselves, but unfavourable for their competitors.

Complex adaptive systems have an underlying order or structure (Thietart & Forgues, 1995). Within the apparent randomness of a chaos system, patterns can be found by geometrically mapping the data.

These patterns are known as **attractors**, the fifth important complexity concept. The edge-of-chaos attractor, known as a 'strange attractor', reflects the area where maximum creativity and innovation happens (Herbig, 1990; Lewin, 1992). This transition between order and chaos is the point at which sensitive dependence on initial conditions causes small inputs to cause big changes. A unique feature of the strange attractor is that it has a coherent pattern and always stays within certain boundaries (Holbrook, 2003). Behaviour is never identical within these boundaries, but is broadly predictable. Nilson (1995) refers to this as non-repetitive repetitiveness. Exactly where the system will go next cannot be predicted, but it will not go outside certain limits (Doherty & Delener, 2001). In other words, the strange attractor allows change while maintaining some order. This bounded stability allows the system to continually adapt, coming close to the edge of chaos where creativity and innovation occur, but pulling it back from plunging over the edge into the disorder and chaos that signify failure (Frederick, 1998). Strange attractors in business could include corporate vision and values (Frederick, 1998; Bates, 1999), market entry and development activities (Black & Farias, 1998) and customer relationship management (Kurtyka, 2000). Strange attractors have also been shown mathematically or via simulations in customer behaviour (Herbig & Golden, 1991), inventory levels (Rasmussen & Mosekilde, 1988), and advertising (Feichtinger, Hommes & Milik, 1994).

Management and strategy in a complex and turbulent environment

Most managers have been brought up in, and trained for, an environment of certainty, whereas they now have to cope with increased complexity, uncertainty and turbulence. The traditional authoritarian, control-oriented management style, when applied in an uncertain environment, can lead to destabilisation of relationships and behaviours, and also to unanticipated behaviours and possible explosive instability (McElwee, 1998; Dolan et al., 2003). There is general agreement amongst chaos and complexity authors that traditional strategy making is ineffective in turbulent environments. Traditional strategy making is not innovative, creative or original, but leads to strategic rigidity (Nilson, 1995; Edgar & Nisbet, 1995; Brown & Eisenhardt, 1998 and Roos, 1999). Strategic success formulae become rapidly obsolete and inappropriate in volatile markets (Conner; 1998; Dohert & Delener, 2001), and competitors make strategies irrelevant by rewriting the rules of the game (Fradette & Michaud; 1998). This ineffectiveness of traditional strategic planning is partly due to the inability to predict in turbulent environments that are near the edge-of-chaos (New Marketing Imperatives Roundtable, 1994; Kurtyka, 2000). This is because the system in which a company operates is continually being subjected to discontinuities, is continually changing, and therefore managers have to continually obtain new information to understand the environment. Any plan is therefore obsolete before it has been fully implemented, and staff that would be expected to cope with the environmental shocks would be restricted by a detailed, prescriptive plan (Glass, 1996). Therefore, strategy making is being done in different ways, such as involving more people in the process, delegating it to those closest to the customers, using cross-functional teams to develop strategies, and generally making strategy everyone's responsibility. Strategy has become a trial-and-error process, evolving through the discovery of what works. As a result planning cycles are shorter, and because quick responses are required, tactics often dictate strategy. Strategy making should be a spontaneous, flexible, reactive, self-organising, learning process (Stacey, 1992; Sengupta, Unadkat & Jain, 2000; Doherty & Delener, 2001).

A complexity/chaos strategic framework for coping with turbulence suggests that a firm must produce chaos through repeat innovation (Chakravarthy, 1997). This can be achieved through ‘adaptive innovation’ at the edge of chaos (Brown & Eisenhardt, 1998). This means balancing between the two attractors of too much structure and too much chaos, which requires lots of experimentation and different competitive moves, to destabilise the market and push it to the edge of chaos, but with sufficient structure (priorities, deadlines and responsibilities) that change does not tip over into total randomness. Some degree of chaos is necessary in a business because in a knowledge-based industry (such as information technology) competencies are often not imitated but side-stepped by competitors, so it is essential to innovate continuously to the extent of making one's own products obsolete and replacing them before a competitor does (Loewen, 1997), which equates to Schumpeter's ‘creative destruction’ (McKelvey, 2004). Clearly, therefore, strategy making in a turbulent environment requires not only coping with chaos but encouraging it in the environment.

Chaos/complexity theory applied to marketing

Although relatively few authors have related chaos and complexity theory to marketing activities, the body of literature is growing. Chaos and complexity theories have been shown to be applicable in supply chains (Rasmussen & Moskilde, 1988; Priesmeyer, 1992), promotions (Forrest & Mizerski, 1996; Paladini, 1999), selling (Herbig & Golden, 1991; Priesmeyer, 1992; Forrest & Mizerski, 1996), advertising (Herbig, 1990; Feichtinger, Hommes & Milik, 1994; Dru, 1996), sales promotion (Priesmeyer, 1992), word-of-mouth (Herbig, 1990), pricing (Priesmeyer & Baik, 1989; Hibbert & Wilkinson, 1994; Smith, Sinha, Lancioni & Forman, 1999; Oda, Miura, Ueda & Baba, 2000), product development (Priesmeyer, 1992; Phillips & Kim, 1996; Millier, 1999; Kopel, 1996), product life cycle (Meade & Rabelo, 2004), brand management (Marks, Midgley, Cooper & Shiraz, 1998), market segmentation (Meade & Rabelo, 2004), market research (Diamond, 1993; Casti, 1999), and consumer behaviour (Benhabib & Day, 1981; Samli, 1993; Farrell, 1998).

A consistent theme that runs through most of this work is the categorisation of the marketing tactics into stabilising or destabilising activities. Stabilising activities encourage the marketing system to behave within boundaries, reducing the rate of change by encouraging negative feedback which brings the system back towards its equilibrium point, or to within its attractor boundaries. It is what Hibbert and Wilkinson (1994) refer to as 'damping change.' In stable environments, stabilising leads to better performance, while in turbulent environments it produces worse performance. Stabilising activities are advantageous in stable environments, but dangerous in turbulent environments (Thomas, **1996**, in D'Aveni, 1999).

Destabilising activities, on the other hand, cause unanticipated consequences that break the system boundaries (McGlone & Ramsey, 1998). They disrupt a 'stable' environment, reinforcing or increasing change in a particular direction by encouraging positive feedback, also known as 'the nudge' or 'butterfly effect,' thereby moving the system away from the status quo (Nilson, 1995). Thus, destabilisation can be either small, seemingly insignificant, actions that influence the environment (i.e. sensitive dependence on initial conditions), or large dramatic actions that cause dramatic shifts in the environment. These destabilising actions provide a shock to the system that permanently alters the market position - in chaos terms a change in phase state. However, it must be remembered that the outcome is uncertain, but Garcia (2004) stresses that such risk-taking leads to greater marketing competencies and innovation in turbulent environments, especially when related to product development.

Nilson (1995) believes there are two ways of managing chaos in a marketing environment: focus on tactics that stabilise the system (distribution, communications, including advertising and personal selling) or change the marketing environment by creating dynamic chaos through rapid change in marketing mix areas other than distribution. Support for the latter approach is provided by Young and Kiel (1997) who maintain that only 'chaos can handle a chaos system,' by Kashani (1995) and Mavondo (1999) who found product innovation to be important in a turbulent environment, by Hibbert and Wilkinson (1994) who found it advantageous to change the 'rules of the game', by Millier (1999) who found successful companies experienced chaos, by Addison (2000) who suggests destabilising the relationship between competitors and their customers and by Doherty and Delener (2001) who stress the importance of product range diversification. Furthermore, Mavondo (1999) found destabilising tactics to be preferable as they developed heterogeneous approaches, rather than homogeneous, 'me too' type tactics.

Nilson's (1995) stabilising approach is supported by Morris, Hansen and Pitt (1995) who stress the importance of partnerships and personal selling in a turbulent environment, and Hibbert and Wilkinson (1994: 230) who believe that "disequilibrium mechanisms to absorb or dampen fluctuations" are required in a chaotic environment.

Adopting this approach to marketing tactics, Nilson (1995) ranked the various marketing tactics in terms of stabilising/destabilising as follows:

↑ **Most destabilising**

Totally new products
Price change
Product innovation (new product development)
Sales promotion
Product enhancement (old product development)
PR and other forms of non-advertising communication
Advertising
Personal selling
Own distribution system

↓ **Most stabilising**

From the above discussion it can be concluded that proaction and destabilising type activities are necessary in turbulent environments. For example, Thomas (in D'Aveni, 1999: 129) found that companies following a "strategy of controlling and muting competition produced better returns in the more stable ... environment" and that the successful and less successful companies in stable environments had similar levels of performance. However, when turbulence increased, companies following a stabilising strategy produced worse results and the gap between successful and less successful company performance increased. This implies that destabilising tactics used in more turbulent markets should lead to greater success than when stabilising tactics are used in such markets. This is implied in McKelvey's (2004) suggestion that entrepreneurial start-ups should be understood and dealt with through complexity techniques to achieve order creation, but not equilibrium.

Marketing tactics proposed by chaos/complexity theory

From the above, it is concluded that companies operating in complex and turbulent environments would use different marketing mixes (product, price, distribution and promotion) than companies operating in more simple and stable environments. Such marketing mixes would place emphasis on tactics that can be changed quickly in reaction to unexpected environmental changes. This would be consistent with issues such as flexibility, quick reactions, and spontaneity, which have been shown to be important methods of coping with complexity and turbulence. From the importance placed on coping with chaos and complexity in the literature, it can also be concluded that businesses that are good at handling complexity and turbulence will be more successful than those who do not handle it well.

From the above analysis of the literature a model for marketing successfully in a complex and turbulent environment was developed. Such a model would include:

- Adoption of tactics that increase volatility by destabilisation, namely, rapid new product development and culling of old products, aggressive price cutting, and short term sales promotional activities.
- Less emphasis on equilibrium mechanisms such as distribution, including inventories.
- Where equilibrium mechanisms are used, they are likely to be in areas that don't change over the longer term, such as building long term relationships with customers.

On the other hand, a less successful company in a turbulent industry would be more likely to adopt the tactics of stabilisation, namely:

- Product enhancement (improving product efficiency).
- Price stability, namely status quo pricing strategies.
- Distribution buffers (e.g. use of agents and buffer stocks).
- Product and image advertising.

Propositions

The problem to be researched was defined as understanding how a more successful South African company, operating in a turbulent environment, differs in its use of marketing tactics from a company that is less successful. Due to the paucity of research in this field and the resulting need for exploratory research, two propositions to explore this problem were developed, based on the review of the literature:

Proposition 1: It was proposed that the more successful company (ITA) would use more destabilising marketing tactics.

Proposition 2: It was proposed that the less successful company (ITB) would use more stabilising marketing tactics.

Research Method

Inherent in the research problem are the difficulties of understanding marketing mix combinations, the assessment of success, and the lack of research in the specific field. These difficulties dictated the need for a qualitative exploratory study. The approach chosen was the case study method to enable the problem to be studied intensively (Welman & Kruger, 1999). Two companies in the most complex/turbulent industry in South Africa were selected to represent a more successful and a less successful company.

Maximal variation sampling was used to select the companies. This method strives "to integrate only a few cases, but those which are as different as possible, to disclose the range of variation and differentiation in the field" (Flick, 1998: 70). The sample was selected through a two-stage process.

First the most complex/turbulent industry was selected via a questionnaire completed by six experts (stock brokerage industry analysts and management consultants). It questioned the experts on the complexity and turbulence in seven external environment sub-categories in nineteen industries. The results highlighted the Information Technology (IT) industry as the most complex/turbulent.

Within the IT industry, a more successful and a less successful company was chosen, based on a Delphi process, using a panel of four experts specialising in the IT industry (consultants, journalists and buyers). A two-iteration, ranking process of the more successful and less successful companies resulted in the panellists nominating ITA as the more successful company and ITB as the less successful company in the IT industry. To obtain the companies' co-operation anonymity was necessary.

Data was collected via semi-structured focussed depth interviews (Yin, 1994) with 31 C.E.O.s, directors, managers and marketing and sales staff in the four companies. All 31 met Morse's (in Flick, 1998) criteria for being good informants. Interviews took between an hour and an hour and a half each, were based on an interview guide and were audiotape recorded and, in addition, notes were taken. Furthermore, various company documents were collected and analysed, for example, annual reports, stock exchange prospectuses, brochures, leaflets, web pages, advertisements, meeting minutes and agendas, and policy and procedure manuals. The interview guide and the document summary sheets were structured mainly in terms of the marketing tactics as ranked by Nilson (1994), namely, destabilising tactics such as rapid new product development and culling of old products, aggressive price cutting, and short term sales promotional activities, and stabilising tactics such as distribution, including inventories, product enhancement (improving product efficiency), price stability (status quo pricing strategies), distribution buffers (e.g. use of agents and buffer stocks), and product and image advertising. In addition, issues relating to organisation, management, planning and controlling of the marketing activities were also included.

A combination of techniques was used to analyse the material. Thematic coding, using NVIVO software, was used to deconstruct and reconstruct the transcripts so as to categorise findings according to the perspective being studied (more/less successful). Content analysis was used to paraphrase, summarise and reduce the field note data and the documents to generalisations in order to compare them with the research problem and propositions. This analysis was done manually by summarising and aggregating the interview notes and the documentary evidence into tables to compare the two companies against each other and against the proposals.

'Method-appropriate criteria' such as data triangulation, methodological triangulation, prolonged engagement and an audit trail were used to validate the procedures and to ensure trustworthiness in the study (Flick, 1998). These multiple data collection methods provided both an 'etic', or outsider, and an 'emic', or insider, perspective, thereby increasing rigour and trustworthiness (Denzin & Lincoln, 1994). Construct validity was increased by using multiple data sources, internal validity was increased by comparison and pattern matching across the cases, external validity was increased by using cross-case analysis of multiple cases (thereby allowing some generalisation), and reliability was increased by the use of a data collection protocol, and the keeping of a data base of the empirical data and a chain of evidence (Yin, 1994; Riley, Wood, Clarke, Wilkie & Szivas, 2000). The method adhered to the ten design considerations of Lincoln and Guba and therefore met the criteria for a high quality, rigorous and trustworthy study (Rudestam & Newton, 1992).

Findings

The average ranking by the respondents of the importance of the various marketing tactics is given in Table 1. Note that the lower the ranking or rating, the more important the activity is perceived to be.

It can be seen from the *rankings* that little difference is perceived in the two companies about the importance placed on the various tactical activities. However, when the *ratings* are examined it can be seen that personal selling is perceived as less important by Company ITA (2.1 versus 1.0), whereas they perceive product innovation (2.4 versus 3.0) and new product development (2.7 versus 5.8) to be considerably more important than Company ITB does. It is also interesting to note that Company ITB perceives product enhancement (4.0 versus 5.4) and price changing (5.4 versus 6.7) to be more important than Company ITA does. Moreover, of the three most important tactics, for Company ITA two are destabilising, whereas for Company ITB two are stabilising. These findings are consistent with the model developed previously, namely that the more successful IT company would place more emphasis on destabilising innovation and development, while the less successful company would emphasise stabilising personal selling, product enhancement (also known as old product development), and price changing.

TABLE 1. Average importance of marketing tactics

TACTICS	Company ITA		Company ITB	
	Ranking	Rating	Ranking	Rating
Personal selling	1	2.1	1	1.0
Product innovation	2	2.4	2	3.0
Develop new products	3	2.7	6	5.8
PR/other communications	4	3.9	3	3.8
Product enhancement	5	5.4	4	4.0
Media advertising	6	6.6	8	7.4
Price changing	7	6.7	5	5.4
Sales promotions	8	6.9	7	6.8
Distribution	9	8.3	9	7.8

In order to gain a better understanding of the perceived importance of the marketing tactics, an analysis of the in depth interviews compared each company against the profile expected as specified in the propositions.

Company ITA – more successful company **Company ITA's tactics were mostly what would be expected of a successful company in a turbulent market:**

- Place more emphasis on new market development than efficiency in current markets, and prepared to aggressively disrupt the market in order to take the lead in, and control, the market.
- Structures and decision making processes are loose and autonomous, encouraging independent action.
- Clear strategic vision with strategies both being planned from the top and evolving dynamically from elsewhere in the company, quickly and radically. The emphasis is on adapting quickly to changes, and maintaining flexibility to assist in such adaptation.
- Their management style is characterised by openness, encouraging self-control and informal communications, which supports innovation. Achievement and performance is enhanced by the promotion of uncertainty and change which keeps staff 'on their toes.'
- Leaders in marketing strategy, changing faster than the market does.
- Product management activities are aggressive, quick and flexible, incorporating customers and suppliers in their activities, which lead the market. They are prepared to be ruthless with under-performing products.
- Although not too important, they will use aggressive price-cutting to win a specific, strategic customer.
- Place/distribution does not play a major role in their marketing activities, except for the use of partnerships.
- Not much use is made of destabilising promotions. However, they do go out of their way to surprise/amaze the industry, and occasionally will use guerrilla tactics. They also make

good use of public relation activities to encourage word-of-mouth promotions and to create a 'buzz' about the company.

As can be seen from the above, most of Company ITA's strategic and marketing activities are consistent with what is expected of a successful company in a turbulent market, but the following are aspects that are not consistent:

- Emphasis on the stabilising activities of relationship building, including partnerships and alliances.
- Little use of pricing as a tactical tool, tending to follow suppliers in terms of price changes.
- The insignificant use of sales promotion as a destabilising weapon to disrupt the market.

Company ITA appears to use product strategies (mainly new product development) and public relations and word-of-mouth to destabilise the market and thus keep one step ahead of competitors, and use the stabilising tactics of relationships to maintain their hold on customers. Thus, the more aggressive tactics of price-cutting and sales promotion may not be necessary until they face competition that is itself more aggressive and destabilising. Overall it can be concluded that Company ITA behaves as predicted by the proposed model.

Company ITB – less successful company **Many of the activities of Company ITB were similar to those of Company ITA, but conducted at a lower level of intensity. The activities consistent with a less successful company in a turbulent market are discussed below:**

- More emphasis on stability and efficiency, and reliance on acquisitions for growth, rather than new markets.
- Strategic vision revolves primarily around people issues, with some emphasis on the technical issues of quality and IT solutions to customers' problems. Although they claim to plan quickly and radically, the emphasis seems to be on cautious efficiency rather than adaptive flexibility to change.
- Their management style provides stability and security for staff.
- They are market followers, change slower than the market, and plan over a longer time horizon.
- New product development is mostly customer driven, with customers intimately involved. They are not first movers, waiting for the market to change, and lead times are slower than the rest of the industry.
- Although pricing is an important tactical weapon, it is not used aggressively. Their pricing method strengthens relationships through its openness, and ensures that projects are costed to set a premium price.
- Much emphasis is placed on building relationships, or partnerships, with both customers and suppliers. Other aspects of 'place' are considered unimportant.
- The stabilising activities of personal selling by account managers and, to a lesser extent, the public relations activities of customer entertainment are important. These events are also used to encourage word-of-mouth promotions. Little use is made of the stabilising effects of advertising.

Activities undertaken which are not consistent with the less successful firm in a turbulent market were:

- A loose and flat organisational structure, with autonomous decision making and independent action encouraged. Staff are trusted with full disclosure of all corporate information and are also trusted to control their own activities.
- Formal, rational planning was absent, but has recently been introduced to the company. Although long-term plans are developed, the reality is that useable plans are more short term.
- They perceive word-of-mouth to be important, but do not do too much to encourage it – mainly playing golf with customers and taking prospective customers to visit successful customers' sites.

Thus, in general it appears as if Company ITB's activities, with a few exceptions, are consistent with what would be expected of a less successful company in a turbulent industry, as predicted by the proposed model.

Table 2 summarises these findings relative to the propositions and shows that both Propositions 1 and 2 may be accepted.

TABLE 2. Comparison of Results against Propositions

	LESS SUCCESSFUL	MORE SUCCESSFUL
COMPLEX/TURBULENT ENVIRONMENT	Company ITB matches Proposition 2	Company ITA matches Proposition 1

Discussion of findings

The fact that the findings of this study have supported Propositions 1 and 2, indicates that the use of complexity and chaos theories may be helpful to understand the dynamics in a complex and turbulent market. However, the accuracy of the marketing tactics predicted by this approach can still be questioned. The model is clearly not foolproof, as the exceptions and anomalies listed above show. Possible reasons for these may be:

- Since the entire South African environment has become complex and turbulent, even less successful companies may be adopting tactics predicted for more successful companies. In fact, the predicted model may even apply to unsuccessful companies, but by definition the unsuccessful companies are no longer in business, and so cannot be examined.
- How a company perceives its market may be more important than the actual state of the market. Since all interviewees believed their industry to be changing significantly, their strategic and tactical actions could well be copied, but poorly implemented, from those they perceive to be more successful in their industry.

- Although the nature of the environment may determine the marketing tactics to use, these tactics may have little effect on success. It may be that other issues are more important determinants of success, for example, the quality of the implementation of the tactics.
- Although the Information Technology industry is complex and turbulent, the conservatism inherent in South African business may lead companies to adhere to traditional tactics, as 'they are the right thing to do', or because 'the competitors are doing them'.

As a general conclusion it is felt that the overall objective of the study has been met by showing that, in a complex and turbulent environment, the more successful company did differ, to a considerable degree, in its use of marketing tactics from those of the less successful company. Furthermore, the differences were more or less to the extent anticipated in the proposals. Although this conclusion appears to be valid for the two companies studied, care would have to be taken when trying to generalise the results more broadly. However, as mentioned in the Research Method section above, the design of the study does permit some degree of generalisation. Although firm, definitive conclusions cannot be extrapolated to other companies, other industries or other countries, the findings can be seen as indicative of the probable dynamics in other complex and turbulent environments and a tentative conclusion can be drawn that marketing tactics can be determined by the nature and dynamics of the external environments in other industries and countries. However, much more research is required before such a proposition can be made definitively.

Implications for African businesses

This study has highlighted the relevance of chaos and complexity theories, as techniques to better understand the market dynamics being experienced by companies in developing countries. It has further highlighted the complex nature of the problem and the difficulty in making conclusive statements about marketing success or failure in rapidly changing markets.

Despite the tentative nature of the findings, it is believed that this approach can help in developing countries, many of which have complex, turbulent and volatile environments. It could help in three ways. Firstly, viewing the environment and markets through a chaos and complexity theory perspective may enable marketers to identify opportunities and the relevant actions sooner and more clearly than when using traditional marketing approaches. Secondly, this approach could help African companies to adopt management and marketing strategies that are different to those developed by more traditional international marketers, and which therefore may be more relevant to the African business environment. Lastly, at a micro level, it may help companies to develop superior marketing tactics more suitable for the environment in which their firms operate, and also to better understand the behaviour and dynamics of competitors in their markets.

Although the research was done in the South African environment and the findings are tentative, it is believed that these findings could be relevant to companies operating in similar environments. Therefore, it is possible that companies in other African countries could benefit from using this marketing approach.

Recommendations for further research

It is hoped that some of the anomalies and difficulties outlined above can be resolved by further research involving a wider range and number of companies, in different industries and in different countries, especially African countries, which are also experiencing complex and turbulent environments. Such research could involve replication studies in other industries and other countries to confirm or refute whether the findings of this study are generalisable. Furthermore, it is believed that quantitative research focussing on multiple companies in a specific industry could be very helpful in more conclusively identifying if a deterministic relationship between the external environment and marketing tactics does in fact exist. Quantitative research could also provide a clearer understanding of such dynamics and more clearly differentiate the marketing tactics of more successful from less successful companies.

References

Addison, G. 2000. A new paradigm for info age marketing. *The SA Journal of Marketing and Sales*, 6(1): 24–26.

Ahmed, P. K., Hardaker, G., & Carpenter, M. 1996. Integrated Flexibility - Key to competition in a turbulent environment. *Long Range Planning*, 29(4) Aug: 562–571.

Bar-Yam, Y. 2000. *Guide to Complex Systems*. New England Complex Systems Institute.www.necsi.org/guide. Accessed 29/6/2000.

Baskin, K. 1998. *Corporate DNA: Learning from life*. Boston: Butterworth-Heinemann.

Bates, C. 1999. Corporate vision statements as an attractor for the movement of the company through time. *Managing the Complex*, Proceedings of conference at New England Complex Systems Institute, Boston, 18 March. www.Proceedings.Net/MTC/schedule.html Accessed 12/11/1999.

Benhabib, J., & Day, R. H. 1981. Rational choice and erratic Behaviour. *Review of Economic Studies*, XLVIII: 459-471.

Black, J., & Farias, G. 1997. *Genesis of complexity cycles*. Paper read at Eighth Annual International Conference of The Society for Chaos Theory in Psychology & Life Sciences, Boston University, Boston, 31 July 1997.

Black, J., & Farias, G. 1998. *The creation of complexity: Staying one step ahead of the game.* http://www.dartmouth.edu/~anderson/informs/ Black/Black.html Accessed 8/6/1998.

Boisot, M. 1999. *Introduction - Panel 2: Managerial insights from complexity science.* Proceedings of Complexity and Management - Two Interacting Sciences conference, Chicago, Aug. 1999.www.Proceedings.net/PDW/mambers/index.html. Accessed 25/10/1999.

Briggs, J., & Peat, F. D. 1999. *Seven life lessons of chaos: Timeless wisdom from the science of change*. New York: Harper Collins.

Brown, S. L., & Eisenhardt, K. M. 1998. *Competing on the edge: Strategy as structured chaos.* Boston: Harvard Business School Press.

Burgess, S. M. 1998. *The new marketing: Building strong marketing strategies in South Africa today*. Halfway House: Zebra Press.

Casti, J. 1999. Firm forecast. *New Scientist,* 162(2183), 24 April: 42–46.

Chakravarthy, B. 1997. A new strategy framework for coping with turbulence. *Sloan Management Review*, Winter: 69–82.

Chattell, A. 1995. *Managing for the future*. Chatham: MacMillan Business.

Coffee, A., & Atkinson, P. 1996. *Making sense of qualitative data: Complementary research strategies*. Thousand Oaks: Sage.

Conner, D. R. 1998. *Leading at the edge of chaos: How to create the nimble organization.* New York: John Wiley.

Cronje, G. J., du Toit, G. S., & Motlatla, M.D.C. 2000. *Introduction to Business Management* (5th ed.). Cape Town: Oxford University Press.

D'Aveni, R. A. 1999. Strategic supremacy through disruption and dominance. *Sloan Management Review*, 40(3), Spring: 127-135.

Diamond, A. H. 1993. Chaos Science. *Marketing Research*, 5(4) Fall: 9–15.

Doherty, N., & Delener, N. 2001. Chaos theory: Marketing and management implications. *Journal of Marketing Theory and Practice*, Fall, 9(4): 66–75.

Dolan, S. L., Garcia, S., & Auerbach, A. 2003. Understanding and managing chaos in organisations. *International Journal of Management*, 20(1): 23–35.

Dru, J-M. 1996. *Disruption: Overturning conventions and shaking up the marketplace*. New York: Wiley.

Du Plessis, P. J., Rousseau, G.G., & Blem, N.H. 1994. *Buyer Behaviour: Strategic Marketing Applications*. Halfway House: Southern.

Edgar, D. A., & Nisbet, L. 1995. Strategy in a small business - A case of sheer chaos. *International Journal of Contemporary Hospitality Management.* Paper presented at Internet Conference - Hospitality Industries: Strategies for the future. www.mcb.co.uk/services/conferen/liblink/ ijchm/intpap.htm. Accessed 11/11/1995.

Farrell, W. 1998. *How hits happen: Forecasting predictability in a chaotic marketplace*. New York: Harper Business.

Feichtinger, G., Hommes, C. H., & Milik, A. 1994. Complex dynamics in a threshold advertising model. *OR Spektrum*, 16: 101–111.

o Flick, U. 1998. *An introduction to qualitative research*. London: Sage.

Forrest, E. & Mizerski, R. (Eds.). 1996. *Interactive marketing: The future present*. Lincolnwood: NTC Business Books.

Fradette, M. and Michaud, S. 1998. *The power of corporate kinetics: create the self-adapting, self-renewing, instant-action enterprise*. New York: Simon and Schuster.

Frederick, W.C. 1998. Creatures, corporations, communities, chaos, complexity: a naturological view of the corporate social role. *Business and Society*, 37(4) Dec: 358-376.

Gault, S. B., & Jaccaci, A. T. 1996. Complexity meets periodicity. *The Learning Organization*, 3(2): 33–39.

Garcia, R. 2004. *Encouraging failure in new product development*. Paper presented at New Priorities and Challenges for Business-to-Business Marketers, 5 –6 August, Harvard Business School, Boston. www.smeal.psu.edu/isbm/seminars/boston04/Garcia.pdf. Accessed 17/9/2004.

Gibson, R. 1996. *Rethinking the future*. London: Nicholas Brealey.

Gilmore, J. H., & Pine II, B. J. 1997. The four faces of mass customization. *Harvard Business Review*, Jan–Feb: 91–101.

Gladwell, M. 2000. *The tipping point: How little things can make a big difference*. London: Abacus.

Glass, N. 1996. Chaos, non-linear systems and day-to-day management. *European Management Journal*, 14(1) Feb: 98-105.

Goldberg, J., & Markoczy, L. 1998. *Complex rhetoric and simple games*. Cranfield University. www.Cranfield.ac.za/public/cc/cc047/papers/ complex/html /complex.htm. Accessed 2/2/1999.

Hamel, G. 2000. *Leading the revolution*. Boston: Harvard Business School Press.

Herbig, P. A. 1990. Marketing chaos - when randomness can be deterministic. *Journal of International Marketing and Market Research*, 16(2): 65–84.

Herbig, P.A., & Golden, J. 1991. Marketing and chaos. *Canadian Journal of Marketing Research*, 10: 50-57.

Hibbert, B., & Wilkinson, I. F. 1994. Chaos theory and the dynamics of marketing systems. *Journal of the Academy of Marketing Science*, 22(3): 218–233.

Holbrook, Morris B. 2003. Adventures in complexity: Dynamic open complex adaptive systems, butterfly effects, self-organizing order, coevolution, the ecological perspective, fitness landscapes, market spaces, emergent beauty at the edge of chaos, and all that jazz. *Academy of Marketing Science Review*, 6. www.amsreview.org/articles/holbrook06-2003.pdf. Accessed 2/2/2006.

Joubert, D. 1998. *Competitive firms thrive on instinct.* Cape Town: Queillerie.

Kashani, K. 1995. Marketing futures: Priorities for a turbulent environment. *Long Range Planning*, 28(4): 87-98.

Kelly, S., & Allison, M. A. 1999. *The complexity advantage: How the science of complexity can help your business achieve peak performance.* New York: Business Week Books.

Koch, R. 2000. *The power laws - the science of success.* London: Nicholas Brealey.

Kopel, M. 1996. Periodic and chaotic behaviour of a simple R & D model. *Ricerche Economiche,* 50: 235-265.

Kurtyka, J. 2000. *Adaptive marketing: The changing relationship of business to the customer.* Paper read at the International Conference on Complex Systems (ICCS), Nashua, New Hampshire, 22 May, 1 –12.

Lamb, C.W. J., Hair, J. F. Jr., McDaniel, C., Boschoff, C., & Terblanche, N. 2000. *Marketing.* Cape Town: Oxford University Press.

Lane, D., & Maxfield, R. 1996. Strategy under complexity: Fostering generative relationships. *Long Range Planning*, 29(2): 215-231.

Lewin, R. 1992. *Complexity: Life at the edge of chaos.* New York: MacMillan.

Lewin, R. 1993. Order for free. *New Scientist*, 137(1869), 13 February: 10-11.

Loewen, J. 1997. *The power of strategy: A practical Guide for South African managers.* Sandton: Zebra.

Manning, A. D. 1998. Radical strategy: The new marketing mantra. *The SA Journal of Marketing and Sales*, 4(4): 24-25.

Marks, R. E., Midgley, D. F., Cooper, L. G., &Shiraz, G. M. 1998. The complexity of competitive strategies. *Complexity International*, 6: 1-12.

Mavondo, F.T. 1999. Environment and strategy as antecedents for marketing effectiveness and organizational performance. *Journal of Strategic Marketing*, 7: 237–250.

McElwee, M. 1998. *Chaos theory and complexity as fountainheads for design of an organization theory building workshop*. Paper read at XIVth World Congress of the International Sociological Association, Montreal, Canada, July 1998.

McGlone, T. A., & Ramsey, R. P. 1998. *Getting realistic about reality: Using chaos theory to explain marketing phenomena*. Proceedings of Society for Marketing Advances conference, New Orleans, 4 - 7 November 1998.

McKelvey, B. 2004. Toward a complexity science of entrepreneurship. *Journal of Business Venturing*, 19: 313–341.

Meade, P. T., & Rabelo, L. 2004. The technology adoption life cycle attractor: Understanding the dynamics of high-tech markets. *Technological Forecasting and Social Change*, 17: 667–684.

Merry, U. 1998. Organizations and Natural CAS. *Thresholds e-Journal.* www.thresholds.com/journal/articles/merryone.htm. Accessed 16/9/1998.

Millier, P. 1999. *Marketing the unknown: Developing marketing strategies for technical innovations*. Chichester: Wiley.

Ministry of Welfare and Population Development. 1997. *Draft white paper on population policy*. Pretoria: Government Printer.

Mix, R. A. 1993. *Is there chaos in marketing*? Proceedings of Annual Summer Marketing Educators' Conference, American Marketing Association, 444 - 445.

Morris, M. & Schurink, C.v.E. 1993. Pricing behavior on industrial markets: The impact of environmental dynamics. *The Journal of Business and Industrial Marketing*, 8(3): 28–43.

Morris, M. H., Hansen, S. D., & Pitt, L. F. 1995. Environmental turbulence and organizational buying: The case of health benefits in South Africa. *Industrial Marketing Management*, 24: 305–315.

Morris, M. H., Marks, A. S., Allen, J. A., Peery, J. R., & Newman, S. 1996. Modelling ethical attitudes and behaviours under conditions of environmental turbulence: The case of South Africa. *Journal of Business Ethics*, 15: 1119–1130.

Morris, R. 1992. *Marketing to black townships: Practical guidelines*. Kenwyn: Juta.

Morrison, D. J., & Quella, J. A. 1999. Pattern thinking: Cutting through the chaos. *Marketing Management*, 8(4) Winter:1-7.

Narus, J. A., & Anderson, J. C. 1996. Rethinking distribution: Adaptive channels. *Harvard Business Review*, Jul–Aug: 112-120.

Nasser, M. E., & Vivier, F. J. 1993. *Mindset for the new generation organisation*. Kenwyn: Juta.

New Marketing Imperatives Roundtable. 1994. Preparing for a point-to-point world. *Marketing Management*, 3(4): 30–40.

Nilson, T. H. 1995. *Chaos marketing: How to win in a turbulent world*. London: McGraw-Hill.

Oda, S. H., Miura, K., Ueda, K., & Baba, Y. 2000. The application of cellular-automata and agent models to network externalities in consumers' theory: A generalization-of-life game. In W.A. Barnett, C. Chiarella, S. Keen, R. Marks, & Schnabl, *Commerce, Complexity and Evolution: Topics in Economics, Finance, Marketing and Management, Proceedings of the Twelfth International Symposium in Economic Theory and Econometrics*: 351-371 Cambridge: Cambridge University Press.

Oliver, D., & Roos, J. 2000. *Striking a balance: Complexity and knowledge landscapes.* London: McGraw-Hill.

Paladini, M. 1999. Changes need not be big to create a big result. *Marketing News,* 18 January, 4: pp..

Peron, J. 1999. *Die, the beloved country.* Saxonwold: Amagi Books.

o Peters, E. E. 1999. *Patterns in the dark: Understanding risk and financial crisis with complexity theory.* New York: Wiley.

Phillips, F., & Kim, N. 1996. Implications of chaos research for new product forecasting. *Technological forecasting and Social Change,* 53(3) Nov: 239-261.

Prendergast, G., & Berthon, P. 2000. Insights from ecology: An ecotone perspective of ,marketing. *European Management Journal,* 18(2), Apr: 223-231.

Priesmeyer, H. R. 1992. *Organizations and chaos: Defining the methods of nonlinear management.* Westport: Quorum Books.

Priesmeyer, H. R., & Baik, K. 1989. Discovering the patterns of chaos. *Planning Review,* Nov/Dec: 14-47.

Puth, G. 1996. *Dynamics of the marketing environment: Implications for marketing training in South Africa.* Unpublished monograph, Department of Business Economics, University of Pretoria.

Rasmussen, D. R., & Mosekilde, E. 1988. Bifurcations and chaos in a generic management model. *European Journal of Operations Research,* 35: 80-88.

Riley, M., Wood, R. C., Clark, M. A., Wilkie, E., & Szivas, E. 2000. *Researching and writing dissertations in business and management.* London: Thomson Learning.

Roos J. 1999. Presentation on strategy making. *Managing the Complex.*_ Proceedings of conference at New England Complex Systems Institute, Boston, 18 March. Available from: http://www.Proceedings.Net/MTC/ schedule.html. Accessed 12 November 1999.

Rudestam, K. E., & Newton, R. R. 1992. *Surviving your dissertation: A comprehensive guide to content and process.* Newbury Park: Sage.

SA 2000: South Africa at a glance. 1999. Craighall: Editors Inc.

Saisse, M. C. P., & Wilding, R. D. 1997. Short-term strategic management in mass customized markets. *Logistics Information Management,* 10(5): 1-7.

Samli, A. C. 1993. *Counterturbulence marketing: A proactive strategy for volatile economic times.* Westport: Quorum Books.

Sengupta, A., Unadkat, C., & Jain, N. 2000. *Surviving chaos.* Business School, XLRI, Jamshedpur. http://iil.indiainfoline.com/cgi-bin/print.pl. Accessed 12 November 2000.

Smith, M. F., Sinha, I., Lancioni, R., & Forman, H. 1999. Role of market turbulence in shaping pricing strategy. *Industrial Marketing Management,* 28: 637-649.

South African Yearbook 2001/02. 2002. Pretoria: Government Communications and Information Services.

Stacey, R. D. 1992. *Managing chaos*. London: Kogan Page.

Stacey, R. D. 1995. The science of complexity: An alternative perspective for strategic change processes. *Strategic Management Journal*, 16: 477-495.

Stacey, R. D. 1996. *Complexity and creativity in organizations*. San Francisco: Berrett-Koehler.

Tedesco, B. G. 1998. *Neural network complexity models for the marketing mix*. Paper read at the Advertising Research Foundation Media Accountability Workshop, New York, October 1998.

Terblanche, N. 1998. *Retail management*. Halfway house: Thomson International.

Thietart, R. A., & Forgues, B. 1995. Chaos theory and organization. *Organization Science*, 6(1): 19-31.

Van der Walt, A., Strydom, J. W., Marx, S., & Jooste, C. J. 1996. *Marketing management*. Kenwyn: Juta.

Waldrop, M. Mitchell. 1992. *Complexity: The emerging science at the edge of order and chaos*. New York: Simon and Schuster.

Wall, S. J., & Wall, S. R. 1995. The evolution (not the death) of strategy. *Organization Dynamics*, Autumn: 7–19.

Welman, J. C., & Kruger, S. J. 1999. *Research methodology for the business and administrative sciences*. Cape Town: Oxford University Press.

Wheatley, M. J. 1996. The unplanned organization. *Noetic Sciences Review*, Spring: 16-23.

Wilkinson, I., & Young, L. 1998. *On Competing: Firms, relations and networks*. Paper read at Research Conference on Relationship Marketing, October 1998, Emory University.

Yin, R.K. 1994. *Case study research: Design and methods*. Thousand Oaks: Sage.

Young, T. R., & Kiel, L. D. 1994. *Control, prediction and nonlinear dynamics*. Red Feather Institute Series on Non-Linear Social Dynamics, December. www.tryoung.com/chaos/029management.html. Accessed 12 November 2000.

RAISING PRIVATE SECTOR COMPETITIVENESS THROUGH FOREIGN DIRECT INVESTMENT: THE CASE OF TANZANIA

CRANMER RUTIHINDA

Williams School of Business
Bishop's University
2600 College Street
Sherbrooke, QC, J1M 0C8
Canada
Tel: 8198229600
Fax: 8198229720
e-mail: crutihin@ubishops.ca

ABSTRACT

Investigating the impact of foreign direct investment on Tanzania's private sector this study finds Tanzania to have consistent growth of foreign direct investment (FDI) with evidence of positive impact on private sector development including new capital, modern technology, effective management, marketing methods, product innovation and human resource development with a positive correlation between FDI and Tanzania's economic growth as well as export growth. On the other hand, the study finds weak linkages between FDI and indigenous firms with most of the value-adding activities being done outside Tanzania, and a greater portion of inputs imported, with evidence of negative balance of payment effects.

Key words
Foreign direct investment, private sector competitiveness, Tanzania, entry mode, location specific advantage, economic impact.

INTRODUCTION

With the rapid rate of globalization and the widening economic gap between the world's least developed countries and developed countries, there has recently been growing interest in the role of foreign direct investment (FDI) as a viable means for economic growth. Most economists and policy makers believe that FDI provides the very basic pillars for private sector development currently lacking in these countries, including access to direct capital financing, effective product and process technology, employment creation, human capital development, tax revenue and access to global markets by linkages into the multinational's global value chains. Through technology transfer, FDI can further contribute to dynamic effects that would shift further the production possibility frontier and enable developing countries to break away from the vicious circle of poverty. Arguments for the unique position of foreign direct investment were further supported after the global financial crises (Asia 1997, Mexico 1995, Latin America debt crisis 1980s), where it was found to be more resilient compared to other forms of private capital flows.

However, although these arguments are intuitive and compelling, empirical evidence on the impact of foreign direct investment on host developing countries is still mixed. Some empirical studies (Haddad and Harrison, 1993; Aitken and Harrison, 1999) have found no evidence of FDI positive spillovers in the host country. Surveys on spillover literature (Hanson, 2001; Lapse, 2002) have found empirical evidence of positive spillovers for host countries to be weak or negative (Aitken and Harrison, 1999), while other empirical studies have found positive spillovers (Caves, 1974; Kokko, 1994). Some have come to the conclusion that foreign investors may not always be the best alternative to a host country (Razin, Sadka and Yuen 1999; Hauman and Fenancez-Arias, 2000). Spillovers are not automatic (Bloomstrom and Kokko, 2003), and for positive spillovers to take place a country must meet certain requirements that facilitate spillover effects. Borrensztein et al. (1998), Xu (2000), and Alfaro (2003), for example, suggest that for a host country to enjoy positive spillover effects, the country should have higher education levels and developed financial markets. It has also been argued that, rather than filling the gap between saving and investment, FDI may lower domestic savings and investment by extracting rents and siphoning off capital through local capital markets and local supplies of foreign exchange. Foreign direct investment can also lead to crowding out domestic producers and substituting them with imported inputs.

This lack of theoretical and empirical consensus on the positive impact of FDI on host countries can be partly explained by inadequate analytical methods used to measure the intended variables. Some of these studies have mainly used secondary data to examine productivity trends across countries in relationship to FDI. These studies can only provide presumptive evidence of causation, but fail to address the transmission mechanism, and are not able to explain the impact of FDI on the growth of domestic firms. Case studies have also been used to address specific FDI and technology transfer effects but without using quantitative methods. Even when addressing specific countries, studies have taken a holistic approach without paying attention to the type and nature of FDI. Complicated with the lack of appropriate data to meet the more rigorous econometric methods, researchers have found themselves using variables that do not match the models. On the other hand, most of the evidence on the impact of FDI in developing countries has mainly been limited to the relatively affluent developing countries of Asia and Latin America. Very few empirical studies exist that address the impact of FDI on the least developed countries of Sub-Saharan Africa. Until now, there has been no systematic study of the impact of FDI on Tanzania. The aim of this paper is to contribute towards filling in this gap by exploring the contribution of foreign direct investment on Tanzania's private sector development.

ANALYTICAL FRAMEWORK

The suggested framework (Figure 1) assumes that foreign direct investment influences a country's competitiveness through direct and indirect interaction with host country firms and other institutions in the host country. Direct interaction with host country firms comes through the establishment of forward and backward linkages. Through backward linkages foreign firms work with host country firms to supply inputs, such as raw materials, products or services that are part of the foreign firm's global value chain. On the other hand, with forward linkages host country firms are contracted by foreign firms to channel products and services to final consumers as distributors or intermediaries for foreign firms. Indirect interaction takes place when foreign firms compete with host country firms for resources and markets. Other forms of indirect interaction may come from the movement of labor between foreign firms and host country firms. The greater the interaction between foreign firms and local firms the higher the likelihood that FDI will enhance the host country's competitive advantage.

Interaction between FDI and host country firms will lead to enhancing the host country's competitiveness by stimulating the host country's product and process innovation, management and marketing know how development, entrepreneurship development, human resource development, export and economic growth. As interaction between foreign firms and local firms intensifies through competition, host country firms will be pushed to improve their product and process quality to meet the changing market demand. In their efforts to compete with foreign firms, local firms may imitate and learn from foreign firms' new methods of production and management leading to product development and innovation. This upgrading can also take place as foreign firms instill additional capital and modern management practices into acquired host country firms.

FIGURE 1

Analytical Framework

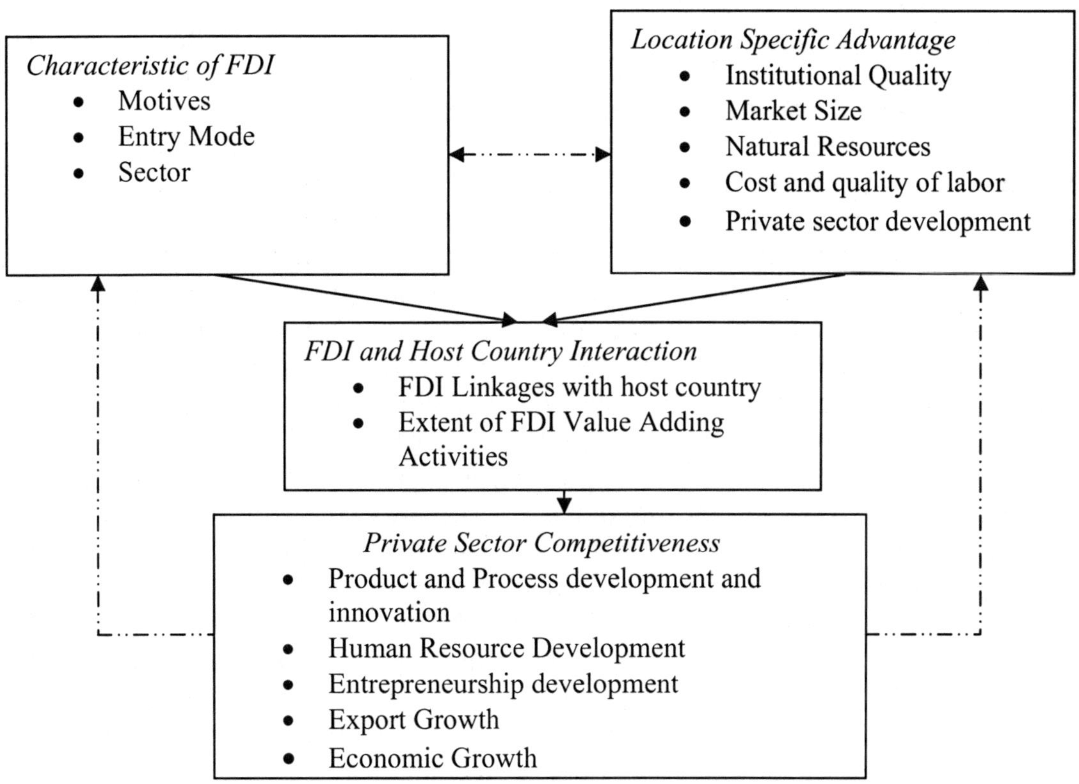

Linkages between foreign firms and local firms may also lead to greater product and process innovation. Since foreign firms have higher quality standards, by sourcing inputs from local firms they raise the quality requirement of inputs. As local firms struggle to meet these demand conditions they become more competitive. In an effort to guarantee and maintain long-term supplies of inputs, foreign firms may provide information and know-how to enable these local firms to meet globally accepted standards of quality and service delivery.

Through the interaction of foreign firms with host country labor markets, FDI can also develop the host country's human resources as they upgrade their skill gaps to meet global standards. Employees who work for foreign firms may be required to upgrade their skills through organizational learning or training, to meet the higher skill needs of those firms. This knowledge learned from foreign firms may spillover to other firms as employees move to other firms or start their own businesses. The demand for specific skills by multinational firms may also lead to the host country upgrading or setting up educational institutions to ensure local supply of such skills. Since multinational enterprises are expected to generate more profits and pay more taxes, these taxes can provide the host government with the funds needed to finance the education budget. The fact that foreign firms are also likely to pay higher wages than host country firms attracts host country nationals to opt to work in their home countries, rather than look for greener pastures outside their home country. In this way, the host countries can retain their best and brightest and avoid the brain drain, or even lead to reverse migration where host country nationals working abroad may return home to take up lucrative jobs offered by foreign firms in their host countries. This assumption is further strengthened by the example of Ireland's FDI success in the early 1990's that lead to Ireland's shift from a net emigration of 35,000 to a net immigration of 45,000, most of which were Irish returnees (Slaughter, 2002). As a part of corporate social responsibility, foreign firm may also upgrade the human capital development through sponsorship of educational programs and curriculum development.

In the same manner, through interaction with local firms foreign firms can stimulate entrepreneurship development in host countries. Foreign firms are likely to subcontract most of their non-core activities to local firms, as this allows them to concentrate on their core activities. This provides new investment opportunities for local entrepreneurs as new markets of products and services are made available by foreign firms. Foreign firms may also upgrade the host country's capacity to export by providing international market access to local products through linkages to their global value chains. Local firms in the least developed countries have greater difficulties having access to foreign markets, mainly due to their limited marketing and production capacity, as well as other international barriers such as the lack of brand recognition. Through linkages with FDI host country nationals can become part of the multinational global value chain and therefore boost the host country's exports.

Ultimately, the increase in competitiveness of the host country will lead to higher economic growth. However, the enhancement of a host country's competitiveness through foreign direct investment is not automatic. The possibility of FDI to enhance a country's competitiveness will be based on the characteristics of the FDI, as well as the business environment of the host country. The characteristics of FDI and the host country's business environment are also interrelated. The characteristics of FDI may be mapped by looking at the motives for FDI, entry modes, the sector in which the FDI is in the host country, and the extent of value adding activities that the foreign firm has at site in the host country. The host country environment can be mapped by looking at the quality of its institutions, market size, natural resources and private sector development.

The motives, entry mode, sector and extent of value adding activities of FDI are more likely to be influenced by the host country characteristics. The generic motives for FDI in a host country are distinguished as market seeking, resource seeking and efficiency seeking. Resource seeking FDI refers to FDI that is geared towards extracting resources from the host country and is most likely to be in the mineral extraction or agricultural sectors. Efficiency seeking FDI is mainly geared towards sourcing of low cost labor from the host country, while market seeking FDI mainly uses the host country to provide access for its output. It is, thus, natural to assume that host countries that have low cost and qualified human capital are likely to attract more efficiency seeking FDI, while countries with relatively abundant natural resources will attract greater resource seeking FDI, and countries with access to larger markets are likely to attract market seeking FDI.

The sector in which the foreign firm enters the market does have an impact on the extent to which FDI will enhance the host country's competitiveness. Hirschman (1958) argues that not all sectors have the same potential to absorb foreign technology or create linkages with the rest of the economy. Agriculture and mining are considered to have weak linkages and foreign investment has limited effect in enhancing the host country's competitiveness. Rodiguez-Clare (1996) theoretically demonstrates that foreign firms that intensively use intermediate goods are likely to enhance host country's production efficiency. Some studies have shown that FDI in the primary sector tends to have a negative effect on economic growth while investment in manufacturing tends to have a positive effect (Alfaro, 2003). We therefore expect to see least developed countries with greater investment in the manufacturing and services sectors experiencing greater economic growth than those with more FDI in the primary sectors. Since the extent of value adding activities is always associated with risk of the host country, countries that have better quality institutions are more likely to have foreign firms committing more value adding activities. On the other hand, linkages between foreign firms and host countries highly depend on the availability of a viable private sector and an educated workforce that is capable of serving the needs of foreign firms. I, therefore, expect least developed countries with more viable private sectors and human capital to have foreign firms establishing greater linkages with their local firms.

The entry method that foreign firms choose to enter host countries can influence the extent to which they interact with the host country firms. Foreign firms that enter a host country through acquisition take over an existing concern that has already established a network of linkages with other domestic firms. Since green-fields are new firms starting from scratch, they are more likely to start gradually and expand as the foreign firm gains experience. I, therefore, expect foreign firms entering host country markets through acquisition to have more linkages with host country firms than those through green-fields.

On the other hand, acquisitions do not necessarily lead to enhancement of the host country environment. Unlike green-fields, acquisitions are less likely to create new jobs – they take existing firms and, at times, may replace the existing workforce with foreign nationals. Since industries are relatively underdeveloped in the least developed countries, there are normally very few firms available for acquisitions. The only candidates that are available are the large state-owned enterprises, which, in most cases, have a monopoly in the domestic market. Most of these state-owned enterprises are largely inefficient with poor management and outdated technology. Although foreign firms may choose to start up new green-fields to avoid taking over those existing inefficiencies of the state owned enterprises, due to the monopoly position and the already established networks and goodwill that these firms have, it may be in the interest of foreign firms to acquire these state owned firms for rapid market growth. Their inefficiencies may also work to the advantage of the foreign firm in acquisition price negotiation. The monopoly position of these firms may be in the interest of foreign firms but may create market barriers for new firms that want to enter the market.

RESEARCH METHOD

Due to the lack of appropriate data for more rigorous time series analysis, especially considering that it was only in the early 1990's that FDI began to flow into Tanzania, this study uses the triangulation method where both qualitative and quantitative methods are used to gather evidence on the role of FDI in raising the competitiveness of Tanzania's private sector. Ordinary least square regression is used to examine the relationships between foreign direct investment, economic growth, manufacturing value added and exports.

Foreign direct investment data is drawn from the UNCTAD's World Investment Report data base of 2005. The business investment environment in Tanzania is mapped by using benchmark data from UNCTAD's Investment Compass data base of 2005. Data for Tanzania's manufacturing and agriculture value added and export data are gathered from the

World Development Indicators (2005) from the World Band database. The rest of the secondary data is drawn from Tanzania's Economic Survey 2004, the Tanzania Investment Report (2004). For evidence on the interaction of FDI with domestic firms in Tanzania, data is drawn from interviews with foreign affiliates in Tanzania. The survey sample comprised 51 foreign firms with Head Offices in Dar-es-Salaam.

FINDINGS

Tanzania's FDI Competitiveness and FDI Growth

When the average stock of inward flow of FDI into Tanzania for the past decade (1994 to 2004) is compared to other least developed countries in Sub-Saharan Africa, we find that Tanzania has done relatively well with an average stock of US$ 2762 million, an average inflow of US$ 340 million. During the same period the proportion of FDI inflow in relation to gross fixed capital formation was 22 percent and 31 percent as a percentage of gross domestic product.

TABLE 1

FDI Inflows 1994-2004

	Tanzania	Zambia	Mozambique	Rwanda	Uganda
FDI Inward Stock (million US$)	2762	2388	1084	274	822
FDI Inflows (million US$)	340	160	204	4	157
Inflows as (% GFCF)	22.0	18.8	26.9	17.0	13.5
Inwards stock as (% GDP)	30.58	64.87	27.96	18.11	13.33

Source: UNCTAD World Investment Report 2005

Using a comparative global benchmark of 100 (Figure 2), Tanzania compares well with favorable labor costs and a very open and liberal FDI policy. Tanzania has also had a successful macroeconomic policy, with an economic growth rate of 6 percent during the past decade and inflation rates have remained low. Human capital development is at half the global benchmark.

Compared to global standards, the market size of Tanzania is very small and available raw material is limited, while the quality of government institutions is still below the global average. In terms of population, Tanzania has a population of 34 million and is a member of regional economic groupings of Southern African Development Community (SADC) and the East African Community (EAC), but its relatively small benchmark of market size reflects the country's low level of economic development and low income levels with a very low per capita GDP (PPP$700).

FIGURE 2

Tanzania's FDI Global Competitiveness

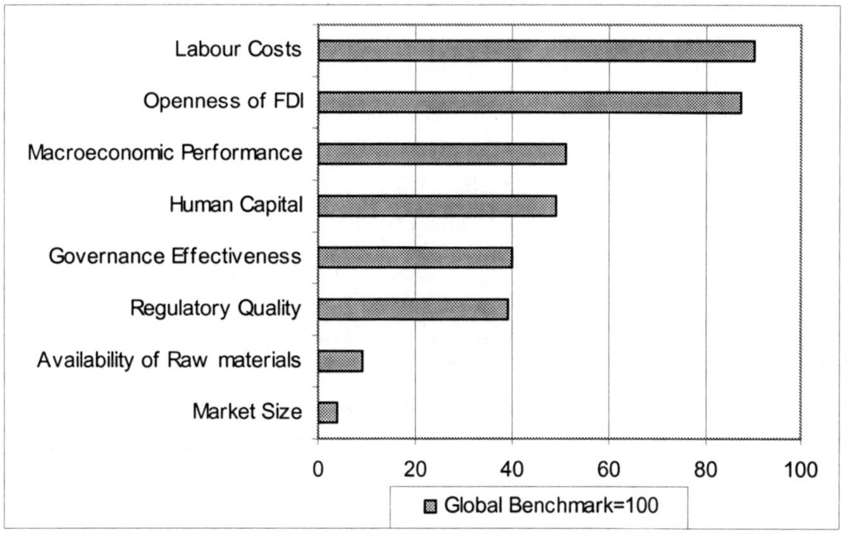

Source: UNCTAD Investment Compass 2005

FIGURE 3

Tanzania's Distribution of FDI Stock by Sector

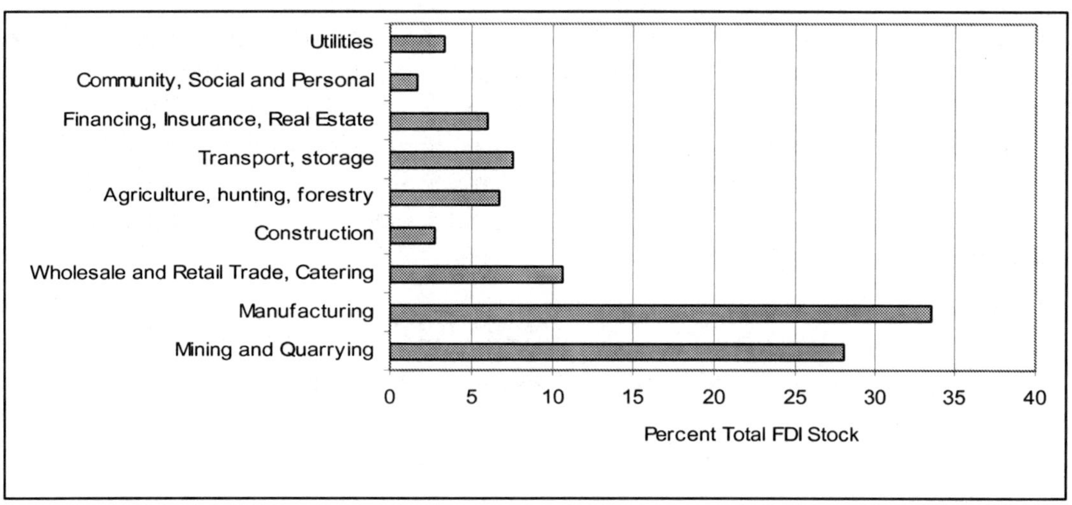

Source: TIC 2005

Human capital development in Tanzania is lower than the global average. This is partly due to low student enrollments in both secondary and tertiary educational institutions. The educational system has been deteriorating with vocational training relatively underdeveloped, leading to a lack of qualified craftsmen and technical professionals. Although Tanzania ranks very low on the global benchmark for raw materials, the distribution of FDI by sector in Tanzania (Figure 3) shows a high percentage of FDI in the mining and manufacturing sectors where the two sectors share a total of more than 60 percent of total FDI stock.

As found in Figure 3 the main motive of FDI in Tanzania is resources seeking, followed by access to low cost labor and favorable tax incentives. A high percentage of Tanzania's FDI is in the mining and manufacturing sectors, with more than 60 percent of total FDI stock. The attractive mining policy introduced in 1997, Mineral Act 1998, coupled with successful mining exploration, has attracted the attention of global mining giants such as Barrick Gold Corporation that acquired Bulyanhulu Mine in 1999. Other large mining companies include South Africa's Anglo-Gold and London based Ashanti Goldfields. Up to 2004, Tanzania had been opening one modern gold mine every year. Most manufacturing in Tanzania is mainly concentrated in the agro-processing industries including textiles, food and beverages. This again fits well with Tanzania's comparative advantage in the agriculture sector, especially in the produce of cotton, coffee, sisal, tea and cashew nuts. Low FDI in Tanzania is driven by market motives mainly because Tanzania's local market is too small to attract market-seeking FDI. Most of the FDI stock in Tanzania is concentrated in the manufacturing and mining sectors, suggesting that current FDI is geared to take advantage of Tanzania's available natural resources.

Linkages between FDI and Local Firms

When the percentage of inputs sourced from local firms is used to examine the linkages between local firms and foreign owned firms, we find that a greater percentage of the raw materials and equipment are sourced from abroad (see Figure 4). The low levels of local sourcing of raw material suggests that most manufacturing taking place in Tanzania has a relatively low percentage of value adding activities suggesting an unfavorable balance of payments as value imported is greater than local value created. However, most of the financial and marketing services are sourced within the local market. Based on these findings we can conclude that foreign firms in Tanzania are sourcing a major part of their equipment and material inputs from abroad, while a greater proportion of the financial and marketing services are locally sourced.

FIGURE 4

Percentage of Inputs from Local Sources

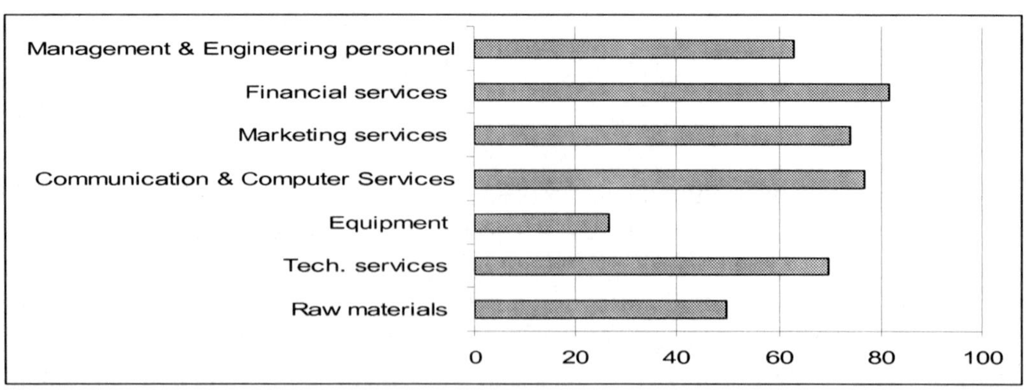

Source: Survey results

From our interviews we find that most foreign firms were more satisfied with the quality of local financial services but less satisfied with local technical services and material inputs

(Figure 5). These survey results provide evidence that low levels of training and technical competence are major obstacles to local sourcing. Even the quality of human and marketing resources is considered to be relatively low.

FIGURE 5

Quality of Local Inputs

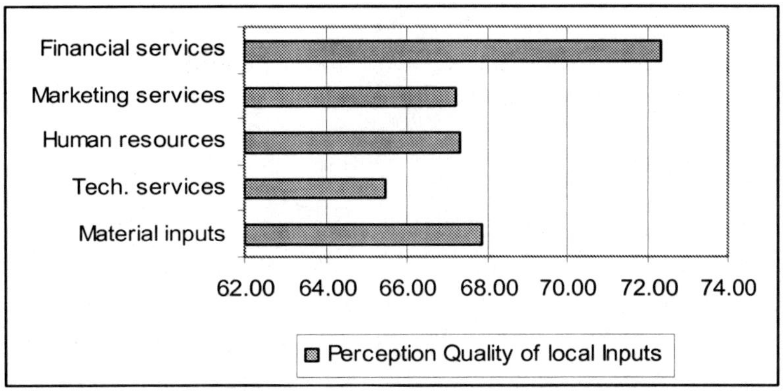

Source: Survey Results

FDI and Extent of Value Added

Value adding activities at site were measured by the proportion of local managerial and engineering work at site to total managerial and engineering work of the products sold by the affiliate in Tanzania. The proportion of locally produced goods to the value of total goods sold was also used to indicate the extent to which manufacturing activities take place in Tanzania. In this way we are able to have an idea as to the proportion of managerial and engineering work that is carried out in Tanzania. Based on the percentage of total product sold by foreign firms in Tanzania to total sales, we find that a very small percentage of goods sold by foreign firms in Tanzania go to their parent companies, suggesting that these firms are not integrated with their parent companies. The percentage of locally produced value over total value of products sold is also small (less than 40 percent), which again suggests that very little value adding of the products sold is done in Tanzania.

FIGURE 6

Extent of Value Adding

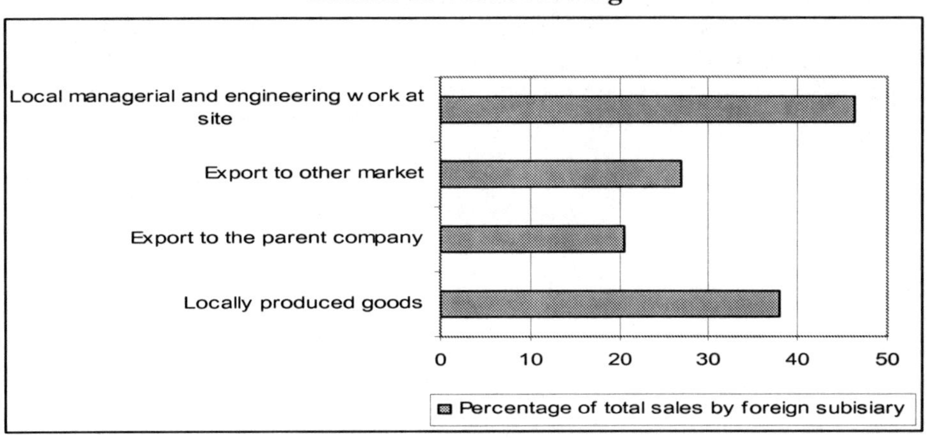

Source: Survey Results

Regression results (Table 2) on the relationship between value added by sector and economic growth shows a positive relationship between the rate of increase in each sector and economic growth, except for the agricultural sector that shows no significant relationship. The relationship between FDI and economic growth is significant and positive, suggesting that increases in FDI are positively correlated with increases in economic growth. These findings suggest that foreign investment geared towards increasing manufacturing and service value added is likely to stimulate greater economic growth. The relationship with the agriculture sector is not significant. With these results we can conclude that FDI in the manufacturing and service sectors is likely to have greater impact on economic growth.

FDI and Export Performance

Tanzania has relatively low export levels and most of the export is in the traditional commodity sectors of coffee, sisal, cotton, tea, tobacco, cashew nuts and cloves. However, recently there has been a shift towards more non-traditional exports taking a greater share in the exports. Foreign investments in the sector have contributed a great deal towards increasing the share of minerals to total exports. Mineral exports as a percentage of total exports grew from 7 percent in 1998 to more than 51 percent in 2004.

This trend is in line with our earlier prediction that FDI is likely to upgrade Tanzania's exports from agricultural raw materials to more manufactured exports. However, it is important to note that most of the exports are mainly being dominated by the mining sector, a leading recipient of FDI. The increasing share of mining in exports has also been boosted by the increasing prices of gold in the world markets. The role of FDI in increasing export performance in Tanzania is further supported by regression results (Table 3) that show a positive correlation between FDI growth and export growth in Tanzania, suggesting that foreign direct investment has substantially contributed to the increase in export growth in Tanzania.

TABLE 2

Relationship between Economic Growth and FDI

	Coefficient	t-values	p-values
(Constant)		-0.78	0.44
Manufacturing Value added (%GDP)	0.78	3.44	0.00
Service value added (%GDP)	0.53	2.29	0.03
Agriculture value added (%GDP)	-0.28	-1.66	0.11
FDI Flows (% GFCF)	0.42	2.37	0.02
Dependent Variable: GDP growth $R^2 = 0.62$ $F = 8.20$ $p = 0.0001$			

FIGURE 7

Exports by Sector

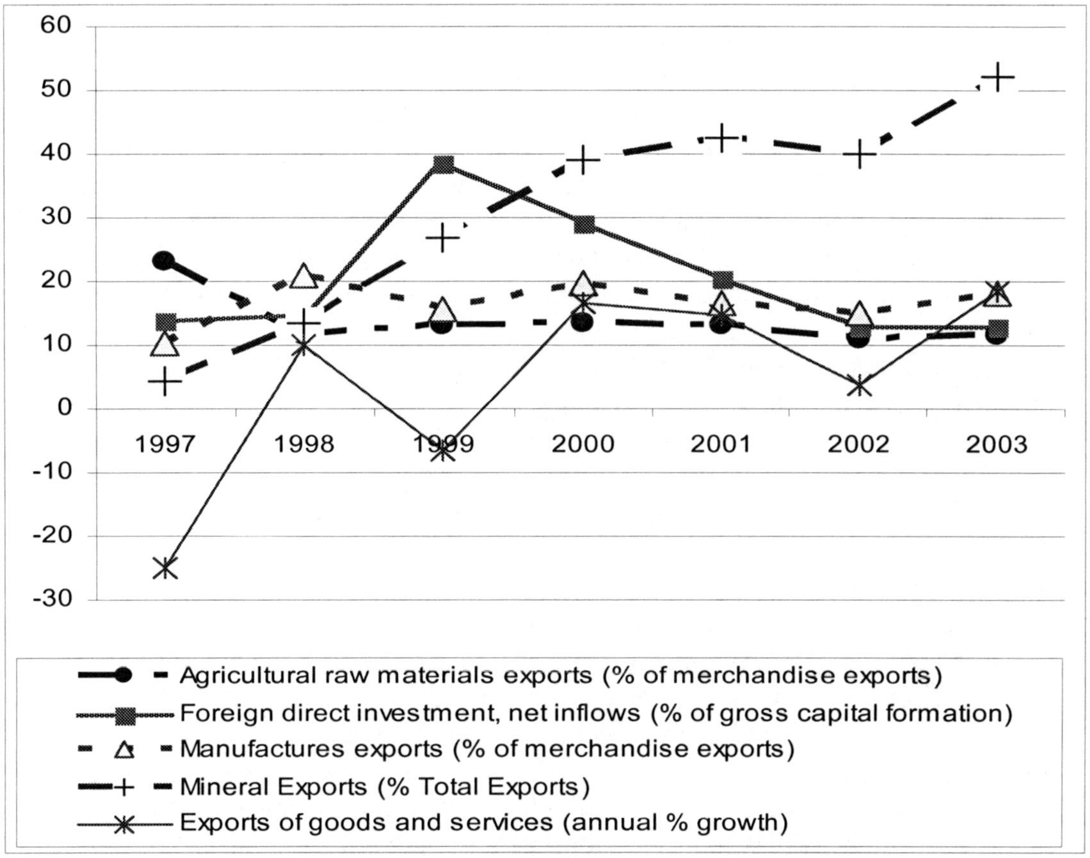

Source: World Development Indicators and Ministry of Planning and Privatization

TABLE 3

Foreign Direct Investment and Exports in Tanzania

Variables	Coefficient	t-values	p-values
Constant		9.15	0.00
FDI Flows (% GFCF)	0.35	2.02	0.05
GDP growth rate	0.46	2.67	0.01
Dependent Variable: Exports of goods and services (constant 2000 US$) $F = 9.976$ $P = 0.001$ $R^2 = 0.47$ $DW = 1.87$			

FDI and Tanzania's Private Sector Competitiveness

Tanzania's private sector is largely dominated by foreign owned firms. Prior to the arrival of FDI, the private sector was mainly dominated by state owned monopolies that were highly inefficient with poor quality products and services, high prices and frequent breakdown of supplies and shortages. On the other hand, the non-state sector was dominated by a large informal sector. Today, the private sector is underdeveloped, but with the entrance of FDI into Tanzania the private sector has begun to grow. The underdeveloped nature of the private sector in Tanzania can be seen by evidence of registration of investment projects (1990 to

2000) at the Tanzania Investment Centre (TIC registers investment projects with an investment capital greater than US$ 300,000), that shows that more than 60 percent of the investments were either joint ventures or wholly owned foreign affiliates. Based on the mode of entry, 53 percent of FDI value for all major foreign investors in Tanzania was green-fields while 47 percent were acquisitions. Most of the major foreign investments in the manufacturing sector were through acquisitions, while those in the tourism sector were green-fields. Major investors in the manufacturing sector include South African Breweries that acquired Tanzania Breweries, and Japan Tobacco that acquired Tanzania Cigarette Company, formerly owned by RJ Reynolds who had earlier acquired the company through privatization. Other major acquisitions in the manufacturing sector include Mtibwa Sugar and Illovo Sugar Company. All of these manufacturing companies in the agro-processing industries have been more closely linked to local producers where new methods of farming have been facilitated through contract farming. Through their linkages with small farmers, these manufacturing firms have provided these farmers ready market access. Local input suppliers that supply components to these manufacturing firms have also improved their competitiveness. For example, Kioo Ltd, a local manufacturer of glass bottles, has dramatically improved both its product quality and its production and management system to match Tanzania Breweries quality demands.

More than 64 percent of investment in the mining sector has been through green-fields. In the mining sector, there has been the largest inflow of capital along with infrastructure development and employment creation, and human capital development. For example, the case of Kahama mine shows that Barrick Gold has installed state of the art mining technology, with safe and efficient mining methods including high tech load-haul drills and dumpers. A major part of Tanzania's FDI in the service sectors is dominated by tourism, banking, telecommunications and retail trade. The telecommunication industry has also seen a substantial inflow of FDI and technology upgrading, with more than 55 percent of FDI gained through acquisitions. A major acquisition in the telecommunication industry is the Tanzania Telecommunication Company (TCC) that was acquired by a company from the Netherlands. Major green-fields investments in the telecommunication industries include VodaCom of USA/South Africa and MIC of United Kingdom. Through FDI, Tanzania has seen its hotels change from poor facilities that took clients for granted to having world class hotels, including global brands such as Sheraton (now Royal Palm) and Holiday Inn. Tanzania's tourist potential has been highly undermined by the lack of viable tourist facilities with global standards. However, with the coming of global franchises in this industry, Tanzania has seen the upgrading of tourist facilities and is offering new products and services.

A remarkable development in the service sector has been in the growth of FDI in the banking sector, where acquisitions of the National Bank of Commerce (NBC) and the Commercial Rural and Development Bank (CRDB) have successfully instilled new banking technology and trained Tanzanian staff to international standards. New banking products and services that are taken for granted in other parts of the world, such as ATM machines and credit cards, were until recently unheard of, but they are now available from the leading banks in Tanzania. Banks that entered the market as green-fields include Barclays Bank (UK), Citibank (UK), Standard Chartered (United Kingdom), International Bank of Malaysia, and Stanbic (South Africa). Entrance of these new banks has enabled other local banks to introduce new products, and to extend their product and client portfolio to serve small and medium size enterprises, a segment that is still yet to be served by commercial banks. The Standard Chartered bank, for example, introduced internet services for corporate clients and has all of its branches linked to computerized satellite networks. It has taken a proactive step in allocating special funds for staff training through in-house training and holding specific workshops, as well as sending its staff for training to foreign affiliates in the United Kingdom and elsewhere in the region.

CONCLUSION

Contrary to the growing consensus that, due to their limited human resource and investment capacity, least developed countries are not able to benefit from foreign direct investment, this study provides evidence that FDI has played a key role in transforming Tanzania's private sector to international standards by instilling new capital, modern technology, effective management and marketing methods, as well as product innovation and human resource development. Local firms that prior to FDI injection, were loss making and required government funding to survive, are now earning profits and paying dividends to their shareholders and paying taxes to the government. Evidence also shows that FDI has contributed to economic growth and exports. Greater investment in manufacturing and service sectors has contributed to greater economic growth. However, evidence also shows that there are still very low linkages with FDI and local firms in Tanzania. Most raw materials and inputs are largely imported, leaving very little value adding being done in Tanzania. This has a negative impact on the country's balance of payments. For policy makers this study suggests that efforts should be targeted towards measures for encouraging more FDI in the manufacturing sector. Policy makers should also find measures to encourage more linkages of FDI with local firms, and encourage sourcing of local inputs. This may be a problem with the low quality of local inputs and the relatively underdeveloped private sector in Tanzania. The dominance of mining FDI may also be a challenge for the country's future. Mining has a very short life and has negative long-term effects on the environment with very little linkages with local firms. Further research can look into the cost and benefits of long-term effects in this industry, especially when the average mine life is only 25 years. Since the time period in which Tanzania began its economic reforms is still recent, by building upon this initial evidence, further studies can replicate this study by examining FDI effects when more time series data is made available. Further studies can also build upon this study to examine the effects of FDI on poverty alleviation in Tanzania, as well as issues related to corporate social responsibility.

REFERENCES

Aitken, B. J. & Harrison. 1999. Do domestic firms benefit from direct foreign investment? Evidence from Venezuela. *American Economic Review,* 89:605–618.

Alfaro, L. 2003. Foreign direct investment and growth; Does the sector matter? *Harvard Business School,* Boston.

Blomstrom, M. & Kokko, A. 1996. Multinational corporations and spillover. *Journal of Economic Surveys,* 12: 247–277.

Bloomstrom, M.& Kokko, A. 2003 The economics of foreign direct investment incentives. *National Bureau of Economic Research Working paper* no. 9489.

Borensztein, E., J. De Gregorio, & Lee, J. W. 1998. How does foreign direct investment affect economic growth? *Journal of International Economics,* 45:115–35.

Caves, R. 1974. Multinational firms, competition and productivity in host country. *Economica,* 41:176–193.

Caves, R. 1996. *Multinational enterprise and economic analysis*. Cambridge: Cambridge University Press.

Haddad, M. & Harrison, A. 1993. Are there positive spillovers from direct foreign investment? *Journal of Development Economics,* 42:51–74.

Hanson, G. H. 2001. Should countries promote foreign direct investment? G-24 Discussion paper no. 9. New York: United Nations.

Hauman & Fenancez-Arias. 2000. *The strategy of economic development*. New Haven: Yale University Press.

Hirschman, A. 1958. *The strategy of economic development.* New Haven: Yale University Press.

Kokko, A. 1994. Technology, market characteristics and spillovers. *Journal of Development Economics,* 43:279–293.

Lipsey, R. E. 2002. *Home and host country effects of FDI. National Bureau of Economic Research Working Paper* no. 9293.

Razin, A., E. Sadka, & Yuen, C. 1999. An information-based model of FDI: The gains from trade revisited. *National Bureau of Economic Research Working Pape*r no. 6884.

Rodriguez-Clare, A. 1996. Multinationals, linkages and economic development. *American Economic Review,* 86:852–873.

Rutihinda, C. 2004. *Specific needs assessment regarding foreign direct investment in Tanzania*. Report for Danida's Market Access Program

Slaughter, M. J. 2002. *Does inward foreign direct investment contribute to skill upgrading in developing countries? Centre for Efficiency and Productivity Analysis Working Paper* no. 2002-8, New York.

Tanzania Investment Centre. 2004.http://www.tic.co.tz/ June 2004

Bank of Tanzania. 2005 http://www.bottz.org/Publications/TZInvestmentReports/Tanzania_Investment_Report_2004.pdf.

. The Presidents Office, Ministry of Planning and Privatization. 2004 Tanzania's Economic Survey. 2004 http://www.tanzania.go.tz/economicsurveyf.html. June 2005

UNCTAD' Investment Compass. 2005. United Nations Conference on Trade and Development. http://compass.unctad.org/. July 2005

UNCTAD's World Investment Report data base. 2005. United Nations Conference on Trade and Development *http://www.unctad.org/Templates/Page.asp?intItemID=3277&lang=1*. July 2005

World Bank. 2005 World Development Indicators Database. *http://publications.worldbank.org/subscriptions/WDI*. June 2005

Xu, B. 2000). Multinational enterprises, technology diffusion, and host country productivity growth. *Journal of Development Economics*, 62: 477 – 493.

BIOGRAPHICAL SKETCH

Dr. Cranmer Rutihinda has a PhD in International Business from Stockholm's University. He is an Associate Professor teaching International Business at Bishop's University, Canada. His current research interests include Globalization and Entrepreneurship Development.

THE SLOW GROWTH OF SMES IN SUB-SAHARAN AFRICA: MARKET, LEADERSHIP AND POLICY FAILURE

KWAME ASUMADU
Managing Director, Asumadu Pty Ltd,
Melbourne 3187
Australia
Tel: 61-3-9593 2435
Fax: 61-3-9593 2437
e-mail: kasumadu@bigpond.net.au

PREM RAMBURUTH
University of New South Wales
School of Organization and Management
Sydney 2052
Australia
Tel: 61-2-93855846
Fax: 61-2-96628531
e-mail: p.ramburuth@unsw.edu.au

Abstract

Universally, small to medium enterprises (SMEs) are considered the engine for economic growth, wealth creation and poverty eradication in both developed and developing economies. Compared with the newly emerging economies of Asia, and to some extent South America, the growth and development of SMEs in Sub-Saharan Africa since the end of colonialism, has been minimal. Many of the now emerging economies of Asia and South America were at the same level of socio-economic development as Sub-Saharan Africa in the 1950s and 1960s, prior to the achievement of political independence. This paper examines some of the factors which have contributed to the growth and development of SMEs in other economies, and explores why SMEs have not been successful to a similar extent in Sub-Saharan Africa. The paper argues that the lack of sufficient growth and development of SMEs in Sub-Saharan Africa since the end of colonization is a classic case of market failure i.e. the inability of the market forces to allocate scare resources efficiently in a way that achieves the highest total social welfare or benefit. We also argue that the lack of sufficient growth and development of SMEs in Sub-Saharan Africa is due to policy failure i.e. the inability of governments to develop and implement policies that support the continual and sustainable growth of SMEs. As classical economic theory justifies government intervention when market failure has occurred, the paper argues for strong intervention by governments and leaders in Sub-Saharan Africa to assist the economic take off of SMEs.

Key words: ***SMEs in Africa, African economic development, market and policy failure***

INTRODUCTION

Since many Sub-Saharan African countries gained political independence in the late 1950s and throughout the 1960s, the region's overall economic development has been less than impressive. This can be partly explained in terms of factors such as low level of appropriate and relevant skilled labour; inadequate financial resources; low level of technology; poor governance at the government and enterprise level; lack of adequate infrastructure; lack of market access, and events including civil war (Albaladejo 2002; Beyene, 2002; Kauffmann, 2005; Radwan and Al-Kibbi, 2001).

Several initiatives have been implemented through the activities of non-governmental organizations (NGOs), multilateral organizations and bilateral arrangements to address the problem of low economic development in Sub-Saharan Africa, with mixed results. In recent times, the growing poverty and economic deprivation in Sub-Saharan Africa has firmly been put on the international agenda again through initiatives such as:

- the New Partnership for Africa's Development (NEPAD) aimed, among other things, at improving transparency and facilitating good governance in Sub-Saharan Africa;
- Prime Minister Blair's Commission for Africa, which produced an Action Plan for Sub-Saharan Africa's development;
- the July 2005 Gleneagles G8 Leaders' meeting which foreshadowed the writing off of debt owed by some of the world's poorest economies, including many in Sub-Saharan Africa amounting to some US$40 billion; and
- the World Trade Organisation's 6th Ministerial Conference held in December 2005 in Hong Kong, which agreed to implement a program to improve market access, particularly for agricultural produce, from developing to developed countries.

An important ingredient which has been lacking in the quest to improve economic development in Sub-Saharan is the private sector, particularly the development and growth of small to medium enterprises (SMEs). The significant role SMEs play in the economies of developed countries and the emerging economies of Asia is recognized universally. Equally, the important contribution SMEs can make to socio-economic development and poverty eradication, particularly in Sub-Saharan Africa, has been the subject of many academic conferences, seminars and publications (Albaladejo, 2002; Asiedu, 2005; Beyene, 2002; Kaufmann, 2005; OECD, 2004; Uzor, 2004). As well, many multilateral organizations and NGOs have commissioned several studies that have produced an extraordinary number of reports on the subject.

The fact that little progress is occurring, despite the world-wide interest in effecting sustainable change, has led the authors to revisit the subject in this paper. We examine the factors that impede the sustainable performance of SMEs in Sub-Saharan Africa, and argue that there has been significant market and policy failure, which justifies active intervention by governments to address the problem.

REVIEW OF LITERATURE

Definition of SMEs

A review of the literature (Albaladejo 2002; Beyene, 2002; Kauffmann, 2005; Radwan and Al-Kibbi, 2001) indicates that there is no single universally accepted definition for SMEs. This is because, defining whether an enterprise is an SME or not, depends, to a large extent, on the relative level of economic development of the country under consideration. Generally, however, SMEs are defined or classified by the number of employees and/or value of capitalization. Universally, there is a minimum as well as a maximum size threshold for SMEs.

In Australia enterprises come in many different forms and structures. The Australian Bureau of Statistics' (ABS, 2004) definitions for enterprises, which come under the generic term SME, are provided below:

- SMEs (small and medium enterprises) have less than 200 employees;
- a small business is defined as a business that employs less than 20 people;
- medium businesses employ between 20 and 200 people;
- micro businesses employ less than 5 people;
- non-employing businesses such as sole traders and many partnerships do not employ people;
- SOHOs (small office home office) are small businesses operating mainly from home.

The threshold size for SMEs in the USA is 500. In Saudi Arabia, enterprises employing less than 10 workers are classified as SMEs (Radwan and Al-Kibbi, 2001). In Sub-Saharan Africa, the threshold sizes that are used to define SMEs in Australia and the USA may represent medium to large enterprises. According to Beyene (2002), in Mauritius, manufacturing enterprises using capital production equipment with a total CIF value of less than 10 million rupees (approximately US$326, 000) are defined as SMEs. Beyene (2002) reported that in Namibia, manufacturing SMEs are defined by the government as those with less than 10 employees, a turnover of less than N$1 million (approximately US$164,000), and capitalization of $N500, 000 (US$82,000). In other business sectors, an SME is defined as an enterprise employing less than 5 people, with a turnover of $N250, 000 (US$41,000) and capitalization of less than N$100,000 (US$16,400). Nigeria, on the other hand, defines SMEs as enterprises employing less than 100 people with capitalization of 100 million naira (approximately US$778,000).

Within the Sub-Saharan African context, the definition of SMEs is further complicated by the large informal sector, which is relatively absent in economies such as those of the USA and Australia. For this reason, Albaladejo (2002), while recognizing the importance of size in defining SMEs, argued that it is more appropriate to define or classify SMEs in Sub-Saharan Africa in terms of the factors which affect their competitiveness and growth. Factors used by Albaladejo (2002) to define SMEs in Sub-Saharan Africa include: location, ownership, legal status and sectoral specialization. Applying the traditional definition of SMEs to Sub-Saharan Africa, it can be argued that SMEs in the classical sense are very scarce. The private sector landscape in the Sub-Saharan African region is characterized by two extremes: a few large multinationals at one extreme and several micro-enterprises operating largely in the informal sector at the other. SMEs in the true sense constitute what Kauffmann (2005) describes as the "missing middle". For the purposes of this paper, we have adopted the definition that classifies enterprises by the number of employees and/or size of capitalization. It is recognized that the specific definition will differ from country to country, and will also depend on the level of economic development, including the extent of diversification within the economy. How a country defines an SME is inconsequential in this context. The most important consideration is the recognition by governments of the potential contribution the small business sector can make to economic development, and thus implement policies that will enable SMEs to develop and grow.

Economic importance of SMEs

In China, SMEs' contribution to national employment is estimated at 75%. SME contribution to employment in the economies of the European Union is around 66%, whereas in Japan it is around 70%. Beyene (2002) reported that in the USA, SMEs employ approximately 72 million people. In Asia SMEs represent more than 90% of industries in Indonesia, Philippines, Thailand and Hong Kong, Japan, Korea, India and Sri Lanka. According to Fadahunsi and Daodu (1997), in employment terms, SMEs accounted for 98% in Indonesia, 78% in Thailand, 81% in Japan and 87% in Bangladesh. SMEs and the informal sector account for about 63% of employment in low income countries (Ayyagari et al 2003). Because very few Sub-Saharan African countries have a working definition of SMEs, it is difficult to compare data. However, information summarized by Kaufmann (2005) and presented below, provides an overview of the economic importance of SMEs in selected countries in Sub-Saharan Africa:

- Congo has 2,100 firms in the formal sector and 10,000 in the informal sector;
- Benin, in 1997, had 666 SMEs of which 50% were in commerce and the balance was mostly in construction, pharmacies and restaurants, with only 17% in manufacturing;
- Kenyan SMEs employed some 3.2 million people in 2003 and accounted for 18% of national GDP;
- Senegalese SMEs contributed 20% of national value added;
- Nigerian SMEs account for 95% of formal manufacturing activity and 70% of industrial employment;
- South African micro and small businesses provided more than 55% of total employment and 22% of GDP;
- Small firms in South Africa accounted for 16% of both jobs and production;
- South African medium and large firms provided 26% of jobs and 62% of production.

Sub-Saharan Africa's economic picture

According to World Bank reports (2004), most Sub-Saharan African economies have been stable since the mid-1990s. IMF-instigated macroeconomic stabilization and reform programmes implemented by several Sub-Saharan African countries since the 1980s have achieved some encouraging results. For example, the rate of inflation for the whole of Africa declined from 23.3% in 1991-2000 to 10.1% in 2001-2004, largely as a result of reducing fiscal deficits and inflationary finance. On average, fiscal deficits declined from 5.2% of GDP in 1993-2000 to 1.68% in 2001-2004. The overall current account deficit reduced from 3.8% in 1981-1990 to 2% in 1991-2000 and 1% in 2001-2002. Effective macroeconomic reform is an important *sine qua non* for attracting foreign direct investment (FDI). Given Sub-Saharan Africa's stable macroeconomic environment for nearly a decade, the question that needs to be answered is: Why, when compared with emerging economies in other regions, SMEs in Sub-Saharan Africa are lagging behind in their ability to contribute their full potential to the economies of their region? In a region where unemployment is the second highest in the world, at 9.7% in 2005 (http://www.ilocarib.org.tt/news/2006/job-report.htm)[10], SMEs offer the greatest prospects for sustained job creation in Sub-Saharan Africa in the short to medium term because of the region's present lack of competitiveness in attracting foreign direct investment. In addition, the traditional role of the state as the largest

[10] The Middle East and North Africa remains the region with the highest unemployment rate in the world at 13.2 % in 2005.

employer in Sub-Saharan Africa has been declining as a consequence of these macroeconomic reforms. Indeed, one of the objectives of these reforms was to reduce government involvement in the areas of economic activity which the private sector is best able to handle most efficiently and effectively.

CONSTRAINTS TO THE GROWTH AND DEVELOPMENT OF SMES IN SUB-SAHARAN AFRICA

Factors listed in the literature (Albaladejo 2002; Beyene, 2002; Kauffmann, 2005; Radwan and Al-Kibbi, 2001) as contributing to the slow development and growth of SMEs in Sub-Saharan Africa include corruption, poor infrastructure, small local markets, difficult business conditions, cumbersome official procedures, underdeveloped legal systems, unattractive tax regimes, and lack of access to finance and simple technology. These factors are examined below.

Corruption

There are as many definitions of corruption depending on the forms it takes. Corruption can be overt or covert. For the purposes of this paper, we have defined corruption as any activity or behaviour that lacks integrity, undermines public transparency and accountability systems and measures, and leads to sub-optimal allocation of scarce resources (Deresky, 2006; Lane and Simpson, 1984). In Sub-Saharan Africa, payment of bribes is generally associated with the activities of governments, and the incentive to demand bribes arises from the inability of Sub-Saharan African countries to pay satisfactory or appropriate wages to government officials. One of the main impacts of corruption in Sub-Saharan Africa has been the misallocation of scarce resources, which has limited the ability of the private sector to create additional wealth. In a region where shortage of affordable capital is already a major challenge, the ability of SMEs to re-invest profits is seriously reduced through corruption. It also has an impact on the ability of the state to establish appropriate infrastructure and other support systems and services required for the sustainable development and growth of SMEs. Beyene (2002) reported that, in Nigeria, available business support services were often diverted to unintended sectors due to corruption.

Bribery, the most common manifestation of corruption, adds to the cost of doing business and has an effect similar to imposing a tax. Fisman and Svensson (2002) reported that, in Uganda, bribes added approximately 8% to the total cost of firms. In Kenya, bribery payments amounted to 5% of the sales of firms (Svensson 2003). With limited cash flow, SMEs are more adversely affected by the payment of bribes than large firms. Large firms, which in most cases are multinational corporations, are better able to absorb the impacts of bribery payments. Firstly, because of their political influence they can often avoid paying bribes or, where they have to pay to buy political influence, they can offset these payments through the tax system in their home countries as part of their normal business costs.

It is important to address corruption in Sub-Saharan Africa; however, it cannot be the unique factor that holds back the development and growth of SMEs in Sub-Saharan Africa. Transparency International's report for 2006 indicates that Sub-Saharan African countries are less corrupt, on average, than countries at the same income level in other parts of the world. For example, Burkina Faso, Ghana, Mali, and Rwanda ranked much higher than Bangladesh, Indonesia, Pakistan, and Vietnam. Yet the Asian countries' economies have tended to grow much faster over the past generation than those in Sub-Saharan Africa (http://www.project-syndicate.org). While corruption exists in all economies, in Sub-Saharan Africa its impacts on socio-economic development are far greater than in comparable economies in Asia and South America. The substantial economic growth achieved in the so-called Asian tiger economies suggests that, even where corruption exists, the private sector (including SMEs) can still develop and grow, provided public policy outcomes are effectively achieved. These include establishing appropriate infrastructure, and implementing business support systems necessary for the development and growth of businesses.

Poor Infrastructure

Infrastructure that supports the sustainable development and growth of the private sector can be divided into two broad categories: physical and soft infrastructure. Physical infrastructure includes energy, clean water, efficient road and rail transport systems, and an effective telecommunications system (postal, fax, telex, telephone network and ICT connectivity). Soft infrastructure encompasses technical and managerial skills, as well as easy access to knowledge and information. The lack of good physical infrastructure is one of the major causes of limited inter- and intra-African trade, an important ingredient for the development and growth of SMEs in Sub-Saharan Africa, given the small domestic markets of many of the countries. Figure 1 below, modified from UNECA data (2004a), illustrates the difficulty of cross border trade in Sub-Saharan Africa compared with other regions and/or economies.

Figure 1 compares the procedural requirements for exporting and importing a standardized cargo of goods, and includes all official procedures from the contractual agreement between the two parties to the delivery of goods along with the time necessary for completion. It shows that, on average, cross border trade within Sub-Saharan Africa takes the longest. The absence of infrastructure such as good road networks, and efficient and reliable air links, has also made it difficult for Sub-Saharan Africa to participate effectively in, and benefit from, globalization. UNECA (2004a) estimated the road density in Africa at 6.8 kilometres per 100 square kilometres, compared with Latin America's of 12 and Asia's of 18. Countries with relatively good physical infrastructure in Sub-Saharan Africa include Mauritius, Namibia and South Africa due to their colonial history. The deficiency of critical infrastructure in Sub-Saharan Africa is further illustrated by the data presented in Figures 2 to 5. Unreliable supply of energy affects the private sector through increased production costs compared with other parts of the world. In Senegal, the costs of power outages were estimated at 10% of sales (UNECA, 2004a).

The situation with ICT infrastructure is even worse. Whilst broadband connectivity has taken off rapidly in the developed world, the story in Africa is different. Sub-Saharan Africa has one of the lowest fixed line penetrations in the world, estimated at the end of 2002 at 2.8% compared with Europe's of 41% (UNECA, 2004a). Broadband market in Africa is currently at a nascent stage in development with users numbering only in the thousands at the end of 2002. The roll out of high-speed broadband services in Sub-Saharan Africa is limited by fixed line infrastructure. With fixed line penetration per 100 inhabitants ranging from 0.24 in the Central African Republic, 0.5 in Ethiopia, 1.03 in Kenya to 10.77 in South Africa, fixed line infrastructure is limited, and tends to be focused on urban areas, thus limiting the rollout of broadband technology. Not only is broadband growth constrained by the lack of fixed infrastructure, amongst other reasons, but it is also limited by a lack of bandwidth i.e. the range of frequencies through which voice, data and Internet traffic are transmitted. In addition, Africa has some of the world's highest costs for international calls and bandwidth, making it far more expensive for African internet service providers (ISPs) to operate than their developed world counterparts.

FIGURE 1
Time for Import (Days)

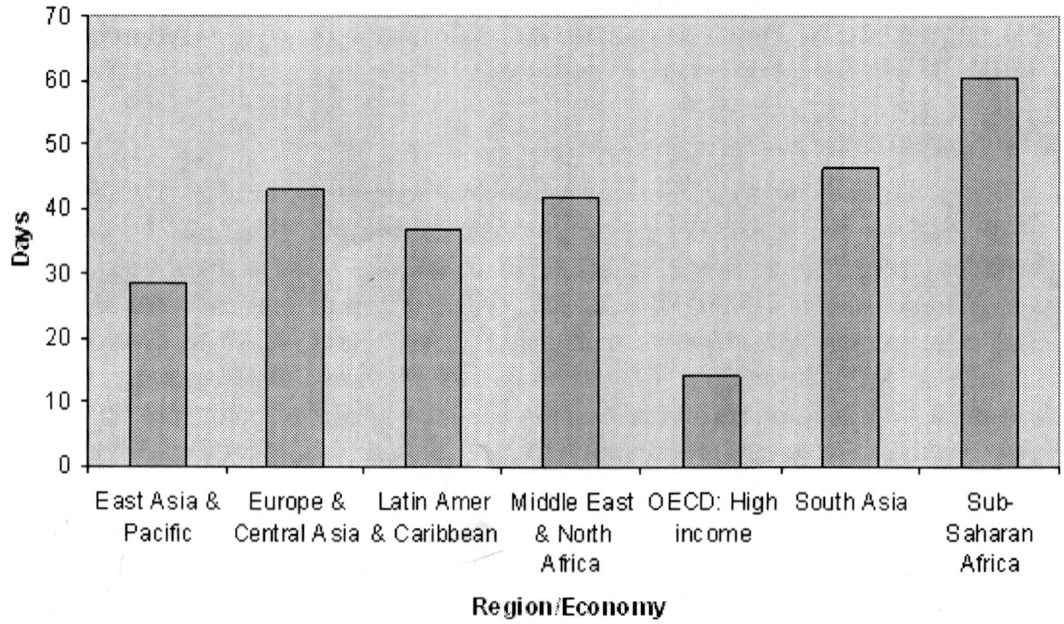

(Source: UNECA 2004a)

Figure 3 shows that only 12% of Sub-Saharan African roads are paved, compared with nearly 80% in Middle East and North Africa. Paved roads in Latin America and the Caribbean and East Asia and Pacific are around 30% and 25% respectively.

FIGURE 2
Electricity Consumption per Capita (kWh) in 2000

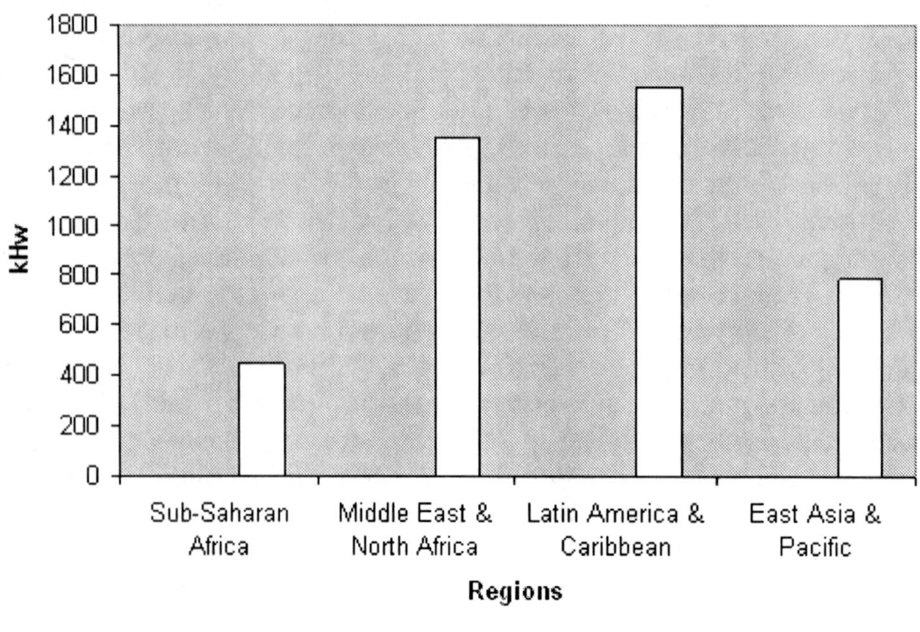

Source: UNECA 2004a

FIGURE 3
Paved Roads (% of Total Road Network, 1995-2000)

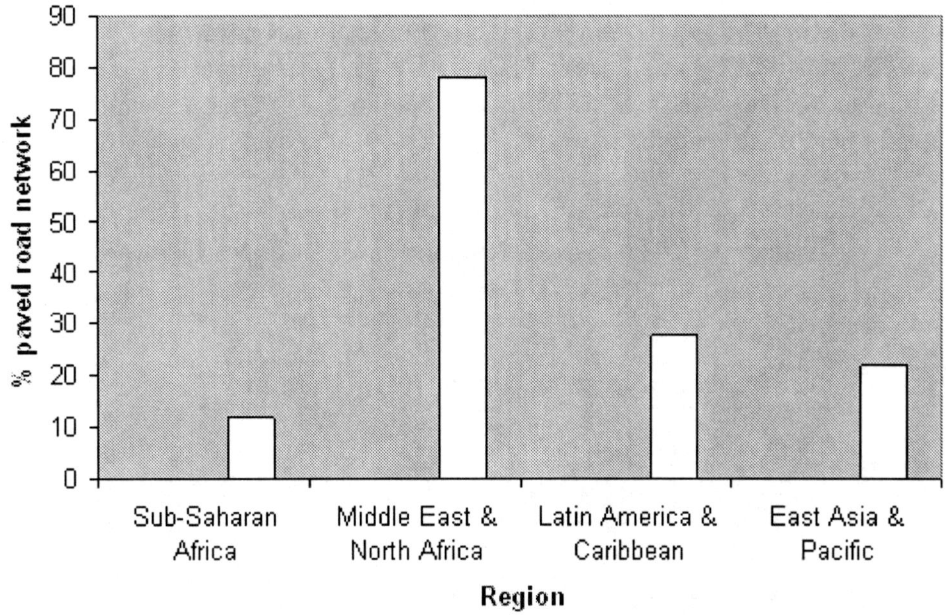

Source: UNECA 2004a

FIGURE 4
Telephone Mainlines (per 1,000 people) 2001

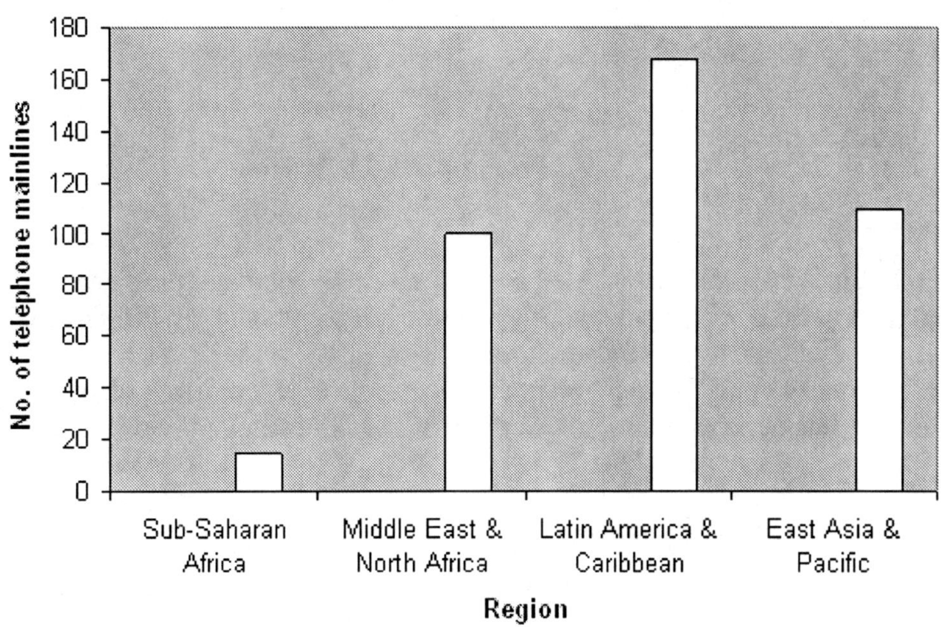

Source: UNECA 2004a

Figure 4 shows that in terms of telephone mains and related infrastructure, Sub-Saharan Africa is weaker compared with other developing regions. Not only is Sub-Saharan Africa deficient in the critical infrastructure required to support business activity, but costs for the use of available infrastructure are equally high.

Figure 5 (based on UNECA 2004a data) shows that transport costs in Sub-Saharan Africa are the highest among comparable regions and economies. The transport cost rate is the ratio of transport cost as a percentage of the value of imports. The high transport cost in Sub-Saharan Africa is associated with low network distribution which is estimated at 2.7 kilometres per 10,000 people.

FIGURE 5
Transport Costs World, Regional and Country Groupings, 2000

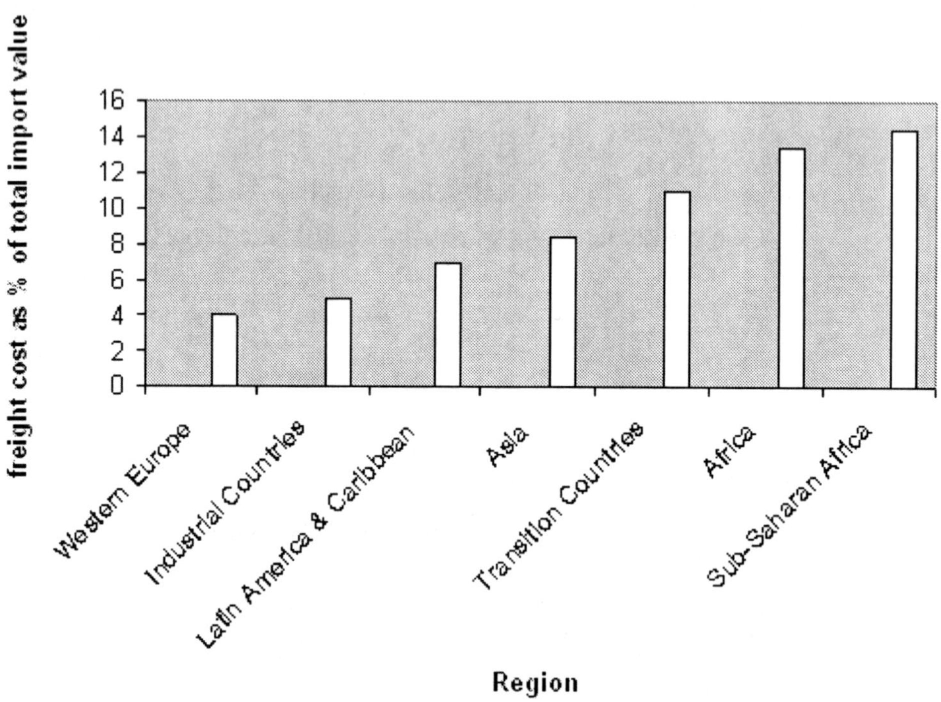

Source: UNECA 2004a

Essentially, Sub-Saharan Africa is not globally competitive in attracting foreign direct investment because of the perception of high overall risk, and the difficulty of doing business due to its rudimentary infrastructure. Sub-Saharan Africa's lack of good and reliable infrastructure can only be addressed through effective government policy i.e. by governments identifying this deficiency as a major priority and allocating appropriate resources to address it.

Small local and regional markets

Although Sub-Saharan Africa has over 10% of the world's population (some 650 million people), it has just 3% of its trade and only 1% of its Gross Domestic Product (Saul and Leys, 2000). A dynamic domestic or regional market is usually an important first step to gaining manufacturing experience. In most developed economies, active domestic markets linked to manufacturing industries underpin the development of the private sector. Except for the oil rich countries such as Angola, Gabon and Equatorial Guinea, the economies of many Sub-Saharan countries are fuelled by small-scale retailing i.e. micro-enterprises importing manufactured goods from overseas and selling them in markets and on street corners. This cannot be sustainable in the long term.

The importance of market size in economic development and world trade is demonstrated by the proliferation of free trade agreements and regional economic blocks in the world today, such as the North American Free Trade Area (NAFTA), Association of South East Asian Nations (ASEAN) and the European Union.

In Sub-Saharan Africa, dynamic domestic and regional markets could provide the much-needed training ground for "would be" entrepreneurs. At present, Sub-Saharan Africa's low economic development is impeding the development of dynamic domestic and regional markets. This situation is not likely to change in the short to medium term, unless governments in Sub-Saharan Africa implement policies that enhance employment growth and increase the purchasing power of their people through the rapid growth of the private sector.

Difficult Business Conditions

Favourable business conditions that support the development and growth of SMEs globally include:

- stable fiscal and monetary frameworks with reasonable interest rates;
- a financial market regime that provides incentives for increasing personal savings, and effective mechanisms for channelling savings into productive investments;
- a fair tax system that enables firms to retain some of their profits for re-investment;
- a diversified economy, with effective linkages between and among the various productive sectors: manufacturing, retailing and services;
- a simple and flexible compliance and regulatory framework devoid of excessive bureaucracy; and
- a well-developed legal system for the protection of ownership rights and the enforcement of contracts.

These enabling business conditions are lacking in many Sub-Saharan African countries. According to Beyene (2002), it is only in Mauritius and Namibia, and, to some extent in Kenya (through the assistance of the British aid agency DIFID), where explicit government policy measures are in place to reduce bureaucracy on SMEs. Government-related constraints described by Beyene (2000b, 2000c) include the lack of a legal regulatory framework for supporting SMEs, and customs duties and tariff regimes that favour overseas businesses but discriminate against local firms, including SMEs.

Beyene (2002) reported that even in South Africa, the most advanced and dynamic economy in Sub-Saharan Africa, despite more than 10 years having passed since apartheid ended, many of the barriers to effective black African participation in the private sector, including SMEs, still exist. In Nigeria, Beyene (2002) reported that, while rules and regulations were in place for leasing and corporate tax, as well as export and fiscal incentives, enforcement was weak due to the lack of political will. One of the reasons for the absence of effective and supportive enabling business conditions for the private sector in many Sub-Saharan countries is that government recognition of the role the private sector can play in socio-economic development is recent, and has only resulted from IMF imposed structural adjustment measures introduced in the late 1980s, which in most cases, were accepted reluctantly. In Asia, Singapore created these conditions within 30 years after independence.

Malaysia achieved these in less than 25 years, and Vietnam is emulating the examples of other so-called Asian tiger economies in less than 20 years.

The weak development of these private sector enabling conditions in many Sub-Saharan African countries can only be attributed to public policy failure, when it is considered that, Ghana, the first to achieve political independence in Sub-Saharan Africa did so nearly 49 years ago. Indeed in 1957, when both Ghana and Malaysia achieved political independence, the levels of socio-economic development in the two countries were similar (Asare and Wong, 2004).

Cumbersome Official Procedures

Compared with the rest of the world, the private sector in Sub-Saharan Africa faces some of the most cumbersome official procedures for formalizing a business, as illustrated in Figures 6 and 7 (based on World Bank Data, 2005). Excessive bureaucracy and unnecessary over-regulation by government institutions is one of the main causes of bribery payments. Excessive bureaucracy can cause considerable delays for businesses, and paying bribes is one mechanism to accelerate action. Figure 6 is a measure of the bureaucratic and legal hurdles an entrepreneur must overcome to incorporate and register a new firm. It includes the procedures, time, and cost involved in launching a commercial or industrial firm with up to 50 employees and start-up capital of 10 times the economy's per-capita gross national income (GNI).

FIGURE 6
Number of Procedures Required to Establish a New Business in Sub-Saharan Africa Compared with the Rest of The World

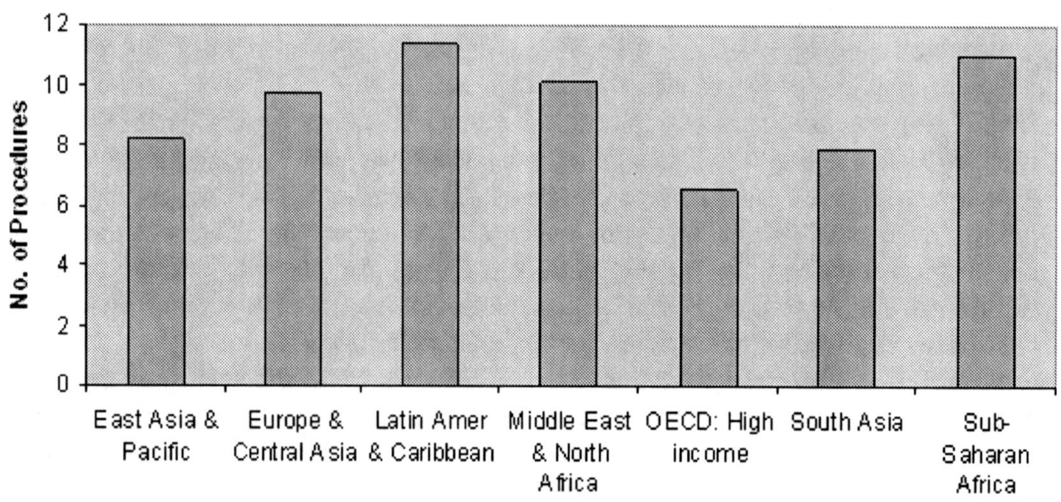

Source: World Bank, 2005

Company registration confers on businesses formal legal identity, and enhances the ability to obtain finance and credit, enter into and enforce contracts and receive government benefits such as business support services. In many developed economies such as Australia, business registration is a simple administrative procedure which takes only a few hours involving the completion of the appropriate forms either online or in hardcopy. According to the World Bank, of the 10 most difficult countries to register a business, seven are in Sub-Saharan Africa.

FIGURE 7
Number of Days (Duration) Required to Complete Each Procedure

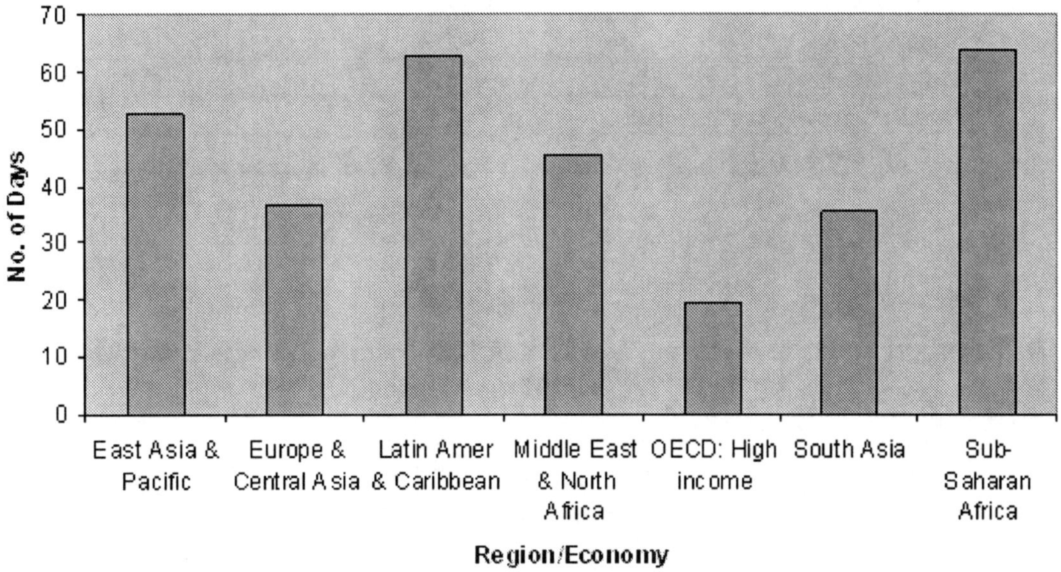

Source: World Bank, 2005

The cost of registering a business in Sub-Saharan Africa is equally high as shown in Table 1. As an illustration, a business can be registered in Denmark with no fee. In New Zealand, the world's second most efficient country for business registration, a new business can be registered for just $39. The average cost of registering a business in Africa is estimated at $785, with Ethiopia the lowest at $74 and Angola the highest at $6, 621 (World Bank 2004a). Sub-Saharan Africa is almost four times as expensive as in Latin America. Compared with East Asia and Pacific and South Asia, Sub-Saharan Africa is approximately five times as expensive, whereas it is almost 16 and 32 times as expensive respectively in Europe and Central Asia and OECD High Income countries.

As a further illustration, Table 2 shows the difficulty of hiring and firing workers in Sub-Saharan Africa compared with the rest of the world. Sub-Saharan Africa has the highest Difficulty of Hiring Index. The index measures the flexibility of labour regulations. It also measures the difficulty of hiring a new worker, rigidity of rules on expanding or contracting working hours, the non-salary costs of hiring a worker, and the difficulties and costs involved in dismissing a redundant worker. The relatively low hiring cost is due to the low wages paid to workers in the region. However, compared with an OECD economy, a fired worker in Sub-Saharan Africa can afford not to work for almost one year, a major disincentive to increasing productivity in the region.

TABLE 1

Official Cost of Each Procedure Required to Start a New Business in Sub-Saharan Africa, Compared with the Rest of the World

Region or Economy	Cost (%GNI per capita)
OECD: High Income	6.8
Europe and Central Asia	13.5
South Asia	39.7
East Asia & Pacific	42.9
Latin America & Caribbean	56.2
Middle East & North Africa	62.4
Sub-Saharan Africa	215.3

Source: World Bank, 2005

TABLE 2

Difficulty of Firing and Hiring Workers in Sub-Saharan Africa Compared with the Rest of the World

Region or Economy	Difficulty of Hiring Index	Hiring cost (% of salary)	Firing costs (weeks of wages)
OECD: High Income	30.1	20.7	35.1
Europe and Central Asia	34.5	29.6	32.8
South Asia	41.9	5.1	75
East Asia & Pacific	26	8.8	44.2
Latin America & Caribbean	40.5	15.9	62.9
Sub-Saharan Africa	48.1	11.8	53.4
Middle East & North Africa	30.8	15.9	62.4

Source: World Bank, 2005

Underdeveloped legal systems

Table 3 illustrates the relatively underdeveloped nature of the legal systems in Sub-Saharan Africa compared with the rest of the world. Among developing economies, the private sector in Sub-Saharan Africa has to contend with the highest number of procedures and delays for contract enforcement. Costs are similarly among the highest in the world, second only after East Asia and the Pacific. The undeveloped legal systems, coupled with the in-built inefficiencies, partly explain the existence of a high informal sector in Sub-Saharan Africa's private sector.

TABLE 3

Difficulty of Enforcing Contracts

Region or Economy	Number of Procedures	Time spent (days)	Cost (% of debt)
OECD: High Income	19.5	225.7	10.6
Europe and Central Asia	29.6	393	17.4
South Asia	29.7	385.5	36.7
East Asia & Pacific	30	406.8	61.7
Latin America & Caribbean	35.5	461.3	23.3
Sub-Saharan Africa	35.9	438.5	41.6
Middle East & North Africa	39.5	432.1	17.7

Source: World Bank, 2005

As can be seen in Table 3, on average, it requires almost 36 procedures and 434 days to enforce a contract in Sub-Saharan Africa, compared with 29 procedures and 386 days in South Asia, the easiest region for contract enforcement among the developing regions. If a transparent and efficient legal system for enforcing commercial contracts does not exist, it adds to the cost of doing business because, unless contracts can be legally and easily transferred, they cannot be used as security for acquiring new or additional capital. Being able to register a title or ownership rights enables *bona fide* claims to be ascertained for credit or collateral purposes. It also enables the lending institution to recover either all or part of the loan in situations of default or bankruptcy.

Another impact of an antiquated legal system is that it drives away Foreign Direct Investment. Investors are unlikely to invest in a country where they cannot be assured of effective legal protection for property rights. World Bank data (2005) shows that it takes more than six months to register a property in Ghana, Rwanda, the Ivory Coast, Angola, Nigeria and Togo. Ghana has the longest delay with more than 382 days. Similarly, the cost of property registration in Sub-Saharan Africa exceeds the average in the other regions. On a brighter note though, South Africa, Namibia and Mozambique are among the most efficient countries in the world for property registration, even faster than the average for OECD countries.

Unattractive Tax Regimes

For a country's tax system to assist national revenue generation, savings and private sector growth, it must be simple, fair and efficient to administer. Simplicity relates to the types and rates and makes it easier to understand. A fair tax system is not regressive i.e. it does not impose disproportionate burden on disadvantaged groups. An efficient tax system is less costly to administer, leading to more revenue being collected by the state. It is important that the tax system is not an incentive for evasion. An inefficient tax system encourages tax evasion and loss of revenue to the state.The experience in many Sub-Saharan African countries is that the tax systems are designed only to collect revenue from firms and individuals but make it either difficult or impossible for businesses and pay-as-you-earners (PAYEs) to claim legitimate costs incurred in earning an income. In theory, Ghana's Value Added Tax (VAT) is similar to Australia's Goods and Services Tax (GST) i.e. it is a tax levied on outputs rather than inputs. In practice, however, the VAT is commonly collected on inputs, which disadvantages the private sector.

FIGURE 8
Total Number of Taxes Paid

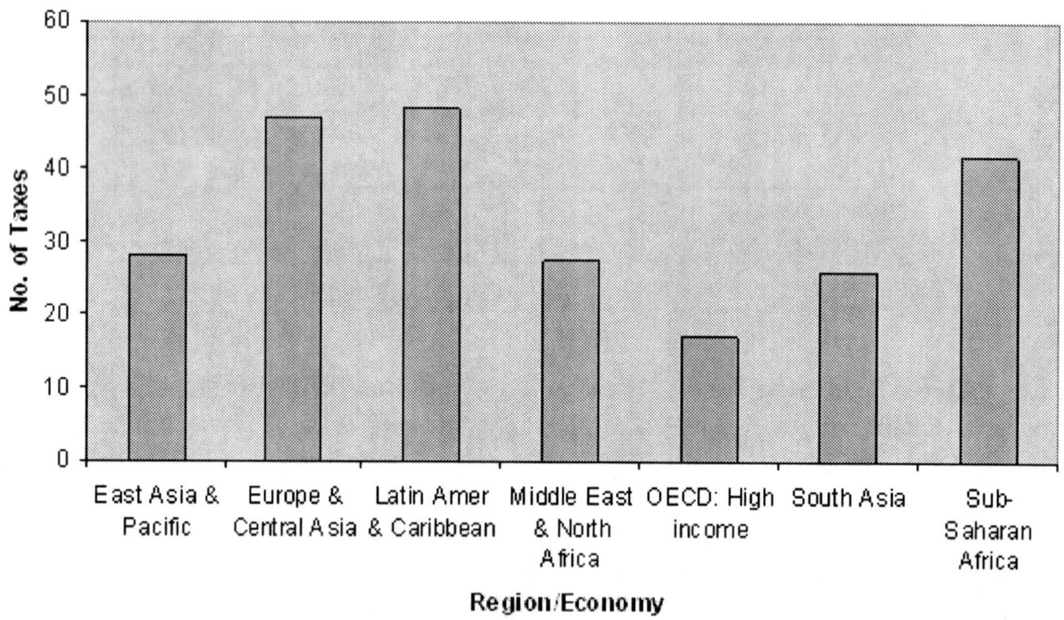

Source: World Bank, 2005

Figure 8 shows that Sub-Saharan Africa is among the regions with the highest number of taxes, comparable only to Europe and Central Asia and Latin America and the Caribbean regions. The relative improvement in Sub-Saharan Africa's taxation system, as shown in Figure 8, has been the result of taxation reforms implemented by some countries in the last 20 years, which have brought them in line with other developing regions. However, countries such as the Democratic Republic of Congo and Egypt still retain some of the highest marginal corporate tax rates at 40%. This is 10% higher than the norm of about 30% recommended by the World Bank (2004a). Compounding the adverse impact of the tax system on the business sector in Sub-Saharan Africa is the narrow tax base, caused in part by high unemployment and the large informal sector. Consequently, the private sector generally bears a disproportionate amount of the tax burden. The narrow tax base also explains the large number of taxes paid as shown in Figure 8. Growing the SME sector will contribute to broadening the tax base and assist in spreading the taxation burden equitably.

Figure 9 illustrates the high taxation burden in Sub-Saharan Africa compared with the rest of the world. With a simple, efficient and a fair tax system, Sub-Saharan African countries will not need tax holidays as incentives for attracting Foreign Direct Investment.

Tax holidays create distortions in economies, and disadvantage domestic firms to whom the incentives do not apply.

FIGURE 9
Total Tax Payable (% Gross Profit)

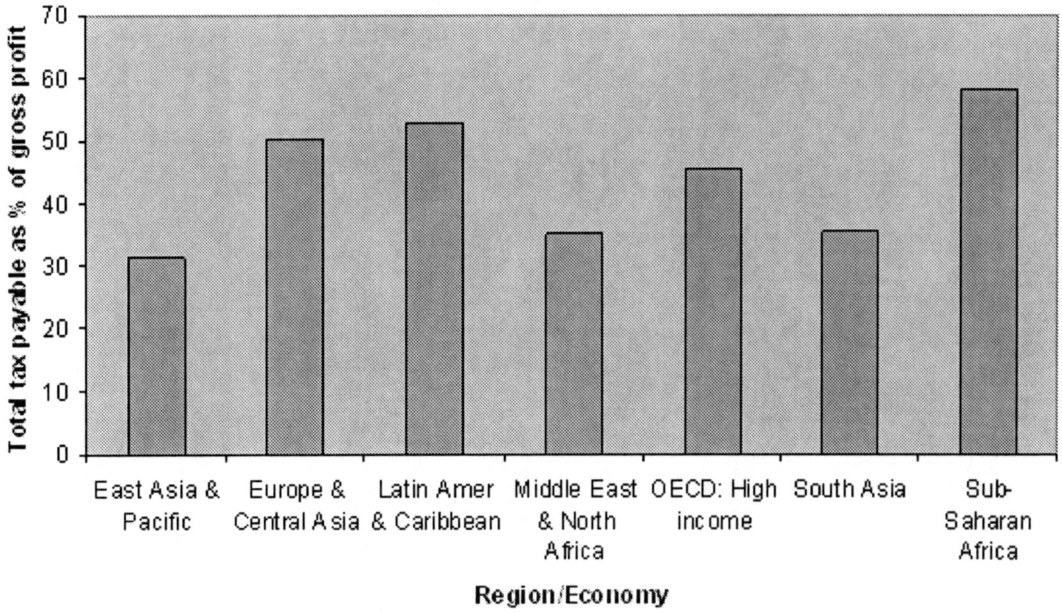

Source: World Bank, 2005

Lack of Access to Finance/Capital

One of the major factors listed in the literature (Albaladejo 2002; Beyene, 2002; Kauffmann, 2005; Radwan and Al-Kibbi, 2001) as hampering the sustainable growth of SMEs in Sub-Saharan Africa is the lack of access to finance or capital. Kaufmann (2005) reported that the main sources of capital for Sub-Saharan African SMEs are retained earnings and private savings. The legal Rights Index shown in Figure 10 is a measure of the extent to which collateral and bankruptcy laws facilitate lending. Sub-Saharan Africa is among the regions with the lowest Legal Rights Index, although it is higher than comparable regions in Latin America and the Caribbean, Middle East and North Africa and South Asia.

The experience universally is that, in developing countries, the main problem with finance relates to access rather than the lack of its availability *per se*. The high cost of money arises from the high level of risk financial institutions such as the banks attach to lending money to SMEs. In most Sub-Saharan African countries the cost of money as reflected by interest rates is very high. In 1999, the International Monetary Fund (IMF) estimated that the average domestic lending rates ranged from 17% per annum in Liberia to a fixed 22% in Cameroon, Gabon and the Congo. In Ghana it was 26%. Only in Togo and the Cote d'Ivoire are domestic interest rates around 5% per annum. The UNECA survey in 2002 reported that in Gabon and Cameroon interest rates were as high as 25%. In Uganda, rates were between 22 and 27% and in South Africa they were between 30 and 40%. The high cost of finance affects the ability of borrowers to service the loan. Although structural adjustment and improved economic management is gradually changing the situation in many sub-Saharan

African countries, commercial bank interest rates still remain too high for many SMEs. High interest rates in Sub-Saharan Africa are not only a function of the level of assessed risk. In most Sub-Saharan African countries, the financial system is under-developed, due to inadequate government policies and support. This has resulted in the underdevelopment of capital markets and minimal or non-existent shareholding.

FIGURE 10
Legal Rights Index

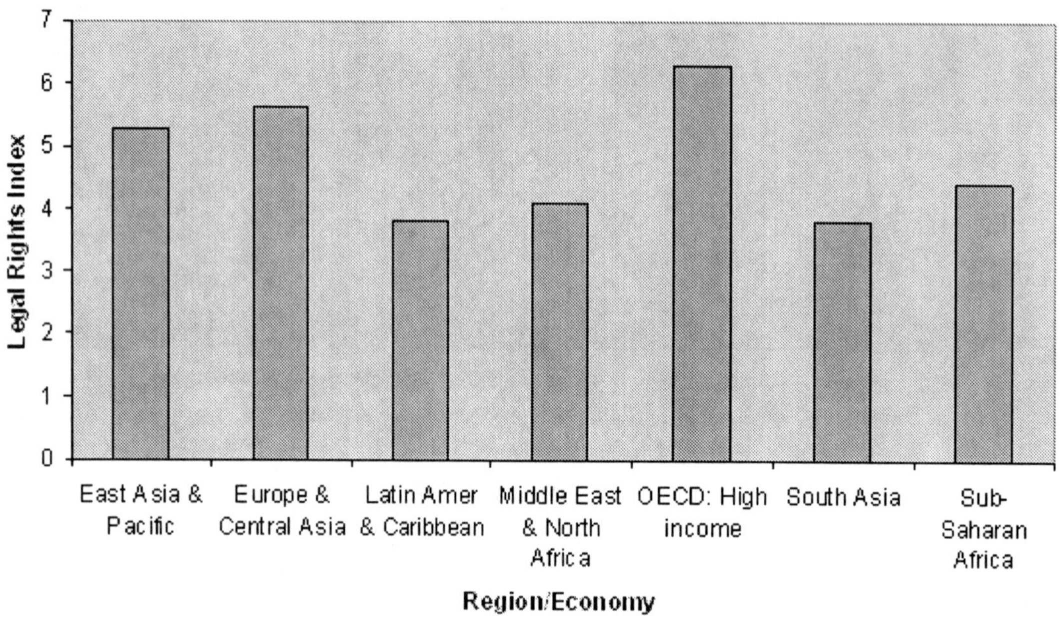

Source: World Bank, 2005

With a few exceptions such as South Africa and Mauritius, the financial sector is still controlled in many respects by governments, thus making it impossible for them to be creative in offering a wide range of products and services to meet the needs of the different sectors within the economy. This situation has arisen because of the failure of governments to provide adequate public resources to support the growth and development of the financial systems in a manner that allows them to be the backbone for SME growth. Similarly, policy failure arises because government control of these institutions makes it impossible for them to operate based on private sector/commercial principles, as occurs in developed and some emerging economies.

Enabling Policy and Regulatory Environment

One of the fundamental roles of governments is to develop and implement policies that enable the private sector to develop, flourish and grow. Elements that constitute favourable or enabling policy and regulatory environment for strong private sector development and growth include:

- articulated public policy with clear support and assistance measures including incentives, and backed by adequate resources for their implementation and delivery;

- a legal system that protects individual civil and ownership rights, and enables commercial and business disputes to be addressed based on the rule of law, and at arms length from government control or influence;
- on-going public investment in hard and soft infrastructure that enhances efficiency and effectiveness, and improves competitiveness through reducing transaction cost;
- machinery of government that enhances rather than impedes private wealth creation;
- a visionary and innovative public policy framework that communicates confidence and welcomes both domestic and overseas investment;
- structures and systems that enable governments to seek and appropriately consider inputs from the private sector in policies relating to the private sector; and
- a system of government which encourages and nurtures the growth and development of private sector organizations and institutions such as professional associations and bodies and chambers of commerce and industry.

An enabling policy and regulatory environment as described above is lacking in many Sub-Saharan African countries. Indeed, in most Sub-Saharan African countries, the private sector is either weak or rudimentary due to neglect by governments.

The private sector is often neglected in public policy considerations in Sub-Saharan Africa because it is not usually considered the responsibility of government to nurture and assist its growth. It can be argued that in some countries, the private sector is seen as the "enemy" rather than a partner with government to achieve socio-economic development. This is partly historical, arising from the legacy of military coups in Sub-Saharan Africa in the 1970s and 1980s when wealthy private business people were alleged to have been the financiers for some of the coups. This ill-feeling against the private sector continues to exist in some countries today. Added to this is the phenomenon we describe as the "politics of envy" whereby in many Sub-Saharan African countries, politicians and government officials consider that it is not in the national interest for the indigenous business sector to be successful in creating wealth. Wealth creation is seen as the exclusive preserve of elected politicians and senior public servants.

Stability of Government

The lack of "democratic" systems of government in some Sub-Saharan African countries is often cited as one of the causes of the under-development of a robust private sector in many of the economies. Democracy, as defined by the election of the government of the day by popular mandate, is growing in Sub-Saharan Africa. The trend started in the 1980s with the imposition of structural adjustment on struggling economies by the IMF, and has gathered pace since the creation of NEPAD in 2001. Today, NEPAD estimates that there are over 18 democratically elected governments in Sub-Saharan Africa and growing. However, democracy in terms of holding elections is not the issue. Many of the emerging economies in Asia, which have achieved extraordinary growth in their economies and the private sector, cannot be described as democracies in the classical sense. Examples are China and Vietnam.

In terms of the development of the private sector, what is important is stability of government and therefore predictability of policy as shown by the examples of Singapore and Malaysia. The private sector can cope provided it knows the rules of the games in advance, and it is confident that the rules are not going to change drastically midstream. Policy failure with respect to political institutions in Sub-Saharan Africa has arisen from the fact that since the end of colonization, there has been little stability in governmental structures, with its attendant lack of continuity of public policy development and implementation. One common factor among both developed and emerging economies in terms of the development of the private sector is the stability of government, irrespective of its type and nature.

Lack of Support for Entrepreneurship Development

There is no shortage of entrepreneurship in Sub-Saharan Africa. Entrepreneurship abounds in Sub-Saharan Africa, and is exhibited visibly in the streets and market places of several Sub-Saharan African cities every day. According to Beyene (2004), entrepreneurship is a function of opportunities, technical, managerial and commercial skills, availability of finance or capital, infrastructure and an overall environment which supports the growth and development of business. The lack of these prerequisites for entrepreneurship development in Sub-Saharan Africa since the end of colonialism can be attributed to the failure of governments to develop and implement policies which would have enabled these conditions to exist. Even today, except in South Africa and to some extent in Mauritius, very few Sub-Saharan African countries have policies specifically designed to support SMEs. In Malaysia, government policy is in place with adequate public resourcing ostensibly to encourage SME linkages. In Sub-Saharan Africa, where similar policies exist, they do so in name only, with inadequate resources provided to enable their effective implementation. Government commitment to, and support for, SME development in Sub-Saharan Africa must be demonstrated through the development and implementation of policies that lead to:

- measurable increase in technological and managerial competence and skills; and
- access to real market opportunities and resources (finance, information, skilled personnel etc.).

Competition

Private enterprises including SMEs develop and grow where public policy ensures fair and open competition. In Australia, government policy is continually reviewed to ensure that it does not disadvantage SMEs in favour of large companies. It is universally accepted that free market forces, critical as they are to the growth and development of the private sector, cannot be relied on entirely to ensure fair and effective competition. An effective regulatory environment is equally important and necessary.

Since the introduction of a goods and services tax (GST) in Australia in 2000, governments (Federal and State) have been reviewing their compliance requirements to ensure that they do not burden SMEs with unnecessary bureaucracy and paperwork. There is very little evidence that Sub-Saharan African governments are reducing the cumbersome processes and requirements on the private sector, let alone SMEs. In Australia, the Australian Consumer and Competition Commission (ACCC) promotes competition and fair trade in the market place to benefit consumers, business and the community at large. It also regulates national infrastructure services. Its primary responsibility is to ensure that individuals and businesses comply with the Commonwealth competition, fair trading and consumer protection laws. The role of Australia's ACCC demonstrates how government policy can be used to ensure the development and growth of SMEs in a meaningful and supportive manner.

CONCLUSION

The literature is replete with advice, suggestions and recommendations on how to jump start SMEs in Sub-Saharan Africa. Amid the doom and gloom, ample evidence exists to demonstrate that macroeconomic reforms started in Sub-Saharan Africa are bearing fruit in some countries. However, successful economic management is a journey, not a destination. Economies are only successful if reforms are on-going. Experience in other regions has shown that Foreign Direct Investment flows freely to countries with stable political and economic environments. Open markets, minimal regulation, good infrastructure facilities, and low production costs are also key factors in attracting and holding Foreign Direct Investment. Bringing these factors together has proven difficult for many countries in Sub-Saharan Africa.

We believe that the lack of reforms to achieve these outcomes is the result of both market failure and policy failure, which justify effective government intervention. As commented by the World Bank (2004) creating an enabling environment for the private sector to grow and create jobs is an important government responsibility. This does not mean that governments have to go it alone. Private-public partnerships are being adopted, even by many developed economies such as Australia, to boost the establishment of critical infrastructure to underpin continual economic growth. In a region where there seems to be a perpetual scarcity of public resources, private-public partnerships may be useful in assisting to address the chronic scarcity of functional infrastructure. Building the infrastructure is not sufficient in itself. The infrastructure has to be maintained to ensure that a return on the investment can continue to be realized. In the past, Sub-Saharan African countries have not proven to be good at maintaining critical public infrastructure, providing another justification for private sector involvement. To achieve sustainable economic development outcomes, Sub-Saharan African countries should not re-invent the wheel. The emerging economies of Asia provide the blueprint for what is required. What is needed is strong and committed leadership, with a vision for the future, to make it happen.

REFERENCES

Albaladejo, M. 2002. *Promoting SMEs in Africa: Key Areas for Policy Intervention*, UNIDO.

Asare, B., and Wong, A. 2004. An Economic Development of Two Countries: Ghana and Malaysia. http://www.westafricareview.com/issues5/asare-wong.htm, accessed 20 April 2006.

Asiedu, E. 2005. *Foreign Direct Investment in Africa: The Role of Natural Resources, Market Size, Government Policy, Institutions and Political Instability*. Helsinki, Finland: The World Institute for Development Economics Research.

Ayyagari, M., Beck, T., and Demirguc-Kunt, A. 2003. *Small and Medium Enterprises Across the Globe: A New Database*. Policy Research Working Paper 3127. Washington, D.C.: World Bank.

Beyene, A. 2002. Enhancing the Competitiveness and Productivity of Small and Medium Scale Enterprises (SMEs) in Africa: An Analysis of Differential Roles of National Governments Through Improved Support Services. *Africa Development,* 27 (3): 130-156.

Derseky, H. 2006. *International Management: Managing Across Borders and Cultures* (5th Ed.). Upper Saddle River, New Jersey: Pearson Education.

Fadahunsi, O. and Daodu, T. 1997. *Small and Medium Enterprise Development: Programmes and Prospects.* Lagos: West African Management Development Institutes Network.

Fisman, R., and Svensson, J. 2002. Are Corruption and Taxation Really Harmful to Growth? Firm-Level Evidence. Stockholm University: Institute for International Economic Studies. http://www.iies.su.se/~svenssoj/corrgrowth.pdf, accessed 20 April 2006.

International Monetary Fund. 1999. *World Outlook.* Washington D C.

Kauffmann, C. 2005. *Financing SMEs in Africa: Policy Insights #7.* OECD.

Lane, H.W. and Simpson, D.G. 1984. Bribery in International Business. *Journal of Business Ethics*, 3: 35-42.

NEPAD. 2004: *Personal Communication.* Johannesburg, South Africa.

OECD (Organisation for Economic Co-operation and Development). 2004. *Women's Entrepreneurship: Issues and Policies.* Paper prepared for the Second OECD Conference of Ministers Responsible for Small and Medium-Sized Enterprises, June 3-5, Istanbul.

Radwan, I. and Al-Kibbi, J. 2001. *Small and Medium Enterprise Development: A Vision for Action in Saudi Arabia.* Washington D C: World Bank Group.

Saul, J. S., and Leys, C. 2000. Sub-Saharan Africa in Global Capitalism. Monthly Review, 1(3). http://www.monthlyreview.org/799saul.htm, accessed 20 April 2006.

Svensson, J. 2003. Who Must Pay Bribes and How Much? Evidence from a Cross Section of Firms. *Quarterly Journal of Economics,* 118 (1): 207-230.

UNECA (United Nations Economic Commission for Africa). 2004a. *Economic Report on Africa 2004: Unlocking Africa's Trade Potential.* Addis Ababa, Ethiopia.

UNECA, 2001b. *Emerging Issues in Private Sector Development: Enhancing the Competitiveness of SMEs in Africa.* ECA/DMD/PSD/01/02.

Uzor, O. 2004. *Small and Medium Scale Enterprises Cluster Development in South-Eastern Region of Nigeria.* Universitat Bremen, Germany: Institute for World Economics and International Management.

World Bank. 2004. Enabling the private sector to create jobs. http://www.uneca.org/era2005/chap7.pdf, accessed 26 April 2006.

World Bank. 2004a. *Doing Business in 2005 Sub-Saharan Africa: Regional Profile.* Washington, D.C.: Investment Climate Department, Monitoring, Analysis and Policy Unit.

World Bank. 2005. Doing Business in 2005: Removing Obstacles to Growth. http://www.doingbusiness.org/documents/DoingBusiness2005.pdf, accessed 16 April 2006).

SECTION 4

SPECIAL ISSUES IN LEADERSHIP AND MANAGEMENT IN SUB-SAHARAN AFRICA

MANAGEMENT PREROGATIVE, DIVERSITY AND RELATIONSHIPS: PANDORA'S BOX REVISITED

PIETER NEL

PROFESSOR OF HUMAN RESOURCES MANAGEMENT
School of Management and Entrepreneurship
Unitec
New Zealand
Tel: Int. + 09 815 4321 ext 7026
Fax: Int. + 09 815 4374
e-mail: pnel@unitec.ac.nz

Abstract

Today businesses operate in a fast changing global environment with many legislative and competitive influences affecting them continuously, albeit to a greater or lesser extent. The business environment includes "management prerogative" which refers to the "right to manage" and is vested in management. It is reflected in the formal contract of employment between the employer and employee. It is influenced by, for example, diversity, customs and social capital. This diversity leads to the concept of "employer prerogative" being fragile in nature.

Relationship building is becoming increasingly important for cross-cultural management as more and more countries do business across borders. Current research findings in this regard have so far mainly focused on marketing relationships or on cross-cultural dimensions. This paper explores relationship building from a social capital, culture and diversity perspective while incorporating relevant intercultural dimensions in the context of "management prerogative", based on dove tailing the results of two research studies.

A model to integrate diversity management and management prerogative but also capitalising on social capital applications is proposed to deal with uncertainties in the multi-cultural and complex current day business environment in South Africa.

Key words: management prerogative, communication, business relationships, social capital, diversity, South Africa.

Introduction

Doing business is increasingly subject to challenges. To be successful in business under the fast changing circumstances worldwide, an emphasis on diversity and cultural issues is important.

The question therefore arises whether "successful management" still includes "management prerogative" in the context of diversity, employment equity and often complex employment legislation, which exists in many countries. A further question that arises is whether compliance with the prescribed legislation requirements in a country is possible while management autonomy and prerogative currently vested in management is being preserved. However, in countries where democracy is the form of government practised a tripartite relationship usually also exists between labour, management and government. This approach usually also supports a market driven economy such as that of the United Kingdom, Australia, the United States of America and South Africa. The governmental approach mentioned above would largely influence the nature and the way in which business is conducted in a particular country.

Whilst appreciating the aforementioned concepts Van Dyk (2001) states that in the context of labour and employment law, "management prerogative" refers to the employers' "right to manage" a business. It is generally accepted that the basis for this right is the formal contract of employment entered into by the organisation (regarded as the employer) and the employee. However, when "managerial prerogative" is approached in terms of culture, religious sensitivities, diversity, customs and employment equity, it becomes apparent that the concept is very fragile and difficult to apply in practice. This fragility and difficulty is due to the rigidity and narrowness of the legal and other statutory restrictions on the one hand and the subjective interpretations by society of, for example, customs and culture on the other hand regarding the interpretation of the concept of management prerogative in practice.

The business of businesses is commonly accepted to include being able to apply economic principles to remain competitive, keeping stakeholders satisfied and retaining managerial prerogative. Attempts to increasingly limit management's prerogative will reduce long-term survival prospects of businesses in a market driven economy, regardless of good communication and relationship building efforts. Relationship building is, however, becoming increasingly important in cross-cultural management as more and more countries do business across borders worldwide, whilst trying to enhance social capital as well. Furthermore, there appears to be limited research in Southern Africa in particular, which acknowledges management prerogative in the context of various cultures and relationship building, to determine its pervasiveness and conversely its limitations.

A fruitful area for research is to investigate the concepts and relationships between relationship building, social capital and managerial prerogative. The research would enable the establishment of a model to accommodate the preceding factors, which impact upon businesses and management in South Africa in particular. It implies that by utilising a model as a roadmap, it will assist organisations to identify their goals and objectives in the aforementioned context via its strategic planning process. This approach would therefore incorporate the aforementioned elements, which impact on and enhance the functioning of businesses in the South African business environment.

The paper is organised in the following manner. First, a discussion of the concept of management prerogative and diversity is undertaken. Secondly, the focus is on developing a framework based on intercultural communication, relationship building and social capital. Thirdly, some background information is provided about culture in South Africa. Fourthly, the methodology and results from the culture dimension interviews and the case study on management prerogative are discussed. Fifthly, relationship building research and management prerogative is discussed to establish a model to observe management prerogative, combined with social capital and culture interventions. Finally some implications for management in South Africa are presented in terms of the identified issues.

Literature Review

Various concepts are analysed to determine the approach to and impact of management and "management prerogative" as well as diversity. These concepts are then linked to relationship building, social capital and culture.

A theoretical framework for cultural characteristics based on social capital theory using Hofstede's (1991) intercultural taxonomies and culture-specific theories needs to be noted as having an impact on the concepts discussed in the paper. It is, however, not discussed in any detail as it does not form the focus of this paper. It is meant to act as an aid to contextualize management prerogative related concepts.

An analysis of the concept "prerogative" The term "prerogative" is defined in the electronic version of the Concise Oxford Dictionary (1999) as denoting a right or privilege, which belongs to a particular institution, group or person. Theoretically this right or privilege is unlimited, but in practice it is restricted by common law, labour legislation and social as well as religious customs and traditions.

"Employer prerogative" is taken to imply the "right to manage" an organisation (Industrial Law Journal 1989:705). It refers to the right to make decisions regarding the aims of the organisation and the ways in which it is to achieve these aims (Industrial Law Journal 1996:582). A further refinement is to demarcate "management prerogative", which is defined by Van Dyk (2001:26) as follows: "The residue of discretionary powers left to management when the restrictive impact of the common law, legislation, delegation of power, economic bargaining power, collective agreements, the legal employment contract and the psychological contract have been subtracted."

The abovementioned concept regarding the management context of an organisation is twofold in nature. The first meaning of management prerogative relates to decisions of an economic nature, such as the acquisition and/or use of physical assets needed by the organisation, its aims, and products or services it provides (Industrial Law Journal 1992:407). The second meaning refers to decisions relating to the human resources utilised by an organisation. This distinction is not watertight and many of the decisions that fall within one category will exert an influence on the other category. A further aspect raised by Van Dyk (2001) is why the owner of a business has the power to manage, as opposed, for example, to a "workers committee" or a body that represents the interests of the other stakeholders in the business? This also points to the difference between ownership (the employer) and management where, for example, shareholders with only a few shares in a business are theoretically also the owners (therefore the employer), but have insignificant, if not non-existent, direct managerial prerogative. This aspect is also highlighted elsewhere in the paper.

The most convincing argument for employer prerogative is that it is contained in the legal contract of employment, which has subordination to authority as one of its legal components (Brassey, Cameron, Cheadle & Olivier 1987). Since this concept is well governed by legislation such as the Labour Relations Act No.28 of 1956 as amended (which was superseded by Act No.66 of 1995) and the Employment Equity Act No.55 of 1998, these aspects are not discussed in more detail in this paper.

The concepts of diversity management and culture are reviewed in the next section.

Diversity management and culture Diversity in the workplace is complex and can be examined at the international or cross-national level. Diversity can therefore include different national cultures in a country's workforce. Intranational diversity, however, refers to diversity within the people of one country, also called ethnicity within one national culture (Allard, 2002). Intranational diversity is thus broadly similar to the term workforce diversity. It is, however, acknowledged that intranational diversity does not precisely equal workforce diversity in that a nation's workforce does not necessarily perfectly mirror the ethnic/gender/ racial makeup of its population. Bearing this in mind, intranational diversity is the term used for the purpose of this paper.

Thomas & Ely (1996) outline various approaches to managing diversity. They all involve focus on equal opportunity, fair treatment, recruitment and compliance with legislation. Furthermore an expanded concept would be to accept and celebrate differences, which would mean an emphasis on multi culturalism as well. It is this approach that is followed in this paper to deal with the issue of managing diversity. Van Dyk (2001) supports this approach and states that the term "managing diversity" encompasses more than just race and ethnicity, but rather the full spectrum of differences represented in the general population. It is also necessary to undertake diversity management in order to cope with the long-term task of creating a work setting geared to the upward mobility of all kinds of employees, and to avoid the loss of morale and motivation. Diversity is, however, not about removing prejudices in the workplace. It is about recognising that prejudices exist and then questioning them before acting (Sono and Werner: 2004). It is therefore not a distraction from more important business issues, but instead forms part of the standard by which the business is measured in terms of fairness in managing its human resources. Martins (2000) claims that in order to meet a diverse population's needs and to be perceived as being fair to all, a shared vision needs to be developed. A shared vision should reflect the diverse values of the cultural groups in the organisation, as well as the business priorities.

Various opportunities are created through managing diversity well. This leads to a competitive advantage for an organisation. Advantages arise from several sources as discussed below.

Resource acquisition: In a study conducted in South Africa, it was pointed out that females in general, prefer to work for organisations that value diversity so that they do not have to compromise themselves to make unwilling cultural sacrifices. They can then work in working environments which suit them (Tinarelli, 2000).

Increased productivity: The improved ability to attract talented persons from diverse backgrounds can result from the merit-based evaluation of employees, bearing in mind that under the previous apartheid based (pre 1994) government, race was a major criteria for employment (Nel, Van Dyk, Haasbroek, Schultz, Sono, & Werner, 2004).

Marketing: People may prefer to buy from organisations that value diversity. Sweat shop manufactured goods have become unacceptable in society and not buying such products could take precedence over cost and convenience factors (Tinarelli, 2000).

Problem solving: Diverse groups have a broader and richer base of experience from which to approach a problem. Homogeneity can be detrimental if it results in absence of stimulation (Daft, 1995).

Creativity: It is well known that innovative organisations deliberately establish heterogeneous teams in order to create a marketplace of ideas (Tinarelli, 2000).

It should be borne in mind that diversity management cannot take place in isolation since culture also plays a role. Hofstede (1991:4) defines culture as "The collective programming of the mind which distinguishes the members of one category of people from another." Hofstede's definition is appropriate here as it rightly refers to understanding culture as a value system that applies to one particular culture.

Schein (1992:12) offers the following classic definition of organisation culture: "A pattern of shared basic assumptions that the group learned as it solved its problems of external adaptation and internal integration, that has worked well enough to be considered valid, and therefore, to be taught to new members as the correct way to perceive, think, and feel in relation to those problems". The challenge of cultural diversity for organisations is in recognising that employees bring their cultural values, attitudes and behaviours into the workplace as well, because employees do not have mutually exclusive "domestic" and "business" profiles. However, it is acknowledged that South African society is currently significantly more influenced by business culture and vice versa than previously, due to the democratically elected Government's impact on people's labour mobility in a business and society context.

Now that the issues that impact on managerial prerogative have been analysed, the issues relating to relationship building in terms of social capital are analysed and contextualized to establish the links to management prerogative.

Social capital and business relationship building concepts Relationship building is often interpreted as a business construct in the light of marketing relationships, which may well reflect the importance of business orientation in the global economy (Zhu et al, 2005b). Relationship building is a social construct, which leads to the need to focus on social capital theory as well. The concept of social capital embodies the concepts of reciprocity and co-operation. There is also a need to understand social capital in relation to human capital. Human capital involves customer relationships as well as those with suppliers, competitors, alliance partners, shareholders and governmental departments. Human capital goes beyond the concept of customer relationship marketing and provides a matrix of relationship building networks. Social capital is a more embracing concept that began to draw management researchers' attention in relation to the competitive advantage of the firm (Tsai & Ghoshal, 1998, Varner, 2000, Adler & Kwon, 2002).

Social capital theory is therefore a much broader dimension than human capital and offers more potential links to communication strategies and other cultural dimensions. This theoretical basis therefore makes it possible to compare cultures and to focus on the culture-specific perspective of relationship building. Zhu (2005a) states that this cultural dimension can help to enhance understanding relationship building across cultures and to indicate links to communication strategies as well.

The nature of South Africa's culture in general and the business environment in particular is discussed in the next section.

Overview of South African culture In this section the focus is placed on the so-called national culture of South Africa. The full South African democracy was established in 1994. At the time accelerated moves towards Afrocentric management in businesses also gained momentum. However, South Africa is currently a complex amalgam of several cultures and sub-cultures and the dominant management culture is, for historical reasons, Western and currently still mainly Eurocentric (Manning, 1997, Jackson, 1999; Prime, 1999, Nel et al., 2004). This is also confirmed by Booysen (2000:10) who states that the cultural constellation of European orientated South African management is a high level of Performance Orientation, above average levels of Uncertainty Avoidance, Future Orientation, High Power Distance and Assertiveness. Conversely, the cultural constellation of black South African management is different from that of white management in that it reflects high levels of collectivism and Humane Orientation. This profile places the emphasis on Afrocentric management, which emphasises collective solidarity, inclusively, collaboration, consensus and group significance, concern for people as well as working for the common good (Booysen 2001, Booysen, Nkomo, & Beaty, 2003).

Hofstede's (1991) model for understanding cultural diversity helps to illustrate the link between cultural differences and work related attitudes. It identifies the importance of and the need for intercultural understanding of diverse workforces. The perception of individualism as a cultural dimension is the pursuit of individual goals, freedom and self-interest in the South African context, which impacts on the management of businesses as well.

Thomas and Bendixen (2000:507) also clearly state that it is inappropriate to talk about a uniform national culture in the South African context, but that the concept "ethnicity" is more relevant. Indeed they observe that cultural diversity characterises the South African population. Furthermore, the cultural identity of employees may not be congruent with the existing organisational culture. This may be to the extent that one cultural group may dominate the organisation culture, which again has an impact on management and in turn on management prerogative.

Khoza (2002:22) proposes to redirect business culture in order for the community concept of business to be pursued. This approach views the organisation as a community to which the individual belongs, not just by way of a legal contract, but as a member by choice. This community is built on close interpersonal relationships and group interactions and held together by a feeling of security and harmony on the part of all its members. It is also suggested that the community concept of management culture should be enhanced by the concept of Ubuntu. In essence Ubuntu could be interpreted, as "a person is a person through other human beings". Mbigi (1997) states that Ubuntu means fundamentally relying on traditional African management values and practices, like leading as an oral culture using parables and African proverbs as well as traditional healers, folk singers, market women and traditional peasant farmers as role models for inspiring and empowering leadership. Other African based Ubuntu principles are about creating an inclusive enterprising community and establishing intimate relationships. Furthermore the view in Africa is that a group needs stroking, nurturing and attention. Much has been written about individualism-collectivism philosophies and their impact on management, but the large body of literature does not provide an adequate explanation of African communalism although generally traditional African society may be regarded as being low in individualism. Ubuntu is an orientation to life that is opposed to individualism and insensitive competitiveness, and that is not comfortable with collectivism where collectivism stresses the importance of the social unit to the point of depersonalising the individual.

From the preceding discussion of the concepts of Euro and Afrocentric management and Ubuntu it is clear that different authors' views need to be acknowledged. These concepts are currently evolving in South Africa to assume a truly South Africanised approach to dealing with cultural concepts in a business context. This also reflects the notion of establishing the African Renaissance more forcefully in South Africa (Nepad, 2001, www.nepad.org).

Therefore to embrace without question management cultures of the West is to impose less than optimum solutions on South African management challenges and circumstances. South African managers need to understand the different cultural expectations of their entire people and must South Africanize their approach more. Ngambi (2003) states that the face of South African management is becoming more diverse and inclusive of all racial groups; the combination of diversity and inclusion pose a challenge to the dominant management values and practices, which are for historical reasons, Western European. This is also confirmed by Khoza (2002) by saying that what appears to be needed then, is an eclectic corporate culture that recognises that Europe and other countries have had and will continue to have, a lot to offer to the body of knowledge crucial for business and economic development in Southern Africa and further a field.

Dadoo, Ghyoot, Lephoko, & Lubbe (2001:130) confirm that the current South African style of management and therefore the implications for management prerogative in a cultural context, still largely reflects the traits of a dominant Eurocentric approach which is autocratic, hierarchical and authoritarian (disciplinary procedures) and individualistic (competition oriented). This creates major dilemmas for traditional Western type organisations trying to adjust to the new South Africa, because they operate on a more narrowly focussed management prerogative basis than most African collectivist orientated businesses. (Booysen, 2000). Decisions are therefore not really discussed and the information system is more top-down. The organisation is generally centralised and the hierarchical structure shows a heavy hierarchy and a large power distance (Jackson, 1999 and Prime, 1999). As a corollary of the Eurocentric dominant vision and management style, the "we-them" syndrome is still strongly prevalent in many South African organisations (Nel, van Dyk, Haasbroek, Schultz, Sono, & Werner, 2004).

The important question that now needs to be reviewed is whether management prerogative can be enhanced within the context of relationship building, social capital, culture and diversity constraints in South Africa by means of a model, which could be utilised for management guidance in organisations.

Problem Statement and Objectives of the Paper

Globally countries increasingly do business across borders and inevitably encounter cross-cultural management conflicts and problems. Research in this regard mostly focuses on marketing relationships or on cross-cultural dimensions. Limited empirical evidence exists regarding relationship building from a social capital perspective while incorporating relevant intercultural dimensions. Furthermore, comparing communication approaches for building business relationships across cultures is also relatively isolated as a focus area of research. The problem is therefore that inadequate knowledge is available on intercultural dimensions, which explores business relationship building in relation to management prerogative.

The objectives of this paper are to identify a way to cross the boundary between building business relationships beyond a marketing approach and to explore it from a social capital and culture perspective, whilst observing the role and importance of management prerogative in businesses as well. It is clear that management prerogative plays an important part in the overall jigsaw puzzle of being an effective business in South Africa with its many facets and cultures. Management style and focus, however, currently oscillate between Afro and Eurocentric management, which reflects changing business culture and society's cultural diversity sentiments. This also reflects the evolutionary process of change from the previous apartheid focussed government to the current democratic government. The latter seems to promote the Afrocentric approach in contrast to Eurocentric management promoted by the previous government, as was alluded to elsewhere in this paper. Finding a model to accommodate and enhance the aforementioned issues in the South African context thus forms the focus of this research.

Research methodology The approach for the methodology of this paper is contained in two empirical research studies that were executed between 2001 and 2004, in order to analyse and apply the possible synergies that arise from it. They jointly form the current research project and provide the basis for the configuration of a revised model for use by management, which enhances relationship building, social capital and management prerogative constructs.

The first project was based on the identification and application of management prerogative constructs. An empirical investigation was undertaken in the form of a case study in a fast growing entrepreneurial organisation in South Africa to assess its functioning by interviewing all 35 personnel to design a management model. After the investigation, a model encompassing strategic diversity management was developed and served to contextualise managerial prerogative as well. The model would enable management to optimise the effect of legislation on its operations, as well as to institutionalise essential basic management principles, skills and organisational culture, all of which are needed to effectively manage the growth of a business. The results of the model could provide the framework for analysing and utilising the relationship building and social capital concepts to enhance management prerogative in organisations.

Interviews were conducted to determine the context and prerequisites for effective management as well as the extent of employee rights. The interviews were scripted and standardised and every interviewee received the same set of questions in the same order. Each interviewee was interviewed by the same researcher. Interviews lasted approximately 30 minutes. Each interviewee was given a guarantee of confidentiality. The results were analysed by the researcher to identify elements to compile the management prerogative model. Subsequently the effect thereof on the exercise of management prerogative was analysed.

As a result of the empirical investigation a model was constructed to address managerial prerogative, equity, culture and diversity issues. Since the model is diversity based and multi phased, it can accommodate alignment and re-alignment of the organisation as it expands. The model also incorporates the organisation whilst it is becoming more complex in its management regarding all aspects of people management in terms of legislation and cultural impact issues.

Subsequently the researchers realised that this model had the potential to be used to enhance building relationships and social capital constructs as well. This was utilised when the research outlined below was planned for execution and difficulties in finding a model regarding interpretation and execution of management prerogative was experienced.

The second research project empirically investigated relationship building across cultures by utilising social capital constructs. It was executed by means of interviews. The questionnaire comprised open-ended questions for interviews with business executives. Narratives were also utilized in collecting success stories from each of the interviewees. The following topics formed the gist of the narratives:

- Identifying the culture-specific meaning of relationship building across cultures in South Africa
- Identifying socio-cultural environments of the target culture in South Africa
- Identifying business executives' views through their narratives of success stories in South Africa

The 25 interview questions covered five areas relating to: relationship building; power distance; individualism versus collectivism; high and low context; and a successful scenario provided by each interviewee. The interviews were scripted and standardised and every interviewee received the same 25 questions in the same order. Each interviewee was interviewed by the same researcher on a one on one basis. Interviews lasted approximately 1 hour. Each interviewee was given a guarantee of confidentiality. The results were analysed by the researcher to enhance the building of business relations and to employ social capital as well. An example of a question is as follows: "What underpins successful relationship building and development? For example, trust and loyalty can be the first priority for certain cultures. Explain issues you regard important in this regard." Lastly, interviewees were asked to provide a success story which reflected the use of social capital in order to build relationships.

For the purpose of the current paper, however, only the first and last section is focused upon. Ten business executives were interviewed. The executives were located in three large cities in businesses that employed between 100 and 1 000 employees in South Africa. They were chosen randomly from the list of businesses of the local Chamber of Commerce, but to participate had to be within the said constraints. The interviews took place in 2004 and were linked to the management prerogative investigation model, which was developed in 2001, since it made a valuable input in this regard.

Information was also collected through narratives. According to Reisman (1993) narratives involve story telling and are an important research method used in linking individual human actions and events to interrelated aspects to gain an understanding of outcomes. In particular narrative analysis is a method of investigating how individuals understand actions and interpret the meaning behind them. Each interviewee was asked to provide a success story on building business relationships by using social capital that had a favourable and positive outcome. This type of analysis is appropriate as it can provide a perspective about business executives' perceptions and actions about relationship building and how these can relate to management prerogative.

Results of the Research Investigations

The results of the two research investigations are discussed first in this section. An integrated approach is then proposed to establish a revised model to accommodate business relationship building and management prerogative for use by businesses in South Africa. It is worth while to note that the combined results could probably be applied in other countries as well.

Results of the investigation to establish a holistic management model As indicated in previous sections personal interviews with all personnel (totalling 35) of were executed. The purpose was to identify current management strategy, equity, diversity, and the impact of legislative limitations on the prerogative to manage. It is self-evident that for a business to survive, grow and reap sustainable profits over time, management needs to incorporate and align all the identified elements into the strategic planning process (Manning 1997). In this regard, a holistic model was developed based on the responses of the interviewees to serve as a conceptual approach to deal with complex and sensitive aspects in organisations. The model would enable management to optimise the effect of legislation on operations, as well as to institutionalise essential basic management principles, skills and organisational culture, all of which are needed to effectively manage the organisation. The model is presented in Figure 1. All the components of the model exert influence on each other, albeit some to a greater or lesser degree. In practice, the entire model is a non-linear interactive process of evaluation and re-evaluation at all stages and at all times. There is no sequenced process to be followed. Everything happens at the same time, all the time. However, to assist in the explanation thereof, the model is depicted in two vertical layers. Each layer is now briefly reviewed.

FIGURE 1
A holistic model for strategic diversity management and existing management prerogatives

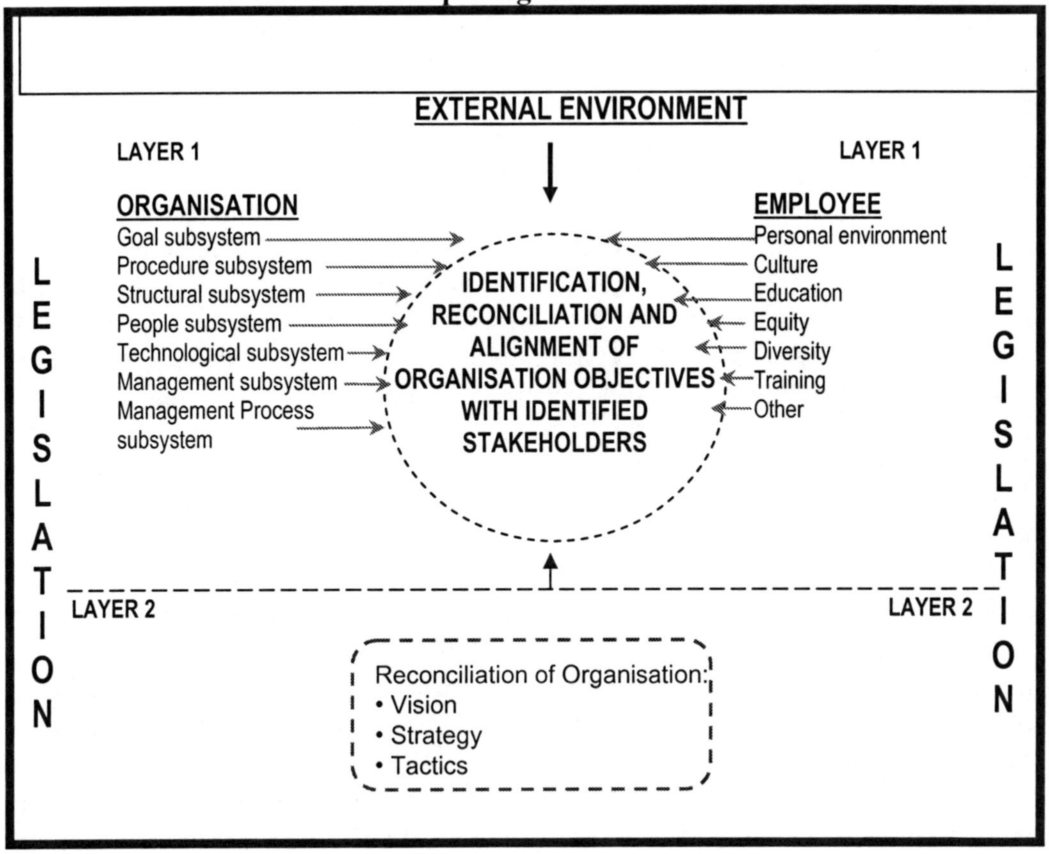

Layer one (top half of the model). In order to provide management with a clearer understanding of the nature of the external environment in which the organisation operates, the assumptions that form the heart of the model are presented. A turbulent external environment exists because "doing business" is executed in terms of uncertainty and constant change in the business environment both nationally and internationally. To develop the ideal theoretical structure and subsystems, an organisation should therefore be able to cope with the external environment as well. Employees are recognised as products of the external environment, as well as critical role players in the success of the organisation. Alignment is also included, which needs to take place between the external inputs of various stakeholders as well.

Layer two (bottom half of the model): The second layer comprises various phases to reconcile aspects of vision, strategy and tactics to synchronize all aspects of an organisation's interaction with its environment. It assists management in exercising its prerogative in aligning and keeping aligned the diverse needs of customers, employees and the organisation in relation to the external environment. The distinction between vision, strategy and tactics is made and management should decide which actions in the implementation of each phase would have the highest probability of success. This is particularly the case in relation to its relationship with the environment it operates in.

The value of the model lies therein that it can be further developed and enhanced for the use of building business relationships and accommodating social capital in a new perspective by combining it with the results of the second investigation.

Building business relationships by utilising social capital in South Africa

The building of business relationships across cultures using a theoretical framework based on social capital provides valuable input into the integration of the components of organisation management based on environmental and internal inputs. This is essential to success in the context of "doing business" in a culturally diverse country, as was outlined in the previous section.

Through interviews with the business executives it was found that relationship building was defined in close relation with the socio-cultural and economic context of "doing" business. Business relationships also evolve alongside multi-culturally characterised multi-national organisations, which operate in a highly diversity sensitive country.

Interviewees revealed that various approaches to building business relationships existed. Building business relationships at the internal level was addressed at top management level first, and then at other levels. Interviewees confirmed that the approach to establish a relationship could vary according to the needs of a business. This is an indication that the traditional dimension of power distance being high in business relationships is starting to shift as managers are becoming less focused on maintaining status stratifications. It should once again be noted that elements of Hofstede's (1991) model are relevant, but do not form the focus for the analysis in this paper.

South African managers seem to prefer long-term relationships. This is in line with the research of Booysen (2000) who stated that future orientation, such as the areas of goal setting, planning and allocation of resources remain very important to South African managers. Communication seems focused on direct and clear styles as part of long-term relationship building. The interviewees placed great emphasis on the importance of building trust to achieve organisational objectives.

Interviewees responded to relationship-based questions by saying that different approaches were used to enhance relationships and that it would also depend on the objectives, such as business spin-offs, which may flow from the relationship. They also mentioned that if quick payoffs and a once-off situation arose, the relationship would be short-term only. It is, however, clear that a more individualistic approach is followed in relationship building for business managers in South Africa as opposed to a collectivist approach. In-depth relationships were, however, less common in building business relations as one interviewee mentioned: "The main goal is to achieve the business' set objectives". This comment is once again characteristic of the Eurocentric management style and alludes to some management's prerogative to manage their businesses in such a cultural context in South Africa. One interviewee in contrast said: "I will meet commitments even if it entails personal sacrifice and cost".

Regarding development of mutually beneficial business relationships in South Africa, interviewees indicated that a direct approach was followed, but they agreed that developing trust was also important. However, when a relationship was developed which was envisaged to be longer-term, the communication was subtler and less direct. Written commitments seem to be the only indicators of trust and there is a tendency to depersonalise relationships and focus on the tasks to be done (Zhu 2005a). As an overall deduction it appears that more participative communication between senior managers is starting to evolve in business dealings in South Africa. This is most noticeable when strategies in the business context are established, which also sheds some light on the approach to management prerogative applications in organisations.

Interviewees furthermore stated that relationship building was attained by mutual understanding of what was important to a business and to the benefit of all stakeholders. One interviewee, for example, expressed it as "a concerted effort by different parties to establish a foundation whereupon they can all co-exist in peace and harmony". Identifiable concepts which underpin successful relationship building were phrased as follows: "Ethics, understanding the needs of others, integrity, empathy, trust, loyalty and, respect for all parties". Once again the dove tailing of relationship building in a particular cultural context and management style and prerogative is evident.

The results also suggest that business executives seem to be moving away from the Eurocentric approach to a more Afrocentric approach in dealing with social capital issues for the various cultures, as was suggested elsewhere in this paper. It could be deduced that by accommodating and applying management prerogative wisely organisations could, within the context of culture, equity and social capital, improve and speed-up the ability to do business with relevant stakeholders. It could thus improve the harmonious yet competitive positioning of organisations in Southern Africa in particular.

Analysing narratives. Various success stories in relationship building were presented by the interviewees. Mr. XYZ provided this outstanding story to the researcher during his interview. He is a senior manager of a business in the service industry.

> "I have developed good relationships with most of the directors and managers on different levels. The value is in future ventures or objectives that need to be achieved. If you have good relationships with key people it is easy to `convince' them to venture on a new idea or concept because they have learnt to trust our motives and abilities. It is then also easier to get the employees involved, because their managers understand what you are doing and are 'on your side'. This has helped especially with the development of a new performance management system we introduced this year."

Narratives of this nature offer further substantiation of the findings regarding the building of relationships within particular cultures and the business environment in South Africa. One of the most significant findings is that there is an overarching theme, namely that business executives regarded relationship building as a process of building trust and reciprocal behaviour. This finding further supports the notion that relationship building is definitely dependant on social capital as well rather than simply business or human capital. It is, however, conceded that relationship building and social capital do rely on some degree of interdependency in order to be separately successful.

The business relationship results have the potential to be integrated with the management prerogative results and to be utilised in organisations to enhance competition. The revised model to accommodate this concept is discussed below.

The Revised model for management prerogative and building business relationship

The revised model focuses on dealing with the flow of complex issues. It could be of significant value to managers in organisations in their quest for better management and improved relations, by using the model in terms of culture, diversity and executing management prerogative appropriately. The model would also enhance African culture and traditions in efforts to build business relations. Social capital, which exists in communities and organisations, would be maximised to enable businesses to grow and be competitive in culturally diverse workforces in an intranational context. The revised model is presented in Figure II below.

FIGURE 2
Revised management prerogative model including relationship building, diversity management and organisational culture

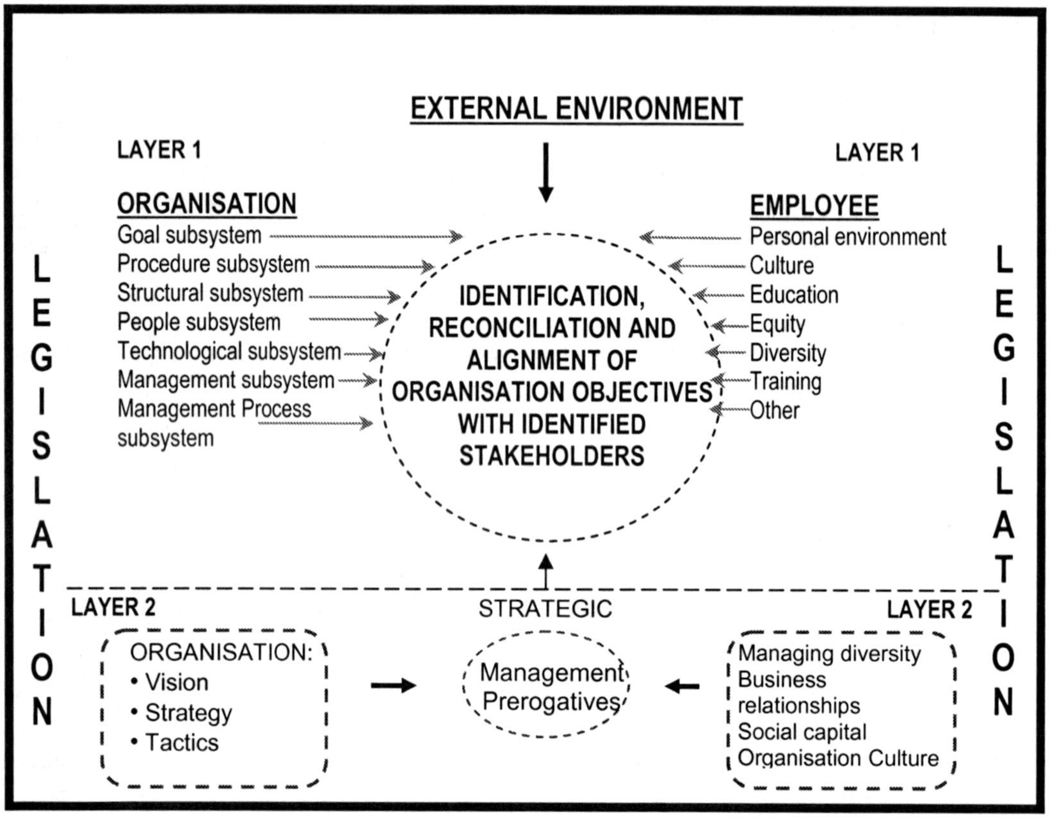

The key elements of the revised model include taking cognizance of diversity, business relationships, social capital and organisation culture being contextualised via management prerogative to identify strategic competencies for the benefit of an organisation. This in turn is linked to the external environment in terms of reconciliation with organisation objectives and alignment with stakeholders to identify a workable mix between the various components. By working through the model businesses could improve their success to employ social capital in building business relationships, whilst maintaining management prerogative at a level which is advantageous to all stakeholders.

The revised model could serve as a point of reference or conceptual road map for the management of organisations in exercising their management prerogative. The revised model could simplify the task of achieving the goals of an organisation, by providing a framework for integrating and aligning diverse and conflicting interests by enhancing the strategic competence of an organisation.

Conclusions and Recommendations

The research findings reported in this paper developed a framework for building business relationships across cultures based on intercultural perspectives, by applying a particular model to enable management prerogative to be viewed in a holistic manner in organisations.

The results of the research investigations could be leveraged to utilise management prerogative as a strategic competence to the benefits of organisations operating in diverse cultures. By applying the revised management prerogative model to the factors that impact on organisations from the external environment perspective, a conceptual "roadmap" model within a "doing business" context is established. It thus reflects the interrelatedness of the factors that impact on the environment in which businesses operate.

Therefore, how to balance management's prerogative to execute the vision to achieve organisational objectives, yet acknowledging diversity and culture to enhance social capital and relationships is an advantage of this integrated approach. An example would be to use social capital networks of an organisation to gain and successfully carry out business across national borders, which could be characterised by a different culture. This could be faster and more efficient than being introduced and trying to do business across national borders (is not that still the case in the latter scenario?).

It is deduced that some implications are that more openness from different cultures and diverse groups confirms that more than a single nation approach exists, which reflects the intranational character of South African society. Therefore, an increased mix between Afro- and Euro-centric management, by making use of more social capital than before to enhance business, seems to be evolving in South Africa.

It is concluded that a greater preparedness to establish relationship building strategies, to manage business and to accommodate management prerogative, are evident in South African businesses. It is also concluded that a new South African approach for doing business across cultures in an intranational manner and across borders seem to be developing. Therefore a model to accommodate a multitude of variables could be a helpful tool to navigate this complex balancing act for business managers to be effective in doing business. In this context it is, however, surprising that cross-cultural management issues in organisations in Southern Africa have been traditionally neglected by the mainstream international management literature until recently (Prime, 1999; Booysen, 2000; Khoza, 2002 and Nel et al. 2004).

It is recommended that a more practical approach to current day South Africa management could be achieved whilst improving the chances of business competitiveness and success by using the topic flows suggested by the revised model. It is furthermore recommended that management strategies could be more inclusive and take more cognisance of other cultures, diversity, employment equity and building business relationships than before to manage organisations effectively.

The findings have far reaching implications for conducting business and management practices by utilising social capital concepts as well as doing business in intra-national cultures, yet retaining acceptable management prerogative to execute the "right to manage". The revised model presented in this paper therefore has extensive application value for managers in businesses in countries with profiles similar to South Africa, of which there are probably a number in Southern Africa.

References

Adler, P. S., & Kwon, S. W. 2002. Social capital: Prospects for a new concept. *Academy of Management Review*, 27(1): 17–40.

Allard, M. J. 2002. Theoretical underpinnings of diversity. In C. Harvey & M. J. Allard, (Eds.), *Understanding and Managing Diversity:*New Jersey: Prentice Hall.

Booysen, L., Nkomo, S., & Beaty, D. 2003. A best practice model for building a valuing diversity culture. *Management Today*, 19(1): 33–36.

Booysen, L. 2001. The duality in South African leadership: Afrocentric or Eurocentric. *South African Journal of Labour Relations*. 25(3-4): 36–64.

Booysen, L. 2000. *Cultural differences between African black and white managers in South Africa.* Paper presented at the Southern Africa Institute for Management Scientists (SAIMS) 12th Annual Conference. 31 October to 2 November. Midrand, South Africa.

Brassey, M. S. M., Cameron, E., Cheadle, M. H., & Olivier, M. P. 1987. *The New Labour Law: Strikes, Dismissals and the Unfair Labour Practice in South Africa.* Cape Town: Juta & Co. Ltd.

Concise Oxford Dictionary (10th ed.). 1999. New electronic edition. Oxford: Oxford University Press.

Dadoo, Y., Ghyoot, V., Lephoko, D., & Lubbe, G. 2001. *Multicultural sensitivity for managers.* South Africa: Tsebanang Group.

Daft, R. L. 1995. *Understanding Management.* Orlando: The Dryden Press.

Hall, D. T., & Parker, V. A. 1993. The role of workplace flexibility in managing diversity. *Organisational Dynamics.* 22(1): 14–15.

Hofstede, G. H. 1991. *Cultures and organisations: Software of the mind.* NY: McGraw-Hill.

Industrial Law Journal. 1996. George v Liberty Life Association of South Africa Ltd. 17(582). (ID).

Industrial Law Journal. 1992. National Union of Metalworkers of South Africa v Atlantis Diesel Engines (Pty) Ltd. 3(405), 407. (IC).

Industrial Law Journal. 1989. "BTR Dunlop Ltd. v National Union of Metalworkers of South Africa." 10(705), 705. (IC).

Jackson, T. 1999. Managing people in South Africa: Developing people and organisations. *The International Journal of Human Resource Management*, 10(2): 306–326.

Khoza, R. 2002. Dancing to our own drum. *People Dynamics*, June/July, 20(5): 20–23.

Manning, T. 1997. *Radical strategy. How South African companies can win against global competition*. Sandton: Zebra Press.

Martins, N. 2000. Employment equity: The challenge of managing cultural diversity. *People Dynamics.* 18(3): 23–33.

Mbigi, L. 1997. *Ubuntu: The African dream in management.* Randburg, SA: Knowledge Resources.

Nel, P. S., van Dyk, P. S., Haasbroek, G. D., Schultz, H. B., Sono, T., & Werner, A. 2004. *Human Resources Managemen.*(6th ed.). Cape Town: Oxford University Press.

New Partnership for African Development (Nepad). 2001. www.nepad.org Accessed 12 January 2006.

Ngambi, H. 2003. Managing diversity. In P. J. Smit & G.J. de J. Cronje (Eds), *Management principles: A contemporary edition for Africa* (3rd ed.). Kenwyn: Juta & Co.

Prime, N. 1999. *Cross-cultural management in South Africa: Problems, obstacles and agenda for companies*. http://marketing.byu.edu/htmlpages/ccrs/proceedings99/prime.htm

Republic of South Africa. 1995. *Labour Relations Act No.66 of 1995*. Government Printer: Pretoria.

Republic of South Africa. 1998. *Employment Equity Act No.55 of 1998*. Government Printer: Pretoria.

Reisman, C. K. 1993. *Narrative analysis*. Newbury Park, Cal.: Sage.

Schein, E. 1992. *Organizational culture and leadership*. San Francisco: Jossey-Bass.

Sono, T. J. & Werner, A. 2004. Employment equity and diversity management. In P. S. Nel, P. S. van Dyk, G. D. Haasbroek, H.B. Schultz, T. Sono & A. Werner.(Eds.?). *Human Resources Management* (6th ed.).Cape Town: Oxford University Press.

Thomas, D., & Ely, R. 1996. Making differences matter. A new paradigm for managing diversity. *Harvard Business Review,* 74(Sep/Oct): 79–90.

Thomas, A., & Bendixen, M. 2000. The management implications of ethnicity in South Africa. *Journal of International Business Studies*, 13(3): 507–520.

Tsai, W., & Ghoshal, S. 1998. Social capital and value creation: The role of intrafirm networks. *Academy of Management Journal*, 41: 464–478.

Tinarelli, S. 2000. *Employers' guide to the Employment Equity Act.* Pretoria: Van Schaik Publishers.

Van Dyk, C. J. 2001. *A model for managerial prerogative in the technological era*. Unpublished MBA dissertation. Pretoria: University of Pretoria.

Varner, I. 2000. The theoretical foundation for intercultural business communication: A conceptual model. *The Journal of Business Communication*, 37(1): 39–57.

Zhu, Y. 2005a. *Written communication across cultures. A sociocognitive perspective on business genres.* Amsterdam: John Benjamins Publishing Company.

Zhu, Y, Bhat, R., & Nel, P. S. 2005b. Building business relationships: A preliminary study of business executives' views. *Cross cultural management,* 12(3): 63–84.

STRATEGIES FOR DETECTING AND AVOIDING THEMES OF DOMINATION AND CONTROL IN MANAGEMENT THOUGHT AND PRACTICE

MICHAEL L. CHASE
Quincy University
Quincy, Illinois, USA

Abstract
Although there has been a decided internationalization of the management sciences over the past two decades, there are still neocolonial traps that can be encountered in the adoption of Western management and leadership practices by organizations in non-Western cultures. This paper describes particular strategies that can be used for identification of Western managerial theory and practices appropriate for non-Western contexts such as Africa. The tools described in the paper are reflexively intellectual and directly participative, thus increasing the probability that they can select organizational concepts and practices that produce patterns of organizational life that will serve African interests by avoiding neocolonial tendencies toward domination and oppression.

Key Words: neo-colonialism management theory Africa

Non-Western cultures face the dilemma of being able to profit from Western management ideas that are already well tested to solve emerging problems such as the need to manage a dispersed workplace, form partnerships across national boundaries, create entrepreneurial activity, etc., while avoiding adopting any Western practices that might foster neocolonial tendencies toward dependency or domination (Begley & Boyd, 2003; Bhagat, Kedia, Harveston, & Triandis, 2020; House, Hanges, Javidan, Dorfman, & Gupta, 2004; James, 2004; Prasad, 2003). The challenge is to find strategies that enable the recipient of Western ideas to control the process of evaluating the Western management theories and practices. This can be a daunting task, if only because of the sheer volume and variety of ideas being generated by Western sources. Koontz (1961), in writing about the difficulty of making sense out of the variety of different theories of organizational behavior that existed over 45 years ago, borrowed an African metaphor, the jungle, to capture a sense of the bewildering variety of theories already in use in the early 1960s. In a retrospective article published in 1980, Koontz (1980) noted that things had become even more complex in the intervening years and concluded that " . . . the jungle appears to have become even more dense and impenetrable" (p. 157). It is clear that in the intervening years since the 1980 Koontz article, the jungle metaphor is still applicable.

Thus, making sense of a vast range of ideas and practices related to the design and operation of organizations is a challenge for everyone. However, for the non-Western organization there is that additional challenge of distinguishing those theories and practices that are appropriate for their context, with special concern that neocolonial dependency or domination not be fostered by their adoption. This task is all the more difficult because control is a feature of even the healthiest organizations (Fiol, O'Connor, & Aguinis, 2001; Jermier, 1998). What is needed is a way to distinguish normal healthy control from control that is oppressive, especially in light of cultural differences related to the control of work teams and organizations.

This paper offers several generic strategies for detecting and engaging forms of oppression that are unhealthy for both individuals and organizations, relative to their cultural distinctives. These strategies will be useful in not only evaluating Western practices that are being considered for adoption, but also for reviewing existing practices that may have been accepted without critique. However, before describing these practices, it should be noted that concerns about domination and excessive control exist in the Western organizational studies as well (Clegg, Hardy, & Nord, 1996) and find expression in various movements to give autonomy to workers, making them active crafters of their work and their place in the organization (Wrzesniewski & Dutton, 2001). For example, the participatory management/employee empowerment movement (Bennis, 1999; Quinn & Spreitzer, 1997) explicitly explores sharing organizational power among multiple stakeholders, and indeed, the very idea of collaboration among multiple stakeholders is in sharp contrast to notions of executive authority, power, and prerogative (Chrislip, 2002; Haskins, Liedtka & Rosenblum, 1998; Jones & Wicks, 1999; Laiken, 1997; Sashkin, 1986). Other lines of inquiry in Western organizational studies such as the nature and function of psychological contracts (Rouseau, 1995; Yan, Zhu, & Hall, 2002), workplace justice (Argyris, 1997; Masterson, Lewis, Goldman, &Taylor, 2000), gainsharing (Welbourne & Mejia, 1995), ethics (Cameron, Bright, & Caza, 2004), humanism (Aktouf, 1992), and trust (Bruhn, 2002; Elangovan & Shapiro, 1998; Horton & Reid, 1991) also probe the nature of the relationship between leaders and followers, especially with respect to equitable and fair treatment. In the midst of the democratization of the workplace over the past half century in Western countries there is also an awareness of countertrends, as noted in a title of a 1991 article: "The Return of the Authoritarian Manager" (Smither, 1991).

Because the struggle against domination and oppression exists in Western cultures and not just in formerly colonial societies, a body of strategies for addressing power and equity issues has emerged in the Western management literature. In reviewing possible tools for consideration in this paper, attention was focused on the requirement that the tool provide both a reflexive intellectual focus and participative engagement, since both of those are antithetical to the characteristics of practices that have the potential to oppress. Thus, the tools described in this paper offer strategies for assisting non-Western societies sort though the bewildering array of Western management practices and select only those that are useful, while avoiding the neocolonial pitfalls inherent in some of them.

Tools For The Analysis of Values

Whether explicitly stated or not, all managerial and organizational practices are built on a values base. Of particular concern to non-Western cultures are the values that underlie the Western management theories and practices that they are considering for adoption. Although differing in approach, the three strategies that follow can be useful in exploring the match between one's culture and a particular management theory or practice.

Hultman's Motivational System Mapping

A major criticism of Western management theory and practice is that typically it is non-reflective and non-reflexive. Western management theory and practice tends to be pragmatically based, with an emphasis on production and effectiveness and little consideration of individual or organizational interests, needs, and values. It would be helpful for non-Western cultures to have tools that assist them in reflective examination before they adopt theories and practices that have originated elsewhere. The Hultman Motivational System Mapping (MSM) instruments offer just such a tool (Hultman, 2002).

Hultman's Motivational Systems Mapping provides a broad conceptual framework and analysis instrument for systematically identifying, examining, and integrating the competing values found in any organization. What make the Hultman MSM tool especially appropriate for use in non-Western cultures is that it is not prescriptive in terms of specifying which values should be embraced by an organization. Rather, the Hultman MSM provides a straightforward method of exploring one's values along a number of dimensions, reviewing the consequences of various values, noting the conflicts among goals, and pursuing a conscious integration of individual and organizational values. A feature that makes Hultman MSM an ideal tool for evaluating a management practice before making the decision to adopt it into an organization is its establishment of a structured process for analyzing the underlying values of that practice. This model is especially useful in multi-ethnic cultures (a situation found in several African countries) because of the structure that it provides for each voice to be heard, understood, and integrated into decisions about the adoption of management practices and organizational priorities.

Integrative Social Contracts Theory (ISCT)

Integrative Social Contracts Theory (ISCT), based on concepts of social justice and stakeholder theories of cooperation, provides both (a) a strategy for making explicit the fundamental, non-negotiable interests and needs of organizational participants and (b) a strategy for integrative negotiation around those fundamental interests and needs in the formation of functional contracts between those participants (Donaldson & Dunfee, 1999; Soule, 2003).

ISCT can be used to analyze individual management theories and practices by addressing a series of important questions related to the consequences of their adoption. Here is just a sample of the kinds of questions that might be asked: Who are all of the stakeholders in the organization and impacted by the organization? What are the fundamental, non-negotiable interests and needs of all of the stakeholder groups? Is the theory or practice consistent with African values? Is the theory or practice consistent with African interests? Does the theory or practice have the potential for advancing the interests of one African group over the interests of another African group? What must be done to adapt a theory or practice to prevent exploitation of one group over another?

The value of ISCT is that it provides a method of explicitly examining the implications of any management theory or practice being considered to ensure that it is consistent with the particular cultural context in which it is being applied. It is evident that the ISCT strategy is reflexively intellectual. In order for it to be participative, all stakeholders must be able to ask questions of and answer questions about the management theory or practice under consideration.

Search and Future Search Conferences

Although differing somewhat in goals and strategies, Search Conferences (Emery & Purser, 1996; Purser, Cabana, M. Emery, & F. Emery, 1997), and Future Search Conferences (Weisbord, 1992; Weisbord & Janoff, 2000) can be powerful tools for helping stakeholders gain a shared understanding that is culturally sensitive, inasmuch as the shared understanding is based on those who participate in the conference. Conferences of this type are widely used to help organizations and communities engage in planned change that is based on the values, needs, and interests of those participating. The conferences are easily scaleable, permitting their use in very small organizations, medium size organizations, large organizations, and communities and have been used in a variety of non-Western cultures.

Conferences like those described by Emery and Weisbord can be used in organizations to gain a shared understanding of the underlying assumptions of Western management practices under consideration and examine the consequences of incorporating them into their organization.

All three of the strategies above are straightforward, enabling individuals to participate in processes that involve a high level of intellectual reflexivity as they probe the realm of values. They share a common assumption that people have the capacity to make explicit their values and talk about their preferences in an evaluative manner that enables them to evaluate the appropriateness of a proposed management concept or practice. Sometimes, however, the underlying assumptions and implications of a practice may not be all that accessible and open to review. What follows are two other strategies for assessing aspects of organizational life that are less visible and not accessible with the above tools.

Tools For The Analysis and Critique of Organizational Discourse

The phrase "the management sciences" suggests that managers are being provided with scientific knowledge about organizations and their management that is universal, neutral with respect to culture, value-free politically, and transferable across social and cultural boundaries. However, even a superficial reading of the leadership and management literature reveals that nothing could be further from reality. Instead, multiple constituencies are being addressed by multiple "authorities." Some writers target the manager or leader who is attempting to use organizational knowledge to achieve economic goals through an enterprise, while other writers champion worker influence over their work and their lives. Others try to find a way to simultaneously help both leaders and followers achieve favorable outcomes. This diversity of perspectives has spawned discussion about the political and power dimensions of organizational and managerial discourse (e.g., Clegg & Palmer, 1996; Boje & Rosile, 2001; Fabian, 2000; O'Connor, 1999; Westwood & Clegg, 2003), the faddish nature of much of managerial writing and consulting (e.g., Abrahamson, 1996; Donaldson & Hilmer, 1998; Staw & Epstein, 2000), and the growing perception that managerial knowledge is not so much "discovered" by the management sciences, as it "constructed" by those with political motives (e.g., Astley, 1985; Gergen & Thatchenkery, 2004; Marshank, Kennoy, Oswick, & Grant, 2000; Scarr, 1986; Tyalor & Robichaud, 2004). Of particular concern to the question of the application of Western management concepts and practices in non-Western cultures such as those found in Africa is the notion that management theory takes on the role as a "discourse of control" (Feldman, 1999; Mizruchi & Fein, 1999; Prasad, 2003; Smith, 2002), resulting in the loss of the person, rather than the integration of the person into the life of the organization (DuPree, 1989; Kramer, 1989; Lawler & Finegold, 2000; McKinlay & Starkey, 1998; Nord & Fox, 1996; Pauchant, 1997; Vaill, 1985).

To address the problems discussed in the previous paragraph, two general strategies have been increasingly applied to the study of organizational discourse: postmodern critique and critical theory (Alvesson & Deetz, 1996; Carr, 2000; Cunliffe, 2003; Kilduff, 1993; Pfeffer, 1997). Although there have been substantive disagreements between these two techniques of discourse analysis, they share much in common, in that both are concerned with the analysis of texts and exposure of the power themes that may be hidden within them. They both take a social constructionist stance toward the role language plays in the development of one's perception of reality (as in, "language constructs reality"). Because of its relatively greater prominence in the organizational studies literature, only the postmodern strategy will receive attention in this section.

Scott (1992) suggests that postmodernism emerged as an alternative model in organizational studies because of a shift that has been taking place in the way in which organizations are viewed. He notes that:

The more open one's conception of organization, the more vague and permeated its boundaries, the more varied its constituent elements, the more diverse the actors and their interests, the more discordant their conceptions and cognitive frames, the less possible it is to embrace a single view of organization as a rational system. Rationalities become multiple, interests and purposes are differentiated and contextualized. (p.312)

Since, for postmodernists, truth is recognized to have many aspects and to speak with many voices, postmodern analysis attempts to understand what is going on in a situation by taking each version to be examined alongside other versions. It is assumed that each possible version and voice is championing power and control for its own subgroup within the organization. This method of analysis is careful not to elevate the version of order or reality promoted by the formal structure of the organization. The analysis goes on to ask why certain accounts or interpretations of events are preferred and examines how organizations attempt to establish legitimacy, hegemony and domination, especially through the determination of the boundaries of rationality. Since postmodernism deals with questions of how people make sense out of their experience, it is particularly useful in examining organizational culture, the relationships within organizations, diversity issues, and the prospects for pluralism.

It contends much of our communication is carefully crafted to obscure rather than reveal intents. Based upon the philosophical orientation outlined above, the postmodernist proceeds with a particular type of textural analysis known as deconstruction which examines themes of power and control that have been covered up through the use of language.

What picture of organizational life emerges from the postmodern critique of the language used in organizational discourse? Scott (1992) summarizes as follows:

A "postmodernist" view emphasizes the diversity of elements that make up organizations. If uniformity exists, it is because diversity has been suppressed; if consistency dominates, it has been arbitrarily imposed (p. 313).

This postmodernist image is quite different than the orderly and predictable ideal pursued in contemporary organizational studies where goals and roles tie people together in coherent unity, leaders provide vision, self-managed work teams pursue quality, and satisfied workers achieve organizational goals while self-actualizing.

Below are some examples of how postmodern analysis might be useful to non-Western organizations in examining the presence and strength of various voices in the life of their organizations. It should be noted that the following examples lend themselves to being pursued in group settings where individuals share with one another their perceptions of the power themes in the discourse of the organization, including both those of Western and indigenous origins (Case & Selvester, 2000; Cunliffe, 2003; Cunliffe, 2004; Fenwick, 2004; Voronov & Coleman, 2003).

1. Formal Communication Including Policy Manuals, Letters, Memos, Organization Newsletters, Posters (including slogans): Examine various sorts of organizational documents in terms of constituents or stakeholders identified, distribution of authority, responsibility, control, power, and methods of legitimizing newly acquired power. Are all stakeholder voices heard or are there some that are muted or silenced?

2. Consistency And Contradiction In Organizational Communication: The basic question to be answered is, “How close is official policy (what is said) to actual practice (what is done)?” If large discrepancies are observed, follow-up analysis investigates the reasons for the discrepancies. Are there ideologies that govern the structure and processes used in the organization? Do the ideologies privilege certain people or groups and oppress certain people or groups? What is the origin of the ideology and is it possible to challenge the ideologies?

3. Non-written Communication: Although the postmodern critique is usually of written

communication, it can also include oral communication and interaction, which can be examined for themes of control and domination using the questions listed above.

4. Contracts: Important analysis questions include: to whom is power distributed, how is control exercised, and what types of punishments are specified? If the contract is touting a "partnership," does scrutiny of the wording confirm shared responsibility and authority?

5. Informal Communication: What does a review of informal documents, graffiti, unofficial slogans, informal modifications to formal documents, and other organizational writing reveal about organization members' perceptions of distribution, sources, and legitimacy of power? Are all constituencies or stakeholders represented?

6. Differences and Inclusivity: Are all stakeholder voices recognized by the formal organization? How are they recognized? Who constructs the "other" and how are they constructed? What constituencies are left out and voiceless? Why?

7. Meetings: How does communication flow in meetings? Does it appear that there are "right" (privileged) and "wrong" (oppressed) answers to questions that come up? If some meeting participants are not heard, why are they without voice? What practice needs to be changed to restore the voices that are not heard?

8. New Management Practices Under Consideration: What are the underlying assumptions of the new management practice? How is power distributed under the new practice? In what ways are the individual person, his/her personal knowledge and skills, his/her personal relationships, etc., subjugated to the organization? Is individuality subordinated to the interests of the organization? Does the proposed practice tend toward justice, fairness, and equity?

The above are some examples of how to engage in postmodern analysis for the purpose of examining control, power, and domination themes. If it becomes evident through this type of analysis that some voices are not heard, then leaders can determine which management practices, whether Western or indigenous, need to be modified or discarded because they interfere with stakeholder expression.

Tools for the Analysis of Unconscious Dimensions of Organizational Life

Most organizational processes are conscious and intentional and can be studied directly, as in the case of the strategies described above for the assessment of organizational values. Organizational researchers and theorists have also wrestled with the problem of studying covert and unconscious dimensions of organizational life (Lau & Shani, 1988; Nevis, 1987; Szilagyi & Wallace, 1990). When unconscious processes are regressive or dysfunctional they can divert energy away from the primary task and thus reduce organizational effectiveness, or even sabotage the formal or primary task of the group or organization. Group Think, popularized by Janis (1972), is an example of a covert process that occurs at an unconscious level which impairs a group's decision-making and problem-solving capacity. Harvey's Abilene Paradox (Harvey, Novicevic, Buckley, & Halbesleben, 2004) describes the problem of collusion in which group members assure each other that they personally want a course of action because they assume that it is the preference of the other group members.

This section focuses on the Tavistock group relations model which is a particularly useful strategy because it not only provides a theoretical framework for understanding several types of covert behavior but also provides a robust training strategy that permits people to experientially explore the complex dynamics involved in those covert behaviors. The Tavistock group relations model was developed by the Tavistock Institute of Human Relations of London in an effort to provide training and consultation in group and organizational behavior from a psychoanalytic and open systems perspective (Bion, 1961;

Miller & Rice, Palmer, 1979; 1967; Rioch, 1970). Affiliates are found in Europe, Israel, India, and the United States. Although no formal affiliate is yet located in Africa, the training methodology can be adapted to any culture. The training methodology would be especially useful in multicultural societies such as those found in many parts of Africa.

The Tavistock group relations work attempts to increase our understanding of the way in which group and organizational anxiety affect group and organizational processes. At the group level, sources of anxiety include concerns about pressure for change and growth from internal and external sources; relationships between the individual and the group (e.g. inclusion, exclusiveness, roles, conformity, power, control, sexuality, aggression, abandonment, differences, etc.); scarcity (e.g. recognition, nurture, support, etc.); and performance of the task of the group (e.g. uncertainty surrounding decisions, planning, and problem solving). Anxiety tends to stimulate fantasy which goes largely unexamined because in group-as-a-whole mode, a group has little capacity for reality testing and tends toward extremes. For example, common fantasies about leaders are that they are all good, or all bad, or all powerful, or the only source of nurture and need satisfaction. Fantasies about groups include such notions as collective incompetence (even though it contains competent individuals), being fused with one another, being fused with the leader, being all alike and all equal (denial of differences), collective weakness (even though it contains strong individuals), culpability, and omnipotence. These untested fantasies give rise to a variety of unconscious and covert group-as-a-whole phenomena.

The following table summarizes some of the common sources of anxiety in work groups and the ways in which they are manifested, using labels developed by Bion (1961) and Babad and Amir (1979):

Table A
Sources of Anxiety and Their Manifestation In Group Behavior

Source of Anxiety	*Unconscious Covert Process Manifested In Work Group*
Anxiety about own and group's adequacy and competence resolved by placing all ability in idealized leader. Scarcity dealt with by finding strong caring leader for nurturing. Anxiety about uncertainty of future expressed by need for omnipotent and omniscient person to take responsibility for what happens and to direct what is believed and done by the group.	Dependency: The group acts as though it is helpless, incompetent, and needy.
Anxiety about being dependent and controlled by designated authority. The perception is that resistance is the only strategy available.	Counter-dependency: The group acts as though its task is to resist authority as the only method of avoiding dependency.
Anxiety about differences, opposition, or scarcity reduced by finding an enemy to focus on. Management of differences through mobilization and attack. Also distortions of group boundaries, particularly relationship with what is "not group."	Fight: The group acts as though it is threatened and its task is survival through fight and aggression.

Source of Anxiety	*Unconscious Covert Process Manifested In Work Group*
Anxiety focuses on avoiding danger and enemies. Management of differences through mobilization and disengagement (passive response). May use diversionary activities to evade fearful tasks.	Flight: The group acts as though there is an enemy or threat that cannot be challenged but must be avoided.
Anxiety about adequacy of formal leader to respond to need for growth and regeneration. Group pins hopes on a solution that could emerge from the collaboration of two members in the group. Bion views this process an expression of covert sexuality through leadership union regardless of the gender of the leaders.	Pairing: The group acts as though its future depends on a new source of life for the group. Looks for the emergence of a new leadership alternative created by the pairing of two of its members.
Anxiety about isolation, differences (belief, gender, age, competence, etc.), and conformity to group rules and norms. Solution seems to be fusion with one another and the universe as a way of obliterating troublesome differences. Managing existential anxiety an issue here.	Oneness: The group acts as though fusion with one another and/or the leader is the central task. Closeness is pursued at the expense of individuality (self-other boundary issue) and the primary task.

Currently, access to the Tavistock training is not very attainable by most African academics and managers because of the distance to the nearest Tavistock affiliate. However, it is included because although all the categories of unconscious behavior described in the model are observed in all cultures, some of the categories (i.e., dependency and counter-dependency) have particular saliency in the postcolonial cultures found in Africa. Also, because of the great multicultural diversity of many of the African urban areas, the Tavistock group relations training can be especially beneficial for helping organization members explore the unconscious dynamics that might negatively affect their work relationships due to the level of diversity. As first steps toward developing competencies in the use of the Tavistock group relations model, persons can become familiar with the conceptual foundation and application through the Group Relations Reader 1 (Coleman & Bexton, 1975) and Group Relations Reader 2 (Coleman & Geller, 1985). Included in the readers are examples of applications in non-Western cultures. Networking with those who have experience in the Tavistock model would also be beneficial. As a community of practice around the Tavistock model develops, developing African training centers becomes a possibility.

Tools for The Design of Participatory Organizations

A variety of tools for identifying and addressing domination and oppression themes in management theory and practice have been described above. They are useful for helping an organization review management theories and practices in terms of their risk of fostering inappropriate use of power, but none of them goes on to offer their own version of a comprehensive management system which the organization can adopt. The next two sections are descriptions of two comprehensive management systems that have built into them the philosophy and practices that are antithetical to domination and oppression because they include an openly reflexive mindset and highly participative style of interaction, thus constructing an organizational culture that institutionalizes mindful attention to values and the fair treatment of people.

Although management thought is evident in non-Western antiquity, the modern management sciences are viewed as Western innovations emerging and expanding during the twentieth century. Because one of the major functions of management is control, there is particular concern about the potential of Western management concepts and practices to be used as tools of domination. This concern is amplified by the suspicion about the risks of globalization that appear to favor the technologically advanced West.

Learning Organizations

The term learning organization is the label now being used for an integration of a set of ideas that have emerged from organizational research and practice over the past several decades. A learning organization is one which seeks to organize work processes in ways that the often-conflicting demands of organizational effectiveness and individual job satisfaction are simultaneously met. The learning organization is, in many ways, a natural evolution of older participatory management themes of the 1970s and more recent emphasis on empowerment and self-managed work-teams. A learning organization is not so much characterized by its altered structure (although it is flatter and less hierarchal) and redesign of work (greater emphasis on teams), but by the transformation of the relationship of the organization to the individual and increased capacity for adaptation and change by the organization. An emphasis on an overriding concern for control (e.g. motivate others, organize work for others, set goals for others, etc.) is replaced by a concern for learning by all organizational members on behalf of the organization. Learning organizations are more deliberate in what they learn about and how they apply that learning. (e.g., learning about external environment, learning about own internal processes). A learning organization expects its members to " . . . act as learning agents for the organization, responding to changes in the internal and external environment of the organization by detecting and correcting errors in organizational theory-in-use, and embedding the results of their inquiry in private images and shared maps of organization" (Argyris & Schon, 1979, p. 29). This tightly packed quote from Argyris & Schon is unpacked below through a discussion of the five disciplines persons in learning organizations pursue. The following are the major features of learning organizations (Garvin, 1991; Senge, 1990, Weick and Westley, 1996):

1. Systems Thinking: Persons in learning organizations engage in systems thinking as they view their role in their work team, the role of their work team in the organization, and the organization's relationship to the larger environment. At the heart of systems thinking is an awareness of the interconnectedness (and varying levels of interdependency) of persons in teams, of teams in organizations, and organizations in the larger environment. To take a systems perspective also means to function individually and as part of a work-team to optimize the organization as a whole (even if that means that one's work-team subsystem is suboptimized).

2. Personal Mastery: In learning organizations the individual's personal and professional development are viewed as crucial to the organization's success. Personal mastery means charting a course of development that leads to a special level of proficiency through life-long learning. This learning is not only in the areas related to the product or service of the organization but includes such areas as enhancing interpersonal competence, personal awareness, emotional maturity, and an enlarging understanding of the ethical/moral dimensions of organizational life. This kind of personal mastery leads people to make a unique contribution because of their deepening understanding of and commitment to their personal vision expressed in concert with others pursuing personal mastery.

3. Mental Models: Our responses to new situations are influenced by our ingrained assumptions and generalizations about how things work in organizations. These mental

models enable us to rapidly size up new situations and take action and can be found at the individual, team, and organizational level. The problem is that sometimes these mental models are limiting or even dysfunctional and prevent adaptation that would strengthen the person, team, or organization. In the learning organization mental models are freely shared, rigorously scrutinized, and revised as necessary at the personal, team, and organizational levels. If an organization is to become a learning organization it must overcome the fear or anxiety that prevents its members from challenging established ways of thinking and doing. Some organizations may also have to overcome a "bias for action" that can prevent a more self-reflective appraisal.

4. Shared Vision: Goals, values, and missions will have the most impact on behavior in an organization if they are widely shared and owned by persons throughout the organization. This larger shared picture of the future emerges from the partial visions of individuals and teams interacting with leadership. A shared vision produces a much higher level of sustained commitment than is possible when the vision is imposed from above.

5. Team Learning: Teams exist in all organizations. They may be called departments, units, divisions, committees, etc. Often a person functions on several teams. For example a person may be part of the X Department, a member of Y Committee, and a member of Z Taskforce. Each of these team settings will have its own dynamic processes. Team learning has to do with improving the processes in a team to improve its effectiveness. Of particular interest is the phenomenon of defensive routines (activities that help a team avoid knowing) that can undermine learning by preventing a team from accurate appraisal of its processes and the consequences of those processes on the work of the team (see Argyris & Schon for a discussion of defensive routines). When effective processes are in place the team can engage in its primary task of providing a product/service.

The five main ideas listed above are not new--what is new is an attempt to integrate all five of the ideas into a single organization. Learning organizations take these five very powerful ideas and pursue them simultaneously. Because the simultaneous pursuit of these is difficult, Senge (1990) calls them "disciplines" in the sense that one has to deliberately and studiously attend to them in the course of functioning as a member of an organization. The exercise of the five disciplines contributes to increased organizational effectiveness in carrying out its primary mission, greater capacity for organizational adaptation to changing internal and external environmental demands, a fuller utilization of the members' abilities and motivation, and higher level of job and personal satisfaction by organizational members.

It is evident that the learning organization culture is very open to input from all members, thus making it difficult to oppress a particular individual or group without it being called out into the open for examination by all organization members. Additionally, learning organizations have great capacity for addressing issues of diversity and inclusion because of their norms of reflectivity, analysis, and action. Although learning organizations were first developed in Western cultures they have equal application in non-Western cultures due to their capacity to openly address issues of fairness and equity through open and transparent communication.

Servant Leadership

Using servant as a modifier of the word leadership, at first, sounds like a contradiction. However, since Greenleaf (1977) introduced the concept in the 1970s, servant-leadership has been subjected to empirical investigation and has become an increasingly wide-spread approach for the management of a wide range of organizations (Autry, 2004, Block, 1996; Greenleaf, 1977; Sendjaya & Sarros, 2002; Spears, 1995). Servant leadership, like the learning organization model, explicitly encourages individual autonomy and participation.

Additionally, through its emphasis on personal development, reconciliation, healing, and community, servant leadership offers additional benefits in cultures where there has been an accumulation of relationship debris due to past repressive practices.

Greenleaf's servant-leadership approach is part of the larger Western employee involvement movement of the past 30-40 years aimed at creating organizations where leaders remove barriers and obstacles that would prevent employees from growing as individuals and performing well in the workplace. Greenleaf places considerable emphasis on the sharing of power in decision-making and the promotion of a sense of community within an organization. Greenleaf's servant leadership model of organizational life is in good company with other formulations such as Argyris' and Senge's learning organization covered above, Deming's quality movement (Deming, 1994), and other participatory approaches to organizational design. Greenleaf's leadership ideas are also very compatible with the emphasis on personal development as a key to organizational effectiveness found in Covey's (1989) seven habits and Goleman's (1995) emotional intelligence concepts.

Although different proponents of servant leadership may emphasize slightly different features of servant leadership, the following characteristics are considered to be at the core of the servant-leadership approach by the Greenleaf Center for Servant-Leadership in Table B.

CONCLUSION

This paper has offered a conceptual overview of some of the tools available to be used to frame discussions about the appropriateness of particular management theories or practices in non-Western cultures and has suggested two comprehensive management frameworks which accommodate the varied needs of stakeholders within a multicultural organization. It is hoped that the descriptions offered and the references will enable the reader to take steps to engage in the kind of analysis suggested.

If necessary, an individual in an organization can simply obtain a copy of a book or article (e.g., Hultman's Balancing Individual and Organizational Values) and start using the instruments contained in it to engage in the analysis of a management practice under consideration. More desirably, that person would join with others in a community of practice (Wenger & Snyder, 2000) so that ideas can be shared and the analysis project strengthened. Note that through the use of modern communications, a community of practice could include individuals at other locations (other companies, academics at universities, etc.). But whether working alone or in groups, persons can find ways to make well-thought through choices in (re)structuring the management practices in their organization.

Table B

Characteristics of Servant Leadership

Listening characterized by • paying close attention and affirming the person speaking • using active listening skills to ensure accuracy of both content and intent of person speaking • remembering what was said • reflecting on and using what was said to enrich one's understanding and inform one's actions
Empathy characterized by • striving to see things through the eyes of others • assuming good intentions of co-workers and colleagues

• accepting the person, while calling for the best from the person
Healing (making whole) characterized by • healing one's self and one's relationship with others • helping others overcome broken spirits from emotional hurts • being able to apologize to followers when wrong in an authentic and healing manner • forgiving and helping others forgive
Awareness characterized by • high level of self-awareness of strengths and limitations • being tuned in to ethics, power, and values dimensions of organizational life • having an inner serenity in order to be sharply awake to the reality of present situation • recognizing the difference between the urgent and the important, and choosing the important • recognizing when and how to change pace and activity in order to find renewal
Leading by persuasion characterized by • attempting to build consensus • striving for shared understanding of all stakeholders • providing reasons for a course of action and involving people in decision making and problem solving • convincing others (vs. coercing and manipulating based on positional authority)
Conceptualization characterized by • being able to see the big picture and think • being able to think about the complexities of the organization in systems terms • being able to think beyond day-to-day realities of the present to future possibilities
Farsightedness characterized by • spotting opportunities early • spotting problems early • helping the organization respond to opportunities and problems early (vs. being forced by events)
Stewardship characterized by • seeing a personal role of holding the organization in trust for the greater common good of society • being accountable and sharing control
Commitment to the growth of people characterized by • affirming the uniqueness and value of each person to the overall mission of the organization • taking active steps toward nurturing the personal and professional growth of employees and colleagues
Building community characterized by • providing opportunities for employees to build personal connections with one another that transcend the work roles of the persons • seeking to build trust throughout the organization

References

Abrahamson, E. 1996. Management fashion. *Academy of Management Review*, 21(1): 254-285.

Aktouf, O. 1992. Management and theories of organizations in the 1990s: Toward a critical radical humanism? *Academy of Management Review*, 17(3): 407-431.

Alvesson, M., & Deetz, S. 1996. Critical theory and postmodernism approaches to organizational studies. In S. Clegg, Hardy, C., & W. R. Nord (Eds.) *Handbook of organization studies* (pp. 191-217). Thousand Oaks, CA: Sage.

Argyris, C. 1997. Justice and effectiveness. *Organization Development Journal*, 15(2), 21-28.

Argyris, C., & Schon, D. 1978. *Organizational learning*. Reading, MA: Addison-Wesley.

Argyris, C., & Schon, D. 1996. *Organizational learning II*. Reading, MA: Addison Wesley.

Astley, W. G., 1985. Administrative science as socially constructed truth. *Administrative Science Quarterly*, 30, 497-513.

Autry, J. 2004. *The Servant Leader*. New York: Three Rivers Press.

Babad, E. Y., & Amir, L. 1978. Trainers' liking, Bion's emotional modalities, and T-Group effect. *Journal of Applied Behavioral Science*, 14: 511-522.

Begley, T. M., & Boyd, D. P. 2003. Why don't they like us overseas? Organizing U.S. business practices to manage culture clash. *Organizational Dynamics*, 32(4): 357-553.

Bennis, D. 1999. The end of leadership: Exemplary leadership is impossible without full inclusion, initiatives, and cooperation of follows. *Organizational Dynamics*, 28 (1): 71-80.

Bhagat, R. S., Kedia, B. L., Halverston, P. D., & Triandis, H. C. 2002. Cultural variations in the cross-border transfer of organizational knowledge: An integrative framework. *Academy of Management Review*, 27(2): 204-221.

Bion, W. R. 1961. Experiences in groups. New York: Basic Books.

Block, P. 1996. *Stewardship: Choosing service over self-interest.* San Francisco: Berrett-Koehler Publishing.

Boje, D. M., & Rosile, G. A. 2001. Where's the power in empowerment? Answers from Follett and Clegg. *The Journal of Applied Behavioral Science*, 37(1): 90-117.

Bruhn, J. G. 2002. *Trust and the health of organizations*. New York: Kluwer Academic/Plenum.

Cameron, K. S., Bright, D., & Caza, A. 2004. Exploring the relationship between organizational virtuousness and performance. *American Behavioral Scientist*, 47(6): 766-790.

Carr, A. 2000. Critical theory and the management of change in organizations. *Journal of Organizational Change Management*, 13(3): 208-220.

Case, P., & Selvester, K. 2000. Close encounters: Ideological invasion and complicity on an

'International Management' master's programme. *Management Learning*, 31: 11-23.

Chrislip, D. D. 2002. *The collaborative leadership fieldbook: A guide for citizens and civic leaders*. San Francisco: Jossey-Bass

Clegg, S. R., Hardy, C., & Nord, W. R. (Eds.). 1996. *Handbook of organization studies*. Thousand Oaks, CA: Sage.

Clegg, S., & Palmer, G. (Eds.). 1996. *The politics of management knowledge*. London: Sage.

Coleman, A.D., & Bexton, W. H. (Eds.). 1975. *Group relations reader 1*. Washington, DC: A. K. Rice Institute

Coleman, A.D., & Geller, M. H. (Eds.). 1985. *Group relations reader 2*. Washington, DC: A. K. Rice Institute.

Collins, D. 1997. The ethical superiority and inevitability of participatory management as an organizational system. *Organizational Science*, 8(5): 489-507.

Collins, D. 1995. Death of a gainsharing plan: Power politics and participatory management. *Organizational Dynamics*, 24(1): 23-38.

Covey, S. 1989. *The seven habits of highly effective people*. New York: Simon and Schuster.

Cunliffe, A. L. 2003. Reflexive inquiry in organizational research: Questions and possibilities. *Human Relations*, 56(8): 983-1003.

Cunliffe, A. L. 2004. On becoming a critically reflective practitioner. *Journal of Management Education*, 28(4): 407-426.

Deming, W. E. 1994. *The new economics*. Cambridge, MA: MIT Center for Advanced Engineering Study.

DePree, M. 1989. *Leadership is an art*. New York: Dell.

Dodgson, M. 1993. Organizational learning: A review of some literatures. *Organizational Studies*, 14(3): 375-394.

Donaldson, L., & Hilmer, F. G. 1998. Management redeemed: The case against fads that harm management. *Organizational Dynamics*, 26: 7-20.

Donaldson, T., & Dunfee, T.W. 1999. *Ties that bind: A Social Contract Approach to Business Ethics*. Boston: Harvard Business School Press.

Driver, M. 2002. The learning organization: Foucauldian gloom or utopian sunshine? *Human relations*, 55(1): 33-53.

Elangovan, A. R., & Shapiro, D. L. 1998. Betrayal of trust in organizations. *Academy of Management Review*, 28 (3): 547-566.

Emery, M., & Purser, R. E. 1996. *The search conference: A powerful method of planning organizational change and community action.* San Francisco: Jossey-Bass.

Fabian, F. H. 2000. Keeping the tension: Pressures to keep controversy in the management discipline. *Academy of Management Review*, 25(2): 350-371.

Feldman, S. P. 1999. The leveling of organizational culture: Egalitarianism in critical postmodern organization theory. *The Journal of Applied Behavioral Science*, 35(2): 228-244.

Fiol, C. M., O'Connor, E. J., & Aguinis, H. 2001. All for one and one for all? The development and transfer of power across organizational levels. *Academy of Management Review*, 26(2): 224-242.

Garvin, D. A. 1993. Building a learning organization. *Harvard Business Reviews*, 71, 78-91.

Gergen, K. & Thatchenkery, T. J. 2004. Organizational science as social construction. *Journal of Applied Behavioral Science*, 40(2): 228-249.

Goleman, D. 1995. *Emotional intelligence.* New York: Bantam Books

Greenleaf, R. K. 1977. *Servant-Leadership: A journey into the nature of legitimate power and greatness.* Mahwah, NJ: Paulist Press.

Harvey, M., Novicevic, M., Buckley, M. R., & Halbesleben, J. R. B. 2004. The Abilene paradox after thirty years: Global perspective. *Organizational Dynamics*, 33(2): 215-226.

Haskins, M. E., Liedtka, J., & Rosenblum, J. 1998. Beyond teams: Toward an ethic of collaboration. *Organizational Dynamics*, 9: 34-50.

Hassard, J. 1994. Postmodern organizational analysis: Toward a conceptual framework. *Journal of Management Studies*, 31(3), 303-324.

Horton, T. R., & Reid, P. C. 1991. *Beyond the trust gap: Forging a new partnership between managers and their employers.* Homewood, IL: Irwin.

House, R. J., Hanges, P. J., Javidan, M., Dorfman, P. W., & Gupta, V. (Eds.) (2004). *Culture, leadership and organizations: The GLOBE study of 62 societies.* Thousand Oaks, CA: Sage.

Hultman, K. 2002. *Balancing individual and organizational values.* San Francisco: Jossey-Bass.

Jams, R. 2004. Exploring OD in Africa: A response to David Lewis. *Nonprofit Management & Leadership*, 14(3): 313-324.

Janis, I. L. (1972). *Victims of groupthink: A psychological study of foreign-policy decisions and fiascoes.* Atlanta: Houghton Mifflin.

Jermier, J. M. 1998. Critical perspectives on organizational control. *Administrative Science*

Quarterly, 43: 235-256.

Jones, T. M., & Wicks, A. C. 1999. Convergent stakeholder theory. *Academy of Management Review*, 24(2): 206-221.

Keenoy, T., Marshak, R. J., Oswick, C., & Grant, D. 2000. The discourse of organizing. *Journal of Applied Behavioral Science*, 36(2): 133-135.

Kilduff, M. 1993. Deconstructing organizations. *Academy of Management Review*, 18(1): 13-31.

Kliener, A. 2003. *Who really matters: The core group theory of power, privilege, and success*. New York: Currency/Doubleday.

Koontz, H. 1961. The management theory jungle. *Academy of Management Journal*, 4(3): 174-188.

Koontz, H. 1980. The management theory jungle revisited. *Academy of Management Review*, (2): 175-187.

Kramer, R. 1989. In the shadow of death: Robert Denhardt's theology of organizational life. *Administration & Society*, 22(3): 357-379.

Laiken, M. E. 1997. Collaborative processes for collaborative organization design: The role of reflection, dialogue and polarity management in creating an environment for organizational learning. *Organization Development Journal*, 15(4): 35-42.

Lau, J. B., & Shani, A. B. 1988. *Behavior in organizations: An experiential approach. Homewood*, IL: Irwin.

Lawler, E. E. III., & Finegold. 2000. Individualizing the organization: Past, present, and future. *Organizational Dynamics*, 29(1): 1-15.

Marchington, M., Wilkinson, A, Ackers, P, & Goodman, J. 1994. Understanding the meaning of participation: Views from the workplace. *Human Relations*, 47(8): 867-894.

Masterson, S. S., Lewis, K., Goldman, B. M., & Taylor, M.S. 2000. Integrating justice and social exchange: The differing effects of fair procedures and treatment on work relationships. *Academy of Management Journal*, 43(4): 738-748.

McKinlay, A., & Starkey, K. (Eds.). 1998. *Faucault, management and organization theory: From panopticon to technologies of the self.* London: Sage.

Miller, E. J. 1989. Leiscester conferences after thirty years. In F. Gabelnick and A. W. Carr (Eds.), *Contributions to social and political science: Proceedings of the first international symposium on group relations*: 1-4. Washington, D.C.: The A. K. Rice Institute.

Miller, E. J., & Rice, A. K. 1967. *Systems of organization: The control of task and sentient boundaries*. London: Tavistock Publications.

Mizruchi, M.S., & Fein, L. C. 1999. The Social Construction of Organizational Knowledge: A study o the uses of coercive, mimetic, and normative isomorphism. *Administrative Science Quarterly*, 44: 653-683.

Nevis, E. C. 1987. *Organizational consulting: A gestalt approach.* New York: Gardner Press.

Nicolini, D., & Meznar, M. B. 1995. The social construction of organizational learning: Conceptual and practical issues in the field. *Human Relations*, 48(7): 727-746.

Nord, W. R., & Fox, S. 1996. The individual in organizational studies: The great disappearing act? in S. Clegg, C. Hardy & W. R. Nord (Eds.), Handbook of organization studies: 148-174. Thousand Oaks, CA: Sage.

O'Connor, E. S. 1999. The politics of management thought: A case study of the Harvard Business School and the Human Relations School. *Academy of Management Review*, 24(1): 117-131.

Ortenblad, A. 2002. A typology of the idea of learning organization. *Human Relations*, 33(2): 213-230.

Palmer, B. 1979. Learning and the group experience. In W. G. Lawrence (Ed.), *Exploring individual and organizational boundaries: A Tavistock open systems approach*: 169-192. New York: Wiley.

Pauchant, T. C. (Ed.). 1997. *In search of meaning: Managing for the health of organizations, our communities and the natural world.* San Francisco: Jossey Bass.

Pfeffer, J. 1997. *New directions for organizational theory: Problems and prospects.* New York: Oxford University Press.

Prasad, A. 2003. *Postcolonial theory and organizational analysis: A critical engagement.* New York: Palgrave Macmillan.

Purser, R. E., Cabana, S., Emery, M., & Emery, F. 1997. *Organization Development Journal*, 15(1): 30-52.

Quinn, R. E., & Spreitzer, G. M. 1997. The road to empowerment: Seven Questions every leader should consider. *Organizational Dynamics*, 25 (2): 37-42.

Randolph, W. A. (2000). Re-thinking empowerment: Why is it so hard to achieve? *Organizational Dynamics*, 29(2): 94-107.

Rioch, M. J. 1970. Group relations: Rationale and technique. *International Journal of Group Psychotherapy*, 20: 340-355.

Sashkin, M. 1986. Participative management remains an ethical imperative. *Organizational Dynamics*, 14(4): 62-75.

Scarr, S. 1986. Constructing psychology: Making facts and fables for our times. *American Psychologist*, 40(5): 499-512.

Scott, W. R. 1992. *Organizations: Rational, Natural, and Open Systems* (3rd ed.). Englewood Cliffs, NJ: Prentice-Hall.

Sendjaya, S., & Sarros, J. 2002. Servant leadership: Its origins, development, and application in organizations. *The Journal of Leadership Studies*, 9(2): 57-64.

Senge, P. M. 1990. *The fifth discipline: The art and practice of the learning organization.* New York: Doubleday.

Shirkin, H. L. 1993. The employee empowerment scam: Without meaningful changes, empowerment is doomed. *Industry Week*, 242 (Oct. 18, 1993): 58.

Smith, K. K. 2002. Violence is the language of the unheard. Journal of Applied Behavioral Science, 38(1): 6-11.

Smither, R. D. 1991. The return of the authoritarian manager. *Training*, 40-44.

Snell, R. S. 2001. Moral foundations of the learning organization. *Human Relations*, 54(3): 319-342.

Solomon, C. M. 1994. HR facilitates the learning organization concept. *Personnel Journal*, 73(1): 56-66.

Soule, E. 2002. Managerial moral strategies: In search of a few good principles. *Academy of Management Review*, 27(1): 114-124.

Spears, L. (Ed.) 1995. *Reflections on Leadership: How Robert K. Greenleaf's Theory of Servant-Leadership Influenced Today's Top Management Thinkers*. New York: John Wiley & Sons.

Staw, B. M., & Epstein, L. D. 2000. What bandwagons bring: Effects of popular management techniques on corporate performance, reputation, and CEO pay. *Administrative Science Quarterly*, 45, 523-556.

Szilagyi, A. D., Jr., & Wallace M. J., Jr. 1990. *Organizational behavior and performance.* Glenview, IL: Scott, Foresman, and Company.

Taylor, J. R., & Robichaud, D. 2004. Finding the organization in the communication: Discourse as action and sensemaking. *Organization*, 11(3): 395-413.

Vaill, P. B. 1985. Integrating the diverse directions of the behavioral sciences. In R. Tannenbaum (Ed.), *Human Systems Development*, San Francisco: Jossey-Bass.

Voronov, M., & Coleman, P. T. 2003. Beyond the ivory towers: Organizational power practices and a "practical" critical postmodernism. *The Journal of Applied Behavioral Science*, 39(2): 169-185.

Wagner, E., & Snyder, W. M. 2000. Communities of practice: The organizational frontier. *Harvard Business Review*, 139-145.

Weick, K. E., & Westley, F. 1996. Organizational learning: Affirming an oxymoron. In S. R. Clegg, C. Hardy, and W. R. Nord (Eds). Handbook of organizational studies: 440-458. Thousand Oaks, CA: Sage.

Weisbord, M. R. 1992. *Discovering common ground*. San Franciso: Berrett-Koehler.

Weisbord, M. R., & Janoff, S. 2000. *Future search: An active guide to finding common ground in organizations and communities*. San Francisco: Berrett-Koehler.

Welbourne, T. M., & Mejia, L. R. G. 1995. Gainsharing: A critical review and a future research agenda. *Journal of Management*, 21(3): 559-609.

Westwood, R., & Clegg, S. (Eds.). 2003. *Debating organization: Point-counterpoint in organization studies*. Oxford, UK: Blackwell.

Wheatley, M. 2002. *Turning To One Another: Simple Conversations To Restore Hope To The Future*. San Francisco: Berrett-Koehler Publishers.

Wrzesniewski, A., & Dutton, J. E. 2001. *Crafting a job: Revisioning employees as active crafters of their work*. Academy of Management Review, 26(2), 179-201.

Yan, A., Zhu, G., & Hall, D.T. 2002. International assignments for career building: A model of agency relationships and psychological contracts. *Academy of Management Review*, 27(3), 373-391.

SECTION 5

THE HISTORICAL CONTEXT OF LEADERSHIP AND MANAGEMENT IN SUB-SAHARAN AFRICA

SUB-SAHARAN AFRICAN LEADERSHIP: EVOLUTION OR DEVOLUTION

ROMIE F. LITTRELL
Auckland University of Technology
Faculty of Business
Auckland
New Zealand
e-mail: romielittrell@yahoo.com

GARY D. GREGORY
University of New South Wales
Director, Centre for Applied Marketing
Sydney, New South Wales
Australia
e-mail: g.gregory@unsw.edu.au

"The future, what's that?"
- BELISARIO, one of a group of hunter-gatherers who left the Colombian jungle to join the modern world. *New York Times*, 11 May 2006

ABSTRACT

Sub-Saharan African countries are among the most diverse of any geographic region. This area has a vast diversity of ethnicity, religion, language, and customs. There is limited interethnic marriage and interaction. Colonial influences tended to be "divide and rule" where colonial governments empowered and coerced local tribal chiefs to regulate local affairs, maintaining ethnic separation during the colonial period. Post-colonial nations were created for the most part with no consideration of ethnic geography. This paper discusses prehistoric and historic influences on the development of leader behaviour and preferences in Sub-Saharan Africa. Data collected in Uganda and South Africa using the Leader Behavior Description Questionnaire XII (LBDQXII) are analysed and discussed. From the LBDQXII, Factor 1: Representation and Factor 11: Integration are universally highly preferred across all national samples, and Factor 3: Tolerance of Uncertainty the least preferred. However, the majority of the managerial leader behaviour sets defined by the LBDQXII appear to be significantly affected by cultural contingencies. *Representation* measures to what degree the leader speaks as the representative of the group; *Persuasiveness* measures to what extent the leader uses persuasion and argument effectively; exhibits strong convictions; *Initiation of Structure* measures to what degree the leader clearly defines their own role, and lets followers know what is expected; and *Integration* reflects to what degree the leader maintains a closely-knit organization; resolves inter-member conflicts, were found to be preferred in Uganda and South Africa.

Keywords: Sub-Saharan Africa, Leadership, History

Since the end of the last Ice Age, less than 20,000 years ago, the northern and Sub-Saharan regions of Africa (SSA) have been separated by the extremely harsh climate of the sparsely populated Sahara Desert, forming a barrier interrupted only by the Nile River. The modern term *Sub-Saharan* corresponds with the European representation of North as above and South as below. The division of Africa into these two, broad regions has also arisen from historical and geopolitical considerations. North Africa's inhabitants have generally been perceived in the West to be predominantly Caucasoid and the Southern Africans Negroid, though such terms are now disputed by anthropologists. North Africans have always been quite distinct from the mostly Black Sub-Saharan Africans. The satellite photo in Figure 1 gives a dramatic depiction of the climactic differences in Africa. This study considers sources of leadership traits in Sub-Saharan Africa, and relates them to research findings in South Africa and Uganda.

FIGURE 1
A composite of satellite images of Africa: It does appear dark

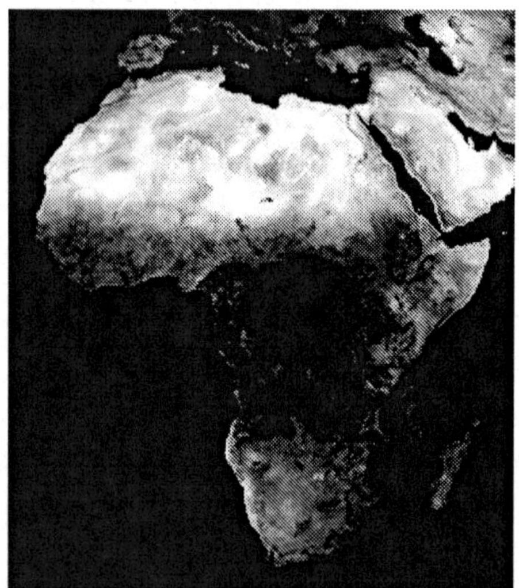

Source: Wikimedia.com[11]

THE CONCEPT OF "NATIONAL" CULTURE

In an analysis of the idea of "nationalism", Anderson (1991) proposes that "imagination" plays a role in any conception of "nation" involving national leadership, identity, geographic boundary, or ideology, and further, that public and popular literature, as opposed to research and first-hand experience, are often instrumental in creating these notions of national group identity. This is particularly applicable to African leadership and society, where most African nations are not based entirely on historical or archaeological facts (Williams, 2003). In the development of concepts of leadership in African nations, Williams proposes that traditional African leadership and authority systems were instrumental in mediating the autocracy of the kingdom but were deeply undermined by colonialism. Some data were collected relating to ethnicity and specific analyses related to these variables will be presented below.

[11] Published under the GNU free documentation license
http://en.wikipedia.org/wiki/Wikipedia:Text_of_the_GNU_Free_Documentation_License

NATIONS IN SUB-SAHARAN AFRICA

An indication of the difficulties in defining "national" culture in Sub-Saharan Africa can be indicated by the 96 major languages of Sub-Saharan Africa identified in the 2005 CIA World Factbook. The people of no nation speak a single language. And the list does not include Niger-Congo languages, Nilo-Saharan languages, or hundreds of minor tribal dialects spoken by small groups.

The Location of Sub-Saharan Africa

The exact position of the dividing line between the Sahara and Sub-Saharan Africa is not well defined due to sometimes indefinite national boundaries, natural ecologies, and ethnicities. Sub-Saharan Africa is usually defined to include forty-eight nations. Forty-two of these nations are on the African mainland, with four island nations in the southwest Indian Ocean (Madagascar, The Comoros, Mauritius, and Seychelles) and two island nations in the Atlantic Ocean (Cape Verde and São Tomé and Príncipe). According to this classification scheme, the countries of sub-Saharan Africa are in Table 1.

PREHISTORIC AND HISTORIC SUB-SAHARAN AFRICA: HUNTER-GATHERER SOCIETIES

Pre-historically and historically Sub-Saharan Africa is a land well-suited to hunter-gather societies. Lee and Hitchcock (2001) note that "...ninety percent of human history –in Africa and elsewhere– is the history of hunting and gathering."

From Sahlins (1972), in the Palaeolithic Era humans lived in small, semi-nomadic clans whose primary function was to hunt and gather food. Mobility was an aspect that was highly valued. Since their food source was primarily game, clans had to be ready to pack up and leave whenever they ran out of food sources. Clans consisted of only 30-50 people, so as to not quickly consume local food sources and to be able to move quickly when necessary. With so few people a clan was a small face-to-face society, where everyone knew one another. Material possessions were not valued, as it was difficult to carry things from place to place. Since there was no desire for material possessions, most things that the clan owned were considered shared property.

During this time, clans had an informal, personalised organization of power. The authority of the clan was given to the elders. Also, there were few, if any, distinctions in status between one person and another, making everyone roughly equal. Women played an important role in society. Most women did not have many children, which allowed the women to be involved in gathering food. Infants were a burden for mothers to carry when they had to leave for a new area. Marital partnerships were formed, however hunter-gatherer bands valued compatibility among their members more highly than continuous co-residence with a single band, and individuals might move from one related band to another (Quale, 1988). This way of life has been idealised by ecologists for holding values of living in harmony with other life forms rather than striving to dominate and exploit them. Not surprisingly, this attitude toward life tends to make the integration of such families into "modern" life a long and difficult process.

In general, the health of the semi-nomadic society was fairly good. There were no widespread epidemics, for as soon as a virus killed everyone in a clan, there was no place for it to go, therefore ending that specific virus within one clan. Humans had few tooth cavities, since their diet was comprised mostly of meat.

Early hunter-gather societies appear to have lived first in small nomadic bands and later, in some locations, in larger, more settled, and hierarchically organized communities (Wenke, 1984). In Africa, observing groups of !Kung, whose lifestyles have remained relatively intact from prehistoric into recorded history, small kin groups of hunter-gatherers tended to be cooperative and relatively egalitarian.

Leadership in Hunter-Gatherer Societies

Jacobson (1997) observed that in the hunter-gatherer band men might hunt individually or in groups, and when they cooperated, leadership was not based on official rank, but rather on one hunter proposing a group hunt and recruiting others to follow him. None were compelled to follow, however, and different hunts might have different leaders based on the relative leader status of different individuals at different times and the nature of the hunt. Women needed even less coordination. With them leadership would be more a matter of the wiser or more skilled giving advice as the need arose.

Riches (1995) finds that leadership notions in hunter-gather/foraging societies imply exemplary behaviour in a particular aspect of life; however, notions of authority are not implied. As Silberbauer puts it, referring to the Khoisan in Africa, leaders are "authoritative" but not "authoritarian" (1982: 29) and owe their position to the fact that others, through choice, have elected to follow them because their performance in some important aspect of social affairs is superior. There is an absence of interpersonal or intergroup ranking.

However, Boehm (1999), in a review concerning modern and prehistoric hunter-gatherer societies, concluded that even in strictly egalitarian bands and tribes, group members exercised differential influence on group decision-making. This is supported by the experimental social psychological literature reviewed by Boehm. When individuals form groups to work on collective tasks, leader-follower patterns emerge quickly and spontaneously, even when groups initially lack a leader (Bales, 1951; Mann, 1959). Leadership functions appear to extend beyond the human species. In studies of nonhuman primates and other social mammals, there have been numerous observations of social interactions that resemble leader-follower patterns in humans (Boehm, 1999; De Waal, 1996; Wilson, 1975). For example, De Waal (1996: 129) observed the following in a captive chimpanzee colony at Arnhem Zoo in the Netherlands: "On one occasion, a quarrel between Mama and Spin got out of hand and ended in fighting and biting. Numerous apes rushed up to the warring females and joined in the fray. A huge knot of fighting, screaming apes rolled around in the sand until Luit (the alpha male) leapt in and literally beat them apart. He did not choose sides in the conflict, like others; instead anyone who continued received a blow from him".

TABLE 1
Nations of Sub-Saharan Africa from various sources

Central Africa
Angola (also sometimes considered part of Southern Africa)
Burundi (also sometimes considered part of East Africa)
Cameroon (also sometimes considered part of West Africa)
Central African Republic
Chad (also sometimes considered part of West Africa)
Democratic Republic of the Congo
Equatorial Guinea (also sometimes considered part of West Africa)
Gabon (also sometimes considered part of West Africa)
Rwanda (also sometimes considered part of East Africa)
Republic of Congo
Zambia (also sometimes considered part of Southern Africa)
East Africa
Burundi (also sometimes considered part of Central Africa)
Kenya
Mozambique (also sometimes considered part of Southern Africa)
Rwanda (also sometimes considered part of Central Africa)
Tanzania
Uganda
North East Africa
Djibouti
Eritrea
Ethiopia
Somalia (including Somaliland)
Sudan (also often considered part of North Africa)
Southern Africa
Angola (also sometimes considered part of Central Africa)
Botswana
Lesotho
Malawi
Mozambique (also sometimes considered part of East Africa)
Namibia
South Africa
Swaziland
Zambia (also sometimes considered part of Central Africa)
Zimbabwe
West Africa
Benin
Burkina Faso
Cameroon (also sometimes considered part of Central Africa)
Chad (also sometimes considered part of Central Africa)
Côte d'Ivoire
Equatorial Guinea (also sometimes considered part of Central Africa)
Gabon (also sometimes considered part of Central Africa)
The Gambia
Ghana
Guinea
Guinea-Bissau
Liberia
Mali
Mauritania
Niger
Nigeria
Senegal
Sierra Leone
Togo
African island nations
Cape Verde (West Africa)
Comoros (Southern Africa)
Madagascar (Southern Africa)
Mauritius (Southern Africa)
São Tomé and Príncipe (Central Africa or West Africa)
Seychelles (East Africa)
Territories, possessions, departments
Mayotte (France)
Réunion (France)

TRANSITION: THE NEOLITHIC REVOLUTION

The "Neolithic Revolution" occurred from 10,000 to 3000 B.C. (Price & Feinman, 1993). This era defines the transition from a food gathering society to a food producing society, when humans settled down to cultivate their food instead of following their food. Many significant economic, political and social changes, both beneficial and detrimental, occurred during this change in lifestyle. No single factor or set of factors has been identified to explain this global phenomenon. Farming appeared and then spread out from many different regions all over the globe. Kimball (1998) provides these dates:

▪ In **Southwest Asia**, agriculture took hold about 10,000 years ago with domestication of grains, goats, sheep, cattle and pigs;
▪In **Mesoamerica**, it happened about 9,000 years ago beginning with the cultivation of gourds;
▪ In **South Asia**, it occurred about 8,000 years ago with domestication of cattle;
▪ In **South America**, agriculture appeared about 7,500 years ago with the cultivation of gourds, squash and lima beans;
▪ In **East Asia**, it happened about 8,000 years ago, this time with the cultivation of rice;
▪ **Central Europe** about 6,700 years ago;
▪ **Western Europe** about 6,000 years ago;
▪ In **Scandinavian Europe** cultivation of cereals began about 3,100 years ago;
▪ In **North America**, domestication appears about 3,200 years ago with sunflower and amaranth cultivation

In Africa the transition to agriculture occurred about 7,000 years ago with the domestication of donkeys. Agriculture in the African rain forest zone farther south evolved independently 4,000 years ago, and was based on root crops such as cassava and tree crops such as bananas and palm nuts.

Characteristics of Societies in the Neolithic Era

- Domestication of plants and animals (and the introduction of domestic animal derived diseases such as tuberculosis from bovine tuberculosis, smallpox from cowpox, rickettsial typhus from murine typhus, influenza, "cold" viruses, rabies, anthrax, tularaemia, etc.)
- More advanced tools, use of pottery
- Spread of village-living
- First systematic war between groups

Characteristics of Societies in the Neolithic-Mesolithic Era

- Cities emerge
- States emerge

- Political, military, and priesthood classes emerge
- Development of hierarchical, paternalistic leadership forms

Changes in the Life of the Individual in the Neolithic Period

Sahlins (1972) found that causes of mortality shifted; the biggest mortality factor in women was ***childbirth***. Since there were more pregnancies, more women died in childbirth. In men, the greatest cause of death was ***warfare***. Eventually, a new type of political structure had to be established to manage larger groups of people.

As society went from small and informal to a large, impersonal hierarchy, military and religious leaders were given authority over the group, and distinctions in social class began to arise based on the acquisition of valuable material goods. Property wealth was based on private wealth, not on the wealth of the group.

The new structured society established specified tasks for people of these communities. Women stayed home with their children, while men went out and ploughed the fields or did other specific tasks.

Benefits arose from a consistent food source, new materials, and quality improvement from specialisation of tasks. On the other hand, health declined, the social and political atmosphere became impersonal, and a gap was created between the wealthy and the poor.

The Neolithic Revolution in Sub-Saharan Africa

In some areas of the world the domestication of animals gave rise to *pastoralism*, the development of economies based upon herding animals, which has proven the strongest cultural/economic competitor to sedentary agriculture throughout most of the world. Pastoralism has thrived in semiarid areas such as central Asia, the Sudanic belt south of the Sahara desert in Africa, and the savannah zone of East and South Africa._These areas were incapable of supporting dense or large populations. The nomadic, herding way of life has tended to produce independent and hardy peoples, well-versed in the military skills needed not only for their survival but also to challenge more heavily populated agrarian societies. The cattle-herding peoples of central, East, and South Africa produced some of the most formidable pre-industrial military organizations. Only with the rather recent period of the Industrial Revolution has the power of nomadic peoples been irreparably broken and the continuation of their cultures threatened by the steady encroachment of sedentary peoples.

Paternalistic Leader Heritage in Pastoral Communities

Most herders and pastoral nomads tend to have patriarchal families and a tendency toward polygyny (Schneider & Gough 1961; Maccoby 1966). Women's productive work tends to be limited to herding of small animals, dairying, and food processing and preparation (Quale 1988). Where exchange relationships must be set in place over widely dispersed territories due to grazing requirements, marriage partnerships may be strategically located, and the exchange of daughters in marriage may help to cement economic alliances. These families are again difficult to integrate into contemporary society because their mobility interferes with the schooling of their children and the continuous health care of their members. Pure forms of nomadic family types may be the exception rather than the rule. The Dinka of the Sudan, for example, grow about one-third and gather and hunt two-thirds of the food types that they use

(Zeitlin, 1977). Dinka women and old men tend to be sedentary year-round, while young men are nomadic pastoralists for a part of the year (Deng, 1972).

In a case study of the contemporary Maasai society in Northern Kenya, Nicholson (2005) found this semi-migratory animal herding culture to have leadership and management behaviours similar to the above mentioned prehistoric and early historic societies. Leaders are charismatic, and are chosen by the group. Leader traits include "good behaviour", good temperament, and a reputation for morality. Requisites of good leader behaviour are "Never quarrel with anyone. Don't demean anyone." (Nicholson 2005: 261). The leader is more of a mediator of disputes than a director of behaviour, a stewardship, consensus, servant-leader model. The power and decision-making remain in the hands of the male elders employing consensus decision-making.

AGRARIAN TRADITIONS

Societies engaged in traditional agriculture, crafts, and trade have been broadly divided into those practicing communal land ownership and those practicing private land ownership (Caldwell & Caldwell 1990). Most populations of Europe and Asia made the transition from communal to private land ownership from 4,000 to 5,000 years ago, in response to the accumulation of significant agricultural surpluses, or possibly wealth from other sources such as mining. In Sub-Saharan Africa, isolated by the desert, and with growing conditions that did not require the accumulation of surpluses, communal land ownership remained predominant.

Polygyny as a family form is well suited to an agricultural system using abundant low-yielding communal land farmed by labour-intensive technologies (Caldwell & Caldwell, 1990). Each additional wife and her children permit the family to farm more territory and to achieve economies of scale in domestic labour and trade. The family unit, which is headed by the husband and the elders of his lineage, starts with one wife and adds more after accumulating the bride-wealth needed for each. The more wives and children, the larger and more affluent this unit can become. Sexual fidelity of the wives is not a top priority, and all children born to a man's wives are legally his. Societies with this family form appear to place the highest cultural and religious value on child-bearing. According to Quale (1988), it may not be reasonable to assume that all early agricultural societies fit this model, when agriculture evolved in rich localized topsoil deposits of annually flooding rivers.

Monogamous marriage, with strong cultural safeguards for the sexual fidelity of women, is important for the maintenance of traditional subsistence agriculture on privately owned farms. Family lands must be passed to male heirs whose paternity is beyond question. For greater security in land transmission, cross-cousin marriage may be preferred. Brothers whose children marry reunite land and other possessions separated by inheritance. Such cousin marriage has been common in many cultures, with the highest rate of about 60 per cent of all marriages claimed for Pakistan (Hussain and Bittles, 1998). It may also reduce property-related feuds common among societies of peasant farmers in the Middle East and elsewhere (Sweet 1970).

In spite of ethnographic variations, agrarian families are recognizable as a type. Throughout the world, these settled institutional families are organized around agricultural production, traditional crafts, or other family business ventures. They have large kinship networks and hierarchical authoritarian governance. These families are producers, employers, consumers, and social welfare agencies in one. Family management tends to be well developed. The highest family value is responsibility (Doherty 1992). Marriage in institutional families is a functional partnership rather than a romantic relationship. Children tend to be valued as apprentices and next-generation managers of the family lands and enterprises.

NEOLITHIC/MESOLITHIC SOCIETAL CHANGES: THE BANTU MIGRATION

Approximately 2000 years ago a massive migration of peoples, which continued for 1500 years, began in Central Africa. This migration is sometimes called the "Bantu Migration". It is given this name as it involved the movement of people whose indigenous language belonged to the Bantu language family of the Kongo-Niger language group. Historians are not in agreement as to why Bantu speaking peoples began to move away from their home areas in Central Africa. Some historians believe this area experienced rapid population growth that resulted in a shortage of land. Other historians point to the development of centrally-governed kingdoms. The process of bringing people under the control of a central authority resulted in the dislocation of defeated peoples, some of whom migrated in search of autonomy. One speculates that divisions occurred between groups accepting egalitarian leadership or hierarchical, paternalistic leadership.

WAR CHIEFS

When hunter-gather societies in denser population areas encountered serious competition for food from other bands, a war chief emerged to coordinate any organized violence (Jacobson, 1997). Relatively large military organisations formed as warriors from several households combined under one leader. This war chief might hold the position formally and for long periods of time. Clan-sized military units were based on blood ties (sometimes via adoption, sometimes via marriage). Especially charismatic war chiefs might have been able to assemble several clans into a military alliance to defeat a common rival clan. These alliances would have been easier where the allied clans were thought to be blood kin. Members of hunter-gatherer bands would have known of the existence of other bands which had blood relations to them, which spoke a common language, and which shared many customs. These related bands would have been distinguishable from other, non-related bands with differing language and customs. Military and other advantages eventually encouraged associations of clans to form as "tribes", larger groups speaking a common language and thought to be descended from a common ancestor. But sub-tribal, clan-level family activity continued to thrive. In part this may have been due to the formation of cities and the rise of "nobility" based upon blood or adoptive relationship with leaders, because the nobles saw clan-level family as more natural, seeing as they themselves stayed together primarily in order to dominate the city.

The emerging nobility could also invigorate their own ranks by recruiting new noble families, clans without noble standing, from time to time. Eventually this diffusion of nobility happened to such an extent that leadership in many cities passed to a new class, the politicians. A politician might or might not be noble, despite the fact that hereditary wealth and influence (more easily acquired by nobility) was still a major factor in the politics of the community. Eventually the influence of the class of politicians began to exceed that of the non-politician nobles. Thus individual non-noble politicians could rule over individual noble non-politicians, and eventually over individual noble politicians, and even perhaps over all nobles.

In some ways social mobility as a politician gave commoners tremendous opportunities for acquiring power. But such power had to be gained and held within the traditional order of the society. Hereditary power and wealth continued to wield considerable influence. Various institutional assaults were made against rival clans by the politician/noble tribes in association with the priestly tribes. Various programs of religious oppression were sometimes tried as well. Rebellion was fomented from time to time against the political order by non-noble clans who would form "criminal" syndicates (thus rival tribes).

COLONIALISM, IMPOSITION OF THE INDUSTRIAL REVOLUTION

Establishment of colonies for mining in mineral-rich areas of Sub-Saharan Africa (1920-1950) brought the local economy immediately into the global economy. The most dramatic economic and social changes occurred as a result of worker migration due to the demand for workers in the mines (and eventually, but slowly, to higher levels of income for locals in mining). Labour migration and urbanization resulted in a dramatic increase in the demand for purchased food, and in rural areas where many men migrated to work in the mines, there was a substantial reduction in food production. Malnutrition and poverty-related diseases spread in, for example, Northern Rhodesia.

In the 1930s and 1940s in Northern Rhodesia a small, but significant, group of European settler farmers were encouraged to grow maize and raise cattle to meet food needs. These farmers were sold choice land that was taken away from African subsistence farmers, who were forced to move to less productive land.

When Northern Rhodesia gained its independence as Zambia in 1964, it inherited a unique economy and social structure. Zambia's mines had produced over a billion dollars of sales for the mining companies; however, outside the "Copperbelt" there was little evidence of Zambia's wealth. The vast majority of profits had been taken out of the country by the Anglo-American and Roan Select Trust. Colonialism had done little to develop the economic infrastructure outside the mines and the commercial farming areas dominated by European farmers

Colonial states were weak and lacked economic and governmental infrastructure. The inability of a government to meet the needs of their citizens is a key cause of current political dissatisfaction and unrest; the colonists are gone, the present government is here and now. Colonial states were not democratic and had little respect for human rights, leaving a non-democratic heritage. Hence, as African leaders faced opposition, partially because of their inability to meet the needs of their citizens, it was easy for them to fall back on the examples of the colonial states. Many post-colonial governments resorted to the same undemocratic practices as the colonial states used to control and deal with opposition.

Ethnicity in Post-Colonial African Nations

All modern African countries split, to some degree, traditional ethnic group geographic boundaries. The colonial policies of "divide and rule" and the use of local chiefs as surrogate colonial rulers helped to establish ethnic rivalries that have become a common part of politics in post-colonial Africa. The populations of arbitrarily bounded states see their nation as an entity alien to their history (Davidson 1992). "We are the rightful rulers" said an Ashanti chief at the independence of Ghana in 1957 (Apter 1968). At times there was a reasonable approximation between pre- and post-colonial states both in terms of existing political cultures and geographical boundaries. In these latter cases, the colonial period is a period of foreign occupation in the existence of the state. The colonial occupier did not create the state but temporarily deprived it of its sovereignty. The populations of states retaining historic boundaries experienced the end of colonialism as the restoration of their statehood.

Bierschenk (2003) and Geschiere (1993) reviewed French and British rule in colonial Africa. Typical of their conclusions, Geschiere, in a study of colonial Cameroon, indicates a continuous tug-of-war between the imposition of the management practices of the colonial powers and the ethnic practices, opinions, attitudes, and beliefs of the local peoples. A not unexpected result of this tug-of-war is the formation of a hybrid culture accommodating sufficiently the needs of the members of the leadership and management cadre, proposed by Graen and Hui (1996) and Heimer and Vince (1998), and supported by Littrell (2003). In a case study of multi-ethnic work teams Heimer and Vince found that at the initial stages of their formation, the teams seem to move in one of two directions; towards the setting up of a "safe hybrid culture" for highly heterogeneous teams; or towards a "dominant culture" in more moderately heterogeneous contexts. Sustainable learning and change within international teams, is created out of a further stage of development, the "challenging hybrid culture", capitalizing upon the multicultural synergies. Depending upon the initiative and competence of the leader and manager players in hybrid colonial-leader-local-leader interactions, we expect to see hybrid cultures of various characteristics emerging. The lasting effect of these hybrid cultures is, of course, a function of the time in power of the colonial government, the kinds of programs and interactions between the colonial and local leaders, and the "strength" of a local culture in maintaining itself.

COLONIAL LEADERSHIP HERITAGE

Ugwuegbu (2001: 65) states, "Problems of leadership in African organizations are responsible for the underdevelopment of organizations in many African countries." He also states that many of the problems are due to the heritage of colonial governments and due to the fragmented ethnic and religious societies in Africa (see pp. 68-69). Chisholm (2001), in a qualitative analysis of interviews with managers in education in South Africa, found that leadership competence was associated with "masculinity, rationality, and whiteness" (Chisholm 2001: 387), and a further comment, "white, male, middle-class, and heterosexual" (Chisholm 2001: 389).

Effects of the Colonial Heritage on Demands of Leadership

Griffiths (1986), and the several works of Samatar (e.g. 1997), provide a thorough analysis of the relationship of the post-colonial state and tribal ethnicity. As noted above, a frequent legacy of post-colonial nation-states is the assignment of boundaries with no consideration of local ethnicity. The perception of legitimacy of the modern African state is a function of its congruence with pre-existing political systems and norms of political authority. Although all African states but Ethiopia and Liberia were imposed by European colonial empires, not all of them ended up being completely arbitrary to existing historic local societies.

Somalia provides an example of incongruent statehood in Africa. Although greatly homogeneous in terms of ethnicity, its boundaries fail to incorporate large segments of Somali populations living now in Kenya, Ethiopia, and Djibouti. Meanwhile, within Somalia itself, the clannish nature of the political system conflicts with the idea of centralized statehood (Samatar, 1997).

The Democratic Republic of Congo (formerly Zaire) provides another case in point. An artificial creation derived from exploitation of ivory and wild rubber in the river's basin by King Leopold II of Belgium (Hochschild, 1998), the country brings together different state systems and non-state societies and splits across its borders important kingdoms or political culture areas such as the Lunda and the Bakongo. With *over 200 African ethnic groups, the majority are Bantu; the four largest tribes, Mongo, Luba, Kongo (all Bantu), and the Mangbetu-Azande (Hamitic), make up about 45% of the population. This artificial creation is subject to continuous ethnic warfare.*

At the other end of the African state perceived legitimacy continuum lie countries such as Botswana, Lesotho, or Swaziland. Based on pre-colonial kingdoms, or federation of kingdoms in the case of Botswana, these contemporary states by and large approximate the contours and political cultures of their pre-colonial roots. In all three cases, the encroachment of Boer settlers from South Africa at the end of the nineteenth century led national authorities to request the establishment of a British protectorate, choosing colonization over the threat of institutional extinction (Brownlie, 1979). As voluntary colonies they were therefore much less arbitrary than most of their African counterparts. Upon reaching independence in the 1960s, Lesotho and Swaziland resumed their monarchic structures. Botswana became a republic but the hegemony of the traditional Tswana cattle-owner hierarchy remained unchallenged and a descendant of the royal family assumed the presidency. These are in fact modernized "traditional" African kingdoms, and are unfortunately relatively unique in Sub-Saharan Africa.

Assuming leadership of a state with arbitrary boundaries places enormous demands upon those who wish to lead. Van Vugt and Hogan (2005) pointed out that sanctions of undesirable behaviours of leaders include wilful disobedience and abandonment of leaders by followers. When this is coupled with the considerable emphasis placed on a leader's ability to honour his or her obligations to ethnic affiliates, without denying others to an extent that causes conflict to break out into the open (Nzelibe, 1986), and the expectation that the organization will in fact not pull together because of ethnic and/or family-based cleavages, successfully governing an arbitrarily created nation might be impossible.

Fractionalisation, Effects, and Validity

The construct termed "Ethnolinguistic Fractionalisation" arises from the *Atlas Nardov Mira* (Department of Geodesy and Cartography) of the State Geological Committee of the USSR in 1964. The *Atlas* was an extensive project to provide an extremely accurate depiction of the historic ethnic and linguistic compositions of the peoples of the world. An index, Ethnolinguistic Fractionalisation (ELF), was constructed by Taylor and Hudson (1972). The ELF measure reflects the likelihood that two people chosen at random will be from different ethno-linguistic groups.Initially no economic or political variables were considered.

William Easterly and Ross Levine (1997) published an article, "Africa's Growth Tragedy: Policies and Ethnic Divisions" that found a statistically and economically important negative effect of ethnic diversity on economic growth in a cross-section of countries. Easterly and Levine found that moving from an ethnically homogeneous country to one with a diversity of ethnic communities was correlated with a decrease in annual economic growth. They then applied this finding to Africa, reasoning that, because African countries are typically ethnically diverse, the strong link between ethnic heterogeneity and slow growth was quite likely an important part of the explanation for that region's "growth tragedy."

A significant problem with an ELF index, pointed out by Posner (2004), is that contrary to the assumptions of most scholars who seek to test the effects of ethnic diversity on growth, there is no single "correct" accounting of the ethnic groups in a country, and thus no single "correct" ELF. Countries possess multiple dimensions of cultural cleavage and multiple possible accountings of the salient ethnic communities. Researchers must choose the one that provides the appropriate enumeration of ethnic groups for the specific causal mechanism that is being tested and then calculate their ethnic fractionalization value from that enumeration.

Posner discussed examples of misclassification of African indices where multiple ethnicities are catalogued as part of a larger umbrella category with a single population count. The "cluster" or "grouping" problem refers to the fact that these umbrella categories sometimes subsume groups that are clearly distinct in most ethnographic and political accounts.

In Uganda, for example, the Acholi and Lango are collapsed into a single category despite a lengthy history of political rivalry between these groups. In Tanzania, the Nyamwezi and Sukuma are lumped together despite the fact that most descriptions of Tanzania's ethnic politics treat these groups not only as geographically, linguistically, and culturally distinct but also as keen political competitors. By grouping them into a single category, an important cleavage is hidden from view.

The most glaring example of this kind involves the cases of Rwanda and Burundi, where the fundamental cleavage between Hutus and Tutsis is totally absent in the *Atlas* accounting. In Rwanda both groups are collapsed into a monolithic "Banyrwanda" category; in Burundi Hutus and Tutsis share a common designation as "Barundi."

In the *Atlas* Kabre are classified along with two other groups as a subgroup of the Tem. Yet, the literature on contemporary Togo identifies the Kabre, but not the Tem, as a central actor in the country's politics. Because the Kabre are grouped under the Tem umbrella, it is impossible to determine exactly how large a group they, in fact, are. As a result, their size is not (and cannot be) reflected correctly in the index.

Similarly, in Mozambique, the Ndau, an important political group, are not even included in the *Atlas*'s listing of the country's ethnic groups. We must infer their size (or, at any rate the upper bound on their size) from the figures provided for the Mashona, of which the Ndau are a subgroup.

Numerous additional examples of this sort can be identified. In 2003 Easterly along with Alesina and others (Alesina, Devleeschauwer, Easterly, Kurlat, & Wacziarg, 2003), proposed religion as a significant source of fractionalisation, finding it positively correlated with economic development. Ultimately, it is difficult to precisely evaluate the effect size of religio-socio-ehtno-linguistic fractionalisation due to the strong correlation of the variables with other variables with explanatory potential.

CHARACTERISTICS OF LEADERSHIP AND CULTURE IN CONTEMPORARY SUB-SAHARAN AFRICA

Identifying cultural "clusters" and characterising nations, regions, and ethnicities should be an exercise on the part of the researcher of minimising the obscuring of real differences by the imposition of a grouping system. With this in mind, the following traits appear frequently in studies in Sub-Saharan countries.

Traditional Ways of Controlling Leaders in Sub-Saharan Africa

Van Vugt and Hogan (2005) point out findings in the literature concerning strategies followers use to curtail the power of leaders:

- Leaders' decisions in hunter-gatherer societies are largely overridden by group decision-making, often in public meetings and through the manipulation of minorities by the majority (Meggitt, 1977).

- A second control strategy is to criticize and ridicule leaders openly. In Africa people shout down leading hunters who fail in their role. In modern society, it is largely the role of the media (TV, newspapers, and internet) to criticize self-serving leaders, who are often caricatured in cartoons. We also find desperate attempts to control public media by standing leaders.

- In traditional African societies, leaders cannot order people to do things that they do not want to do. Disobeying leaders can be effective, because they are sanctioned without being replaced.

- Fourth, followers ostracize or shun exploitative leaders. Moore (1972) (see also Williams and Sommer, 1997) reports that, when aggressive tribal leaders start a feud the tribesmen distance themselves by no longer regarding them as one of theirs. This allows rival groups to kill the ostracized leader with impunity because he is no longer defended by his group.

- Related to immediately above, sometimes followers simply desert an exploitative leader. This reaction has been observed in African American societies (Boehm, 1999).

- In some African tribes, selfish, stingy leaders are routinely removed from office (Lewis, 1974), suggesting the importance of sharing.

Specific Characteristics of Leadership in Contemporary Africa

According to Blunt and Jones (1997), *i*n Sub-Sahara Africa economic psychology is generally characterized by powerful connections between objects, humans and the supernatural; the emphasis put on each of these elements and the interrelationships among them can vary from one ethnic group or tribe to another. Self-reliance and self-interest tend to take a back seat to ethnicity and group loyalty (Dia, 1994: 176).

In Africa individual achievements are frequently much less valued than are interpersonal relations. The value of economic transactions lies as much, if not more, in the ritual surrounding them and their capacity to reinforce group ties as it does in their worth to the parties involved. Wealth is, first, extended family or clan wealth, and second ethnic or tribal wealth; often it can be acquired legitimately at the expense of the organization (Dia, 1994). In many circumstances, ceremony, ritual, interpersonal relations, reciprocity and the distribution of scant resources to clan and ethnic affiliates are therefore natural responsibilities of leadership in Africa (Kolawole, 1996; Nzelibe, 1986; Warren, Adedokun, & Omolaoye, 1996).

African societies tend to be egalitarian within age groups, but hierarchical or gerontocratic between age groups (Linquist and Adolph, 1996). As a result, leaders often behave, and are expected to behave, paternalistically (Jones, Blunt, & Sharma, 1995). Leaders bestow favour and expect and receive obeisance or deference. Consensus is highly valued and decision-making within levels can therefore take a long time (see Cosway & Anankum, 1996). Between levels (downwards) observance of hierarchy means that consensus can be achieved relatively quickly (Blunt, 1978 and 1983; Dia, 1994).

African societies seem to have a great capacity also for tolerance and forgiveness, which can explain the attempts at reconciliation with former oppressors by African leaders like Jomo Kenyatta, Robert Mugabe and Nelson Mandela. Many observers have wondered at this capacity to forgive and forget. This image of the benign acceptance of past wrongs is epitomized by Nelson Mandela who, after three decades of imprisonment comes out, becomes an architect of black/white reconciliation, goes to beg white terrorists who are prepared to fast until death, "Please, please, don't kill yourselves. Please eat." This man, who had just lost twenty-seven of the best years of his life, goes to beg white terrorists not to fast until death. "Where else but in Africa will you find this sort of thing?" (Mazrui, 1994: 134).

Considerable emphasis is placed on a leader's ability to honour his or her obligations to ethnic affiliates, without denying others to an extent that causes conflict to break out into the open (Nzelibe, 1986). It is expected that the organization will not pull together because of ethnic and/or family-based cleavages.

Followers appear to prefer a leader who is kindly, considerate and understanding to one who is too dynamic and productive and, possibly, too demanding. Leaders are seen to possess genuine authority but are expected by their subordinates to use it only sparingly and in a humane and considerate way.

The studies suggest that African managers are concerned overwhelmingly with the quality of their relationship with their boss, rather than, for example, with individual or organizational effectiveness. That is, internal interpersonal issues predominate over those associated with the organization's performance, its long-term strategies, its clients and its external environment. The effective manager is perceived to consult subordinates, treat them considerately, promote their self-development, support and help them, and provide them with clear direction. In this view, good managers are people-oriented rather than task-oriented. The phrases used by several respondents in the Botswana research (Jones *et al., 1995) to describe the ideal boss - "teacher" and "father figure" - illustrate the relationship with the boss that seems to be valued.*

Reciprocity and Mutual Obligation in Gift-Giving Societies

The importance of sharing among in-groups brings us to another set of issues. Younger (2005) finds that reciprocity was a key factor in the social dynamics of many primitive peoples. Numerous ethnographic studies demonstrate that hunter-gatherer peoples developed elaborate and strict rules for sharing, rules that had the effect of optimizing resource use, especially in cultures that lacked storage capacity. The !Kung of the Kalahari hunted in small groups and then shared the results with everyone in the tribe. Villagers in some Polynesian societies collectively gathered food and then distributed it to all of the members of the village. In the case of the !Kung, Yellen (1998) observed that "security was obtained by giving rather than by hoarding, that is, by accumulating obligations that could be claimed in times of need."

Such customs promoted a degree of social equity that was essential in situations where food collection by individuals was not sufficiently reliable to meet daily needs and where storage was not practiced or practicable. However, the functionalist argument that hunter-gather peoples gave gifts to assure future economic return should not be overstated. The basic necessities of life were easily obtained in many such societies so that sharing was not required to sustain an individual. There were important non-economic social functions associated with reciprocity, including the establishment of reputation, social prestige, and the creation of a power base for leadership.

Sahlins (1972) proposed a "spectrum of [three] reciprocities...defined by its extremes and midpoint". These are:

1. Generalized or positive reciprocity (sharing).
2. Balanced reciprocity (trade).

3. Negative reciprocity (theft).

Positive reciprocity in its pure form constitutes altruistic giving, generosity without an expectation of return. But, positive reciprocity need not be exclusively altruistic and it is not solely economic in nature and can be an aspect of gaining and sustaining a leadership position. Gift giving can encourage a sense of obligation in the recipient that provides the giver with confidence that the favour will be returned. Repeated instances of such sharing engender a sense of mutual obligation among the members of a society and in so doing enhance social cohesion. As noted by Ekeh (1974), "Every social exchange transaction creates social bonds that not only tie one person to another and to society but one segment of society to another."

Concerning political motivations for gift giving, Pospisil (1958) stated of the Kapauku Papuans that "society views its ideal man as a most generous individual, who through the distribution of his fortune satisfies the needs of many people. Generosity is the highest cultural value and an attribute necessary for acquiring followers in political and legal life."

In a review and study of Trobriand Islanders, Mosko (1995) reported that a chief won followers through the distribution of food. Generosity increased the reputation of the giver, so aspiring leaders might give to the point of personal penury.

In environments where the basic necessities of life were plentiful, trade could assume roles other than the purely economic. As Firth (1927) observed, "The exchange takes place in gratification of a complex set of social motives - pride, vanity, ambition, sense of kinship bonds - but on the principle of economic utility there is no 'need' for them to occur." Often, exchanges of little practical utility were conducted and in some cases the items traded were destroyed as part of the process. When trade was introduced into some self-sufficient hunter-gatherer societies the result was a focus on toys, unnecessary clothing, or luxury goods rather than utilitarian tools that would enhance economic productivity. The participants thought that these things enhanced their social prestige. One could argue that such peoples had not yet "learned" economics, but this is precisely the point. They operated within a different value structure, one less rooted in countable material assets and services. In primitive societies non-material rewards played a vital role in exchange, as indeed they did and do in other societies. For example, sacrifices common in many religions might be seen as an attempt to exchange material goods for non-material blessings or an expectation of future well-being.

Negative reciprocity ranges from a passive withholding of an obligatory return gift to the aggressive theft of goods owned by another agent. In contrast to positive reciprocity, there may be a limit to the degree to which the members of a society can practice negative reciprocity. Aggression and theft can benefit a sub-group, but only within a victim population that produces the goods to be expropriated. While hunter-gatherer cultures have, like almost all other societies, demonstrated their capacity for acquisitive aggression (Keeley, 1996), few societies consist entirely of thieves. Some degree of cooperation, or at least some moderation of aggression within a social unit, appears to be vital to all functioning societies.

ETHNIC DIVERSITY AND MANAGERIAL EFFECTIVENESS IN CONTEMPORARY SOUTH AFRICA

Ghosh (2001) and Thomas and Bendixen (2000) examined the influence of ethnic diversity on organizational culture and effectiveness in South Africa. Despite the managers' identification with their ethnic group, there was a common national culture at the managerial level. The dimensions of that national culture, including a high degree of individualism and a low tolerance for hierarchical differences in power, resemble those found in the Netherlands, England, and the United States. The authors suggest these similarities may indicate the historical impact of Dutch, British, and American cultures on South Africa, as well as the prevalence of British and American systems of management. Thomas and Bendixen note high scores in individualism that deviate from previous studies on national culture in South Africa and the generally collectivist nature of African culture. They offer two potential explanations for the discrepancy:

1. Organizational cultures, which are largely shaped by American or British systems of management, may have influenced the cultural values expressed by the managers in the study; or,

2. The apparent contradiction can be reconciled by the special nature of African collectivism in which individuals act autonomously, but remain socially united, a concept that has been referred to as communalism. As a form of collectivism, communalism coexists with personal freedom or individualism.

The authors also found that neither ethnicity nor race significantly influenced management culture; similarly, management effectiveness was independent of both ethnicity and race. Together, these findings suggest that management culture and management effectiveness are not affected by either culture or race in South Africa.

On the other hand, Roodt (1997: 16) found the opposite, that the typical South African corporate environment reflects the following characteristics and identified fears of what is to come:

- A "them and us" culture which delineates a predominantly White management minority from the general workforce, which is a predominantly Black and unskilled majority;
- Affirmative action and its prospects as new criteria for jobs and promotion create a lot of stress and a mixture of aspirations, peer group pressure, and fear for job security;
- Adverse labour relations with very strong union backing and the tendency towards conflict and violence;
- Ethnic and language diversity within the workplace, faction-fighting, as well as the way in which people continue to stereotype one other;
- The existing privilege and discrimination practices based mainly on race and ethnicity despite changes in legislation;
- The wealth and poverty gap that exists between the "haves" and the "have-nots", and
- Illiteracy that is rife between the greater portion of the labour force, and the ever-increasing demands of technology and skills, rendering the majority of the Black population unemployable.

Smith, Peterson and Schwartz (2000) found African cultures to depend for guidance upon reliance on superiors and rules, and that these traits are associated with Collectivism and Cultural Embeddedness, Hierarchy, Power Distance, Mastery, and Masculinity. Most of the nations of Africa are especially high on these cultural dimensions. Their regression analysis indicates that Power Distance and Mastery provide the most concise estimate of the country-level correlates of reliance on hierarchical sources for guidance. It's no surprise that kingly authority would be posited as the ideal for people who were often scattered and oppressed.

Williams (2003) presented a thorough study of contemporary political governance. Williams (1998) and Tangwa (1998) reviewed the political structure of pre-colonial African kingdoms, some relatively large such as Ghana, Songhai, Benin, Bornu, and Sokoto, and others relatively small such as Nso', Bafut, and Kom. They found a combination of leadership strategies, including democratic processes (Tangwa, 1998: 2). Tangwa (1998) and Aletum (2001) argue that traditional African leadership and authority systems might be understood as the harmonious marriage between autocratic dictatorship and popular democracy. Specific formal practices (which vary between cultures) found the citizenry authorising, critiquing, and sanctioning the ascension of their ruler, his/her continued reign, and the selection and ascension of his/her successor.

Aletum provides an example of the Bafut kingdom, of Bamenda, Cameroon, where "when the new ruler has been installed, he is presented to the Bafut population for 'stoning'." The ceremonial stoning may consist of tiny, harmless pebbles in the case of an approved and respected new leader, or of large, injurious rocks hurled so as to maim, chase off or kill the undesired incumbent. In either case it reminds the new ruler what could happen if he lost the favour of the people. However, if the leader survived the coronation, dethronement after the fact was unlikely. Ritzenthaler and Ritzenthaler (1964) note that "[t]he stoning indicates that this is the last chance the people have to treat as mortal the man they are elevating to the chieftainship. From this time onward he becomes a king and a god."

Tribes developed checks and balances in the selection of rulers. Tangwa describes a particular strategy where the leader is chosen from a committee comprised of gender and class representatives. Tangwa (1998: 6) notes, "The King (Fon) of Nso', who by original consensus, was always selected by a committee headed by the leader of one of the strands comprising the Kingdom from among the male offspring of a female of another distinct strand (the *mmntar* or free commoner class) and a male of yet another strand (the acknowledged royal *wonto*' or princes class), had very extensive powers which were, however, considered as held in trust and subject to several putative controls."

There were also checks and balances among traditional administrators. While some top offices were lifetime appointments, other titles were graded whereby one could enter in one administrative capacity but might hope, with time and good assessments, to be promoted. Chieftaincies could be graded according to status and population size as first, second, and third class, for example. These grades were also politically important and depending on their level of rank and popularity, chiefs could have lesser or greater influence on community life and resources.

Noble status in pre-colonial African society thus often depended upon both the fact of birth and some form of community approval, both are necessary and neither is sufficient in isolation. Other ritual acts and elements, such as ceremonial objects with an established protocol for usage (for example, stools, palaces, caps, cups, etc.), could not be wielded at the King's whim. The ritual objects were psychologically invested with ancestral power thus inhibiting their abuse. Aletum notes again, "[I]f the transfer of power in the above societies

[did] not follow the customs and traditions dictated by the ancestors, the usurper after sitting on the ancestral stool suffer[ed] a serious mishap such as sterility, madness or even death. This also [was] true for a rightful chief going against the decision taken by the people while at the same time drinking from the ancestral cup to which he swore allegiance to the people," (Aletum, 2001: 206),

The reign of a particular king, however loved or despised, was never more significant than the maintenance of the existence of the kingdom itself. Tangwa (1998: 3) observes that when the ruler was perceived to be a political liability for the existence of the kingdom, "[i]n some traditional African Kingdoms the King/Queen could even be quietly executed or asked to voluntarily drink poison if his/her continued reign was considered dangerous for the survival and/or well-being of the Kingdom."

Auxiliary authorities, often of respected religious and/or elder status (for example, the Queen-Mother, traditional councils, healers, shamans and secret societies) bestowed and/or removed kingship and continually advised the King in roles that mediated the autocracy of the kingdom. For while the King or Queen generally appeared very powerful (especially from outside) and his/her word while ruler could frequently condemn anyone to death, the ruler was nevertheless subject to very strict control, not only by means of taboos but from institutions and personalities of very high moral authority and integrity whose main preoccupation was protection and safeguarding of the Kingdom as distinguished from the King, the interests of the ordinary person, the land, the ancestors and the unborn (Tangwa, 1998: 2).

The distinction between the role of kings and queens before, during and after colonialism is not straightforward. Appiah (1993) in a study of colonial Ghana contended that the subordination to colonial authority was not as extreme as other colonial histories might have suggested. African traditional authority persisted during and after colonialism. Appiah also contends that in some cases what might appear as the persistence of the King's authority despite colonialism might be a result of colonialism, such that colonialism tipped the scale of autocracy and democracy in favour of the King (Tangwa, 1998: 2).

The democratic aspects of traditional leadership were weakened by the colonial process, and kings and queens did not generally allow the lay citizen's interests to take priority in the national response to colonial invasion. Thus, if the King did not suffer much diminishment during colonialism (according to Appiah), a number of his subjects clearly did.

Tangwa argues that in contrast to the balance of authority and democracy exhibited in traditional African leadership, "[i]t is the various colonial administrations which introduced pure dictatorships, that is, dictatorships without any checks and balances, in Africa…." (Tangwa, 1998: 8).

As a case in point, Tangwa analyses the conditions that led to the surrender of the Nso' to German colonial occupation. In a story that seems relatively typical, an existing rivalry with the Bamum Kingdom (historically, "ancestral brothers of the Nso'") was intensified and exploited by the Germans to their advantage, such that Bamum allies participated in the German attack and won a victory over the Nso' that Germany's prior intimidation tactics alone had not produced. Captain Houptmann Glauning received notice of surrender from the Fon of Nso', Sëëm II, on June 6, 1906, marking the formal transition in the region from traditional to colonial rule, at which point many citizens of the Nso' state were conscripted for plantation work and ivory poaching. Sëëm II died not long after, but under his successors the Nso' kingdom continued to operate alongside German colonial authority. Mzeka's (1990) history of the Nso' kingdom notes that during this time, Nso' leadership took a notably different form. While exercising less control of the nation's resources, the Fon, paradoxically, ruled with more brutal intensity than before. "Pre-German survivors in Nso' insist that coercive use of authority in certain areas of Nso' culture was imitated from the German colonial administration, which used physical force as an instrument of administration."

Use of physical force as a means by which African leaders exerted their authority was apparently exceptional before colonialism. Potentially highly exploitative practices such as polygamy and taxation were possible because of citizen deference to kingly authority and via specific ceremonial procedures and limitations. Little coercion was needed in the average case. But new authoritarian demands, such as the widespread seizure and redistribution of land and forced manual labour with minimal compensation, were apparently different matters.

For example, over the course of Cameroon's colonial experience, German leaders gradually began influencing the tribal chains of command. Rudin (1938) reports that "by decree of 1913 no chief was to be removed from his post and no native was to be appointed chief except with the consent of the governor."

This policy suggests that traditional governance structures were co-opted, becoming influenced and sanctioned by and collaborating with colonial rulers in acquiring power and profits at the expense of an increasingly burdened and disenfranchised citizenry. Rudin (1938: 213-14, 327) notes that in a 1909 decree "Governor Satz instructed local officials to show proper respect for native chieftains and warned administrators against whipping chieftains or in other ways weakening their authority over tribesmen." In return for "proper respect," the chieftains maintained sufficient local authority to carry out "the responsibility of collecting taxes in the colony when taxation of natives was adopted as a regular policy, their compensation being 5 to 10 percent of the amounts collected." The taxation policy drove workers to plantations where work conditions yielded little money and an "appalling death rate."

Certainly at this point it becomes important to ask to what extent African leadership remained "traditional," as colonial forces seemed to determine leadership positions and domestic authority structures. It also appears that the presence of more vicious (and thus more pragmatically effective) colonial rulers led traditional leaders to emulate their ways and means.

Some actively adopted the religion and culture of their colonisers in order to assimilate and partake in the power to which they had been subjugated. One example from Geary (1983) regarding colonial religion comes from Sultan Njoya of Bamum, who changed his religion from traditional animism to Islam as a result of a nearby Fulani triumph, then to Christianity following the German invasion, then back to Islam after the Treaty of Versailles. He probably consistently followed the animist belief in gods of different names, powers and properties, by choosing the most powerful god of the day. In the end he declared allegiance to Islam, however, it is said that the Sultan resented giving up alcohol consumption as a Muslim and polygamy as a Christian, and thus synthesized elements of (or vacillated between) the two monotheistic religions

Williams (2003) points out that most of the contemporary notions of African royalty reference a conception of African antiquity rather than the actual state of affairs. At this point in time, the advantages (or prospects) of traditional governance on the continent are varied and dubious for nobles as well as their subjects. Further from Williams:

> "In contemporary Cameroon I have seen malnourished Bafut royals in rags, and Queens who perform traditional dances for tourists asking for a second round of tips (as the first round goes to the Fon). As to the visible economic disparity and depravation among the children, each of the Fon's wives is expected to be self-supporting. However, each receives a minimal stipend from the Fon on behalf of her children, but to which she apparently

contributes.

"In general, these days' advantages of any traditional role probably lie in relation or connection to the ruling party government. Reciprocally, some politicians contend that the chances of being chosen for traditional (royal) leadership might be improved if one has held ministerial or other government offices. I would also venture that in general, traditional leaders from areas that have resisted western capitalism, urbanization or territorial encroachment, do not speak colonial languages such as French or English, and/or do not participate in national elections (such as the Baka, the indigene and most economically oppressed group in Cameroon) are less likely to influence the government and their "subjects" may continue to face problems of poverty and neglect."

IMPLICATIONS

We see myriad ecologies within which leaders operate, and myriad sources of selection of leaders. Prehistoric and historic descriptions of leadership in Sub-Saharan Africa indicate a tradition of egalitarianism. This tends to indicate that hereditary leadership is a problematic model to utilize for the empowerment of Africans. If hereditary authority is socially constructed, then it is necessary to take into account the social processes that created and maintain these institutions. Further, if it is the case that traditional African leadership as such was never without control or accountability to the masses, and that colonialism introduced a dictatorial dimension that legitimised the exploitation of the relatively powerless, one might question the contemporary claims upon which royalty, rule and privileges are supported.

RECENT EMPIRICAL STUDIES OF AFRICAN CULTURE

Hofstede (2001: 369-370) and Noorderhaven and Tidjani (2001) report a Delph-technique/Factor Analysis project developing cultural dimensions for Sub-Saharan Africa survey. With quite small samples, two dimensions of culture receiving high scores in samples from Cameroon, Ghana, White South Africa, Senegal, Tanzania, and Zimbabwe were "Importance of Religion" and "Traditional Wisdom". "Importance of Religion" is self-defining, however the scale was structured as bi-polar with Importance of Religion" as one pole and "Hedonism" as the other; this could indicate an ethnocentric bias by the researchers. "Traditional Wisdom" consists of four items, two expressions of wisdom and two sources of wisdom:

1. It is important to show hospitality to strangers. (An arbitrary addition to the set.)
2. Wisdom is more important than knowledge.
3. Wisdom comes from experience and time, not from education.
4. It is better to discuss a decision than to impose a decision, even if it is a majority decision.

The high scores on these two factors by the SSA samples could indicate a strong inclination to adhere to tradition in many aspects of life.

The Globe Study Sub-Saharan African "Cluster"

In the Global Leadership and Organisational Behaviour Effectiveness (GLOBE) study House et al. (2004: 187) noted that the Sub-Saharan African countries in the sample were the most diverse of any geographic region for which they proposed "clusters". This area has a vast diversity of ethnicity, religion, language, and customs. There is limited interethnic marriage and interaction. Colonial influences tended to be "divide and rule" where colonial governments empowered and coerced local tribal chiefs to regulate local affairs, maintaining ethnic separation.

In South Africa, where there is significant racial diversity with Blacks, Whites, Indian, Chinese, and "Colored" (historically a racial mixture of imported Malay slaves and other races, but later broadened to any mixed race), in addition to the tribal ethnic diversity, racial separation was politically exacerbated for an extended period (Littrell and Nkomo, 2005).

The GLOBE leadership dimensions are defined as follows (House et al., 2004: 675):

Charismatic/Value-Based: The ability to inspire, to motivate, and to expect high performance outcomes from others on the basis of firmly held core values. This dimension includes six primary leadership subscales: visionary, inspirational, self-sacrifice, integrity, decisive, and performance oriented.

Team Oriented: Emphasises effective team building and implementation of a common purpose or goal among team members; includes five primary leadership subscales: collaborative team orientation, team integrator; diplomatic; malevolent (reverse scored); and administratively competent.

Participative: Reflects the degree to which managers involve others in making and implementing decisions; includes two primary leadership subscales: autocratic (reverse scored), and non-participative (reverse scored).

Humane Oriented: Reflects supportive and considerate leadership, but also includes compassion and generosity; includes two primary leadership subscales: modesty and humane orientated.

Autonomous: Refers to independent and individualistic leadership; includes the autonomous subscale.

Self-Protective: Focuses on ensuring the safety and security of the individual or group member; includes five primary leadership subscales: self-centered; status conscious; conflict inducer; face saver; and procedural.

In Table 2 (from House et al., 2004: 713-714) we see a summary of the GLOBE means for leadership dimensions for the Sub-Saharan African nations studied. The GLOBE project places South African Whites in the Anglo cluster, however in Table G the means for the Whites compare more closely with the other scores than do the South African Blacks.

One GLOBE researcher, Booysen (1999, 2000 and 2001) reported results that indicated differences between blacks and whites for both males and females. However, Littrell and Nkomo (2005), comparing leader behaviour preferences among Black, White, Asian, and a small sample of Coloureds found that black and white males and females were more similar to one another than to Asians and coloureds. In general, Booysen's (2001) conclusions that black women emphasized collective mutual support and interdependence, concern for employees, compared to White women's emphasis on independence and individual freedom, employees as workers and planning and future action, were not supported in the Littrell and Nkomo study, where Black and white females opinions, attitudes, and beliefs were similar. Booysen also found the culture of South African male and female, black and white managers to focus on different values. However, the analysis in Littrell and Nkomo indicates that the leader behaviour preferences of the South African blacks and whites of both genders to be quite similar.

The country means for the Sub-Saharan African samples in the House et al. report fall in the moderate range compared to the extreme high and low national means. Further review and analysis of the large volume of data in the GLOBE book is planned.

TABLE 2
GLOBE Dimensions as Leadership Characteristics

	Charismatic / Value Based	Team Oriented	Participative	Humane Oriented	Autonomous	Self Protective
GLOBE high	*6.33*	*6.21*	*6.09*	*5.75*	*4.63*	*4.62*
GLOBE low	*4.81*	*4.74*	*4.5*	*3.82*	*2.27*	*2.55*
Namibia	**5.99**	**5.81**	**5.48**	**5.10**	**3.77**	**3.36**
Nigeria	**5.76**	**5.65**	**5.18**	**5.49**	**3.62**	**3.89**
South African Black	**5.16**	**5.23**	**5.04**	**4.79**	**3.94**	**3.62**
South African White	**5.99**	**5.80**	**5.62**	**5.33**	**3.74**	**3.19**
Zambia	**5.92**	**5.86**	**5.29**	**5.27**	**3.43**	**3.66**
Zimbabwe	**6.11**	**5.97**	**5.57**	**5.18**	**3.37**	**3.20**

EMPIRICAL SUPPORT FOR SOME IDEAS OF SUB-SAHARAN CONCEPTS OF LEADERSHIP

From 2003 through 2005 data were collected in South Africa and Uganda employing the Leader Behaviour Description Questionnaire XII. Concerning the developm*ent of this instrument*, Stogdill (1959, 1963, 1974 pp. 142-155) noted that it was not reasonable to believe that the original two factors of Initiating Structure and Consideration derived for the Leader Behaviour Description Questionnaire were sufficient to account for all the observable variance in leader behaviour relating to group achievement and the variety of social roles. Stodgill's theory suggested that the following patterns of behaviour are involved in leadership, though they are not equally important in all situations.

1. *Representation* measures to what degree the leader speaks as the representative of the group.
2. *Demand Reconciliation* reflects how well the leader reconciles conflicting demands and reduces disorder to system.
3. *Tolerance of Uncertainty* depicts to what extent the leader is able to tolerate uncertainty and postponement without anxiety or getting upset.
4. *Persuasiveness* measures to what extent the leader uses persuasion and argument effectively; exhibits strong convictions.
5. *Initiation of Structure* measures to what degree the leader clearly defines own role, and lets followers know what is expected.
6. *Tolerance of Freedom* reflects to what extent the leader allows followers scope for initiative, decision and action.
7. *Role Assumption* measures to what degree the leader exercises actively the leadership role rather than surrendering leadership to others.
8. *Consideration* depicts to what extent the leader regards the comfort, well being, status and contributions of followers.
9. *Production Emphasis* measures to what degree the leader applies pressure for productive output.
10. *Predictive Accuracy* measures to what extent the leader exhibits foresight and ability to predict outcomes accurately.
11. *Integration* reflects to what degree the leader maintains a closely-knit organization; resolves inter-member conflicts.
12. *Superior Orientation* measures to what extent the leader maintains cordial relations with superiors; has influence with them; is striving for higher status.

These twelve behavioural patterns are measured by the Leadership Behaviour Description Questionnaire (LBDQ) XII. Judge, Piccolo, and Ilies (2004) attempted to identify all possible studies of the relationships between Consideration, Initiating Structure, and relevant organizational criteria. The results of this analysis indicated higher LBDQ scores to be positively associated with greater leader effectiveness ratings.

The LBDQ XII has been used in several countries to study leadership behaviour, Littrell (2002a, 2002b, 2004a and 2004b); Littrell and Valentin (2005); Lucas, Mesner, Ryan and Sturm, (1992); Schneider and Littrell (2003), Selmer (1997), Black and Porter (1991), and Stogdill (1963), with the general finding that patterns of preferred leader behaviours vary significantly and considerably across national cultures.

RESEARCH QUESTIONS

From the literature review we can derive four possible expectations for the behaviour of contemporary leaders in Sub-Saharan African organisations:

1. Tradition 1: Egalitarianism

2. Tradition 2: Paternalism
3. Tradition 3: Authoritarian/Autocratic Colonial Heritage
4. Tradition 4: Post-Colonialism Western Influence

The literature review also leads us to the expectation that the ecology of leadership will be more influential than any overarching tradition. Hence, our expectation is that the null hypothesis that there is no consistent set of preferred leader behaviours will be demonstrated in analysis of the samples for which we have data.

METHODOLOGY

Data were collected from 2003 – 2005 in South Africa and Uganda, employing the LBDQXII. For further discussion see Littrell and Baguma (2005) and Littrell and Nkomo (2005).

Sample in Uganda

LBDQ XII surveys were administered to 307 secondary level teachers in 179 Ugandan public and private schools who voluntarily completed the surveys. The survey was administered in English, with 89.5% of the subjects indicating English as a second language. Details of the sample are discussed in reference to the tables below.

Sample in South Africa

Surveys for the South African sample were distributed to part-time, working MBA students in Pretoria, with 414 surveys providing sufficient demographic information to select subjects. The sample was of varied age (23 - 52 years) and from varied industry sectors. The education level of the sample was high, with 76% having a bachelor's degree or higher, and the rest having formal education at least at the associate or professional qualification level. The breakdown by race and gender appears in Table 3.

ANALYSES

Analysis of variance among nationality, race, and gender across samples from South Africa and Uganda yielded no consistent similarities. Males and females from Uganda (all were Black), tended to cluster together most frequently from Tukey's HSD post-hoc analysis, but consistency was minimal, as these two groups often clustered with other sub-groups.

Mean factor scores for the LBDQXII dimensions were calculated from all available studies employing subjects from the USA and the UK (see Littrell and Baguma, 2005, for sources). To define the "Western" means in Table 4 z-scores were calculated for the mean factor scores for the three groups and compared rationally, as raw data was not available for all the USA samples. These results are depicted in Tables 4 and 5. The common high-mean factors in Table 4 indicate preference for a group-cohesiveness orientation on the part of managerial leaders.

TABLE 3
Demographics for the Samples

Sample x Race x Sex Cross-tabulation

Sample	Black Males	Black Females	White Males	White Females	
South Africa	94	50	109	37	369
Uganda	192	111	0	0	303
Total	286	161	109	37	672

Age Statistics for Samples

	N	Mean	Std. Deviation	Range
Black Males	277	33.9	6.3	23 – 58
Black Females	154	31.7	5.8	23 – 50
White Males	109	33.9	6.5	24 – 52
White Females	35	36.4	8.0	24 – 51
Total	653	33.5	6.5	

Results within Uganda

Due to decisions by collaborators, a richer set of demographic data is available from Uganda than South Africa. Attention is directed to Table 6. Uganda data indicated the smallest differences between males and females, differing marginally but not significantly at $p<0.10$ on Factors 9 and 10.

Differences were observed for 5 factors between speakers of Bantoid languages and English as first languages. However, this observation is further complicated by the fact that the response set for the Bantoid-as-first-language sample had universally lower means and universally higher standard deviations across sub-samples. This indicates that there is a source of diversity that may be related to specific first language and specific tribal ethnicity.

Significant differences were observed for 5 factors comparing Catholics and Protestants, 3 factors between Catholics and Muslims, and only 1 factor for Protestants and Muslims.

These findings indicate that "nationality" in Uganda is not a strong predictor of preferences for managerial leader behaviour.

DISCUSSION AND CONCLUSIONS

Past research employing the LBDQXII (Black and Porter, 1991; Littrell, 2002, Littrell and Baguma, 2005; Littrell and Nkomo, 2005; Littrell and Valentin, 2006; Schneider and Littrell, 2003; and Selmer, 1997) have indicated that the combinations of the twelve factors indicating more and less desirable leader behaviours have varied across cultures. Factor 1:

Representation and Factor 11: Integration are universally highly preferred across all national samples, and Factor 3: Tolerance of Uncertainty the least preferred. However, the majority of the managerial leader behaviour sets defined by the LBDQXII appear to be significantly affected by cultural contingencies.

We find Sub-Saharan African countries to be significantly multicultural and multi-lingual, with frequently small, highly homogeneous and ethnocentric ethnic groups; in this environment, appropriate and effective management, leadership, and governance system(s) remain to be defined.

TABLE 4
Ordering of Mean Factor Scores for Three Cultural Groups

Western			South African			Ugandan		
Factor	Sample Mean	z-score	Factor	Sample Mean	z-score	Factor	Sample Mean	z-score
1. Integration L11	*4.33*	*2.96*	**1. L11**	**4.41**	**1.55**	*1. L1*	*3.95*	*1.38*
2. Role Assumption L7	*4.15*	*1.63*	**2. L6**	**4.31**	**1.19**	*2. L5*	*3.86*	*1.10*
3. Demand Reconciliation L2	*4.08*	*1.06*	**3. L2**	**4.20**	**0.79**	*3. L11*	*3.81*	*0.94*
4. RepresentationL1	*4.05*	*0.87*	**4. L5**	**4.16**	**0.65**	*4. L9*	*3.74*	*0.72*
5. Consideration L8	*3.95*	*0.11*	**5. L4**	**4.04**	**0.22**	*5. L12*	*3.73*	*0.69*
6. Superior Orientation L12	*3.95*	*0.11*	**6. L1**	**4.02**	**0.14**	*6. L4*	*3.63*	*0.38*
7. Initiation of Structure L5	*3.93*	*-0.08*	**7. L12**	**3.98**	**0.00**	*7. L7*	*3.57*	*0.19*
8. Persuasiveness L4	*3.93*	*-0.08*	8. L10	3.96	-0.07	*8. L2*	*3.32*	*-0.60*
9. Predictive Accuracy L10	*3.90*	*-0.27*	9. L7	3.86	-0.43	*9. L10*	*3.31*	*-0.63*
10. Tolerance of Freedom L6	*3.88*	*-0.46*	10. L9	3.82	-0.58	*10. L8*	*3.24*	*-0.85*
11. Tolerance of Uncertainty L3	*3.65*	*-2.17*	11. L8	3.49	-1.77	*11. L6*	*3.00*	*-1.60*
12. Production Emphasis L9	*3.45*	*-3.69*	**12. L3**	3.47	-1.84	*12. L3*	*2.98*	*-1.67*
Mean	**3.94**		**Mean**	**3.98**		**Mean**	**3.51**	
STD	0.13			0.28			0.32	

TABLE 5
Common Factors with Above Average Means – South Africa and Uganda

- **L1** — *Representation* measures to what degree the leader speaks as the representative of the group.
- **L4** — *Persuasiveness* measures to what extent the leader uses persuasion and argument effectively; exhibits strong convictions.
- **L5** — *Initiation of Structure* measures to what degree the leader clearly defines own role, and lets followers know what is expected.
- **L11** — *Integration* reflects to what degree the leader maintains a closely-knit organization; resolves inter-member conflicts.

TABLE 6
Average Scores Related to Demographic Variables for the Uganda Sample (*ANOVA p [0.05)

Avg	N	1	2	3	4	5	6	7	8	9	10	11	12
Gender													
Male	191	3.94	3.04	3.19	3.58	3.84	2.96	2.97	3.21	3.71	3.38	3.81	3.76
Female	111	3.96	2.96	3.13	3.49	3.89	2.96	2.93	3.13	3.79	3.20	3.80	3.67
Sig										**p=0.056**	**p=0.080**		

Language	N=152	1	2	3	4	5	6	7	8	9	10	11	12
English vs Bantoid		0.150	**0.001***	**0.001***	0.257	**0.029***	0.098	0.110	**0.015***	0.103	0.070	**0.009***	0.253
English	Avg	4.07	3.60	3.17	3.65	4.04	3.15	3.68	3.37	3.88	3.52	4.07	3.81
	Std D	0.65	0.58	0.45	0.54	0.51	0.66	0.57	0.53	0.57	0.63	0.65	0.54
Bantoid	Avg	3.90	3.21	2.93	3.54	3.80	2.96	3.54	3.13	3.71	3.29	3.72	3.70
	Std D	0.80	0.84	0.49	0.66	0.77	0.74	0.57	0.68	0.71	0.91	0.94	0.67

Religion	N		**1**	**2**	**3**	**4**	**5**	**6**	**7**	**8**	**9**	**10**	**11**	**12**
Catholic-Protestant		*p*	0.14	**0.00***	0.24	0.07	0.20	0.08	0.10	**0.04***	0.31	**0.02***	**0.02***	**0.04***
Catholic-Muslim		*p*	0.27	**0.03***	0.51	0.56	0.22	0.56	**0.04***	0.19	0.70	0.07	0.14	**0.05***
Protestant-Muslim		*p*	**0.05***	0.91	0.89	0.52	0.83	0.53	0.42	0.89	0.75	0.90	0.83	0.72
Catholic	155	Avg	**3.99**	**3.47**	**3.02**	**3.61**	**3.92**	**3.07**	**3.64**	**3.26**	**3.78**	**3.44**	**3.93**	**3.82**
	Std Dev		0.77	0.80	0.51	0.63	0.69	0.69	0.54	0.64	0.65	0.81	0.85	0.61
Protestant	111	Avg	**3.84**	**3.17**	**2.94**	**3.47**	**3.80**	**2.91**	**3.52**	**3.09**	**3.69**	**3.19**	**3.67**	**3.65**
	Std Dev		1.04	0.97	0.47	0.74	1.04	0.90	0.67	0.72	0.89	1.10	1.18	0.55
Muslim	37	Avg	**4.14**	**3.15**	**2.96**	**3.55**	**3.77**	**3.00**	**3.43**	**3.11**	**3.74**	**3.17**	**3.71**	**3.60**
	Std Dev		0.53	0.61	0.45	0.55	0.54	0.59	0.56	0.62	0.55	0.72	0.78	0.56

Concerning accommodation of religio-ethno-linguistic diversity, Beber (2004) relates an incident in the USA where a delegation of the Indonesian government shared its assessment of current politics in the archipelago at a seminar at Columbia University.

> "One of the speakers was Fu'ad Jabali, a university professor from Jakarta. He introduced himself by noting that when he was working on his doctorate in Canada, he was taken aback by the fact that his university did not consider Bahasa Indonesian to be an Islamic language, unlike Turkish and Urdu. Drawing nods from the other members of the panel, Jabali explained that he submitted a complaint, and the university corrected their 'mistake.'"

While "Muslim language" is a rather religiously ethnocentric lable for a national language, religion, language, and ethnicity are profound issues for socio-linguist fractionalised nations such as Indonesia. How should governments treat diverse languages and cultures when trying to consolidate a state's functional coherence, while protecting the rights of its citizens? What choices should a government make in accommodating or breaking down cultural boundaries? Beber discusses two collections of essays concerning governmental responses to socio-linguistic fractionalisation, Brown and Ganguly (2003) and Duncan (2004). He criticises the paternalistic and politically correct approaches of both publications in seeking solutions primarily in multi-cultural accommodation and autonomy arrangements. Beber notes that the collections fail to provide an adequate defence of why such accommodation should be given priority over the promotion by governments of allegiances beneficial across all socio-ethnic groups in a state, suggesting, for example, providing incentives for acquiring a common language. Beneficial policies crosscutting socio-ethnic cleavages might fundamentally transform social and political identities, effectively eliminating interethnic violence from the set of choices that people would even consider.

Beber (2004) comments on individual freedom in language choice, pointing out that authors in the two works use commentary such as in Thailand, more efforts should be made to "preserve" local languages, and in Vietnam, languages are "dying," some are "lost," others are "endangered". "…it is as if these languages have become more authentic than the people speaking it." Where the struggle is survival and health, "should we be so preoccupied with keeping languages alive? If individuals freely choose to abandon their native language on the basis of expected economic returns, for instance, should we disparage that choice?"

APPENDIX A

Information from the New York Times, May 11, 2006, the original article Copyright 2006 The New York Times Company
http://www.nytimes.com/2006/05/11/world/americas/11colombia.html?_r=1&th=&oref=slogin&emc=th&pagewanted=print

Information from: "Leaving the Wild, and Rather Liking the Change"

By Juan Forero

SAN JOSÉ DEL GUAVIARE, Columbia — The Nukak-Makú tribe have lived a Stone Age life, roaming across hundreds of miles of isolated Amazon jungle, killing monkeys with blowguns and scouring the forest floor for berries for centuries.

However, recently a band of nearly 80 wandered out of the Amazon wilderness, and declared themselves ready to join the modern world. "When I've had some time to talk to them and asked where they came from, they just say 'the bush,' " said Xismena Martínez, who oversees aid to the Nukak for San José. "But that could mean anywhere."

The newly arrived Nukak do not provide much detail about why they left. They just say that "the Green Nukak," a possible reference to Marxist guerrillas, who wear camouflage, told them to leave. "The Green Nukak said we could not keep walking in the jungle, or else there would be problems," explained Va-di, another Nukak man, whose words were translated from Nukak by Belisario. "The Green Nukak told us to go where it is safe."

The Nukak have no concept of money, of property, of the role of government, or even of the existence of a country called Colombia. They ask whether the planes that fly overhead are moving on some sort of invisible road. They have no government identification cards, making them nonentities to Colombia's bureaucracy.

When asked if the Nukak were concerned about the future, Belisario, the only one in the group who had been to the outside world before and spoke Spanish, seemed perplexed, less by the word than by the concept. "The future," he said, "what's that?" He serves as a interpreter for the others. The Nikak are one of a few dozen indigenous communities living in relative seclusion in the Amazon basin. Small groups of Nukak have ventured beyond the borders of the jungle since 1988, and exporers have intermittently found them.

In 2003 dozens of Nukak left the wilderness and arrived at San José del Guaviare, saying Colombia's seemingly perpetual civil war had encroached on their reserve and forced them to seek safety. Some 250 now live in settlements around the town; anthropologists estimate about the same number are still alive in the wilderness. Anthropologists also believe that what little contact the Nukak have had with outsiders has most likely left them reduced by Western diseases such as influenza and the common cold, to which they have no natural resistance. Janet Chernela, an anthropologist who has worked with the Nukak, said a study she had conducted showed that Nukak who abandon their nomadic lives and settle down, even temporarily, become susceptible to illnesses, including soil-transmitted diseases.

What little is known about this latest group is that it abandoned the Nukak National Park, which is nearly half the size of New Jersey, in the state of Guaviare. Belisario — who knows several of the towns outside the reserve, having been reared for part of his childhood by settlers who encroached on the jungle — led the way.

Colombian officials wonder if farmers growing coca, the crop used to make cocaine, may also have displaced the Nukak, who are peaceloving and unlikely to fight. Another theory is that another Nukak clan pushed this one out.

But because it is assumed that they fled the civil war, the Nukak are classified as displaced people, requiring the state to provide aid and help them return home, as long as it is safe. The government, though, cannot guarantee their safety.

But even as the aid arrives, the donors are well aware that the largess could well doom the Nukak to a life of dependency, ensuring not only that they never return home but also that they never learn how to live in their new world. "People want to protect them," Ms. Martínez said. "To help them, we give them food and clothes. That doesn't help them at all in the long term."

What everyone agrees on is that these Nukak must avoid the fate of the Nukak who came here in 2003 and now live in aanother clearing near the same town. Now in their fourth year in the area, the initial Nukak group lead listless lives, lolling in their hammocks awaiting food from the state. They do not work, nor have they learned Spanish. They also have no plans to return to the forest. "I think we will be here always," said Martín, a young man who is considered a leader.

Are they sad? "No!" cried a Nukak named Pia-pe, to howls of laughter. In fact, the Nukak said they could not be happier. Used to long marches in search of food, they are amazed that strangers would bring them sustenance for free.

One young Nukak mother, Bachanede, breast-feeding her infant as she talked, said she was happy just to stay still. "When you walk in the jungle," she said, "your feet hurt a lot."

The Nukak have plans. Ma-be explained that the idea is to grow plantains and yucca and take the crops to town. "We can exchange it for money," he said, "and exchange the money for other things."

But first they need to learn how to cultivate crops. The Nukak say they would like their children to go to school. They also say they do not want to lose traditions, like hunting or speaking their language. "We do want to join the white family," Pia-pe said, speaking of Colombian society, "but we do not want to forget words of the Nukak."

REFERENCES

Alesina, A., Devleeschauwer, A., Easterly, W., Kurlat, S., & Wacziarg, R.. 2003. Fractionalization. *Journal of Economic Growth,* (8)2: 155–194.

Aletum, T. M. (or M.T.?) 2001. *Political sociology.* Yaounde, Cameroon: Patoh Publishers.

Anderson, B. 1991. *Imagined communities: Reflections on the origin and spread of nationalism.* London: Verso Books.

Appiah, A. K.. 1993. *In my father's house: Africa in the philosophy of culture.* London: Oxford University Press.

Bales, R.F. 1951. *Interaction process analysis: A method for the study of small groups*. New York: Addison-Wesley.

Beber, B. 2004. Marginalizing multiculturalism. *Journal of International Affairs*, 58(1): 266–271.

Bierschenk, T. (Ed.). 2003. Administration Etatique Et Societe Locale A Tanguieta (Nord Du Benin). Une Analyse Politique Suite À Des Interprétations Des Événements De Février 1996 À Tanguiéta. Arbeitspapiere (Working Papers). Nr. 20, Tilo Grätz, Institut Für Ethnologie Und Afrikastudien, Department of Anthropology and African Studies. Johannes Gutenberg-Universität. http://www.unimainz.de/~ifeas/workingpapers/graetz2.pdf., accessed 1 November 2003.

Black, S.J.,& Porter, L. W. 1991. Managerial behaviors and job performance: A successful manager in Los Angeles may not succeed in Hong Kong. *Journal of International Business Studies*, 22(1): 99–114.

Blunt, P. & Jones, M.L. 1997. Exploring the limits of Western leadership theory in East Asia and Africa. *Personnel Review*, 26(1): 6–23.

Blunt, P. 1978. Social and organizational structures in East Africa: A case for participation. *Journal of Modern African Studies*, 16(3): 433–449.

Blunt, P. 1983. *Organizational theory and behaviour: An African perspective*. London: Longman.

Boehm, C. 1999. *Hierarchy in the forest: The evolution of egalitarian behaviour.* Cambridge, MA: Harvard University Press.

Booysen, L. 1999. Male And female managers: Gender influences on South African managers in retail banking. *South African Journal of Labour Relations*, 23 (2): 25–49.

Booysen, L. 2000. *Cultural differences between African black and white managers in South Africa*. Paper presented at Southern Africa Institute for Management Scientists 12th Annual Conference, *Africa's Century: Challenges for Management and Leadership*, South Africa, 31 October-2 November 2000.

Booysen, L. 2001. The duality of South African leadership: Afrocentric or Eurocentric. *South African Journal of Labour Relations*, Spring/Summer: 36–63.

Brown, M. E. & Ganguly, S., (Eds.). 2003. *Fighting words: Language policy and ethnic relations in Asia*. Cambridge, MA: MIT Press.

Brownlie, Ian, (Ed.). 1979. *African boundaries: A legal and diplomatic encyclopaedia*. Oxford, UK: C. Hurst & Co. Publishers.

Caldwell, J.C., & Caldwell, P. 1977. The economic rationale of high fertility: An investigation illustrated with Nigerian survey data. *Population Study*, 31: 5–27.

Chisholm, L. 2001. Gender and leadership in South African educational administration. *Gender & Education*, 13(4): 387–399.

CIA. 2005. *CIA World Factbook*. http://www.cia.gov/cia/publications/factbook/. [accessed 11 November 2005]

Cosway, N. & Anankum, S.A. 1996. Traditional leadership and community management in Northern Ghana. In P. Blunt & D.M. Warren (Eds.), *Indigenous Organisations and Development*: 88–96. London: Intermediate Technology Publications.

Davidson, B. 1992. *The black man's burden: Africa and the curse of the nation-state.* London: James Currey.

De Waal, F. 1996. *Good natured: The origins of right and wrong in humans and other animals.* Cambridge, MA: Harvard University Press.

Deng, F. M. 1972. *The Dinka of the Sudan*. Prospect Heights, NY: Waveland Press, Inc.

Department of Geodesy and Cartography. 1964. *Atlas Narodov Mira*. Moscow: State Geological Committee of the USSR.

Dia, M. 1994. Indigenous management practices: Lessons for Africa's management in the `90s. In Serageldin, I. & Taboroff, J. (Eds.). *Culture and Development in Africa*: 165–191, World Bank, Washington, DC.

Doherty, W.J. 1992. *Private lives, public values. Psychology Today, May/June: 32–37.*

Duncan, C. R. (Ed.). 2004. *Civilizing the margins: Southeast Asian government policies for the development of minorities*. Ithaca, NY: Cornell University Press.

Easterly, W., & Levine, R. 1997. Africa's growth tragedy: Policies and ethnic divisions. *Quarterly Journal of Economics,* 112(Nov.):1203–50.

Ekeh, P. 1974. *Social exchange theory*. Cambridge: Harvard University Press.

Firth, R. 1927. The study of primitive economics. *Economica*, 21(Dec.): 312–335.

Geary, C. M. 1983. *Things of the Palace: A catalogue of the Bamum Palace in Foumban.* (Cameroon) Weisbaden: F. Steiner Verlag.

George, D. and Mallery, P. 2003. *SPSS for windows step by step: A simple guide andreference. 11.0 update* (4th ed.). Boston: Allyn & Bacon.

Geschiere, P. 1993. Chiefs in colonial Cameroon: Inventing chieftancy French and British style. *Africa* 63(2): 151–175.

Ghosh, S. 2001. Ethnic diversity and managerial effectiveness in South Africa. *The Academy of Management Executive*, 2(1/2), 136-137.

Goldin, I. 1987. *Making race: The politics and economics of Coloured identity in South Africa.* London: Longman.

Graen, G. & Hui, C. 1996. Managing changes in globalizing business: How to manage cross-cultural business partners. *Journal of Organizational Change Management*, 9(2): 62–72.

Hart K. & Padayachee, V. 2000. Indian business in South Africa after apartheid: Old and new trajectories. *Comparative Studies in Society and History*, 42(4): 683–712.

Heimer, C. & Vince, R. 1998. Sustainable learning and change in international teams: From imperceptible behaviour to rigorous practice. *Leadership and Organizational Development Journal,* 19(2): 83–88.

Hitchcock, R. K. 2001. African hunter-gatherers: Survival, history, and the politics of identity. *African Study Monographs*, Suppl. 26: 257–280.

Hochshild, A. 1998. *King Leopold's ghost: A story of greed, terror, and heroism in colonial Africa*. New York: Houghton Mifflin.

Hofstede, G. 2001. *Cultures' consequences* (2nd ed.). Thousand Oaks, CA: Sage.

House, R.J., Wright, N., & Aditya, R.N. 1997. Cross cultural research on organizational leadership: A critical analysis and a proposed theory. In P.C. Earley & M. Erez (Eds.), *New perspectives on international industrial and organizational* psychology:. San Francisco, CA: Jossey-Bass. (Available at http://jonescenter.wharton.upenn.edu/papers/1999/wp99-03.pdf)

House, R.M., Hanges, P.J., Javidan, M., Dorfman, P., Gupta, V., & GLOBE Associates. 2004. *Culture, leadership, and organizations: The GLOBE study of 62 societies*. Thousand Oaks, CA: Sage.

Hussain R., & Bittles A.H. 1998. The prevalence and demographic characteristics of consanguineous marriages in Pakistan. *Journal of Biosocial Science,* 30: 261–75.

Jacobson, D. 1999. Women still on the road to nowhere. *Sunday Business Times*, 16 May. Johannesburg: Johnnic Publishing.

Jacobson, P. E. 1997. Free families to statist societies and back again. *Formulations,* Libertarian Nation Foundation. Retrieved from http://libertariannation.org/a/f43j1.html, 9 May 2006.

Janine Aron, Janine. 2000. Growth and institutions: A review of the evidence.*The World Bank Research Observer,* 15(1): 99–135.

Johnson, P.L. 2003. *Leaders on leadership: Perpetuating the "glass ceiling".* Digital Dissertations. Ann Arbor, MI, USA: ProQuest Information and Learning. [Accessed 3 December 2004]

Jones, M.L., Blunt, P., & Sharma, K. 1995. *Managerial behaviour, organizational functioning and performance in an African public service organization.* Stockholm: Sida.

Judge, T.A., Piccolo, R.F., & Ilies, R. 2004. The forgotten ones? The validity of consideration and initiating structure in leadership research. *Journal of Applied Psychology*, 89(1): 36–51.

Kelley, L. 1996. *War before civilization.* Oxford: Oxford University Press.

Kilianski, S.E. 2002. Implicit and explicit attitudes toward female authority. *Personality and Social Psychology Bulletin*, 26(11): 1315–1328.

Kimball, M. J. 1998. Global change from local decisions: An archaeologist's perspective. *Human Ecology Review,* 5(2): 19–24.

Landrine, H. 1985. Race x class stereotypes of women. *Sex Roles*, 13: 65–75.

Leonard, D.K. 1987. The political realities of African management. *World Development*, 15: 899–910.

Leung, C., & Moore, S. 2003. Individual and cultural gender roles: A comparison of Anglo-Australians and Chinese in Australia. *Current Research In Social Psychology*, 8(210): 302–316.

Lewis, H. 1974. *Leaders and followers: Some anthropological perspectives.*Reading, MA: Addison-Wesley.

Littrell, R.F. 2002a. Desirable leadership behaviours of multi-cultural managers in China. *The Journal of Management Development.* 21(1): 5–74.

Littrell, R.F. 2002b. *Comparative analysis of management styles: Desirable leader traits across cultures*, Proceedings Academy of International Business Southeast Asia and Australia Regional Conference CD, ISBN 962-8134-05-1. July 18 – 20, 2002, Shanghai, China, Hong Kong Institute of Business Studies, Lingnan University, Tuen Mun, Hong Kong, http://www.ln.edu.hk/hkibs/. (Copy available at: www.romielittrellpubs.homestead.com)

Littrell, R.F., & Baguma, P. 2004. *Leader behaviour preferences of educators in Uganda.* Proceedings First Conference on Cross Cultural Leadership and Management Studies, Seoul, Korea, 10-12 June. (Copy available at: www.romielittrellpubs.homestead.com)

Littrell, R.F. & Baguma, P. 2005. Education, management, and the world's work: Leadership traits of educators in undeveloped and developing countries focusing on Uganda in Sub-Saharan Africa. In I. Alon & J. R. McIntyre (Eds.), *Business and management education in transitioning and developing countries: A handbook*, Chapter 20, Armonk, NY: ME Sharpe.

Littrell, R.F., & Nkomo, S. 2005. Gender and race differences in leader behaviour preferences in South Africa. *Women in Management Review*, 20(8): 562–580.

Littrell, R. F. 2003. *Corporate and national cultures: Influence of the cross-cultural composition of the management team on leadership preferences in a Chinese organisation, a longitudinal study*. Proceedings of the 2003 International Human Resources Management Conference, University of Limerick, Limerick, Ireland, (available at http://www.romielittrellpubs.homestead.com)

Littrell, R. F. & Valentin, L. N. 2005. Preferred leadership behaviours: Exploratory results from Romania, Germany, and the UK, 2005, *The Journal of Management Development*, 24(5): 421–442.

Lucas, P. R., Messner, P. E., Ryan, C. W. & Sturm, G. P. 1992. Preferred leadership style differences: Perceptions of defence industry labour and management. *Leadership & Organization Development Journal*, 13(7): 19–23.

Mangaliso, M. 2001. Building competitive advantage from Ubuntu: Management lessons from South Africa. *Academy of Management Executive* 15(3): 23–35.

Mauro, P. 1995. Corruption and growth. *Quarterly Journal of Economics*, 110(3): 681– 713.

Maznah, I., & Choo, P. F. 1986. The factor structure of the Bem Sex Role Inventory (BSRI). *International Journal of Psychology*, 21: 31–41.

Mazrui, A.A. 1994. Development in a multi-cultural context: trends and tensions. In I. Serageldin & Taboroff, J. (Eds.), *Culture and Development in Africa*: 127–136, Washington, DC: World Bank.

Mbigi, L. 1997. *Ubuntu: The African dream in management*. Johannesburg: Knowledge Resources.

Meggitt, M. 1977. *Blood is their Argument*. Palo Alto: Mayfield.

Montgomery, J.D. 1987. Probing managerial behaviour: image and reality in Southern Africa. *World Development*, 15(7): 911–929.

Moore, S. F. 1972. Legal liability and evolutionary interpretation: Some aspects of strict liability, self-help, and collective responsibility. In M. Gluckman (Ed.), *The Allocation of Responsibility*: 51–107. Manchester: Manchester University Press.

Mosko, M. 1995. Rethinking Trobriand Chieftainship. *The Journal of the Royal Anthropological Institute*, 1(4): 763–785.

Mzeka, P. N., 1990. *Four Fons Nso': Nineteenth and early twentieth century kingship in the Western Grassfields.* Bamenda, Cameroon: The Spider Publishing.

Nicholson, N. 2005. Meeting the Maasai: Messages for management. *Journal of Management Inquiry*, 14(3): 255–267.

Noorderhaven, N.G., & B. Tidjani, B. 2001. Culture, governance, and economic performance: An explorative study with a special focus on Africa. *International Journal of Cross Cultural Management,* 1(1): 31-52.

Norris, P. & Inglehart, R. 2000. *Cultural barriers to women's leadership: A worldwide comparison*. Paper for Special Session 16 'Social Cleavages and Elections' Thursday 3rd August 2000 at the International Political Science Association World Congress, Quebec City, Canada. [http://ksghome.harvard.edu/~.pnorris.shorenstein.ksg/acrobat/IPSA20~1.PDF. [Accessed 6 December 2004]

Nzelibe, C.O. 1986. The evolution of African management thought. *International Studies of Management and Organization*, 16(2): 6–16.

Popper, K.R. 1959. *The Logic of Scientific Discovery.* London: Hutchinson.

Posner, Daniel N. 2004. Measuring ethnic fractionalization in Africa. *American Journal of Political Science*, 48(4): 849–863.

Pratto, F. & Espinoza P. 2001. Gender, ethnicity, and power. *Journal of Social Issues*, 57,(4): 629–849.

Price, T.D., & Feinman, G. M. 1993. *Images of the past*. Mountain View, CA: Mayfield.

Quale, G.R. 1988. A history of marriage systems. *Contributions in Family Studies, Number 13.* New York: Greenwood.

Riches, D. 1995. Hunter-gatherer structural transformations. *Journal of the Royal Anthropological Institute*, 1(4): 679–702.

Ritzenthaler, R. & Ritzenthaler, P. 1964. *Cameroon's Village: An Ethnography of the Bafut.* Milwaukee, WI: North American Press, p. 73.

Roodt, A. 1997. In search of a South African corporate culture. *Management Today*, 13(2): 14–16.

o Rudin, H. R., 1938. *Germans in the Cameroons, 1884-1914; A case study in modern*

Imperialism. New Haven, CT, USA: Yale University Press.

Sahlins, M. 1972. *Stone Age Economics*. New York: Aldine de Gruyter.

Samatar, A. I. 1997. Leadership and ethnicity in the making of African state models: Botswana versus Somalia. *Third World Quarterly*, 18(4): 687–708.

Schneider, J., & Littrell, R. F. 2003. Leadership preferences of German and English managers. *The Journal of Management Development*, 22(2): 130–148.

Selmer, J. 1997. Differences in leadership behaviour between expatriate and local bosses as perceived by their host country national subordinates. *Leadership and Organizational Development Journal*, 18(1):13–22.

Silberbauer, G. 1982. Political processes in G/wi bands. In E. Leacock & R. Lee (Eds.), *Politics and history in band societies*. Cambridge: University Press.

Smith, P. B., Peterson, M. F., & Schwartz, S. H. 2002. Cultural values, sources of guidance, and their relevance to managerial behavior. *Journal of Cross-Cultural Psychology,* 33(2): 188.

Stogdill, R.M. 1948. Personal factors associated with leadership: A survey of the literature. *Journal of Psychology*, 25: 35–71.

Stogdill, R.M. 1963. *Manual for the Leader Behaviour Description Questionnaire -- Form XII*. Columbus: Ohio State University, Bureau of Business Research.

Stogdill, R.M. 1974. *Handbook of leadership: A survey of theory and research*. New York: The Free Press.

Stogdill, R. M. 1963. *Manual for the Leader Behavior Description Questionnaire-Form XII.* Columbus: Ohio State University, Bureau of Business Research Stogdill, Ralph M. 1963. *Manual for the Leader Behavior Description Questionnaire-Form XII.* Ohio State University, Bureau of Business Research: Columbus, Ohio.

Stott, L. & Shunmugam, N. 2002. *Business and gender equality: Lessons from South Africa.* London: Prince of Wales International Business Leaders Forum.

Sweet, L.E. (Ed.). 1970. *Peoples and Cultures of the Middle East: Vol 1, Depth and Diversity; Vol 2, Life in the Cities, Towns and Countryside.* Garden City, NY: Natural History Press.

Tangwa, G.B. 1998. Democracy and Development in Africa: Putting the Horse Before the Cart, essay in *Road Companion to Democracy and Meritocracy: Further Essays from an African Perspective*. Bellingham, WA, USA: Kola Tree Press.

Taylor, C & Hudson, M. H. 1972. *World Handbook of Political and Social Indicators.* New Haven, Conn.: Yale University Press.

Thomas, A., & Bendixen, M. 2000. Management implications of ethnicity in South Africa. *Journal of International Business Studies*, 31: 507–519.

Uguwegbu, Denis Chima E. 2001. *The Psychology of Management in African Organizations*. Wesport, CT: Quorum Books (Greenwood).

Van Vugt, M. & Hogan, R. 2005. *What evolution teaches us about leadership: Some lessons from the past.* Retrieved from http://www.kent.ac.uk/psychology/department/people/van-vugtm/personal/publications/Leadershiprevpsprmvv%204%2012%2005.pdf on 9 May 2006.

Warren, D.M., Adedokun, R., & Omolaoye, A. 1996. Indigenous organisations and development: The case of Ara, Nigeria. In P. Blunt, & D. M.Warren (Eds.), *Indigenous Organisations and Development*: 43-49. London: Intermediate Technology Publications, pp. 43-49.

Wenke, R.J. 1984. *Patterns in Prehistory: Humankind's First Three Million Years.* Oxford: Oxford University Press.

Williams, Al-Yasha. 2003. On the subject kings and queens: "Traditional" African leadership in the diasporal imagination. *African Studies Quarterly*, 7(1): online. Retrieved 20 April 2006 from http://web.africa.ufl.edu/asq/v7/v7i1a4.htm

Williams, J.E., Satterwhite, R.C. & Best, D.L. 1999. Pancultural gender stereotypes revisited: The five factor model. *Sex Roles*, 40(7/8): 513–525.

Williams, K. D., & Sommer, K. L. 1997. Social Ostracism by co-workers: Does rejection lead to loafing or compensation(?). *Personality and Social Psychology Bulletin,* 61: 570–581.

Wilson, D., McMaster, J., Greenspan, R., Mobyi, L., Ncube, T., & Sibanda, B. 1990. Cross cultural validation of the Bem Sex Role Inventory in Zimbabwe. *Personality and Individual Differences*, 11, No 651-656.

Wilson, E. O. 1975. *Sociobiology.* Cambridge, MA: Harvard University Press.

Woodburn, J. 1968. Stability and flexibility in Hadza residential groupings. In R. Lee & I. DeVore (Eds.), *Man the hunter.* . Chicago: Aldine.

Woodburn, J. 1980. Hunters and gatherers today and reconstruction of the past. In E. Gellner (Ed.), *Soviet and Western anthropology.* London: Duckworth.

Woodburn, J. 1982. Egalitarian societies. *Man (N.S.)*. 17: 431–451.

Yellen, J.E. 1998. The transformation of the Kalahari !Kung. In J. Gowdy (Ed.), *Limited wants, unlimited means: A reader on hunter-gatherer economics and the environment*: Washington DC: Island Press.

Younger, S. 2005. Reciprocity, normative reputation, and the development of mutual obligation in gift-giving societies. *Journal of Artificial Societies and Social Simulation*, 7(1). Retrieved 30 April 2006 from http://jasss.soc.surrey.ac.uk/8/2/9.html.

Zeitlin, M. F. 1977. *Report of nutrition survey conducted in Abyei district S. Kordofan Province, Sudan*, by the Nutrition Division of the Ministry of Health, Government of the Sudan and by Harvard Institute for International Development, November and December. Cited in Zeitlin, M. F., Ratna Megawangi, Ellen M. Kramer, Nancy D. Colletta, E.D. Babatunde, and David Garman, Eds., *Strengthening the family - Implications for international development. New York: United Nations University Press.*

Printed in the United States
102439LV00001B/93-142/A

9 781934 269121